PROFITABLE
LOGISTICS
MANAGEMENT

PROFITABLE LOGISTICS MANAGEMENT

Firth
Apple
Denham
Hall
Inglis
Saipe

McGRAW-HILL RYERSON LIMITED
Toronto   Montreal   New York   Auckland   Bogotá   Cairo
Caracas   Hamburg   Lisbon   London   Madrid   Mexico   Milan
New Delhi   Panama   Paris   San Juan   São Paulo   Singapore
Sydney   Tokyo

Profitable Logistics Management is a Revised Edition of Distribution Management Handbook

ISBN: 0-07-549603-8

1 2 3 4 5 6 7 8 9 0   THB   7 6 5 4 3 2 1 0 9 8

Printed and bound in Canada

Canadian Cataloguing in Publication Data
Main entry under title:

Profitable logistics management

2nd ed.
First ed. published under title: Distribution
management handbook.
ISBN 0-07-549603-8

1. Physical distribution of goods — Management.
I. Firth, Don, date.   II. Title: Distribution
management handbook.

HF5415.7.D58 1988   658.7'88   C88-093596-0

CONTENTS

039443

For Pam, Mary Audrey, Lynne, Anne, Catherine and Sharon

Preface

The age of logistics has finally arrived. For years, the logistics (also known as distribution or materials management) functions were viewed as merely cost centres. The responsibilities for these major functions (network planning, customer service, order processing, forecasting, production planning, inventory management, warehousing, transportation and purchasing) were traditionally split among various corporate departments. Over the last five years, however, more and more companies have recognized the benefits of placing these functions under the control of a single logistics department.

As all of these functions are interrelated, the logistics department can balance the trade-offs between each function to provide a highly competitive service at the lowest overall cost. The result: increased profitability.

When competing companies provide products of similar quality at similar prices, the major differentiating factor is customer service. Logistics is responsible for consistently providing a competitive customer service. This in turn leads to increased sales. By achieving this service level in the most efficient and effective way, logistics is a major contributor to a company's profitability. It is for this reason that logistics is now regarded as the critical department by the most successful companies.

In 1980 I had the pleasure to edit and co-author *Distribution Management Handbook*. In 1987 I was asked by McGraw-Hill Ryerson to write a new edition of the book. With all the changes that have happened over the last seven years, almost a total rewrite was required. In addition, I included chapters on distribution resource planning (DRP) and direct product profitability (DPP), two areas that are becoming increasingly popular among progressive companies.

I was supported in my endeavour by five leading authorities in logistics. During the years I spent as a management consultant in logistics, first for Stevenson Kellogg Ernst & Whinney and subsequently for Coopers & Lybrand, I was fortunate enough to work on numerous assignments with each of them.

Although the authors are experienced in all aspects of logistics, I asked each one to write on particular components and issues. A brief introduction to the authors and their contributions follows.

Jim Apple is a partner of Systecon, the warehouse design, operations and systems practice of Coopers & Lybrand in the U.S. Jim, naturally, wrote Chapter 7, "Warehousing." Coincidentally, Jim's father, the late James M. Apple, taught me warehouse design and operations in the early 1970s.

Ron Denham, who pioneered the logistics concept in Canada, is Vice-President of Stevenson Kellogg Ernst & Whinney (SKEW), a management consulting company. I worked with Ron for five years at SKEW and learned a lot from his experience. Ron wrote Chapter 1, "Logistics," contributed to Chapter 2, "Customer Service," and wrote Chapter 12, "Planning for More Profitable Logistics."

Jeff Hall is Vice President, Distribution and Logistics with Price Daxion. I worked with Jeff for five years at Coopers & Lybrand and consider him to be a leader in the fields of inventory management and distribution resource planning (DRP). Naturally, he wrote the chapters on these topics, Chapters 6 and 10.

Paul Inglis is manager of the logistics practice of Coopers & Lybrand. Paul was originally one of my clients when he was Director of Network Planning and Design for Canada Post. He subsequently joined my team at Coopers & Lybrand. Paul wrote Chapter 3, "Order Processing," Chapter 9, "Purchasing," and contributed to Chapter 2, "Customer Service," and Chapter 8, "Transportation."

Al Saipe is a partner of Stevenson Kellogg Ernst & Whinney. I worked with Al for four years and consider him to be a leader in sales forecasting and production planning. He wrote Chapters 4 and 5 on these topics.

For my own part, after eleven years in consulting, I have returned to industry as Vice-President Logistics for Steinberg Inc. My contributions to this book are Chapter 2, "Customer Service," Chapter 8, "Transportation," and Chapter 11, "Direct Product Profitability (DPP)."

I would like to thank a few colleagues who also provided input into the book: Bernie Brunet, Jon Lett, Gord Margolese, Cynthia McCarthy and Barry Seitz from Steinberg; Nancy Pinnington of Coopers & Lybrand; Anna Shepherd of Stevenson Kellogg Ernst & Whinney; Tammy Jordan of Systicon; John Brittain, of Philips Electronics; Andy Apple; and especially Pam Firth.

DON FIRTH

Logistics

THE CHALLENGE

Logistics, as the field is now known, has come a long way in the past decade. Whereas logistics managers formerly focused on efficiency and cost control, they now focus on profitability and return on net assets.

Realizing the full potential of the logistics system correspondingly requires much more than state-of-the-art financial controls. It demands an integrated set of management practices: strategy, organization, performance measurement, information management and effective use of human resources as well as the efficient conduct of each operation. This is the framework for this book.

Twenty years ago Peter Drucker referred to logistics as "the economy's dark frontier." Even though it accounted for up to 30% of the revenue from the sale of a product, few managers saw it as a problem or an opportunity.

The reasons were many. In most companies the responsibility for logistics activities was fragmented among many managers. It was not unusual to find transportation reporting to the financial executive. Warehousing, especially at the factory, was usually seen as an extension of manufacturing. In the field, branch warehousing was part of the sales department's responsibility.

Inventory, which in most organizations represents the second-largest cost element of the distribution system, was ignored. Raw materials inventory was often attached to the purchasing department. In other cases it was seen as part of manufacturing.

Finished goods inventories, which extend from the end of the production line to the customer, were invariably assigned to a number of managers. At the plant, occupying valuable warehouse or manufacturing space or both, they were often assigned to the production manager. In transit to branches or customers, they were obviously influenced by the actions and decisions of the traffic manager. In branches across the country, they were assigned to the local manager, who usually had a sales orientation. In other organizations, where senior management was concerned with the investment of inventories, they might have been assigned to the senior financial officer.

None of these managers felt any responsibility for the level or utilization of these inventories. No one executive had the responsibility of overseeing the full range of activities involved in moving a product from the factory to the customer.

Another reason for the failure to recognize the importance of logistics is a lack of meaningful information. To this day, in many organizations important logistics information is lost within the accounting system. Inventories, always the result of operating decisions, seldom appear on any operating manager's financial statements. They are normally treated as a "balance sheet" item — the responsibility of the financial officer. Transportation costs, which in most Canadian firms are the largest single cost of logistics, were frequently hidden in other accounts. When goods were supplied on a "delivered price," the cost of transportation was hidden in the purchase price. In other instances, the terms of sale resulted in outbound transportation costs not appearing in the shipper's financial statements. Similarly, the costs of warehousing and materials handling were buried in costs of manufacturing or of branch activities, depending on the location of the activity.

Besides fragmented responsibility and the lack of information, the organizational structure and the conventional measures of performance discouraged managers from treating logistics as an entity. Purchasing managers were charged with laying down materials at the lowest cost. The operating statements in that part of the organization highlighted the purchase price and perhaps inbound transportation costs. Since purchasing managers were not accountable for inventories, they would naturally attempt to reduce purchase prices and transportation costs through bulk buying.

Managers of manufacturing were traditionally judged on plant costs. Direct labour and materials and indirect expenses formed the basis of performance reports. What could be more natural, therefore, than to set up and run production lines as long as possible without regard to the level of inventories?

Managers of transportation knew that shipping large quantities meant lower transportation costs. Carload and truckload lots would always move more cheaply than LCL (less than carload) or LTL (less than truckload) lots. Excess inventories resulting from transportation managers "doing their job" were someone else's concern.

If anyone was concerned about inventories, this person would invariably be at loggerheads with the previously mentioned managers. Whenever inventory levels were reduced, the usual consequence was higher costs in transportation, purchasing or manufacturing.

Now, in the 1980s, the situation is gradually changing. A number of conditions have forced management to recognize that physical distribution, or business logistics, has a major impact on profit and return on investment. The most important of these conditions are:

1. the squeeze on margins
2. the search for competitive edge
3. availability of skills and tools
4. increasing awareness
5. emerging professional associations

THE SQUEEZE ON MARGINS

Traditionally management has looked to the production activity as a source of cost savings. Through industrial engineers and, later, automation and robotics, companies have focused on the opportunity for reducing manufacturing costs. In the distributive trades, the search for cost reduction has largely been focused on the efficient use of labour and the introduction of labour-saving devices. Each step in cost reduction reduces the opportunity for further reduction. So it is that after striving to reduce manufacturing costs for 70 years, management must now look elsewhere if margins are to be restored to an acceptable level.

The logical place for this search is in logistics. In many companies it represents 30%, or more, of the revenue received. In some companies it represents the largest single cost component. Management must therefore ensure that logistics are as efficient and effective as all other activities in the enterprise.

THE SEARCH FOR A COMPETITIVE EDGE

Most companies compete in markets in which, with few exceptions, they do not have a strong consumer franchise. There is little product differentiation in terms of quality, features or price. Under these conditions, the logistics system can become an important marketing tool. It can, if managed effectively, provide the competitive edge that is needed to command higher prices or gain additional volume or both.

The logistics system can provide this edge in a number of ways. Fast and reliable service in addition to ready availability of product mark the ideal supplier. Dealing with such a company enables customers to reduce inventories, provide better service to their customers, respond more quickly to customers' whims and obtain a better return on investment.

AVAILABILITY OF SKILLS AND TOOLS

The widespread use of the computer, supported by the necessary analytical skills, allows management to grapple with the complexities of logistics costs. Mathematical models of logistics systems foster a better understanding of the complex interrelationships among various components. They provide answers to speculative questions: "What if . . . ." They also provide insights into the chain reaction that takes place in a logistics system as a result of a stimulus applied at a particular point.

This modelling ability has been paralleled by a steady upgrading of management skills. Managers are no longer prepared to operate on intuition. As they recognize the impact of the logistics system on profits and return on investment, they seek a more rational approach to the complexities of logistics decision-making.

INCREASING AWARENESS

Several changes have occurred during the past decade which have forced a closer look at logistics systems. Improved management skills are one of these changes. But there are others, outside the scope of any individual company, which profoundly affect distribution costs.

The more notable of these changes include:

- The increasing cost of capital and shortage of funds. The surge in the cost of funds, from a level of 6 or 7% ten years ago to a high of almost 20% in 1982, has forced companies to assess the need for, and role of, better inventory control. Managers have become increasingly aware of "lazy capital" not earning a target return and depressing the overall profitability of the enterprise.
- Transportation rates. The search for profitable operation has forced many transport companies to restructure their rates. This has resulted in a significant shift in the relative cost of small and large shipments. In turn, shippers have been obliged to reassess their use of transportation systems. Recently, the trend towards deregulation in both the United States and Canada has led to marked changes in freight rates. These changes, affecting the cost and profitability of many companies, have raised questions about the traditional methods of moving products.

Yet another change in the transportation scene has been the emergence of air freight and the small-package carrier. These companies, offering to move small shipments literally overnight to any point in the country, have prompted a reassessment of traditional distribution systems. In the past, the need for fast service invariably required suppliers to locate warehouses and inventories close to customers, usually within a 24-hour trip. Now, however, the availability of overnight service to almost any point in the country has enabled companies to consolidate distribution centres, resulting in significant reductions in warehousing and inventory expense.

EMERGING PROFESSIONAL ASSOCIATIONS

The growing awareness of the importance of logistics has led people with similar interests to band together for their mutual benefit. The Canadian Association of Logistics Management, formerly the Canadian Association of Physical Distribution Management (CAPDM), the Council of Logistics Management (formerly National Council of Physical Distribution Management [NCPDM]), the International Materials Management Society (IMMS) and the Society of Logistics Engineers (SOLE) typify these groups. By exchanging ideas, sponsoring seminars and promoting the "logistics concept," they have all contributed to a growing recognition that logistics, when well managed, can make a substantial contribution to corporate goals and objectives.

LOGISTICS MANAGEMENT: THE SCOPE

"Physical distribution," "logistics" and "materials management" are all terms used to describe the integrated flow of materials through an organization from the point of supply to the ultimate consumer. The specific terminology and its application depend more on the nature of the industry and its evolution than on any generally accepted definition (see Figure 1.1).

The term "physical distribution" is most widely applied to the distribution of high-volume consumer packaged goods such as grocery products, confectionery, pharmaceuticals and tobacco products. Within this group there is general acceptance of the definition of physical distribution as promulgated by the National Council of Physical Distribution Management/National Council of Logistics:

> The term (describes) the integration of two or more activities for the purpose of planning, implementing and controlling the efficient flow of raw materials, in-process inventory, and finished goods from point of origin to point of consumption. These activities may include, but are not limited to, customer service, demand forecasting, distribution communication, inventory management, materials handling, order processing, parts and service support, plant and warehouse site selection, procurement, packaging, returned goods handling, salvage and scrap disposal, traffic and transportation, and warehousing and storage.

FIGURE 1.1
BUSINESS LOGISTICS, PHYSICAL DISTRIBUTION AND MATERIALS MANAGEMENT

("A ROSE BY ANY OTHER NAME")

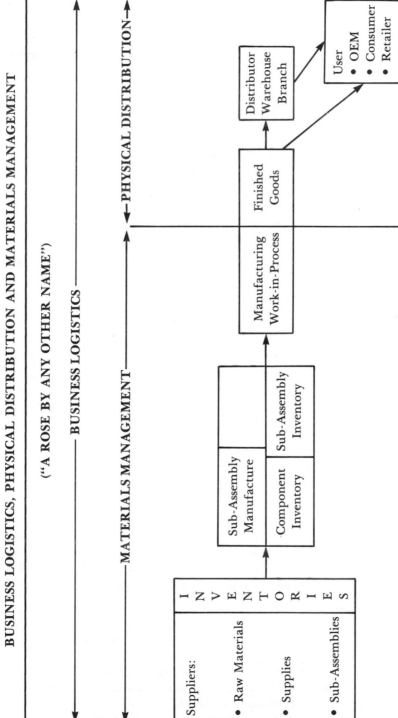

Application of this concept in the consumer packaged goods industry has led to the creation of the position of Manager, Physical Distribution. The incumbent normally has planning and control responsibility over the entire movement and storage of the finished product. The scope extends from production planning to ultimate delivery of the product to the customer. It should be noted that this "planning authority" does not imply line authority. The line activities may be divided among a number of functional groups. The distribution executive does, however, have responsibility for planning logistics operations, including the setting of targets and objectives, ensuring reconciliation between the level of service and overall logistics costs, and monitoring performance.

The "materials management" approach stems from an emphasis on purchasing and the related inbound flow of raw materials and supplies. It may also be extended to work-in-process inventory. It has been defined as

that aspect of industrial management concerned with the activities involved in the acquisition and use of all materials employed in the production of the finished product. These activities include production and inventory control, purchasing, traffic, materials handling and receiving.

This approach reflects the manufacture of industrial products, especially those delivered to original equipment manufacturers (OEMs) or those with a relatively small number of customers. Another characteristic: the value added in manufacturing is relatively high compared to the previous category of packaged consumer goods.

Industries in which this term has gained wide currency are chemical manufacturing, automotive parts and basic industries such as steel or forest products.

The most comprehensive term, and the one gaining rapid acceptance, is "business logistics." It has been defined as

a total approach to the management of all activities involved in physically acquiring, moving and storing raw materials, in-process inventory and finished goods inventory from the point of origin to the point of use or consumption.

The term "logistics" has its origins in the military establishment. There it is related to the acquisition and supply of all goods and materials needed to fulfil a mission. It is now being increasingly adopted by those organizations dependent on widely dispersed points of supply for raw materials and components and, at the same time, on a large number of widely dispersed customers or users. The description is especially appropriate for multinational corporations where fabrication of parts occurs in one or more plant within the same country, sub-assembly takes place in a different location often thousands of miles away, and final assembly occurs at yet another location. Such an arrangement is typical of the electronics and automotive industries.

The actual terminology is not critical. Most important is that management recognize that the flow of materials from the point of supply to the customer is an interrelated and interdependent set of elements constituting an integrated system. This system must be viewed as an entity for the purposes of planning, implementation and control.

The system must also be viewed as extending not only to the immediate customer, but eventually to the ultimate consumer. The ultimate consumer, be it a manufacturer, distributor or retailer, is the source of all revenue to the business. Consequently, any inefficiency or duplication within the system will reduce the revenue and, in turn, the income available to any participant in the distribution system.

This "total system" view of distribution means that the logistics manager must plan and control not only the activities within his or her company's domain, but also the flow through other intermediaries as far as the consumer. When this approach is used, it quickly becomes apparent that inventories are duplicated many times within the total system and that a product is picked from storage, moved and returned to storage, and the process repeated several times, without benefiting the ultimate purchaser of the goods.

TRADITIONAL APPROACHES TO MANAGING LOGISTICS

For the past 25 years or so, management has become increasingly aware of the problems and opportunities to be found in more efficient and effective distribution. Some headway has been made by studying and improving the individual elements.

Some examples of improvements in individual elements which have led to savings, greater sales or profits, or both, are listed below.

TRANSPORTATION IMPROVEMENTS
Transportation costs have been reduced in a number of ways, including:

- holding shipments for a few days to consolidate into a larger load, thereby taking advantage of the lower freight rates for larger or heavier shipments
- better utilization and scheduling of trucks and railcars
- arranging for consolidations of small orders to regional break-bulk points instead of shipping the orders independently
- arranging for a backhaul to improve the utilization of vehicles and drivers

WAREHOUSING IMPROVEMENTS
Warehousing costs have been reduced in various ways. Some of the most notable are:

- establishing work standards for employees and planning the workload and measuring performance accordingly
- introducing mechanized methods such as conveyors, fork-lift trucks and computerized storage systems
- positioning goods in storage according to their popularity (e.g., fast-moving items near the shipping/receiving areas) or with other items in the same family
- reducing the number of items stocked in the order-picking area, thereby reducing the walking time and work content of picking an order

Many other examples could be quoted, all illustrating the improvements made in warehousing methods and technology.

INVENTORY MANAGEMENT

This is frequently the second most costly element, after transportation, in the logistics system. Inventories occur in the form of raw and packaging materials, work-in-process and finished goods. Methods of reducing inventory costs include:

- implementing scientifically determined replenishment rules
- improving demand forecasting: reducing the error in the forecast
- reducing the time lapse between generating information on a transaction and taking action to replenish stocks reduced by the transaction

These are but a few of the better-known approaches. Other cost-cutting measures have been applied to order processing, customer forecasting and packaging; in short, to every element that might offer some chance of cost reduction or better service to the consumer.

PROBLEMS OF THE TRADITIONAL APPROACH

In some cases the previously described techniques produced the desired results, albeit to a limited extent. They did not, however, lead to the major breakthrough eagerly sought by management. Worse still, in many cases they caused adverse effects elsewhere in the system. These effects frequently offset the initial benefits being sought. This problem is illustrated in the following cases.

CASE 1: FREIGHT REDUCTION AT ANY COST[1]

A large company produces its consumer goods in several plants in eastern Canada, including one in Toronto. National distribution occurs through branches located in strategic centres across the country, one of which is in Toronto.

Trucks were originally employed to transfer goods between the

---

[1] F. R. Denham, "Making the Distribution Management Concept Pay Off," *The Business Quarterly* (Winter 1967).

FIGURE 1.2
CONFLICT IN THE SYSTEM: THE SEARCH FOR
LOWER FREIGHT COSTS LEADS TO HIGHER INVENTORIES

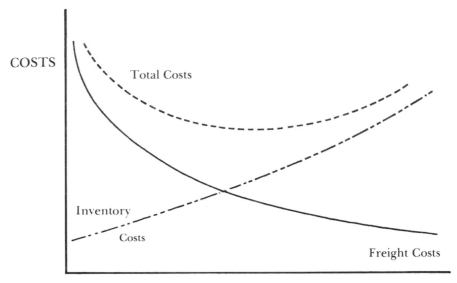

TIME TO DELIVER GOODS

Toronto plant and warehouse, the contract rate being 30¢ per cwt. (hundredweight). As a result of the enquiries and negotiation by the traffic manager, the railroad agreed to haul goods for 25½¢ — a saving of 4½¢ per cwt. or $4,150 per year.

However, the time taken to move goods by rail was about three days, compared to less than eight hours by truck. This difference required an increase of $112,500 in inventories, enough to cover the three days in transit. Valuing inventory at 15% implied an increase in inventory costs of $16,900 per year. Thus the reduction in freight rates led to an increase of $12,750 in total distribution costs. When this situation came to light some time later, management reverted to the former mode.

CASE 2: CONSOLIDATION AT THE EXPENSE OF THE CUSTOMER
A major pharmaceutical company was concerned about the costs of distributing its product to western Canada from the plant in Quebec. Customers were primarily retail pharmacists and hospitals. Orders varied in size. Ethical drugs were shipped in small quantities, frequently with a minimum lead time. Over-the-counter drugs were shipped in larger quantities, often allowing a longer time.

Transportation was costly. Small shipments of less than 50 pounds cost more than $18 per hundredweight. However, as the weight increased the transportation cost fell substantially. Shipments of 500 pounds cost less than $10 per cwt. Shipments of 5,000 pounds were handled for about $7 per cwt.

In an effort to reduce transportation costs, the traffic manager began to accumulate small orders. Initially they were held for one or two days. Later, after receiving praise for his cost-cutting results, the manager delayed for up to a week in order to accumulate a substantial shipment.

Customers became concerned, but their concerns fell on relatively deaf ears. Only when a major account cancelled its business did management wake up to reality. The lower transportation cost had been gained at the expense of the customers, who could no longer depend on receiving their orders when needed. The distribution system delivered space value but no longer time value.

CASE 3: MISPLACED INVENTORY RULES[2]

A company producing and distributing 6,000 different items to the construction industry faced a serious inventory problem. Management could not reconcile the conflict between giving 24-hour service to customers, reducing freight costs and keeping inventories within an acceptable level.

After manufacturing, the products go into a warehouse beside the factory. From there they move on demand to 20 company-owned branches and a greater number of jobbers.

The company's service policy was clear: shipment of goods within 24 hours. It applied equally to the warehouse and to the branches. Initially this policy lead to a sharp increase in inventories. Later, under a "reduce inventory" drive, freight costs soared as branches placed too-frequent orders for small quantities. Finally, when a ceiling was placed on inventories and freight costs, customer service deteriorated.

To resolve these conflicts, an inventory control system was introduced in the branches. Balancing the costs of too much inventory on one hand against the costs of too-frequent shipments on the other, the system called for branches to purchase economic order quantity (EOQ) lots from the factory.

As might be expected, this resulted in lower costs in the branches. But EOQ lots imposed a highly variable demand on the factory. These fluctuations could be absorbed only by lowering the service level or increasing inventories.

In this case, the problem was aggravated because management tried to

---

[2] Denham, "Distribution Management Concept."

"optimize" part of the logistics system without studying the effects on other segments.

A subsequent simulation study of the overall system produced quick and economic operating rules. The service level increased from 87% to 93%, inventories were lowered from $4,900,000 to $2,900,000 and freight costs increased by only $45,000 per year.

These cases, and many others that could be quoted, all illustrate the fundamental issue in managing logistics. It consists of a set of interdependent activities extending from the production line to the consumer. Unless management considers all the trade-offs, or conflicts, in the system when evaluating changes it is unlikely to select the optimal solution.

THE NEED FOR THE SYSTEMS VIEWPOINT

The simple cases quoted previously illustrate the need to study the impact on all elements of the logistics system before making a change in any single element. And many other comparable cases could be cited.

But there are other reasons of a more fundamental nature. They reflect that truly significant breakthroughs in improving logistics efficiency and effectiveness will come only from a radical redesign of the total system. Fine-tuning of individual elements is a good start. But it seldom brings the major improvements in profit that come from drastic revision of the entire system.

Some illustrations will demonstrate the pay-off from this approach.

CASE 1: THE CASE FOR AIR FREIGHT

This company manufactured and distributed records (phonograph discs) from a plant in eastern Canada. Distribution initially was by surface — rail and truck — to a number of company-operated warehouses in strategic centres. Inventories of all current releases were kept at these warehouses.

Customers, mostly retailers, phoned in orders to the warehouses. Goods were delivered the next day in the larger centres and two days later in other locations.

Demand on the warehouses was very unpredictable. Patterns were difficult to discern until too late. A sudden surge in popularity of one item because of the enthusiasm of a local disc jockey would exhaust stocks. Or frequently the opposite would occur: in anticipation of high sales the company would ship large quantities of certain records to the warehouses, then the records would just sit there. Inventories were excessive, and surplus goods had to be returned to the factory.

In short, a costly process. Despite a steady buildup of inventories, stock-outs were approaching 35%. Attempts to overcome this condition by increasing local inventories had little effect — the problem of forecasting defied rational inventory management.

As a first step to overcoming the situation, the company introduced a systematic inventory management system. Based on generally accepted principles of inventory management, it was expected to improve service levels materially. However, the improvement was insignificant.

Shortly thereafter management shifted its attention from warehouse inventories to the total system. Instead of asking "How can inventories be managed more effectively?" it posed the system question "How can customers be served most profitably?" This forced an evaluation not only of demand forecasting and inventory management but of the whole system. It focused on issues such as:

• Are warehouses in the correct location?
• Should warehouses be eliminated entirely and the need for immediate service to customers be satisfied by air freight direct from factory to retailer?

Following the identification of a number of optional ways of serving the customer, it was established that air freight was technically viable. Then, when each system was costed, it was found that air freight, despite its higher transportation cost, gave a lower total system cost (Table 1.1). Further, it had the advantage of flexibility in the use of inventory — better response to sudden surges in demand and a higher level of customer service for any specified inventory investment.

The result of looking at the total system was an annual saving of $186,500.

CASE 2: THE MANY MOVES OF HARDWARE

The distribution of hardware presents an interesting example of the benefits of studying the total system. Typical of such products are electrical goods — conduit, lighting, electric switchgear, etc. — and plumbing and builder's hardware.

The end-user is normally a contractor. It may be the consumer in a do-it-yourself mode. Products normally move from the manufacturer to a distributor to a dealer — the final reseller — to the end-user.

Concerned about the costs of distributing its products, the company studied all activities between the production line and the end-user. The results (Table 1.2) indicated much duplication and needless activity. But this duplication became apparent only from examining the total system. Much of it occurred in the distributor's and dealer's domains. It was not identified in a traditional approach which was limited to activities within any single legal entity.

TABLE 1.1
MODELS OF TWO SYSTEMS

		SYSTEM 1 RAIL-WAREHOUSE	SYSTEM 2 AIR-DIRECT
I	INVENTORY CYCLE COSTS		
	Transit Inventory (days)	5	2
	Plant Warehouse Inventory (days)	10	5
	Field Warehouse (days)	28	0
	Total Days	43	7
	Total Days Saved		36
	Annual Inventory Carrying Costs:		
	Capital	25%	25%
	Obsolescence	5%	2%
	Insurance	1%	1%
		31%	28%
	Annual Sales $10,000,000 Inventory	$\frac{43}{365} \times 10,000,000$ = 1,178,000	$\frac{7}{365} \times 10,000,000$ = 192,000
	Annual Cost of Carrying Inventory	.31 × 1,178,000 = 365,000	.28 × 192,000 = 54,000
	Annual Savings in Inventory Cost		$311,000
II	SAVINGS IN WAREHOUSING COSTS		
	Warehouse Rental	$ 80,000	$ 35,000
	Labour	$175,000	$ 80,000
	Operating Cost	$ 45,000	$ 20,000
	Total	$300,000	$135,000
	Savings		$165,000
III	TOTAL SAVINGS ON INVENTORY AND WAREHOUSE		$476,000
IV	TRANSPORT COSTS		
	Freight Charges	$380,000	$620,000
	Local Delivery Charges	$160,000	$210,000
		$540,000	$830,000
	Savings	$290,000	
V	TOTAL OVERALL SAVINGS $476,000–$290,000		$186,500

TABLE 1.2
ELEMENTS IN DISTRIBUTING HARDWARE
FROM END OF PRODUCTION LINE TO END-USER

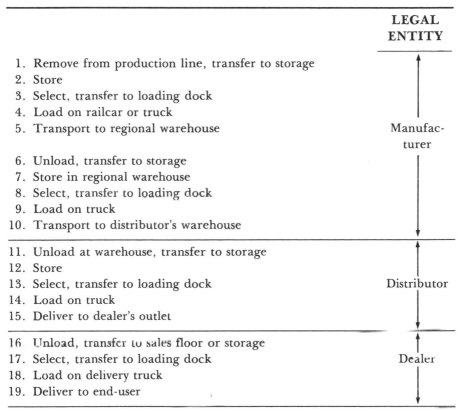

	LEGAL ENTITY
1. Remove from production line, transfer to storage	
2. Store	
3. Select, transfer to loading dock	
4. Load on railcar or truck	
5. Transport to regional warehouse	Manufacturer
6. Unload, transfer to storage	
7. Store in regional warehouse	
8. Select, transfer to loading dock	
9. Load on truck	
10. Transport to distributor's warehouse	
11. Unload at warehouse, transfer to storage	
12. Store	
13. Select, transfer to loading dock	Distributor
14. Load on truck	
15. Deliver to dealer's outlet	
16. Unload, transfer to sales floor or storage	
17. Select, transfer to loading dock	Dealer
18. Load on delivery truck	
19. Deliver to end-user	

Once this duplication was identified, a number of cost-reducing, profit-improving options were identified. They included:

- transporting directly from the plant to the dealer's warehouse
- transporting directly from the manufacturer's regional warehouse to the dealer's premises
- drop-shipping from manufacturer's regional warehouse or distributor's warehouse to the end-user

Selection of the most appropriate routing varied with the customer, product and location. It reflected the total costs of each alternative. However, the critical breakthrough was an ability and willingness to study the total system.

THE IMPLICATIONS OF THE LOGISTICS CONCEPT

Viewing the logistics system as an entity, from the end of the production line to the consumer, has many implications for management. It obviously impinges on the design of the organization, which must be structured to ensure the best trade-off among conflicting functions. It also influences external relationships, between the manufacturer and carriers, customers, suppliers and even competitors. Some insight into these relationships is presented below.

RELATIONSHIPS WITH CARRIERS

The traditional way of dealing with carriers is to assume that they can meet any demand for shipping capacity with relatively little notice. Whenever an order is to be shipped, the traffic manager or shipping supervisor phones a carrier, explains what is needed and expects a truck at the dock within a few hours.

This method works well as long as the shipping pattern is fairly predictable and not too variable. Also, it assumes the carrier has adequate capacity.

If business is highly seasonal and/or unpredictable this approach may break down. The carrier will not have adequate capacity to meet all demands. Some shipments are delayed, tempers are frayed, and a customer is dissatisfied.

A more effective approach is to recognize that carriers are part of the distribution system. They can provide the best, most effective, service if they also are involved in planning logistics. If shipments are highly seasonal they may be in a position to find complementary loads for the slack season, if they have sufficient warning. Alternatively they might be able to offer lower rates if the variability in the shipping pattern is reduced. Levelling out shipments provides economies, just as does levelling out variations in production.

With this knowledge carriers and shippers may work together to move goods to regional storage depots ahead of the peak volume season.

Carriers know how their costs are affected by different shipping patterns. If they are able to reduce their costs they may well be in a position to reduce their charges. The manufacturer/shipper should explore the relationship between transportation costs, shipping patterns and other costs such as inventory and storage charges.

RELATIONSHIPS WITH CUSTOMERS

Finished goods in the supplier's warehouse and purchased materials in the customer's warehouse are usually the same product separated only by time and space. In effect the physical relationship parallels that between goods in the plant warehouse and those in regional distribution centres.

If one company, such as the manufacturer, controls both inventories, they can be and often are managed as one inventory. The replenishment rules reflect the trade-offs between inventory costs and transportation.

The two inventories can be tightly controlled as one system, providing the customer with the desired level of service at the lowest total cost.

Once goods change ownership, this "one system" breaks down. The separate legal entities fail to understand the interdependency between their inventories. As a result, each company attempts to second-guess the actions of the other.

This problem is illustrated clearly in the action and reaction of a supplier and customer under conditions of variable, somewhat unpredictable demand. The sequence generally goes as follows:

- During a stable period both supplier and customer have inventories reasonably well balanced. The supplier's stocks are sufficient to meet the demand from the customer. The customer's stocks are adequate to cover demand during the order cycle lead time (i.e., the time between placing an order and receiving the shipment of goods).
- Demands on the customer increase. Afraid of running out of stock, the customer over-compensates by ordering excess stock.
- The supplier is caught short, able to fill only part of the order; the balance is back-ordered.
- The supplier, faced with this sudden, unanticipated pick-up in demand, increases inventories to guard against a recurrence.
- The customer, concerned that the supplier cannot meet the demand, increases inventories to guard against future short-shipments.
- And the cycle is repeated until both supplier and customer have much more inventory than is required.

This not uncommon situation could have been eliminated if both parties recognized that their inventories were two elements in *one* system. If they had shared information on trends and actions, both could have met the changing demand patterns with a minimum increase in inventories. Further, mutual confidence would have been enhanced, not shattered.

Some companies have recognized this one-system concept. Their policies and actions reflect a conscious effort to manage the overall system so that it makes maximum contribution to profit.

Examples of this practice are seen below.

GREETING CARDS DISTRIBUTION   Unsold cards at the end of the season represent a costly write-off to manufacturer and retailer alike. Consequently the manufacturer's representative sets up a min-max replenishment system which the retailer administers.

The representative studies the demand pattern for a sample of types and families of cards. From knowledge of the lead time to replenish stocks, and the probable variability in demand, the rep calculates appropriate reordering rules. Whenever the stock of cards on the shelf falls to the specified "minimum" level, the retailer orders the prescribed quantity.

Periodic reviews of the system ensure that the reordering rules reflect current demand patterns.

SPARE PARTS INVENTORIES — MOBILE EQUIPMENT   Spare parts inventories represent a costly investment for agricultural implement and industrial equipment dealers. They are expected to stock several thousand different items. Demand for the majority is low and very unpredictable. In fact, inventory may turn over as infrequently as twice a year.

Recognizing the lack of sophistication of many dealers, the equipment manufacturers have developed stock replenishment rules which the dealers can administer. The rules may not coincide with the dealer's best interest. They tend to result in relative overstocking. Nevertheless, the introduction of systematic rules by the manufacturer ensures that the total system provides the end-user with a high level of service at a reasonable cost, and at a reasonable profit to dealer and manufacturer.

This is another example of a supplier crossing legal boundaries in an attempt to manage the total physical distribution system more effectively.

TRANSFERRING INVENTORIES TO CUSTOMERS' PREMISES   Some manufacturers have adopted a total system viewpoint by transferring inventories to the customer's premises and applying rational stock replenishment procedures. This enables the customer to eliminate inventories by drawing on the supplier's stocks as needed.

The best-known example of this approach is the supply of home-heating oil. The fuel supplier monitors the demand and accepts responsibility for filling the tank when necessary. The home-owner is freed of all concerns.

This method allows fuel-oil delivery to be scheduled so that trucks and drivers are utilized efficiently and effectively. A number of homes in the same area can be served on the same trip. Contrast this approach with a method in which oil was delivered only when the customer placed an order!

This method is well suited to bulk products, of which home-heating oil is a good example. Other notable examples include:

• delivery of liquid sugar and glucose to confectionery manufacturers
• delivery of industrial gases to industrial users
• delivery of flour, etc., to bakeries

Many opportunities remain to be explored. The above examples show, however, that some companies are consciously bridging legal boundaries in their search for more profitable distribution.

RELATIONSHIPS WITH SUPPLIERS

This is the complement of the previous concept. Instead of the supplier taking the lead to manage the entire system, the customer may do so. However, the principle remains the same. By managing the total flow of goods through the supplier's facility, total costs can be reduced and levels of service improved.

One example of such a managed system is the case of a cigarette and tobacco products manufacturer that was facing difficulties in the supply of packaging materials.

The printed packet is supplied to the cigarette company by the lithographer. In turn the lithographer purchases board from the board mill. Delays in delivery were being caused by a lack of co-ordination throughout the system. Each firm was attempting to maximize its profits without regard to the effect of its actions on its customers. Manufacturing schedules, run lengths and shipping schedules were being set on individual priorities and requirements. This resulted in excessive inventories and frequent delivery failures.

The cigarette manufacturer recognized that the problem was due to the fragmentation of the one system. Consequently the company developed policies and practices which scheduled and monitored the inventory and flow of materials from the board mill, through the lithographer, to the cigarette-making plant.

Acceptance of the total system concept, from the end of the production line to the consumer, is essential if the distribution system is to maximize its contribution to company profitability. But another essential ingredient must be added: the system must be managed effectively.

MANAGEMENT OF THE SYSTEM: MAKING THE LOGISTICS CONCEPT WORK

Logistics has been defined as a *system* of interdependent activities. The role of management therefore is to *design* and *administer* the system so that it makes the greatest possible contribution to corporate objectives. Essential to this task are (see also Figure 1.3):

• design of the distribution network
• formulation of operating rules and policies
• design of the logistics organization structure
• design of the management information system

In this chapter we are concerned with the principles underlying the design of the network and the formulation of operating rules and policies.

THE NETWORK

The distribution network consists of all the fixed facilities, plant and

FIGURE 1.3

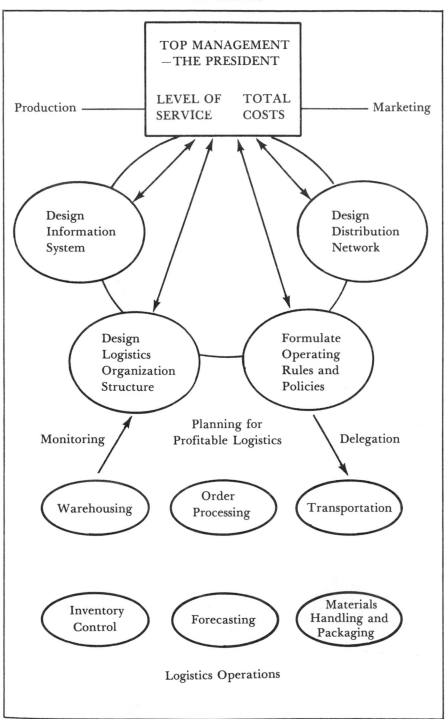

equipment needed to provide value to the end-user. Typically it embraces:

- manufacturing plants
- warehouses
- distribution centres
- break-bulk terminals and consolidation points
- transportation facilities

The key decisions facing management in designing the network are:

- where to locate production facilities
- how many warehouses, distribution centres, break-bulk and consolidation terminals there should be
- where they should be located
- what kind of facility they should be: highly automated, computer-controlled, mechanized or largely manual
- what kind of transportation facilities and equipment are most appropriate

These decisions have a lasting impact on the performance of the system. They represent a major investment of capital and have a prolonged effect on the balance sheet. If a poor choice is made, the error can be corrected only at considerable expense, if at all.

Further, the decision must be made in an atmosphere of uncertainty. The investments must serve the company for many years to come, yet during this period major shifts could occur in the location and nature of the market and in the preferences of the consumer.

Despite these risks, the selection of the "best" network will influence logistics costs and customer service in the long term much more than will the selection of the "right" operating rules and policies.

OPERATING RULES AND POLICIES

This second dimension of managing the logistics system embraces the set of policies and mechanisms that causes products to move through the system. Typically they cover:

- the routing of specific products through the network from plant to end-user
- allocation of products to plants and of customers to shipping points
- inventory replenishment — when an order should be placed with the supplier and how much should be ordered
- the routing and scheduling of trucks
- scheduling of shipments to customers and branch warehouses
- sequencing of production runs
- the production of "lot size" — how much should be produced in each batch
- the procedures for preparing forecasts of the demand for products
- transmission of orders from branches to plant

In short, the rules should cover all situations where a decision in any one element of the system has repercussions on other elements. They should also cover those situations which affect the level of customer service and total system costs.

THE THREE-WAY TRADE-OFF

Management of logistics implies selecting the unique combination of distribution network and operating rules that will maximize the contribution to profit.

It should be noted that management's focus should not be cost minimization. This would encourage subordinates to take cost-reducing action at the possible expense of customer service.

A profit-maximizing approach, on the other hand, forces customer service to the focal point of logistics decision-making. This is reflected in Figure 1.4, which captures the essence of the management problem.

The first and, in the long term, most important set of issues facing management relates to the design of the network. Plant location and, especially, warehouse location are the principal determinants of the speed with which an order is filled. Obviously, a customer needing goods within 24 hours must be served from a closer distribution centre than a customer who is prepared to wait a week or longer. The provision of merchandise within short lead times for all major customers implies a proliferation of warehouses or supply points throughout the market. Costs will increase, but so will revenues, leaving management to evaluate the trade-off implied in Figure 1.5.

However, the design of the network cannot be considered in isolation.

FIGURE 1.4

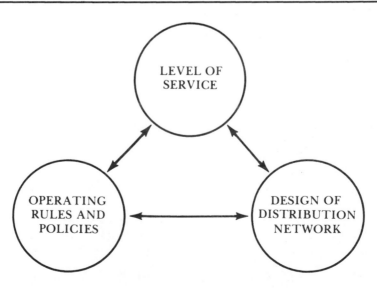

FIGURE 1.5

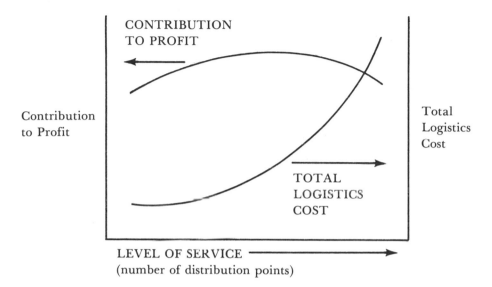

Contribution to Profit

Total Logistics Cost

CONTRIBUTION TO PROFIT

TOTAL LOGISTICS COST

LEVEL OF SERVICE
(number of distribution points)

Customers are satisfied only if they receive the required quantity and quality of goods in the right place at the right time. Therefore the network must be complemented with the appropriate rules and policies.

Policies which reflect the need to accumulate orders until a truck-load or other large shipment is available will largely negate the benefits of having many warehouses close to customers. Similarly, rules governing the flow or routing of goods through the network will affect costs, profits and levels of service.

In short, the network cannot be designed without considering the rules and policies that make goods flow. Similarly, in the short term, a change in rules and policies will materially affect the level of service and profit contribution of a given network.

This is the essence of managing the logistics function. The ensuing chapters give an insight into how the network should be designed and how the rules and procedures should be formulated.

THE CHALLENGE FACING MANAGEMENT

Although there is no universal consensus on the scope of business logistics/physical distribution/materials management, there is widespread agreement that it embraces two or more of the following activities:

• traffic and transportation
• warehousing and storage

- materials handling
- protective packaging
- inventory control
- plant and warehouse location
- order processing
- market forecasting
- customer service

In the early days of logistics management, the objective was to minimize the total costs of all of these activities. This "total cost" approach forced management to recognize the interdependence of the several logistics activities (see Figure 1.6). It called for an estimate of the costs of each element under a variety of possible operating conditions. This ensured, for example, that a transportation cost-reduction strategy which resulted in an increase in inventories would not be implemented without management being aware of the full impact.

This emphasis on total costs was a big step forward. It represented the first serious attempt to address the interdependencies within the logistics system. In extreme cases, however, it failed to serve the best interests of the company.

The focus of any business activity should be on a greater return on investment, or profitability, or both. This is not necessarily synonymous with cost reduction. In fact, as shown in Figure 1.7, the optimal logistics system is seldom the one which is lowest in cost. Nor is it the one which generates the maximum possible revenue. As is always the case in the design of a logistics system, the optimal design represents a compromise between increasing revenues on one hand and cost reduction on the other. More recently, as the emphasis has shifted towards "business logistics," so has management's attention shifted from cost minimization or profit maximization to maximizing the return on investment. This is especially critical when evaluating strategies which might require significant capital investment in plant, equipment or inventories.

The focus on "return on investment" for logistics decisions forces management to consider the full impact of the logistics system on the income statement and balance sheet. It calls for a detailed evaluation of the impact of the logistics system on:

- Revenues. Positioning stocks of goods in locations and facilities where they can be delivered reliably and swiftly to a customer will generally lead to higher sales revenues. This is especially true if a company is thereby able to serve the market better than its competitors can.
- Expenses. All cost-incurring activities and their interdependence must be assessed within the "total cost" approach. Critical here are transportation, warehousing and inventory. Together they frequently represent up to 90% of total logistics costs.

FIGURE 1.6
LOGISTICS MANAGEMENT

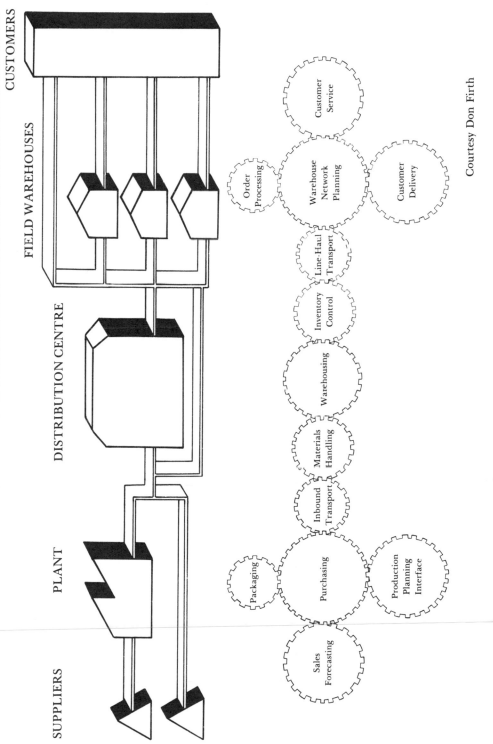

Courtesy Don Firth

FIGURE 1.7
OPTIMAL LOGISTICS SYSTEM

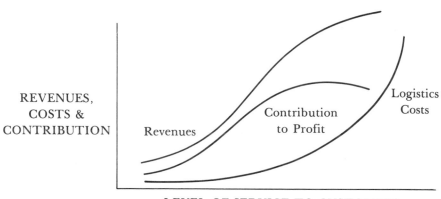

REVENUES,
COSTS &
CONTRIBUTION

Revenues

Contribution
to Profit

Logistics
Costs

LEVEL OF SERVICE TO CUSTOMERS

- Capital investment. The search for improved customer service or lower logistics costs or both may require additional capital investment. An assessment should be made of those areas in which investing seems most beneficial: in plant and manufacturing equipment, in warehouses and the associated materials-handling and storage equipment, or in a proliferation of inventories at strategic locations across the country.

Only by evaluating the interdependence of these three financial components can management be sure that the logistics system is making the greatest possible contribution to corporate goals.

IMPLICATIONS FOR MANAGEMENT

It is apparent that the profitable management of the logistics system has three kinds of implications: strategic, tactical and operational. Just as the physical elements of the system must be closely co-ordinated, so must these three levels of decision making (see Figure 1.8).

STRATEGIC IMPLICATIONS

Strategic decisions have a lasting impact on the efficiency and effectiveness of the logistics system and on the corporate balance sheet. The effects of a wrong decision could be costly. Logistics operations would be impaired, and remedial measures could necessitate a considerable one-time outlay.

Strategic decisions address, for example:

- The number, location and role of manufacturing facilities.

FIGURE 1.8
THE INTERDEPENDENCE OF LOGISTICS DECISIONS

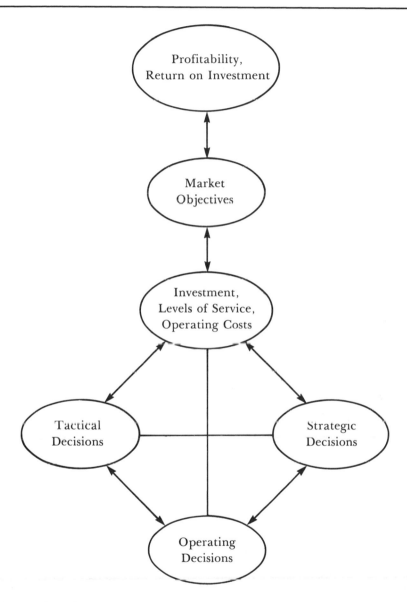

- The number, function and location of warehouses and distribution centres.
- The type of equipment in plants and warehouses: special-purpose, multi-purpose, highly specialized or flexible.
- The staging of inventories within the system. Should the bulk of the inventory be in the form of raw materials or components? Or should it be in sub-assemblies or in finished goods ready for distribution or sale or both?

- Deployment of inventories. Should they be widely dispersed or close to the point of use? Or, in an effort to reduce the investment, should they be consolidated at a small number of retail locations?

TACTICAL IMPLICATIONS

Within a given system comprising physical plant and facilities, a number of tactical decisions influence operational effectiveness. These decisions are the basis for co-ordination. They ensure that the various trade-offs are consistent with corporate objectives. Further, they prevent the excessive pursuit of sub-optimal objectives which would adversely affect the overall performance of the system.

Typical of these tactical decisions are:

- Selecting the mode of transport for line haul from the plant to distribution centres and for local delivery from distribution centres to customers.
- Inventory targets and turnover policy. Inventory, as shown in Chapter 6, is the "lubricant" which facilitates co-ordination among various elements of the system. That is why inventory levels should be planned and budgeted. They then provide the target towards which day-to-day operations are directed.
- Performance goals. The logistics system should be designed to provide the most profitable level of service. As suggested earlier, this represents a trade-off between gaining additional revenues and incurring additional costs and capital investment. Once the trade-off is made, the performance targets of the system become the focus for day-to-day operations, especially at the customer interface.
- Routing of goods. The path, or route, followed by goods from the supplier to the manufacturing facility and from the factory to the customer plays a major role in determining costs and level of service. This is illustrated in Figure 1.9, which shows a number of possible routes from a plant to the customer. The direct path is usually the least costly, provided that there is sufficient volume to justify a large shipment and sufficient time to move the product along this route.

In some instances, in order to make possible the quick and reliable service expected by customers, the product must be stored in regional distribution centres or warehouses. Such a routing decision reflects a trade-off between the search for lower transportation costs (which would come from shipping larger quantities to the warehouse) and the need to reduce investment in inventories. Similarly, the relative roles of a national distribution centre and regional warehouses reflect a trade-off between a number of conflicting operational objectives.

OPERATIONAL IMPLICATIONS

Customers are satisfied, products are moved, and goods are manufac-

FIGURE 1.9
POSSIBLE ROUTINGS – PLANT TO CUSTOMER

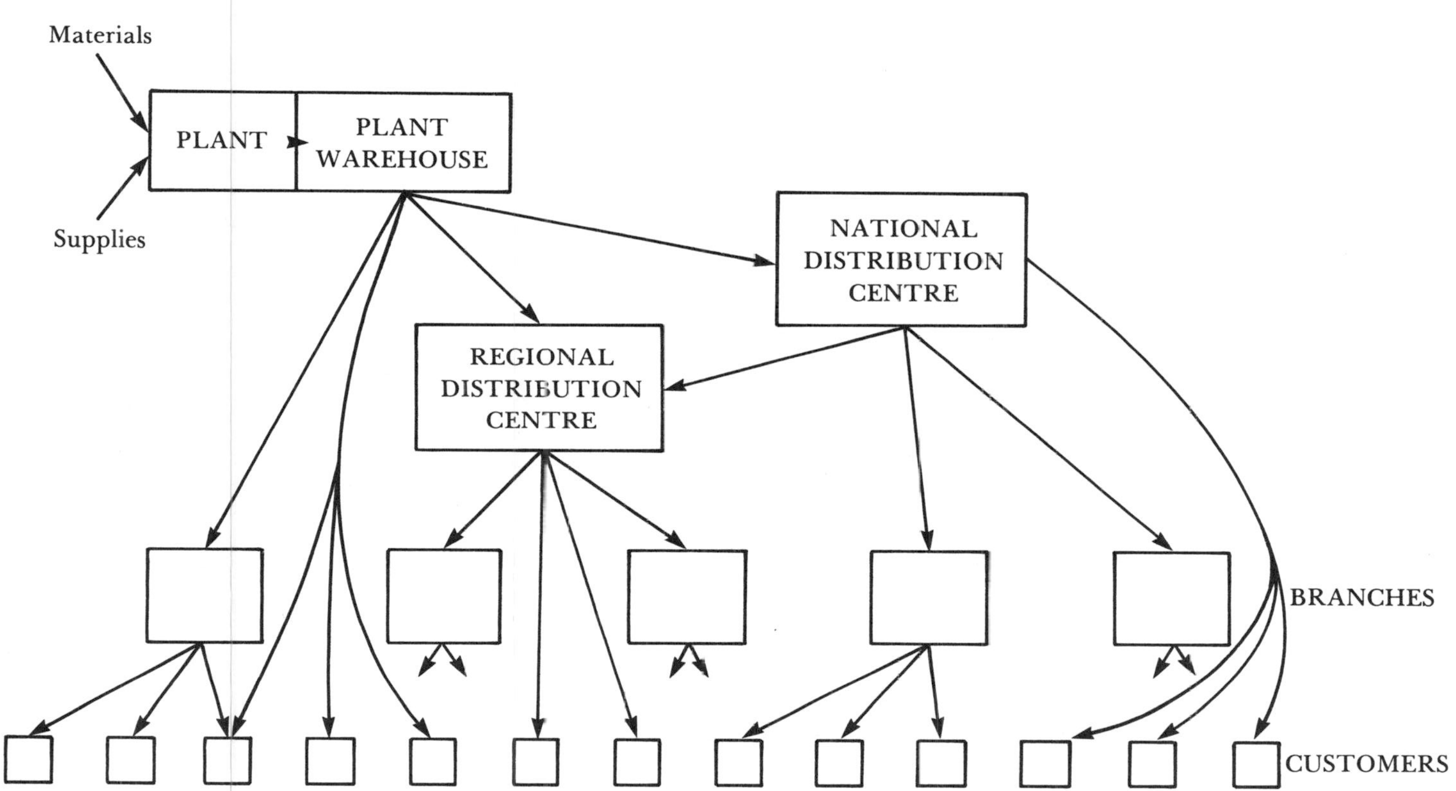

tured as a result of day-to-day decisions made at a number of points along the system. Typical of these decisions are:

• size and frequency of production runs
• size and frequency of shipments from plant to branch
• delivery route or schedule for local deliveries
• staffing level in the shipping department or in the regional warehouse

CONCLUSION

Profitable management of logistics depends on the co-ordination of decisions and activities throughout the entire system. Unless this is recognized — and acted upon — by senior management, logistics will indeed remain the "dark frontier."

CHAPTER 2

Customer Service

INTRODUCTION

Chapter 1 introduced the concept of customer service as the driving force for logistics. Simply stated, customer service is the ability of a supplier to satisfy customers by consistently providing the right product, at the right place, at the right time, in the most convenient and courteous manner. Customer service extends across the chain of logistics activities and often across several companies, as products change hands, from raw materials to the eventual user. Figure 2.1 illustrates the series of customer/supplier interfaces in the automotive industry.

Customer service is a set of activities which occurs at the interface between a supplier and its customers when the underlying purpose of that interface is delivery of the product. The common measures of customer service are:

- order cycle time
- consistency of order cycle time
- availability of product
- order status information
- flexibility to handle unusual situations
- returns — damaged and surplus goods
- response to emergencies
- freedom from errors
- others which are of less general importance but may be critical in certain industries

Under the logistics system, the key to ensuring maximum profitability

FIGURE 2.1
CUSTOMER/SUPPLIER INTERFACES IN THE
AUTOMOTIVE INDUSTRY: A TYPICAL LOGISTICS CHAIN

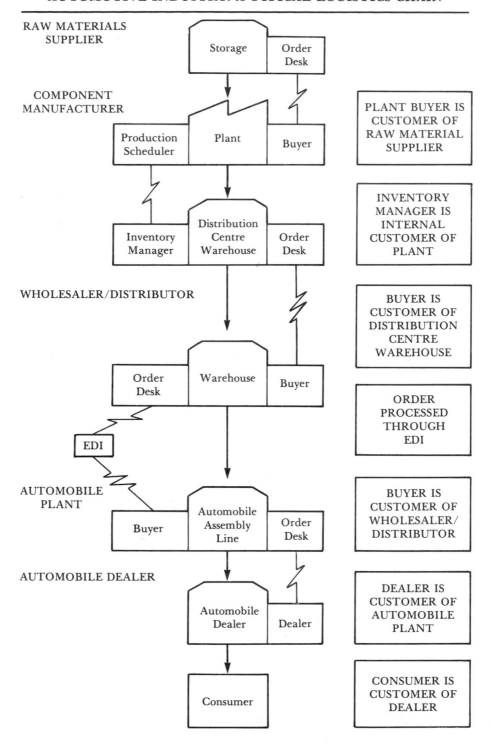

and return on investment is to identify and manage the essential elements of customer service. In this way, the necessary competitive edge may be gained without incurring excessive costs.

Customer service is becoming a major sales and marketing tool. In today's market, where competing products are often identical in both quality and price, customer service performance can be the key differentiation. Many leading companies are recognizing this fact and are developing customer service strategies designed to give them a competitive edge, increase sales and, in some cases, even reduce logistics costs.

In this chapter we initially review the importance of customer service. We then discuss the major components of customer service, and finally we provide an outline of the worksteps needed to develop a customer service strategy program.

THE IMPORTANCE OF CUSTOMER SERVICE

Most companies compete in markets in which, with few exceptions, they have no strong consumer franchise. There is little product differentiation in terms of quality, features or price. Even those companies with unique products or features lose their initial advantage as the product becomes generic through the introduction of competing products. Under these conditions, as suggested in Figure 2.2, the maintenance of market share becomes increasingly dependent on customer service.

Many examples can be cited to illustrate the impact of effective distribution on sales volume and profits. In one case, a distributor of food products to hotel, restaurant and institutional businesses opened a distribution centre some 200 miles closer to the major markets. As a result of this move, the order cycle time was reduced by several hours. This reduction gave the company a significant advantage over its competitors. Sales soared by about 30% in less than a year.

A large merchandise chain introduced an ordering system for catalogue sales which increased on-time delivery from less than 40% to more than 95%. This change boosted sales and contribution. The initial outlay was amortized in less than a year.

A manufacturer of high-fashion goods switched from a branch warehousing system to direct shipment, by air freight, from the factory to retail customers across the country. The improved customer service led to a gain of more than 30% in sales volume. At the same time, inventories and warehousing costs were drastically reduced, by more than enough to offset the higher transportation costs.

The underlying principle of managing customer service is illustrated in

FIGURE 2.2
THE IMPORTANCE OF CUSTOMER SERVICE

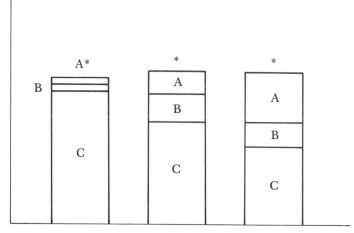

COMPANY
MARKET
SHARE

TIME: STAGE IN PRODUCT LIFE CYCLE

* Proportion of share due to:
A   Customer Service
B   Captive Markets
C   Product and Features

Figure 2.3. It shows the conflict, or trade-off, that occurs at the interface between supplier and customer. The supplier, in an effort to reduce costs, may reduce the level of service. Stock availability may fall. Order cycle time may increase and become more variable. Shipment frequency may decrease due to the consolidation of orders. Such moves may, as suggested by the diagram, reduce the costs which appear on the supplier's accounts. In most cases, however, the supplier has merely shifted certain activities and costs to the customer. Lower stock availability and uncertain shipments will lead the customer to increase stocks. In turn, the customer's investment is increased and return on investment reduced.

The challenge facing the distribution manager is to search for a set of conditions at the interface in which the total cost to supplier and customer is minimized. Similarly, customers who enjoy a strong negotiating advantage over the supplier should take care not to reduce their costs by forcing the supplier to incur excessive costs.

Unfortunately, much of the negotiation between supplier and customer is, by nature, adversarial. Instead of mutually searching for the most efficient overall system, each party tries to shift costs to the other.

FIGURE 2.3
MANAGING THE CUSTOMER INTERFACE

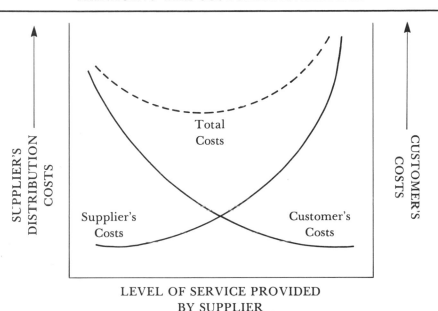

LEVEL OF SERVICE PROVIDED
BY SUPPLIER

THE COMPONENTS OF CUSTOMER SERVICE

In the following sections we discuss the major elements of customer service, namely availability, reliability and convenience, and their potential impact on sales and logistics costs

AVAILABILITY

Availability means that the supplier is able to fill customer orders at the agreed time and place. The two most common components of availability are order fill rate and order lead time. These provide tangible yardsticks against which the company can measure performance and compare targets.

Other components of availability can also be important, depending on the industry. The time required to fill a back order can be as crucial as the time required to fill the initial order, especially if the back-ordered items hold up a manufacturing process or maintenance project. In addition, the ability to handle emergency orders can create a long-lasting bond between supplier and customer. The goodwill that is gained from helping out a customer in trouble is almost as memorable as the annoyance that results from the supplier's falling down on a particular order.

ORDER FILL RATE

Order fill rate is the percentage of an order filled complete at the agreed time and place.

A typical measure is the percentage of lines filled complete, or

$$\frac{\text{number of lines filled}}{\text{number of lines ordered}} \times 100\%$$

Thus, if a customer orders ten product lines from a supplier and receives eight of these at the agreed delivery time, the service level will be 80%.

RELATIONSHIP BETWEEN INVENTORY LEVELS AND ORDER FILL RATES Figure 2.4 illustrates the relationship between inventory levels and order fill rates for a particular item. As the order fill rate increases, the inventory level increases exponentially. Thus, in this example, while an 80% order fill can be achieved with less than one month of inventory, twice as much inventory is needed to achieve 95%, and three times as much to reach 97%. Even five months' supply will result in only a 99.9% order fill. Obviously there is a point of diminishing returns.

In recognition of this fact, most companies set order fill standards below 100%. In the food industry, for example, a 95% order fill rate is the norm. For general merchandise, an 85% to 90% service level is

FIGURE 2.4
RELATIONSHIP BETWEEN INVENTORY LEVELS
AND ORDER FILL RATES

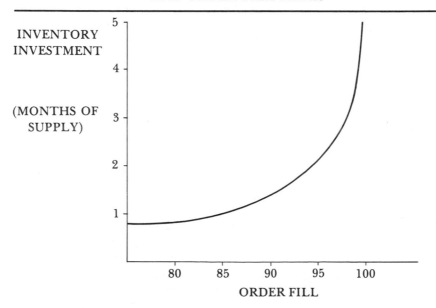

generally acceptable. Thus, companies need to establish order fill objectives which are competitive yet cost-effective.

ABC CLASSIFICATIONS More progressive suppliers divide their product range into ABC classifications according to their importance. A high service level is established for the key "A" items, a slightly lower level for "B" items, and an even lower level for "C" items. Certain "AA" items should never be out of stock. A grocery wholesaler, for example, should never be out of Kellogg's Corn Flakes. However, a temporary shortage of Froot Loops is less serious, because customers will likely substitute a different brand or delay their purchase. Thus a service level target of 99.99% may be established for Corn Flakes, but only 90% for Froot Loops. The overall service average may well be 97%, but customer irritation over stock-outs will be minimal.

The composition of the ABC classification may change periodically, depending on the company's marketing program. For example, if a retailer arranges an advertised special on a certain item, the supplier must have the available stock to fill the order. A stock-out in the retail stores irritates the retail shoppers, reduces the profits for the retailer and ultimately reduces profits for the supplier. Retail store buyers are accountable for the results of their promotions, and they will not tolerate delinquent suppliers for long.

IMPACT OF A STOCK-OUT In developing order fill standards, suppliers should assess the impact of a stock-out. Some important factors to consider include:

- How easily can the product be substituted? If a customer will buy a similar item, there is little impact.
- How competitively priced is the product? If prices are much lower than the competition's, many customers will back-order or take a raincheck.
- Is the item unique and not easily obtained from competitive sources? For these types of items, customers are generally prepared to wait for the item to be expedited.
- Is the item readily available from competing suppliers? A customer whose need for an item is not urgent may remain loyal to the supplier despite an occasional stock-out. If the item is needed urgently, or stock-outs persist, the customer will likely start buying from other sources. Eventually the supplier may lose this customer.

To illustrate, consider the possible effects of a stock-out in the following examples:

- *A record and tape store*
  Impact of a stock-out of the #11 record of the week:
  - Customers purchase an alternative selection.

- Customers purchase the tape, CD or digital version.
- Customers come back and purchase the record when it is back in stock.
- Customers purchase from a competitor.
- *A retail store selling general merchandise*
  Impact of a stock-out of one-litre cans of sky-blue paint:
  - The customer substitutes for a different package size, colour, brand or quality of the item.
  - The customer returns at a later time when the item has been restocked.
  - The customer purchases from another nearby store.
- *A plumbing supply distributor*
  Impact of a stock-out of a valve assembly:
  - The plumbing contractor substitutes a compatible item.
  - The plumbing contractor reschedules work while awaiting the arrival of a back order.
  - The plumbing contractor buys from a competing distributor. (This results in the loss of a sale and the potential loss of a repeat customer.)
- *A component supplier to a production line manufacturer*
  Impact of a stock-out of a critical product component:
  - The production line stops until all parts are available. Idle labour and machinery cost the customer company thousands of dollars, and the production capacity is lost forever.
  - Extra cost is incurred to expedite delivery, perhaps by using air freight.
  - The vendor may be eliminated as a qualified supplier for this and other components.
- *The supply depot of a military base*
  Impact of a stock-out of a weapons system component:
  - The component is transferred at high cost from another depot or manufacturer.
  - Strategic equipment is on downtime.
  - Duties are rescheduled.
  - Operational readiness is reduced.

Thus, the effects of a stock-out on a customer can range from negligible to critical. The customer will treat the supplier accordingly.

ORDER FILL MEASUREMENTS There is no standard method of measuring order fill performance. Typical measurements include:

- percentage of lines (stock-keeping units) filled complete
- percentage of cases filled complete
- percentage of orders filled complete
- percentage of order value filled complete

Each of these methods measures different aspects of order fill and reports different results. Table 2.1 demonstrates how the different measurements can indicate levels of service ranging from 0% to 99.9% for the same order. Accordingly, comparing industry statistics on service level performance can often be very misleading.

TABLE   2.1
SAMPLE ORDER

ITEM #	NUMBER ORDERED	NUMBER SHIPPED	UNIT PRICE $	VALUE ORDERED $	VALUE SHIPPED $
1	1,000	1,000	1	1,000	1,000
2	100	100	10	1,000	1,000
3	10	10	100	1,000	1,000
4	1	0	2,000	2,000	0
Totals	1,111	1,110		5,000	3,000

Orders filled complete: $0/1 \times 100 = 0\%$
Value shipped complete: $3,000/5,000 \times 100 = 60\%$
Lines filled complete: $3/4 \times 100 = 75\%$
Cases shipped complete: $1,100/1,111 \times 100 = 99.9\%$

When selecting an order fill measurement, suppliers should consider several factors. How do customers measure the order fill rate? Ideally, suppliers should measure their performance in the same way. This allows them to define service in the same way, and to be more responsive to problem areas. Why not measure two, three or four of the order fill methods? With the advent of computer power, additional processing time is negligible. The results enable suppliers to more easily identify the reasons for and extent of the problem areas. Is low performance caused by a few specific line items, or are stock-outs widespread? What is the overall impact on dollar sales?

Table 2.2 illustrates a simple order fill report which provides a guideline to performance and identifies problem areas. In this example, immediate attention needs to be paid to the automotive supply division, which should be providing the highest level of service, but which is obviously in deep trouble.

ORDER LEAD TIME

Order lead time is the total time that elapses between the time the customer places an order and the time the customer receives the goods. During this time, many activities take place: order transmission, order entry, order processing, order picking, packing, shipping, transportation and customer receiving.

To consistently meet lead-time expectations, each of these activities must be synchronized, like a production line. The order must be processed through each work centre within a certain time limit to ensure that the overall customer requirement is met.

TABLE 2.2
ORDER FILL RATE

PERIOD:

DIVISION	REGION	# ORDERS	# LINES ORDERED	# LINES FILLED	% O/F	SERVICE LEVEL POLICY
Electrical Supply	E	42	1020	878	86%	85%
	C	40	438	352	80%	85%
	W	46	392	338	86%	90%
Plumbing Supply	E	20	372	316	85%	85%
	C	16	88	76	86%	85%
	W	38	272	272	100%	90%
Automotive Supply	E	16	404	232	57%	95%
	C	32	516	92	18%	95%
	W	24	320	284	89%	95%

For example, a supplier promises delivery of goods the following day for orders received up to 5:00 P.M. To provide this service, all orders are entered into the computer by 6:00 P.M. and the picking slips produced for 8:00 P.M. The warehouse activities (picking, packing and loading) take place on the night shift for dispatch to the customer early the next morning. Failure to accomplish any of the steps in the time allocated results in a late delivery or in extra cost for warehouse overtime or supplementary delivery trips.

LEAD TIMES VARY BY INDUSTRY Customer lead-time expectations vary by industry. Table 2.3 illustrates some typical lead-time requirements, varying from immediate service to several years.

- Retail shoppers generally expect an item to be on the shelf, ready and available. Even a delay of five minutes while the store assistant fetches a product from the back room becomes an irritant.
- In the case of equipment parts, the failure of a bearing may shut down a production line, at a cost of thousands of dollars for lost production and idle labour. Rapid service is imperative. For the normal replenishment of stock of this same item, the customer will likely accept a lead time of one to two days.
- Customers expect rapid copies from a printer. Generally, the printer does not carry inventory of fine paper, but orders supplies from the fine paper distributor after receiving an order from the customer. Thus the whole industry runs on a panic level, measured in hours, not days. If the supplier does not have the stock available, or the transportation to deliver the stock, the printer will merely place the order elsewhere.

TABLE 2.3
EXAMPLES OF LEAD-TIME EXPECTATIONS

PRODUCT	CUSTOMER	TYPICAL ORDER LEAD TIME
1. Food and general merchandise	Retail shopper	Immediate
2. Machinery bearing	Manufacturer	2 hours for breakdown, 1 to 2 days for regular stock
3. Fine paper	Printer	4 hours to next day
4. Packaged food	Grocer	5–10 days
5. Electronic components	Automotive Manufacturer	2–3 months
6. General merchandise	Government Supply and Services	6 months to several years

- Retailers generally accept a five- to ten-day lead time for packaged food products, with longer notice provided for promotions. Supplier performance, however, is measured. Late deliveries are recorded. Poor performance may result in the retailer reducing or relocating a supplier's product shelf space or delisting some or all of the supplier's product lines.
- The automobile industry expects a high order fill rate of close to 100%, to be delivered at a specific time and day to support their just-in-time (JIT) production lines. But because production is planned far ahead of time, the automobile manufacturer can communicate the requirements for components far in advance. The lead time can be several months. The delivery time and day, however, must be faithfully observed.
- Government procurement often entails lead times of at least six months or, for specialized equipment, up to several years. Very little pressure is placed on suppliers to reduce lead times. Most items ordered have unique specifications, usually requiring special production runs. In addition, expediting is usually slow or non-existent. Accordingly many manufacturers produce government supplies as and when they have some downtime.

    Relative to industry, government purchasing practices and lead-time expectations are generally lax. This presents government purchasers with a major opportunity for improvement. If they start to copy industry purchasing practices, they could provide better service to their clients and achieve a multi-billion-dollar reduction in government inventory.

ABC CLASSIFICATIONS   As discussed for order fill rates, many companies also divide their product range into lead-time classifications. In the electrical industry, for example, distributors maintain counter operations across the country. In the smaller communities, counters may carry 1,200 fast-moving items, readily available for a customer pick-up. An additional 4,000–6,000 items may be stocked at regional warehouses, and can be shipped to the counters within a two- to three-day lead time. Slower-moving "C" items may be centralized at a national distribution centre. These can be shipped to the counters within five to ten days for normal orders, or next day by courier for emergency orders. The distributor may sell very slow-moving "D" items from a catalogue and order them directly from the manufacturer on request. Lead times of several months may be the standard for these items.

LEAD-TIME EXPECTATIONS Industry lead-time norms provide a guideline for general lead-time expectations. Nevertheless, customers may request specific delivery days which differ from the general policy. These lead-time expectations are the true lead times against which the customer measures a supplier's service performance.

There are many instances where the agreed lead times are neither realistic nor essential. Too often, a customer may ask for same-day service yet be quite content with next-day service. This often leads to additional costs to process and distribute orders outside the normal order-processing schedule.

Good sales representatives and order desk staff often steer a customer round to more realistic lead-time expectations. They discuss the true lead-time needs and suggest a longer lead time where appropriate.

Unfortunately, many salespeople do not fully understand the implications of agreeing to, and in some cases suggesting, rapid lead times. They are not aware of the additional workload and costs associated with processing and shipping orders outside the normal lead-time policies. And, in some cases, these unreasonably short lead times cannot be met, resulting in an unhappy customer.

It may be good policy to provide occasional emergency service to help the customer out of a jam. The customer will likely remember this incident and show extra loyalty to the supplier. Too often, however, these exceptions become commonplace. The customer no longer regards the emergency order as an exception, but rather as the rule. This results in unnecessarily high distribution costs and a disappointed customer on the odd occasion that the impossible is not achieved.

One company got itself into this bind. Almost 75% of the orders were specified by the sales reps as "rush." This backed up the order-processing activities until even a rush order was taking as long as the normal order lead-time standards. When truly urgent orders came along, sales reps started to denote "rush rush" on the order form.

Eventually, unless an order had "rush rush rush" in big red letters across the order form, it would be merely processed along with all the "rush," "rush rush" and non-designated orders.

LEAD-TIME MEASUREMENTS   Although most suppliers establish customer lead-time goals, few actually measure their performance. These suppliers record neither the time the customer placed the order nor the time the customer received the order. In fact, many companies using outside carriers tend to underestimate true lead times. If they measure lead times at all, they tend to stop the clock as soon as the order is loaded onto the carrier's truck. Many assume that the carrier will now deliver the order post-haste to the customer. Wrong. For less-than-truck-load shipments, the order will likely be unloaded at the carrier's terminal. Here it may stay, in some cases for several days, while the carrier consolidates other orders to make up economical truck routes.

For an agreed fee, carriers will record date and time of arrival. This is often a good way of measuring true lead-time performance and also of determining whether the carrier is responsive enough to achieve the desired times.

Lead-time measurements should include the total time that elapses between the time the customer places the order and the time the goods are actually received. Typical measurements include:

- average lead time for all orders
- deviation from a pre-determined standard, such as:
  - % of orders delivered before requested date
  - % of orders delivered on requested date

TABLE 2.4
LEAD-TIME REPORT

CUSTOMER	ORDER ENTRY #	DATE ORDERED	REQ. DEL. DATE	DATE DEL.	LEAD TIME REQ. (WORKING DAYS)	ACTUAL LEAD TIME (WORKING DAYS)
L. B. Shanks	0591	11/10	18/10	18/10	5	5
Rousseau Electrical Distributors	0592	11/10	13/10	14/10	2	3
Massey & Son	0593	11/10	20/10	22/10	7	9
Volk Machinery	0594	11/10	14/10	15/10	3	4

ORDER LEAD TIME
PERFORMANCE

Delivered on requested date	25%
Delivered one day late	50%
Delivered two days late	25%

- % of orders delivered one day late
- % of orders delivered two days late
- % of orders delivered three or more days late

Table 2.4 illustrates a simple lead-time report which provides a guideline to lead-time performance.

RELIABILITY

Reliability is defined as the consistency with which the supplier achieves the customer service goals agreed to with the customer.

Traditionally, speed or rapid availability has been a major service consideration, with the watchwords being "faster is better." However, customer research in a wide variety of industries has repeatedly confirmed that reliability of service is far more important than pure speed. Customers prefer suppliers whom they can trust and who can reassure them that their orders will be delivered on time.

RELIABILITY FROM A CUSTOMER'S VIEWPOINT

To illustrate the benefits to be gained from reliability, consider the following example. A Food Chain store orders and sells 100 cases of a particular product every week. If there is no sales variance and the supplier is reliable, the order will be delivered just as the customer sells the last unit — an ideal world. Figure 2.5 shows the customer's average inventory to be 50 units.

FIGURE 2.5
NO SALES VARIANCE

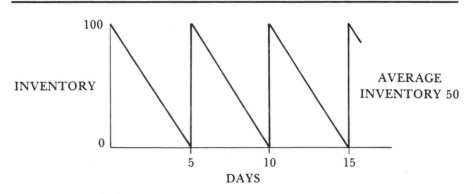

Now assume that daily sales remain constant, but that the supplier is less reliable. Some weeks the order could arrive two days early; others, two days late. To prepare for the possibility of a late delivery, the customer must carry an additional two days' inventory of safety stock. Figure 2.6 shows the customer's average inventory to be 90 units.

FIGURE 2.6
TWO DAYS' LEAD-TIME VARIANCE

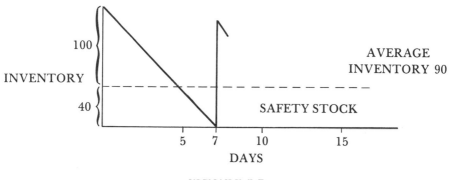

FIGURE 2.7
25% SALES VARIANCE

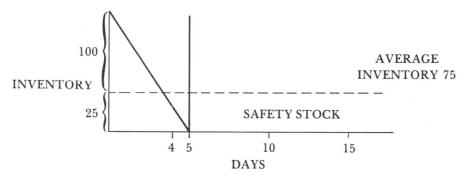

Now let us come closer to reality and assume that the supplier is reliable, but that sales could fluctuate by 25%. Figure 2.7 indicates the need to carry 25 items in safety stock to meet sales fluctuations, giving an average inventory of 75 units.

Finally, we will assume the same 25% sales variance coupled with the less reliable supplier, who could be two days late. The customer must carry sufficient inventory to cover a possible seven-day lead time with sales as high as 25 units/day. Figure 2.8 shows the average inventory level of 125.

As shown by comparing Figures 2.7 and 2.8, the customer can reduce inventory 40% from 125 to 75, if the supplier provides a reliable lead time.

Thus, from a customer's viewpoint, a reliable supplier enables the customer to plan ahead and to reduce inventory to a bare minimum. In fact, it is this element of reliability that drives the just-in-time philosophy. The automotive manufacturers can eliminate safety stock as long as they

FIGURE 2.8
25% SALES VARIANCE AND TWO DAYS' LEAD-TIME VARIANCE

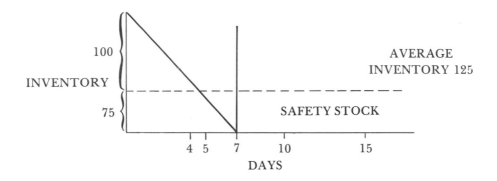

can rely on their suppliers to meet the strict time windows. In fact, many assembly lines carry only a few hours' supply of thousands of items.

CONVENIENCE

The third key factor in customer service is convenience. This can be defined as the ease with which the customer can deal with the supplier. The convenience factor generally deals with the less tangible, more personal side of customer service:

- minimal time in placing, receiving and paying for orders
- accuracy of filling the orders and subsequent paperwork
- efficiency in correcting errors and resolving problems
- communication of changes to product specifications, pricing or availability
- technical, sales and after-sales support
- friendliness and courtesy of order desk, customer service and sales staff.

The convenience factor can include all departments and all personnel within a company. A few case examples show how lack of convenience can lead to customer annoyance and frustration, which in turn can lead to lost sales and lost customers.

INACCESSIBLE SUPPLIER
A distraught customer telephoned a supplier at ten minutes before closing time on an important matter, only to receive a computer-synthesized voice response, "I'm sorry, all our lines are busy. We will contact you when there is a line available." After waiting ten minutes with the message being repeated every minute, the voice message changed to, "Our normal business hours are eight to five thirty. Please call back tomorrow." The caller was trying to reach the "customer service department."

INFLEXIBLE ACCOUNTING PROCEDURES

After considerable sales effort, an electrical distributor managed to persuade a potential customer to switch suppliers. The customer placed the first order, then waited . . . and waited . . . and waited for the order to be delivered. After too long, the irate customer called the sales rep to complain about the service. The sales rep checked the problem. Company policy decreed that all new customers must be approved by the accounting department. The file for opening the new customer's account was sitting on the credit check person's desk, awaiting the person's return from a two-week vacation.

INACCURATE PAPERWORK

A cereal manufacturer changed modes of transportation from road to rail. The first shipment by the new mode was for a railcar-load of cereal from Toronto to a major customer in Winnipeg. After several weeks, the load eventually turned up on a rail siding in Moncton, some 2,000 miles from Winnipeg. The shipper had made an error on the bill of lading, and the error had obviously confused the railway.

LACK OF COURTESY

The president of a company needed to send an urgent document across the country by courier. The president's secretary called the courier's order desk and requested a pick-up, but was informed that the latest time for pick-up was 5:00 P.M. It was approximately two minutes after five. Realizing the importance of the document, the secretary begged and pleaded with the order desk clerk, and finally resorted to clout, reminding the clerk that the company spent thousands of dollars a year with this courier and that this package was from the president. The answer was, "Listen, bitch, I don't care if it's from the President of the United States, I'm not sending a special pick-up for you."

That was the last day that company did business with the courier.

The following checklist addresses some of the convenience factors which help to form a closer relationship between customer and supplier.

CAN CUSTOMERS REACH ORDER DESK STAFF QUICKLY?

The telephone can be a major source of irritation. Whereas a customer can stand for five minutes in a bank line-up without too much annoyance, the same time spent "on hold" at the end of a telephone can drive a person up the wall. It is similarly frustrating to have the receptionist repeatedly switch a customer from one wrong department or person to another.

Reception/telephone operator competence is essential to most suppliers. This is the first point of contact for most customers and sets the tone for the relationship. It is important to train receptionists and switch-board operators in customer service courtesy. Their performance can be monitored through the complaint system, or through periodic blind calls designed to audit their attitude and competence.

Many companies, in a move to cut costs, have reduced the number of order desk personnel. This leads to longer delays in placing an order and can result in customers changing suppliers: "You can never get through to the person you want with that company."

Using modern switching systems, some companies measure the length of time it takes for customers to get through to the order desk. They analyse the results to determine the need for more or fewer access lines, and to ensure that there are sufficient order desk staff available to avoid undue customer waiting time. Some companies will add more people to the order desk for a few hours a day to meet peak periods. Some companies even arrange for scheduled ordering times for regular customers. Often a firm will open WATS lines in major customer areas to reduce the need for long-distance calls, thus improving convenience.

DO ORDER DESK PERSONNEL HAVE READILY AVAILABLE INFORMATION?

With more sophisticated computerized order entry systems, the order-desk staff can immediately provide customers with all the relevant information on stock status, lead times and, if items are out of stock, back-order lead times. This lets customers know where they stand and enables them to decide whether to substitute, back-order or accept a partial shipment.

Companies who cannot provide this information are at a competitive disadvantage. They leave customers unsure of whether, or when, the order will be filled. To avoid uncertainty, customers will tend to call the more knowledgeable supplier first.

ARE CREDIT TERMS AVAILABLE AND WELL UNDERSTOOD?

Sales staff should be fully aware of the scope and limitations to eligibility. Credit checks should always be made prior to a commitment, to avoid embarrassment to both parties. Accounting staff should review the credit status of customers promptly. They should be sensitive to the impact of telling either potential or long-standing customers that they are not creditworthy enough to deal with. The accounting staff should work closely with the sales staff to review each questionable account.

ARE ACCOUNTING PROBLEMS RESOLVED QUICKLY?

It is inevitable that mistakes and disagreements will occur due to returns and credits, clerical errors or price changes. Customers accept the occasional mistake, but if it takes many phone calls and letters to correct mistakes, customers will become disenchanted with the supplier.

In some ways, computerized billing tends to make accounting problems more impersonal and harder to deal with. Corrective information supplied by customers with their payments is ignored by the computer. A human intercept is necessary to resolve such problems.

ARE COMPLAINTS HANDLED PROMPTLY AND COURTEOUSLY?

No one ever won an argument with a customer! Any complaint from a customer is serious. The customer is obviously less than happy with the supplier, rightly or wrongly. Prompt action to resolve the dispute can rectify the situation. Many major department stores, such as Sears or Eaton's, for example, take back merchandise from consumers with no questions asked.

ARE STEPS TAKEN TO IMPROVE ORDER FILL ACCURACY?

Order fill accuracy can have a significant effect on customer/ supplier relationships. From a customer's viewpoint, it is very frustrating to place an order and receive the wrong item or the wrong quantity.

There are many opportunities for a supplier to ship the wrong product. Typical sources of error include:

- order entry
- picking
- labelling
- substitution without consulting the customer
- delivery drivers selecting the wrong items from the back of the truck

Because of the high cost of checking every order, some companies have eliminated the checking activities at the warehouse. Thus, when the order picker selects a wrong item, or arbitrarily decides to substitute an item, the customer suffers. This means that the customer not only does not receive the items ordered, but must also spend significant time and effort to rectify the situation:

- double-checking the order
- repacking the wrong item
- returning the wrong item
- reordering the correct item
- correcting the invoice

Not only is the customer inconvenienced, but the supplier also incurs additional time and costs to correct the mistake.

If order picking errors are significant, companies should take the time to identify and rectify the cause. Errors may be due to poor warehouse layout, inaccurate slotting or undisciplined warehouse staff. The root cause can generally be identified through checking on a sample basis, covering in some cases as few as 2% of the orders, but extending across each area of the warehouse and each employee. These checks should not only identify picking errors, but also provide information on the cause of the error, such as careless picking or items stocked in the wrong slot location.

ARE GOOD COMMUNICATION CHANNELS MAINTAINED BETWEEN SUPPLIER AND CUSTOMER?

Customers are generally tolerant of change if they are kept informed. Good communications start with the sales force and include the order desk, shipping department, service department and accounting department. In each case, honesty is the best policy.

The objective of effective communications is to ensure that the customer is kept up to date on all changes and is never unpleasantly surprised. The kinds of information a customer needs include:

* new product specifications
* order status
* order tracing
* product substitution
* notification of delivery delays

Good communications can downplay problems of supply, particularly if the information is provided early enough. If the stock is not available when requested, the results are obviously negative. But if advice is given in advance, the customer will be able to make alternative plans and will appreciate the thoughtfulness of the supplier. The annoyance level will have been minimized and the account retained.

ARE TECHNICAL SERVICES AVAILABLE?

For some industries technical help on specifications or applications can be a major factor in selecting a supplier. Customers tend to have more confidence in a supplier if the sales and technical staff know their products and applications.

While the convenience factor is less important to most buyers than availability and reliability, it is still a basis of discrimination when selecting suppliers. The customer frustration caused by an inconsiderate supplier can be the underlying reason for changing to a more customer-oriented supplier.

A CUSTOMER SERVICE STRATEGY PROGRAM

For many companies, customer service is achieved more by accident than by design. There are no firm policies or guidelines to direct the sales, distribution or accounting staff to deal with customers. Order fill performance depends on how effectively the inventory controller fights the conflicting demands of production, purchasing, marketing and accounting. Lead times are too often arranged at the discretion of the sales representative or the shipper. Reliability is often a passing phase, and convenience and courtesy depend on the mood of the staff on a particular day. Customer service performance is measured by how many people call the president and complain.

Given that customer service plays an important role in enhancing the profitability of an organization, it follows that management must:

- Identify each relevant component of customer service. At any interface between supplier and customer, only a relatively small number of activities are truly significant in influencing the customer's actions.
- Know the impact of each of these relevant components of service on the customer's buying decision and, in turn, on the projected sales revenues.
- Predict the effect on the customer's buying decision, and, in turn, on revenues, of changing the level of each element of customer service.
- Know the impact of changing the relevant components of customer service on total distribution costs.
- Select that mix of performance measures that will most enhance sales performance while incurring a minimal increase in distribution costs.

In essence, management should be searching for ways to improve the level of service in areas which are most important to the customer and which incur minimal additional cost. At the same time, it should try to reduce the level of service in areas which are not important to the customer and which offer substantial savings opportunities.

To provide the most profitable customer service, more progressive companies are developing customer service and logistics strategies. These are designed to gain market share, minimize logistics costs and increase profitability.

The following section provides a guide to implementing a customer service strategy. For a large company, this project will likely take three to six months to complete. Figure 2.9 illustrates the seven major worksteps in the project. These are discussed below.

1. ORGANIZE THE PROJECT

The intentions of this preliminary step are to define the objectives and goals of the project, and to plan the worksteps, responsibilities and timing.

DEFINE OBJECTIVES AND GOALS
The overall objective of the project is to determine the most profitable

FIGURE 2.9
WORK-STEPS TO DEVELOP A CUSTOMER SERVICE STRATEGY

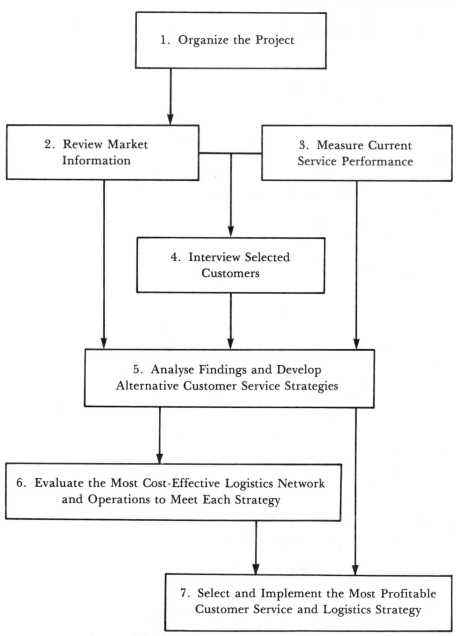

customer service and logistics strategy. This will take into account the trade-offs between improved sales from superior service versus the cost of providing the service. Specific goals could include:

- Identify and establish priorities for customer service requirements.
- Rank the company's service level relative to competitors.
- Identify strengths and weaknesses in current service performance.
- Identify specific service aspects that may provide a distinct competitive advantage.
- Assess the impact on sales and on costs of a higher or a lower service level.
- Evaluate the least-cost logistics network and operations to meet alternative customer service strategies.
- Recommend the most appropriate customer service strategy.
- Develop action plans to implement the recommended service and distribution strategies.

PLAN WORKSTEPS, RESPONSIBILITIES AND TIMING

A customer service strategy involves all departments of a company, and needs top management support. The project should be directed by senior management and should involve a cross-section of staff from all departments.

It is imperative to form a steering committee, comprising the top management in marketing, sales, logistics, finance and production. These people must be aware of the progress of the project, provide direction at key milestone meetings, agree on the strategy and ensure the recommendations are implemented.

In the first meeting of the steering committee, the project manager must discuss:

- project objectives
- scope of the program
- members of staff who will be directly involved in the project and those who can provide valuable input
- project timing and key milestones

At the end of this meeting the top decision-makers must declare their total support and enthusiasm for the project.

2. REVIEW MARKET INFORMATION

The objectives of this step are to obtain background information on the industry and to review the internal perception of customer service requirements and performance.

Much of this information will be obtained from internal interviews and a review of any available marketing reports, service performance reports (if available), and previous customer service studies.

The markets, products and customers should be categorized according to potential customer service differences. Customer service requirements should be established individually for each category. As examples:

- An electrical supply distributor may sell the same products to industrial customers and contractors. The industrial customers may be satisfied with a one-week lead time, whereas the contractor will insist on same- or next-day delivery.
- A customer in Prince Rupert may be delighted with a lead time of four days from a supplier in Vancouver. The Vancouver customer may expect next-day delivery.
- The company may distribute a diverse range of product groups. Each product group may have totally different customer types and service requirements.

Interviews with internal people will provide a wealth of information. In particular, the marketing and sales force can provide good field information on the customers' requirements and on the service provided by competitors. Finance, logistics and production personnel can often identify major problem areas and suggest causes and solutions.

At this stage, however, the information obtained should be used only as a guideline. Some of the data provided will be based on opinions, rumours, hearsay, bias and wishful thinking. This information will, however, provide a few first impressions about what the main issues are. These impressions can then be confirmed from external interviews.

3. MEASURE CURRENT SERVICE PERFORMANCE

To assess improvements, it is necessary to find out initially what service the company is actually providing. In the more sophisticated companies, the computerized order entry system will provide data on current order fill and lead-time performance. However, for most companies, this information will not be readily available. Accordingly, the project team will have to generate the information from raw data, or conduct live measurements over the ensuing few weeks.

The service performance should be obtained for each category of products or customers defined in the market review.

Some of the more important issues in this process are outlined below.

AVAILABILITY OF STOCK, OR ORDER FILL

This measure may exist already in the company's information system, especially when orders are received by mail or data links from the customer. In these events, there is a complete record of what the customer wanted.

Invoices, packing slips, or other shipping documents are the source of data on what has been actually shipped. The two together should give a comprehensive picture of the actual status.

However, most systems are not this simple. In many situations, the customer dictates the order over the telephone. During the course of this conversation with the inside sales desk, it may be discovered that a particular item is not available. In that event, it seldom appears on the order form. Subsequent comparisons between shipping documents, or invoices, and the order would show that the customer apparently received most of the desired items. The only variances are the result of discrepancies in the warehouse or possibly of errors in order picking. The true level of service could be much lower than indicated — and it usually is. In this, as in many other similar cases, it is necessary to document what the customer actually wants. This frequently requires a temporary change at the order desk. A new form is required. It should identify not only those items which are to be shipped, but also those items and quantities which the customer would have ordered had they been available.

The results of this comparison are striking. In one case, management believed confidently that it was providing about 93% service level on the shipment of its industrial products. Documentation of the actual performance showed it to be less than 50%.

ORDER CYCLE TIME AND CONSISTENCY

Many carriers now offer "proof of delivery" or "record of delivery" on request. Some carriers may charge for this service; others provide it free as part of their total service package. In either event, this is likely the most effective way of determining when an order is actually delivered.

Another method used by some companies requires the customer to return a card when the goods are received. Unfortunately, this puts the onus on the customer, who has relatively little vested interest in completing the card at the time the goods are received. In fact, customers are reluctant to be burdened with this additional paperwork. Despite this caveat, there are instances where the use of a card — especially a warranty card — could provide the information in the most cost-effective way.

The elapsed time for the order to come from the customer to the inside sales desk is more easily determined. Telephone calls are instantaneous; there is little lost time unless the customer is kept waiting because of a shortage of lines.

Orders mailed in usually provide the data, either from the postmark or from the order date which the customer might have written on the document.

Orders solicited by the salespeople should be similarly scrutinized. Instances have been recorded where an order was carried in a sales rep's briefcase for several days before it was delivered to the branch. Not surprisingly, the customer complained about the long lead time on that particular order.

Similar steps should be taken with other measures. The principles are simple:

- Determine what is important from the customer's point of view.
- Determine, again from the customer's viewpoint, the most appropriate units.
- Implement a system for collecting the data, either through sampling or through comprehensive analysis.

4. INTERVIEW SELECTED CUSTOMERS

Based on the information developed from the market review and the measurement of current service performance, the next step is to conduct customer interviews. The objectives of this step are:

- to determine customers' current and prospective service requirements
- to rank the company's performance against competitors
- to identify areas for improvement
- to identify customer service strategies which will provide a competitive advantage

SELECT CUSTOMERS

In this step, a representative cross-section of customers should be selected from each of the market categories developed earlier. The selection should take into account size and type of customer and geographic differences and should also include prospective customers and former customers.

DESIGN QUESTIONNAIRE

The project team should develop an interview questionnaire which will cover all aspects of vendor selection, customer buying habits and competitor performance. In addition, the questions can provide good insights into other marketing areas, such as pricing, promotional activities and advertising support. Table 2.5 provides a list of customer service issues to cover.

REPORT TO STEERING COMMITTEE

At this stage, the project team should convene a steering committee meeting to discuss the market review, customers selected for interview and details of the questionnaire. The steering committee may suggest additional or alternative customers to include on the list and request additional issues to discuss with the customers.

CONDUCT EXTERNAL INTERVIEWS

Following approval by the steering committee, the project team should make the necessary appointments with the selected customers and conduct the interviews.

It is often advisable to use outside logistics consultants to conduct the interviews. They can obtain a more accurate impression of the customer's true service requirement and of the competitors' performance. Using an

TABLE 2.5
CUSTOMER SERVICE ISSUES

- product quality
- pricing
- lead times provided
- lead times needed
- reliability of delivery dates and times
- attitude to scheduled deliveries
- product substitution
- order-fill requirements
- order-fill performance
- method of measuring order-fill rates
- back-order policies
- accuracy of order fill
- method of ordering
- ease of placing orders
- electronic data interchange
- incidence of damages
- packaging, handling and shipping requirements
- invoicing requirements
- discount structures and credit terms
- methods used to deal with emergencies
- after-sales service
- technical advice availability
- importance of local warehouse/counter or service centre
- courtesy of staff
- communication on order status, expediting, etc.
- effectiveness of supplier's sales force
- other characteristics considered important
- major problem areas
- examples of punitive action taken for poor service
- service performance aspects which may lead to greater share of business

approach typified by Table 2.6, the customer is asked to rank the performance of three or four competing firms on each of the important service characteristics. A useful ploy is for the consultant to withhold the name of the client until the end of the interview. This provides an unbiased ranking of the company against the competitors. At the end of the interview, when the client's name is revealed, some very rewarding insights are often forthcoming about how the customer really sees the client company.

To obtain customer service information from a broader cross-section of current and prospective customers, the project team may supplement the personal interview with a mailed questionnaire. It should be noted,

TABLE 2.6
EVALUATION OF CUSTOMER SERVICE:
PERFORMANCE VIS-À-VIS COMPETITORS'*

CHARACTERISTIC	SELF	COM-PETITOR A	COM-PETITOR B	COM-PETITOR C
Speed of Delivery	2	3	5	1
Consistency	4	2	3	3
Order Fill Rate	2	4	4	1
Flexibility	5	3	1	2
Information	2	1	3	3
Returns Policy	4	2	4	3
Emergency Response	4	4	2	4

- By product line
- By marketing channel
- By region

*Relative performance vis-à-vis competitors':
1 = Excellent   5 = Bad

however, that as a rule questionnaires generate only about a 10% to 20% response.

5. ANALYSE FINDINGS AND DEVELOP ALTERNATIVE CUSTOMER SERVICE STRATEGIES

The objective of this step is to assess ways of increasing sales by developing customer service strategies which will provide competitive advantages. Three elements provide input into this step: what the customer wants, what the competitor provides and what it will cost.

The results of the previous four steps will give answers to such questions as:

- What are the key criteria used by customers to select suppliers? How important are the individual service factors? If one of the attributes of customer service is important to neither the customer nor the supplier, it can be ignored. This will allow management to concentrate on the relatively small number of measures that are truly significant in generating profit and return on investment.
- Does the service as perceived by customers differ from the actual service provided?
- What service aspects need improvement?
- What service advantages does the company currently enjoy? Can these advantages be developed further?
- In which areas do competitors perform better? Do these areas have a significant effect on supplier selection or their share of the business?

- Is service in some areas unnecessarily high? Can service be reduced without affecting sales?
- How can the company differentiate itself from the competitors? Can strategies be developed which will be difficult for the competitors to copy?
- What must the company do to open specific accounts or increase market share with specific customers?

At this stage the project team can develop alternative customer service strategies and requirements, which should lead to increased sales.

6. EVALUATE THE MOST COST-EFFECTIVE LOGISTICS NETWORK AND OPERATIONS TO MEET EACH STRATEGY

The objective of the logistics assessment is to develop the most cost effective method of providing the alternative service strategies identified in the previous step. Generally, costs increase with increasing levels of service. The increased cost may reflect any combination of:

- strategic change, in which the location of inventories is moved
- tactical change, in which the overall level of inventory is raised or shipping frequency increased to provide a higher level of service
- operational change, in which goods are shipped the day the order is received instead of consolidating for two or three days to reduce transportation costs

Depending on the major service strategies, the necessary changes may include the following:

SERVICE CHANGE: FASTER LEAD TIMES
- Improve delivery methods.
- Simplify order processing procedures.
- Improve warehousing activities.
- Add or relocate warehouses.

SERVICE CHANGE: INCREASE ORDER FILL RATE
- Increase inventory levels.
- Improve inventory management systems.
- Improve purchasing methods.
- Change production schedules.

SERVICE CHANGE: REDUCE DELAY TIMES AT ORDER DESK
- Add more order desk staff.
- Introduce split shifts to meet peak demand.
- Simplify order desk procedures.
- Develop an improved order entry system.

SERVICE CHANGE: PROVIDE GREATER TECHNICAL SUPPORT
- Provide technical training to sales and order desk staff.
- Transfer long-term field salespeople to order desk department. (Often older

salespeople welcome the opportunity to leave the road and settle down into a desk job.) Their wealth of experience and customer knowledge can greatly enhance the image of the order desk department.

• Establish a technical support service to respond to customer enquiries.

SERVICE CHANGE: REDUCE LEAD TIMES ON BACK ORDERS

• Add more items to inventory or improve inventory management procedures to reduce incidence of back orders.
• Develop improved expediting procedures.
• Change production schedules or source of supply.

SERVICE CHANGE: INCREASE BREADTH OF LINE

• Introduce additional items to inventory.
• Find alternative sources of supply which can provide additional items at short notice.

SERVICE CHANGE: IMPROVE DISCOUNT STRUCTURE AND CREDIT TERMS

• Change policies to match or beat competitors.

SERVICE CHANGE: IMPROVE ORDER FILL ACCURACY

• Check selected items or selected customer orders prior to shipping.
• Identify and correct causes of error.

SERVICE CHANGE: PROVIDE IMPROVED COMMUNICATIONS ON ORDER STATUS

• Introduce an on-line order entry system so that order desk personnel can provide up-to-date information on order status.
• Develop procedures to ensure customers are contacted when changes occur in product availability.

SERVICE CHANGE: PROVIDE MORE RELIABLE SERVICE

• Identify reasons for unreliable service — sales force, production, inventory, order processing, warehousing, transportation. Rectify the problems.
• Co-ordinate all logistics activities to ensure that service goals can be met consistently.
• Measure performance and correct problem areas.

SERVICE CHANGE: INTRODUCE SCHEDULED DELIVERY DAY PROGRAM

• Establish frequency of service to each geographic location.
• Prepare program to sell the benefits of reliability, initially to the sales force, then to the customers.
• Consider setting up a special delivery service to supply emergency orders to customers on non-scheduled delivery days.

SERVICE CHANGE: CHANGE PACKAGING OR ORDER QUANTITIES

• Change number of items in a case to meet customer requirements.
• Sell individual items instead of case quantities only. (This will require a broken-case picking section and a packaging section in the warehouse.)

- Change policies on minimum order quantities.
- Provide unitization methods (pallet, clamp or slip sheet) to meet customers' receiving and storage requirements.

For each change in service, the project team should identify the most effective and cost-efficient way of providing the service. The team should then evaluate any increased costs to the company of providing this service. In some cases, the service strategies can be developed by improving the performance of the current operations without increasing the logistics costs. In fact, improvement opportunities identified in this step can lead to both improved service and reduced logistics costs.

7. SELECT AND IMPLEMENT THE MOST PROFITABLE CUSTOMER SERVICE AND LOGISTICS STRATEGY

In this final step, the project team should review the findings of the study with the steering committee. The service improvement opportunities should be prioritized according to the expected impact on sales, effects on logistics and the ease of implementation. The steering committee and the project team should then examine the trade-offs between the service improvement opportunities against the cost of providing that service. The key issues to address at this point are:

- If we improve service, will we improve sales? By how much? What is the cost of providing the superior service?
- If we reduce service in certain areas, what will be the effect on sales? What will be the cost savings?
- Which programs can be implemented rapidly? What will be the effect on sales and costs?
- Which programs will provide a definite competitive advantage? How easy are they for the competitors to copy? What are the benefits and costs?

The meeting should result in a well-documented customer service policy and a detailed implementation guide. The new customer service policy will be used by the logistics department to develop a logistics strategy, providing the desired service at the lowest overall cost.

The normal steps in implementing the policy are:

- Communicate the target levels of service and the projected impact on sales revenues, costs and profitability to key members of the firm.
- Obtain feedback, review and modify the initial trade-off, if appropriate.
- Review and discuss with customers the implications for the interface between the two organizations.
- Prepare an explicit operational statement of customer service policy. It should contain target levels of service as they are to be measured, as well as whatever qualitative or special procedures may be included as part of the overall customer service policy. Without such a specific statement, managers will

interpret the standards as best suits their divisional objectives, undermining the cohesion which is so essential to gaining the competitive edge.

• Implement a performance measuring system. It should be built around the relatively small number of performance measures that are important in terms of the market. It should also focus on the trade-offs between customer service and significant elements of distribution costs such as transportation, local delivery, inventories and warehousing. The performance measuring system could be based on sampling of data, or it could reflect 100% of the transactions. The important issue is: will it provide the control in the most cost-effective way?

Current evidence in Canada and in the United States suggests that a relatively small number of firms, usually the most sophisticated, have developed customer service strategies in the manner outlined above. These companies report substantial benefits from the approach, although they realize that it is not yet an exact science.

Interest is increasing among those who have not implemented a rational approach to managing customer service. The search for the competitive edge and the recognition of the increasing importance of distribution and/or logistics in determining profitability and return on investment are increasingly forcing management to re-examine this "unmanaged" component of the organization.

CHAPTER 3

Order Processing

INTRODUCTION

The time that elapses between placing the order and receiving delivery was defined in Chapter 2 as the *order lead time*. The activities that take place between the time when the customer starts the process and the time the order is submitted to the warehouse is the *order processing time*.

This chapter discusses how order processing can affect customer service, describes a typical order processing system and reviews the emergence of electronic data interchange (EDI).

ORDER PROCESSING AND CUSTOMER SERVICE

The order processing functions are vital to logistics efficiency. If orders are not taken and entered in a timely and accurate manner, sales may be lost or extra costs incurred or both. The result will be a longer lead time and, therefore, poorer customer service.

Order processing comprises the activities of order entry and document preparation to enable order fill to proceed. Order entry starts when the customer contacts a representative of the supplier firm with the intent of placing an order, and ends when the supplier hands the order to warehousing. The following activities may be included:

- initial client contact
- transmission of order from client to supplier
- supplier internal transmission, including "salesperson pocket time"

- supplier internal document preparation
- credit check
- order confirmation to client
- data processing
- information transmission within the supplier organization (including to warehouse)

The supplier and the purchaser can work together to minimize delays in placing the order, and thus improve availability, reliability and convenience — the three main customer service goals. The supplier may consider the lead time to start from the time he or she receives the order, while the purchaser considers it to start when he or she completes the paperwork. The difference is the information transmission time. The supplier has control only over the activities *within* the corporation and cannot be held responsible for any delays in initial transmission *to* the corporation. A successful supplier will, however, take the initiative to streamline the process, recognizing the competitive advantages to be gained.

THE ORDER MESSAGE

In order to properly transmit the needs of a purchaser to the supplier, the purchaser must prepare a clear and concise message. Each of the following elements is a source of error:

- identification of items — incorrect catalogue number, size, colour, package size, etc.
- incorrect quantity — confusion over units, for example, cwt. with crt.
- incorrect delivery location — often confused with address for sending the invoice
- incorrect delivery date — inconsistent convention for numeric designations (e.g., month/day/year sometimes transposed to day/month/year)

PLACING THE ORDER

There must be an effective communication channel for placing orders, and the supplier must be able to receive and interpret the message.

In many cases, the elapsed time between identifying a need for goods or services and preparing the order is significant. The purchasing department may have a backlog, competitive quotes or tendering may be necessary, or an extensive approval process may be required. Strategies to minimize this time lag are discussed in Chapter 9.

The buyer must determine exactly what is needed and convey those requirements to the selected supplier through one of the following methods.

DIRECT CONTACT BY A SALES REPRESENTATIVE

The main reason for using sales representatives is to maximize sales through pro-active selling as opposed to reacting to a specific need. Personal contact by a sales rep gives the customer a sense of importance, and the needs of the customer can be more readily investigated. It is clearly a labour-intensive and therefore costly mode. Since the information taken by the representative must be entered into the system, there is a built-in delay and a higher cost. Special accommodations such as dedicated lines, automatic answering machines or remote data entry may be made to facilitate the transmission of information. While "salesperson pocket time" may vary widely, this is not normally a large source of delay, and information transmission is reasonably accurate.

DIRECT PLACEMENT AT THE ORDER COUNTER

It is less costly for the supplier but more costly for the customer to have one of the customer's employees travel to the supplier site. For items that are in stock, the lead time can be minimized, and supplier costs are reduced. Since there is one less channel to go through, accuracy is also improved. In order to service this trade reliably, a greater amount of inventory must be carried by the supplier.

TELEPHONE CONTACT WITH THE ORDER DESK

For many small and medium-size suppliers, the telephone is the main channel of communication for orders. It is vital that the order desk be properly equipped to provide service. Procedures must be established. Staff must be trained and their performance monitored. A sufficient number of lines must be provided and, if needed, special WATS lines used to improve customer convenience. The order desk must be open when the customers want to place their orders.

For both parties, this is a convenient channel. Information transmission time is minimized, and costs are low. Product availability and delivery time can be verified. However, accuracy will not be as high, because there is no written document to refer to.

WRITTEN COMMUNICATION BY MAIL

To avoid the misunderstandings that can result from verbal communication, many companies require that written purchase orders be sent for all orders. Unless there is a great urgency, the cheapest method of transmission of written material is still the mail service. Cost and accuracy are advantages. However, transit time can vary from one day for some local mail to weeks for international surface mail. And delivery time for the same local message can vary from one to five or more days. This mode is, therefore, considered slow and unreliable. Many companies have substituted courier delivery for the mail to ensure fast and reliable service. This increases the transmission cost by a factor of at least ten.

TELEX OR FACSIMILE TRANSMISSION

Both telex and facsimile transmission of orders are speedy and accurate. But not all customers are equipped to transmit or receive in these modes, unless the population of customers has a special agreement. Transmission costs are high compared to local telephone or mail, but both provide the hard copy necessary to start the process for many buyers. Telex is slightly less accurate because it requires retyping the information for transmission.

DATA TRANSMISSION

The personal contact modes are costly, very reliable and moderately speedy. Telephone contact is speedy, but suffers in accuracy. Written communication is accurate but, if transmitted through the mails, can be unreliable and slow. Telex and facsimile are more reliable, but slightly more costly. By far the most desirable method of contact is data transmission, which combines the best characteristics of the other modes. It seems more costly if only the order placing costs are taken into account, but if all logistical costs are recognized, efficiencies can be achieved and costs reduced in most industries. A network of users must be set up; this requires a protocol for transmission and the necessary hardware to send and receive the signals. The transmission network is in place and is operated by telephone companies.

In general, the faster the mode, the higher the unit cost to transmit the order. The cost is offset, however, by the assurance that the message will be received accurately and on time. This, in turn, leads to better inventory control and less expense. In evaluating the methods to be used, this cost and service trade-off must be considered.

ORDER ENTRY

The order message, in whatever form, must then be interpreted by the supplier into a code which is used by the supplier's organization. The order clerk is responsible for transferring the information from the customer purchase order to the supplier order, and ensuring that the two documents are cross-referenced. A credit check is made prior to release of the order.

Most firms have progressed as far as automating at least part of their operation. At the very least, they have a system to manage the accounts and, likely, the invoicing. Often there will be separate systems for each of these activities, but these systems should be integrated to save effort and processing time. However, at some point in the process the data concerning the orders must be entered into a data base. The data thus coded are then available to feed the processing programs which help to run the company.

The most common process is through the key-punch operator, or the data-entry clerk, who works at a console translating the written orders, produced from the various sources discussed above, into machine-readable code. Initially, this code was in the form of key-punched cards, a method which has been largely discarded in favour of electronic data base storage.

The next step in sophistication is the elimination of the operator and one step in the cycle by having the order desk or a salesperson input the orders using a desktop terminal. The use of remote terminals at distributed locations feeding the central computer via telephone lines extends this capability.

In order to minimize error and further streamline the process, the data can be input on the customers' premises. This is done using portable, hand-held terminals to record the needs. Either the supplier's employee enters the information, as in a bread route, or the customer is supplied with the equipment and any necessary training.

More sophisticated customers have information systems which automatically produce orders, requiring only a release by the purchasing department. These "point-of-sale" data-capture devices can be used to record sales, control inventory and send requirements to the supplier via telephone lines. The information systems can have order enquiry and forward planning features. In steady-state conditions, human intervention is not required except for approval. Elapsed time is minimal, accuracy is high, and the cost of data capture is low, although the initial capital investment is significant. Bar coding of each item is the key which enables the information to be entered into the data base quickly and accurately.

BAR CODING

The food industry has progressed farther than any other industry in the application of bar code technology to control inventory, monitor status, price orders, etc. The Universal Product Code (UPC) symbols are found on most packaged food products throughout North America. The most visible use is for pricing an order at the check-out counter of the local grocery store, but before it reaches that point, the code has likely been used many times.

The bar code is merely a label that is machine-readable. By affixing the label to a product, it is possible to use machines to read the labels and thus relate the location to the package characteristics. Using this information, computers can:

• determine the remaining inventory level, as in the check-out example
• check bills of lading during loading or unloading of shipments
• speed stock taking and increase accuracy
• direct packages to the right lanes in conveyor sorting systems
• direct AGVs or AS/RS to the appropriate station
• verify that the correct items are being picked from warehouse bins, and record the debit (or addition) from inventory records
• facilitate any other task which requires location or volume information

Bar codes are thus used to validate every single transaction from packaging (including labelling) through to customer delivery.

Bar codes have been used in the manufacturing sector since before 1971. Whole plants may be controlled, using a bar code system to track component parts from receiving to storage to picking to the production line, the work-in-process from one line to another and, finally, the finished inventory from the line through the distribution process.

The key benefits are:

• shipment accuracy
• better customer service through higher reliability
• fewer rush orders and emergencies
• better inventory control and thus less inventory
• near-perfect inventory records
• more streamlined processes
• higher productivity
• reduced wastage
• superior error detection earlier in the cycle
• higher morale
• reduced paper flow

A bar code system comprises the label printer, a method to affix the label, various fixed and wand scanners including their data-storage hardware, communications hardware and a communications link, processing hardware and, most importantly, the software which is used to process the data into useful information.

There are eight symbologies, or languages that are commonly in use, each of which is designated with a Uniform Symbol Description number (USD), as follows:

- USD-1 (interleaved 2-of-5)
  - high-density numeric code
  - used for external markings
  - codes are contained in the bars and spaces
- USD-3 (Code 39) and USD-2 (Code 39 subset)
  - alphanumeric code
  - used by auto and health industries
  - three of the nine elements are wide and weighted differently
- USD-4 (Codabar)
  - numeric code with control characters
  - used by libraries and blood banks
  - applied to category and sub-category inventories
- USD-5 (Matrix Code)
  - alphanumeric based on absence/presence criteria
  - used on conveyor lines
  - developed for the Charge Couple Device
- USD-6 (Code 128)
  - second-generation all-character code
  - used for small electronic components
  - compatible with laser, dot-matrix or ink-jet printers
- USD-7 (Code 93)
  - 43 data characters, alphanumeric plus control
  - compatible with Code 39 applications
  - higher density
- USD-8 (Code 11)
  - high-density numeric code
  - scanning is possible in either direction

USD-1 and USD-3 make up about 90% of industrial applications.

COMMUNICATING ORDER REQUIREMENTS

One of the key concepts in information systems design is the concept of entering data as early as possible in the cycle, preferably at source. A second concept is entering data only once. These notions led to the integration of all the internal logistics functions from order entry to shipping. Data entered at the order desk are transmitted to the warehouse and used to create picking slips. Likewise, they are used for shipping documents and billing to accounts. In every system which is not integrated in this way, additional resources are being used and the possibility of error is compounded.

Once the data on each order are in the system, the information is available for use by many operations in the distribution function.

- An open order file is created, and checks are made for other open orders for the same customer which can be consolidated for delivery.

- Hard copies of orders or notices of back order may be printed and sent to the customer.
- Picking slips are produced and sent to the warehouse.
- Bills of lading are printed.
- Invoices are prepared.
- Historic customer records are updated.
- Inventory records are updated.
- Sales records are updated and commissions are calculated.
- Account status is revised.

It is essential that accurate information be available to ensure the efficient use of resources in all of these areas.

ELECTRONIC DATA INTERCHANGE

Electronic data interchange (EDI) encompasses the transmission of transaction information between locations using electronic channels. While many enterprises have had company-wide programs for many years, it is only comparatively recently that they have been integrated with customer systems.

Recent advances in computer technology have improved the feasibility of computer-to-computer messaging. The result is the elimination of requisitions, purchase orders and other paperwork. The system is fast and virtually error-free. With higher order and inventory reliability, both supplier and customer can reduce inventories. There are fewer middle parties, and thus administrative labour costs are reduced.

Many companies initially developed electronic data interchange within their plants and between their divisions. These private networks were then expanded to include key suppliers. The third stage was the creation of public clearing-houses which managed the transmission of information between large numbers of users in different industries.

WHO IS USING EDI?

In the U.S., the Transportation Data Coordination Committee (TDCC) spearheaded the first formal development of the concept. In the late 1970s, it published the U.S. EDI message standard for shippers, the various modes of transport (air, rail, marine and motor carriers) and their agents, brokers and bankers. This was closely followed by the warehouse standard. Other industry standards have been developed through the American National Standard Institute as an offshoot of this effort. The key is that each of these systems is compatible with all other systems.

The following communications standards have been set by organizations in the U.S.:

Air Transportation — AIR
Motor Transportation and Trucking — MOTOR
Ocean Shipping — OCEAN
Rail Transportation — RAIL
Warehousing — WINS
Electrical Distribution — EDX
Chemical Industry — CIDX
Automotive Industry — X12

The banking, office products, retail and aluminum industries have also set communication standards.

The first organized efforts in this direction in Canada started in 1982 when the Grocery Products Manufacturers of Canada initiated a pilot project. Initial transmissions of purchase order and invoice data began in 1984, followed in 1985 by the addition of debits, credits and adjustments, and shipping advice.

This led to the formation of the Electronic Data Interchange Council of Canada (EDICC) to manage standards and be the governing body of the industry. The Council is supported by the following organizations:

Canadian Food Brokers Association
Canadian Grocery Distributors Institute
Canadian Warehousing Association
Canadian Wholesale Drug Association
Grocery Products Manufacturers of Canada
Pharmaceutical Manufacturers Association of Canada
Proprietary Association of Canada
Retail Council of Canada

More recently, the trucking industry has formed the Trucking Task Force Group, with the support of the Canadian Trucking Association.

HOW IS EDI USED?

Communication requires initiating a message, transmitting the information between two points without interference, receiving the signal and decoding the message.

To be effective, first, the sending and receiving hardware must be compatible, and the protocol consistent. The manufacturing and consumer products industries through the EDICC have adopted the U.S.-developed uniform communications message standard (UCS) as the specification for electronic data transmission.

Second, the content of the transmissions for each of the types of document must be agreed on: purchase order, credit note, etc. The coding of component parts, finished products and so forth must be compatible, so that any number of companies in the same industry can communicate on a common ground without the need to translate into "in-house" languages. New trading partners can be quickly integrated into the business. As with the development of UPC bar codes in the grocery industry, common product numbering systems have been a major road-block to effective implementation of EDI. As an alternative, it is possible to develop the necessary software to translate the coded information into the internal forms of each of the participating firms.

Direct communication between a large number of firms is unwieldy because of scheduling restrictions (i.e., the receiving computer cannot always be ready to receive a transmission from a sending machine). Therefore, the larger networks are operated by third parties who manage a "mailbox" of messages which is accessed as needed. The information is received from all senders at their convenience, analysed for completeness and compatibility and stored in the receiver's file(s). The trading partner can then choose to access its file when it is convenient or, alternatively, schedule a regular transmission. Such a system increases security as well, since the sender never interfaces directly with the receiver's computer.

WHAT ARE THE BENEFITS OF EDI?

EDI can significantly change the relationships between buyer and supplier, to the benefit of both. The system is convenient and increases the opportunity to co-operate. Specifically it:

- reduces purchase-order preparation and delivery time
- reduces invoice preparation and delivery time
- increases order accuracy
- eliminates data entry for the supplier
- facilitates two-way communication of order status
- facilitates JIT (just-in-time) manufacturing practices and CIM (computer-integrated manufacturing)
- permits shipping/receiving scheduling
- facilitates sourcing searches
- allows for increased reliability
- increases customer convenience
- improves supplier performance monitoring
- reduces paper flow, document storage and filing costs
- permits purchasing, accounting and traffic functions to be centralized
- makes seven-day, 24-hour access available
- enables electronic funds transfer and shipment verification
- streamlines credit procedures for returned goods

IMPLEMENTATION OF EDI

EDI will not be applicable to all transactions. Suppliers must consider whether their operation can fit into this concept.

Keep abreast of developments in your industry. Are your major customers encouraging your participation? Are your competitors taking market share because they can communicate better and thereby provide better service? Is there a trade organization with an EDI initiative?

Ensure that the company is ready internally. Does the company have the logistics capability under control, and is it prepared to extend the co-operative attitude to competitors and customers alike? Can it operate in a disciplined manner?

Analyse the benefits and weigh them against the cultural changes and cost implications. Assess the appropriate timing. Many of the savings will be modest until there is greater penetration of EDI in your particular industry sector.

Investigate all options and work with your peer companies and clients to minimize cost and ensure compatibility. Most industry associations have begun to establish standards and procedures. This is the starting point.

Your internal systems must be made consistent with the selected protocol for your industry. Early involvement of departments which will use the strategy is essential to obtain their support, and to take into account all your corporate needs.

Prepare for a gradual transition. Undertake extensive training of all staff involved.

After the commitment is made, the implementation process can take from six weeks to six months.

Be prepared to act quickly, for progress is being made. For example, between 1985 and 1986, Chrysler increased its supplier base on EDI from 125 to 500 of its 1700 suppliers.

SUMMARY

Order entry is a vital component of the logistics process. To process information efficiently, buyers and suppliers must co-ordinate their efforts. Current methods are labour-intensive and very error-prone. The successful suppliers must look to technology to become more efficient.

Bar code applications are being used in all sectors of our economy. EDI is improving customer service and reducing costs significantly. These advances will mean great gains in efficiency for distributors and manufacturers in the 1980s and 1990s.

CHAPTER 4

Sales Forecasting

INTRODUCTION

Sales forecasting is an integral part of business logistics. Forecasting permits planning, and planning is one of the cornerstones of good management. Forecasts are also woven right into a company's daily operating routine — a forecast of some kind is a part of every materials procurement, production planning and finished goods stocking decision. Companies that do a good job forecasting their sales usually perform better: their customer service is more reliable and their operating costs are lower.

Yet a truly effective approach to sales forecasting can be elusive. Many companies struggle for years and still do not get their forecasting working as it should. In fact, a great many senior managers rate sales forecasting as the weakest link in their overall logistics system.

Can forecasting accuracy be improved? Who should be responsible? What is the right role for the computer? These are some of the questions that need to be answered as a company selects its approach to sales forecasting. We will deal with these and related issues in this chapter.

DIFFERENT KINDS OF SALES FORECASTING

Logistics managers use different kinds of sales forecasts for planning than for day-to-day operations.

It is fascinating how many important business decisions are made, often of necessity, with surprisingly little solid information about the future. *Long-term forecasts*, which look two to five years ahead, are difficult, costly and not very reliable. As a result, when companies look several years ahead, they often use simple projections of current trends. Such forecasts are only useful if conditions do not change.

Annual sales forecasts, usually made at the product group level, look ahead at the coming business year. These forecasts, which provide the basis for annual budgeting, are usually more financial than they are operational. The numbers are often chosen and adjusted to develop an overall financial plan that makes sense; the numbers may not be particularly good estimates of how much product will actually be sold.

What we will call the *operating sales forecast* is, arguably, the most important forecast of all. It is certainly the most detailed. This forecast covers every end-item that the company sells, is made in units (not dollars) and looks forward for some number of time periods, usually months. This is the forecast that most influences short-term business operating performance.

Although companies plan based on longer-term forecasts, they commit resources based on their operating forecast. When this forecast is reasonably accurate, things go well. Performance suffers when forecasting errors are too large: if the forecast is too high, inventories grow; if the forecast is too low, service falters or unplanned overtime and other costs are incurred.

No two companies develop their operating sales forecasts in exactly the same way. Some rely heavily on the computer for projections; others do not use projections at all. Some companies get sales estimates from customers, others from salespeople; some from branch managers, others from buyers. Some companies forecast 12 months or longer into the future; others look ahead for a much shorter period of time.

Although each company's situation is somewhat different, three basic approaches to detailed sales forecasting are common. These are:

• the product manager's forecast
• the computer projection
• the key customer forecast

Many companies use a variant of one of these approaches. Some companies combine features from more than one to suit their particular situation. In this section we will discuss each one in turn. Table 4.1 summarizes the highlights of the three.

THE PRODUCT MANAGER'S FORECAST

The product manager's forecast is most common among companies that manufacture and distribute consumer case goods. This includes grocery

TABLE 4.1

THREE COMMON APPROACHES TO FORECASTING

	PRODUCT MANAGER'S FORECAST	COMPUTER PROJECTION	KEY CUSTOMER FORECAST
Who's Responsible	Marketing	Operations	Sales
Number of Items	Relatively few	Large number	Small number
Accuracy Level	• Can be very good • ± 25% per month	• From fair to good • ± 50% per month, but exceptions must be identified and dealt with	• Can be excellent • ± 10% per month, but subject to major adjustments when customer's situation changes
Methodology	• Estimate large accounts carefully and scale up from there	• Trendline or smoothing plus seasonal index	• Close links with the customer at all levels
Limits to Accuracy	• Forecast forced to agree with financial plan • Inexperience	• Change • Quality of data	• Lack of effort • Poor planning by customer • Conflict with sales targets

products, pharmaceuticals and cigarettes. But versions of it are used whenever a company produces and sells standard products from stock to retailers and wholesalers.

The basic idea is that a marketer, often a product manager, is responsible for forecasting his items. This person may manage as many as 10 brands and a total of 30 end-items. A new forecast is prepared each month for each item: it is in units and looks forward for 12 months. Normally the forecast that the product manager submits is for total company sales. If necessary it is later split into sales regions or distribution territories.

Forecasting methodology is normally quite simple. Aware of the current situation, the forecaster estimates most carefully for the large accounts, then scales up the results to cover the rest of the business. Certain information and analysis is available to the forecaster, including detailed sales reports by product and by customer. Sometimes a computer-generated projection is also available, but in most companies of this kind, computer projections are of limited use.

There are good reasons why this kind of company forecasts this way. The product managers are responsible for forecasting because they are in the best position to estimate sales for their products. A product manager's job, after all, is to market the product, which includes setting the price and arranging deals and advertising. For many consumer products companies, as much as 90% of all volumes that are sold move out as part of a deal or promotion of some kind. The person who pulls the strings can best predict how the puppet will dance.

Computer projections are often less important for this kind of company because, at the detailed end-item level, the pattern of sales depends so heavily on deals and promotions, pricing, positioning, package changes, line extensions and the like. The timing and impact of every change from the status quo needs to be considered and weighed in the balance. Clearly this is not a computer task.

In some companies a forecasting department is set up between the product managers and the users of the sales forecast. The department gathers the forecast from marketing and transmits it to the users. Sometimes the job is largely clerical. But if staff members are knowledgeable and experienced, they can actually improve the forecast, correcting errors and providing continuity when marketing staff changes.

Finally, forecasts look ahead for as much as 12 months for this kind of company, so that plant capacities can be carefully planned and materials with longer lead times can be procured.

THE COMPUTER PROJECTION

Some companies rely much more on a computer-generated forecast as the "driver" of day-to-day operating decisions. Among this group are distributors and retailers of industrial products and supplies, building products, maintenance and repair parts and other staple items.

What these companies have in common is that the number of stock-keeping units is extremely large. Whereas a product manager must forecast 30 or so items, this type of company can have thousands of items to deal with. It is just not practical for each item to get much attention.

On a regular basis the computer looks back over the sales history for each item and makes a projection of sales for the coming one to three months. (Often the computer will also determine if a rebuy is needed for the item and, if so, the quantity that should be bought.) Methodology may be simple or more complex. We will discuss methodology later in this chapter.

Although the computer plays a vital role in forecasting in this kind of situation, it is best considered only an aid or a support. Forecasting is still a management job. The computer's projection only becomes accepted as a forecast once it has been reviewed and approved by someone — either the branch manager or the corporate inventory control manager, who is also responsible for providing forecasts for new items, deal and promotion items and other exception items.

THE KEY CUSTOMER FORECAST

One other situation is so common and important that it deserves discussion here. Many companies find that a few customers account for an extremely large portion of their business. These companies often develop specialized ways to forecast sales for these key customers.

Suppliers of custom packaging often have a few key customers that require special forecasting attention. So do many suppliers to large original equipment manufacturers (OEMs) such as auto makers and electrical and electronics products companies. The common element here is a repetitive custom product being sold at least partly from stock and almost entirely to one customer.

Nowhere is good customer service more important than in a key customer situation. Consider an industrial supplier with a maintenance systems contract for a large nearby factory, or a windshield manufacturer with a sole-source supply contract with an automobile assembly plant. In this kind of situation, service failures put the business at risk. With service at a premium, distribution and inventory costs are dependent on the quality of the sales forecast. The operating forecast takes on a special importance for companies in this kind of situation. That is why companies pay a lot of attention to these "high-leverage" situations.

The sales manager, or the sales manager's boss, is usually responsible for the forecast. This is the individual who has the closest relationship with the customer and whose job it is to manage the dealings between the two organizations. Typically supplier and customer forge links at many levels. This facilitates easy exchange of information.

In these situations it is in the best interests of both the supplier and the customer for the two companies to work as closely together as possible. The trend is for customers to provide suppliers with firm orders to cover as large a portion of the supply lead time as possible. It has become quite common for telecommunications links to exist between customer and supplier. In this way, the issue becomes less one of forecasting, and much more one of joint planning and co-ordination.

HOW ACCURATE SHOULD FORECASTS BE?

Most of the management difficulties with sales forecasting relate to the matter of forecasting accuracy: how to minimize the consequences of poor accuracy, how to improve accuracy and how to manage the inevitable internal conflicts that surround it.

The forecaster knows how difficult it can be to anticipate the future accurately. Forecasts are never perfect; there is always some degree of error. Forecasters learn to think of their job as a little like taking a regular gambling vacation in Las Vegas; they think of themselves as lucky if they do not lose too badly.

The user of the forecast, on the other hand, suffers the consequences of the forecasting errors that occur. If only forecasts could be more accurate, business performance would improve to some extent, and, in any event, life would be easier.

Just how accurate can forecasts be? Unfortunately no standards exist. Not many companies systematically measure forecasting accuracy. Those that do rarely make the results public.

Stevenson Kellogg Ernst & Whinney has developed a forecast rating scheme to help gauge forecastability. The scheme, which is most suitable to higher-volume, mass-market products, is reproduced in Table 4.2. By selecting a particular end-item and answering the questions, you will get an idea of how difficult your forecasting situation is.

The rating scheme is not meant to be scientific, but it has been completed by hundreds of seminar participants over the past five to ten years. A small sampling of their results is presented in Table 4.3.

The key message here is that a whole host of factors influence just how accurate a forecast will be. Differences will exist from company to company, and even from product to product within any given company.

TABLE 4.2
STEVENSON KELLOG ERNST & WHINNEY FORECAST
RATING SCHEME

Is forecasting easy or tough in your company? Pick a particular end-item and a forecasting situation you want to rate. Score each question and total the results.

Question	*Score*
1. Is the item seasonal? No 10 points; Mildly 5 Points; Strongly 0 Points	_____
2. Can the customer buy a ready substitute? No 5; At times 3; Yes 0.	_____
3. Is the purchase discretionary? No 5; At times 3; Yes 0.	_____
4. How long has the item been on the market? More than 4 years 20; From 2 to 4 years 0; Less than 2 years minus 20.	_____
5. Does the selling price fluctuate quite a bit? No 10; At times 5; Yes 0.	_____
6. How much is sold through deals, promotions and specials? 0% 20; Less than 25% 10; More than 25% 0.	_____
7. How many pieces are sold in the slowest quarter? More than 200 20; Between 50 and 200 10; Less than 50 0.	_____
8. How many customers are there for this particular item? More than 20 10; Between 5 and 20 5; Less than 5 0.	_____
9. How many items are there in the product group? Less than 10 10; Between 10 and 100 5; More than 100 0.	_____
10. How long a period is the forecast for? More than 3 months 5; From 1 to 3 months 3; 1 month or less 0.	_____
11. How far ahead is the forecast made? 3 months or less 10; 3 to 12 months 5; 12 months or more 0.	_____
12. What is the market share? The largest 20; Relatively large 10; Relatively small 0.	_____
13. Rate the competition. Relatively easy 10; Moderate 5; Tough 0.	_____
14. As well as operational planning, is the forecast used for other purposes, such as general business planning and/or budgeting? No 20; Yes 0.	_____
15. How long has the current forecaster been at the job? More than 2 years 10; From 1 to 2 years 5; Less than a year 0.	_____
TOTAL	======

125 or more = Easy.   90-124 = Rather easy.   50-89 = Getting tougher. 49 or less = Tough.

TABLE 4.3
A SAMPLING OF FORECAST RATING RESULTS

PRODUCT	RATING	REPORTED AVERAGE MONTHLY FORECAST ERROR (%)
Baby food	155	15
Cigarettes	140	20
Cement	165	25
Rubber	120	40
Paper plates	110	15
Lube oils	105	30
Electrical parts	85	60
Light bulbs	70	40
Gas lawn-mowers	75	100 +
Grain bins	45	200
Agricultural chemicals	45	75
Repair parts (auto)	45	90

Many of the factors are external and outside of management's control. These factors mean that some level of forecasting error is inevitable and should be expected.

Experienced management knows what level of forecasting accuracy to expect. They are able to anticipate risks and opportunities. New management often does not have the same feel for the business. They may ask for better forecasting than is practically possible, or, worse, they may plan on it.

HOW TO IMPROVE FORECASTING ACCURACY

We have noted that many of the factors that determine forecasting accuracy are external and beyond management's ability to control or even influence. On the more positive side, there are many factors that management can influence to improve forecasting accuracy. These are the keys to a forecasting improvement program.

ORGANIZATION AND ACCOUNTABILITY

The first question to address is whether the right people are doing the forecasting job. In each of the three common forecasting situations that we presented earlier, the responsibility for developing the detailed operating sales forecast lay in a different part of the company: marketing, operations and sales. Clearly there is no single answer to the question of who should be responsible for forecasting.

The detailed sales forecast should be developed by the people who are in the best position to judge what will be sold. The trick is to organize forecasting so that the right people play the right roles. What this means in one situation, for example, is that the branch operations manager develops the forecast, with appropriate computer support. Then the branch manager, actually a sales position, approves the forecast, reviewing selected high-volume, new and promotional items in detail each month.

In many companies the cause of poor forecasting performances is not that the wrong people are doing the work, but that those who are forecasting are not doing a very diligent job. It is not difficult to see why. Some people view forecasting as tedious in the extreme — almost as bad as budgeting. Add to that the facts that it usually attracts darts instead of laurels, and that the consequences of shoddy work will most likely be overcome by extra efforts elsewhere in the company.

A lack of accountability in forecasting shows up in many small ways. Forecasts may be late and incomplete. Serious omissions may happen regularly. Obvious factors may be missed: the Easter promotion is forecast in May instead of April, or requirements for a new account don't show up on the forecast for several months.

It is not practical to hold people responsible for creating highly accurate forecasts, but it is appropriate to ask for a little discipline and common sense. If a lack of accountability is part of the problem, it should be dealt with first, or else it will undermine the success of any other accuracy improvement efforts. Fortunately, the problem is often quite easily solved. The situation will often improve if senior management agrees that it is important and then takes an active interest in the improvement program.

GOOD METHODOLOGY

On the technical side of forecasting, often the first key step to making improvements is to improve the quality of historical sales records. Surprisingly, even in today's information society, good, accurate, well-organized historical sales and shipments information is still a common weak spot.

The appropriate use of computer projections is also often an opportunity. In many situations a computer projection can serve as a useful starting point for the forecaster. If the assumptions that underlie the calculation remain valid, and if the number looks reasonable, the forecaster may often be able to use the computer's projection as the forecast. This can save time and free up the forecaster to work on more important things.

Methodology for computer projections normally does not have to be complicated. In fact, the simpler, the better.

MONITORING FORECASTING ACCURACY

Forecasting accuracy should be monitored at the most detailed level. Doing so provides extremely useful information. By monitoring forecasting errors you can:

- Identify exception items that need attention — often some deliberate operating action as well as a new forecast.
- Detect unexpected sales patterns early.
- Provide visibility for undesirably poor sales forecasts.
- Identify product groups that require higher levels of safety stock to ensure adequate customer service levels.
- Provide a basis for measuring the overall improvement in forecasting accuracy that you achieve.

One way to develop a forecasting accuracy measure is to define an error limit for each forecast item. For example, for an item that is forecast each month, the limit might be 25% of the last 12 months' average monthly sales. At the end of the month you then determine the percentage of all items where forecast and actual sales agreed within their error limit. A score of 50% or 60% would mean that there is considerable scope to improve performance.

This kind of scheme can be refined in a number of ways. Lower-volume, more erratic sales items might be given a higher percentage error limit. Items on contract or with programmed deliveries could be given tighter error limits. The whole scheme could be applied to all items, or might be restricted only to the most important groups or "A" items.

MAKING COMPUTER PROJECTIONS

Detailed sales forecasting — in units at the end-item level — is often a matter of adjusting recent sales patterns to the current business situation. In many cases a computerized projection can play a very useful role, but just how useful depends on how accurate the projection is. If it is accurate enough, the forecaster will often be able to use the projections without changing them.

When you look beyond the arithmetic, mathematical forecasting boils down to finding sales patterns and projecting them forward. To see if projections can be useful in your situation, and to decide what kind of projection to make, the first step is always to plot sample sales data on a graph. If you can see a pattern, the computer can probably give you back a useful projection. If you cannot see any pattern, the best you are likely to get from the computer is some kind of average sales rate.

Some situations are more prone to accurate projections than others. Accurate projections require stable sales patterns. Products such as beer and cigarettes are the easiest to make accurate projections for, because of the following characteristics:

• low price
• standard product
• many customers
• high brand loyalty
• mature and stable markets
• few deals and promotions

TREND LINES AND SEASONAL INDEXES

Figure 4.1 shows some sales data from a sales branch of a food service distributor. The company sells coffee and related items to restaurants, hotels and institutions. The graph shows the sales of one of their higher-volume coffee items in cases for a year and a half.

The product shows a clear-cut downtrend. A straight line — technically a trend line — drawn through the middle of the data would do a fair job of forecasting sales for this item. In fact in any given month the forecast error would have been roughly 200 cases or less. This is about 20% of the average month, which is good accuracy. (The accuracy for this item could actually be improved a bit by correcting the data for the fact that the months are accounting months with four, four and then five selling weeks in each quarter.)

Figure 4.2 shows another item from the same branch. This one is a hot chocolate powder. It shows both a downtrend and a seasonal pattern — good sales in the winter months, but much less in the warmer weather. This kind of pattern is easily projected with a simple seasonal index.

Whenever you need a projection for several periods into the future, the trend line and seasonal index can usually do the job. These are among the simplest methods available, do not require much historical data and are easy to understand.

SMOOTHING

Most sales histories do not show the neat patterns of Figures 4.1 and 4.2. Many times what you see is essentially a random pattern: some action in some months, little or no action in the rest and no recognizable trend or

FIGURE 4.1
A HIGH-VOLUME SALES ITEM

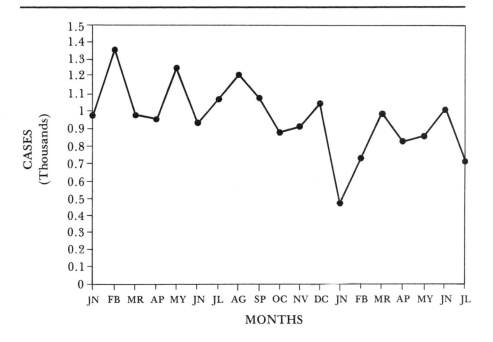

FIGURE 4.2
A SEASONAL ITEM

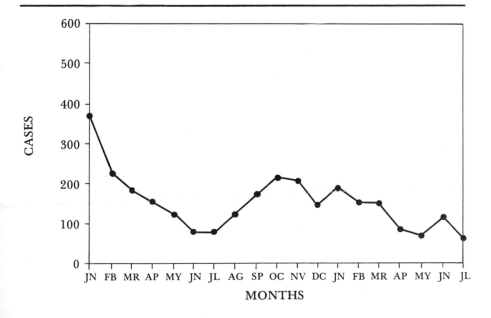

seasonal effect. What the computer can do in these situations is calculate the average rate of sales over some appropriate recent number of periods.

The method is called *smoothing*. The name adds an authoritative aura to what is a very simple calculation. Whether done by means of a moving average or by simple exponential smoothing, the result is really just an estimate of the recent average rate of sales. Smoothing methods can also be used along with seasonal indexes.

Although the accuracy of the estimate is not always the best, having the computer automatically calculate a reasonable number can be a tremendous time-saver when there are hundreds or even thousands of stock items to manage. This can free the staff to manage on an exception basis, devoting more time to more important aspects of the business.

SIMPLE METHODOLOGY IS BEST

Many sophisticated methods for mathematical forecasting have been and continue to be developed. Some of the best-known are time series analysis, multiple exponential smoothing and multiple regression analysis. It has long been the dream of many to apply these methods to logistics forecasting. Regrettably, they rarely work very well.

The single largest obstacle to using fancy projection methods in business logistics is that conditions change too fast. Most complex methods require a lot of historical data to work on — in some cases three years of monthly history. Nowadays, getting hold of the data is usually not much of a problem. The problem is that three years in the life of most companies brings so much change that the history is almost irrelevant.

Here is a list of some of the things that have caused abrupt shifts in sales patterns for the food service company we have been using as our example:

- losing/gaining a large customer
- introducing a new product
- extending/trimming the product line
- changing the package size
- changing the pricing concept
- changing the number of sales drives
- buying another company

All of these changes can wreak havoc on existing sales patterns. We show some examples in Figure 4.3. In each case, what went on before the change is of no value when forecasting after the change.

Another plus for simple methodology is that it is easy to understand. This can be extremely important for accountability purposes. The person who is responsible for forecasting needs to understand how the computer

FIGURE 4.3
ABRUPTLY CHANGING PATTERNS

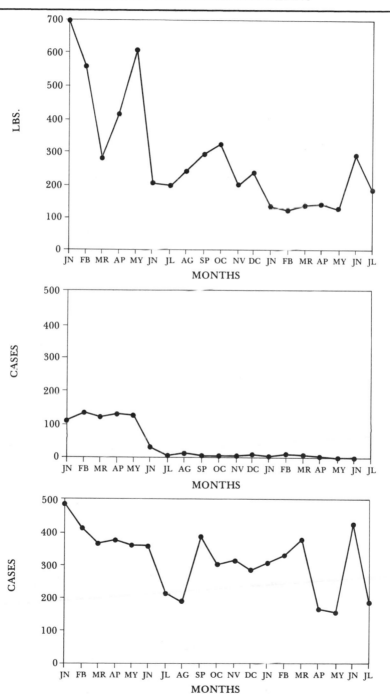

makes its calculations. Ideally, the forecaster should be able to reproduce the calculation on a calculator, in order to know where the numbers come from and feel comfortable changing the computer projection when that proves necessary. This way, the computer cannot be blamed for a poor forecast.

Although very sophisticated projection methods have generally been ineffective, three other ideas have proven useful. These are focus forecasting, demand stream forecasting and developing separate forecasting data bases, each of which we discuss below.

FOCUS FORECASTING

Bernard Smith developed focus forecasting when he was working in the hardware business. The basic idea of this method is to keep on trying until you get it right — or, more accurately, until you get it best. Smith bases his approach on the assumption that no single forecasting method is going to be right for all of your items at the same time. In fact, the best way to forecast any one item today may not be best several months from now.

Smith's approach is to test a number of different forecasting methods for each item being forecast, every time the forecasting calculation is made. He tests them by determining which method would have provided the most accurate forecasts for the item in question over the last several months. Whichever method would have worked best is the one that is used to calculate the forecast this time.

The approach will work no matter what kind of forecasting methods are used, but Smith favours simple rules like setting next month's forecast equal to:

- sales in the same month last year
- average monthly sales in the same quarter last year
- same as above, but scaled up by the year-to-date change in unit sales volume this year over last
- and the like

Smith's approach has proved successful in a number of companies. It is now being written into some computer software packages. Focus forecasting can improve forecasting accuracy. Its only drawback is that it can gobble up a lot of computer time. But today, with computing costs lower than ever before, that can be a small price to pay for better forecasting.

DEMAND STREAM FORECASTING

Demand stream forecasting is another very effective forecasting method. It is based on separating the different types of demand that you have and forecasting each one in its own most effective way. A company often sells the same end-product either to different groups of customers or for different kinds of end-uses. These different "demand streams" sometimes even have different customer service requirements. It may be possible to forecast more accurately and operate more efficiently if you treat each different stream in its own best way.

To illustrate, think of a distribution centre that supplies repair parts to about 30 branches across North America and sells to end-users in its own local region. For any given part, the shipments — that is, sales and transfers — arise from three sources:

• local sales, which in this situation are subject to a seasonal pattern
• branch stocking orders (in this case there is not much of a seasonal pattern for this stream because the branches are spread out across the country)
• initial stocking orders for new branches (the company is expanding and several new branches are opened each year)

As Table 4.4 shows, each separate demand stream has a recognizable pattern over the year — a pattern that is easy to interpret and to project. There is no meaningful pattern, however, for total shipments. Projecting total shipments forward is just a numbers game. As a result, it is difficult for someone reviewing that kind of projection to judge how reasonable it might be.

The power of demand stream forecasting is twofold. First, splitting the sales history into natural streams makes it easier to use simple methods to

TABLE 4.4
DEMAND STREAM FORECASTING

MONTH	LOCAL SALES	BRANCH TRANSFERS	NEW BRANCHES	TOTAL SHIPMENTS
January	2	37	0	39
February	7	22	0	29
March	21	43	0	64
April	5	19	25	49
May	1	21	50	72
June	1	41	25	67
July	2	49	0	51
August	9	27	0	36
September	19	35	0	54
October	8	41	0	49
November	3	40	50	93
December	1	16	0	17

project them forward. It also makes it easier to interpret the results. Second, and this can be a real money-maker, the separate streams may well be subject to different customer service requirements. Efficiencies may be achieved by handling the customer groups differently. In the repair parts example above, the parts for the new branches' initial stocking orders need not be carried in stock in the distribution centre. In fact, new branch openings are planned well ahead. The required parts can actually be brought in just ahead of the shipment date, resulting in an overall reduction in inventory.

The key to implementation lies in keeping sales and shipments history separately for the different demand streams.

SEPARATE FORECASTING DATA BASES

A long-standing problem with computerized sales forecasting lies in the kind of data that has been available for analysis. The purpose of the forecasting exercise is to predict demand, but the input data is usually historical sales data from the accounting system.

Sales data has its limitations, some of them serious:

• Sometimes sales are lower than they could have been because product is unavailable, perhaps because of a supply problem. The sales record does not show what might have been sold, only what was sold. A forecast based on this history could well be a sizeable underestimate.
• Sales records show sales timing, which is not necessarily the same as shipping or delivery timing. Also, accounting cut-offs can cause sales from one period to be reported in another.
• Sales records can also contain adjustments, such as returns. These can be troublesome, sometimes forcing sales quantities to be negative, particularly if not reported in the same period as the actual sale.

Companies are overcoming these kinds of problems by developing and maintaining separate forecasting data bases. These files are built using the same transaction data that are used to prepare sales reports, but that information is edited and modified to make it more suitable for forecasting purposes.

An example of this idea comes from a company that supplies dishes and cutlery to restaurants. They found that their forecasts were being distorted by large, non-recurring sales such as first-time sales to new locations of expanding restaurant chains. The solution was to exclude these non-recurring sales from the history file used for computer sales projections. Forecasting accuracy improved measurably, and stock levels came down.

DEALING WITH FORECASTING ERRORS

Many companies pay a good deal of attention to the question of improving forecasting accuracy, but not enough to finding ways to minimize the impact of the forecasting errors that are bound to occur. Yet practical techniques are available, and the benefits of finding them can be worthwhile.

Most logistics systems are geared to deal routinely with small forecasting errors. Companies that operate formal inventory management systems aim to carry adequate safety stocks to absorb reasonable variances between actual and forecast sales. If actuals exceed forecasts by larger amounts, supply orders can often be hastened or expedited.

But safety stock and expediting can only take you so far. Most companies find inventory carrying costs too high for them to rely on safety stock to cover more than the most modest forecasting errors. As for expediting, even the most willing supplier is only able to pull the rabbit out of the hat once in a while. Other means are needed to deal with unanticipated demand variations.

Brewers' Warehousing Company, the distributor and retailer of all beer in Ontario, Canada, has developed a number of effective operating methods that helps it achieve peak performance levels, even for the harder-to-forecast, low-volume brands and package sizes. Among them:

- *Last-minute fine-tuning of supply orders*. The supply system in the company operates on a rolling three-week planning cycle. In the first week a detailed shipping schedule is prepared for all 460 beer stores across the province. In Week 2, the schedule is reviewed and approved by the store managers and the brewers. In the third week the shipments are made. Thus, two or three weeks elapse between the initial stocking order for the stores and the actual delivery. Many things can happen during that time, and frequently store managers find that they need a few more cases of a particular end-item. The company has put a last-minute change-order procedure in place. Store managers can call up to 36 hours ahead of shipping day and make adjustments to their orders, swapping up to several pallets of product. This catches many potential stock-out and overstock situations before they happen.

- *Repacking in the field*. Beer is sold in a range of different packages. The most popular package is still the case of 24 bottles, but most brands are also available in a 12-pack and a 6-pack as well. Some brands are also available in cans. Certain lower-volume brands will sell as little as three or four cases of beer per week from any given store. Sometimes a package that is normally a slow seller will experience an unusually high demand, say 10 or 12 cases, which will exhaust the safety stock and cause a stock-out. To handle this situation, the stores carry empty packaging. If they are out of 12-packs, the store will break into a 24-pack and repackage the required product.

Last-minute adjustments to supply orders and repacking in the field are two useful ways to keep service levels high in the face of variations in demand. Another is transfers from nearby branches. These techniques help Brewers' Warehousing achieve an extremely high service level while keeping inventories low and product fresh.

Taking full advantage of substitution opportunities is another powerful antidote to the ills of poor forecasting. The ultimate substitution gambit happens at the airport car rental desk. You have reserved a mid-sized car, but may well be offered a full-sized car instead, at the same price. Most people are happy with the switch. From the rental company's point of view, they have serviced a customer and made a sale, even though they have had a stock-out. Substitution is to logistics what standardization is to product design. For many companies it remains an important opportunity that is still largely untapped.

Finally, increased use of central warehousing is another way to reduce the problem of poor forecasting. Many manufacturers and distributors push product out to field warehouses rather than keep it close at hand where it is made or first received. Their reasons include capacity limitations, handling costs and the lack of enough central storage space. The result can too often be that product in short supply at one location is gathering dust somewhere else — possibly too far away to justify a costly transfer.

Forecasting total demand is always easier than forecasting regional requirements. Companies that keep more product centrally and dole it out in small doses as required avoid a difficult forecasting problem and often operate more efficiently.

CHAPTER 5

Production Planning

INTRODUCTION

If you trace far enough back along the distribution channel, you inevitably find a production plant. Production is the process of physical creation — the transforming of natural and raw material into either finished or semi-finished goods.

The primary industries convert natural substances into raw materials: bauxite into aluminum, wood into pulp and then paper, crude petroleum into its many fractions from asphalt through waxes and greases to gasoline and petrochemicals. The secondary industries transform these materials into pens, erasers, printing presses and books; tires, plastics, motors and cars; wire, transistors, tuners and television sets — the numerous products that form the material fabric of modern life.

Production is often highly mechanized, using expensive, specialized equipment and requiring well-developed skills and expertise. The knowledge of how to harness labour, energy, science and technology to create society's material goods is some companies' most valuable asset.

The great bulk of the assets used in many companies — the capital invested, the people employed and the management time and effort — is involved in the production and distribution of goods. Other chapters in this book deal at length with the many aspects of distribution. In this chapter we discuss the planning of production and its co-ordination with other business activities, principally distribution.

ORGANIZING THE PRODUCTION RESOURCE

It has been said that the purpose of a business is to create a customer. Similarly, the purpose of the operating arm of the business is to service the customer. Management must assemble and organize its resources to accomplish this objective.

There are a number of basic questions that must be answered in deciding how to arrange the company's production efforts. Among them are:

• How many production plants should be operated?
• Where should the plants be located?
• What size should they be?
• Which products should be made at which plant?
• What technology should be used?

The answers to these questions determine the nature of the physical plant and result in the company's approach to production. In short, they specify the overall production plan. As times goes on and as conditions change, the production plan comes under continuous review. This keeps the production resource in constant evolution.

In the longer term the number, size and location of production facilities are determined by the mix of products the company makes, and by:

• the size and location of markets
• the technology that is available
• the location and availability of labour, raw materials and energy
• trade-offs between production and distribution costs
• other economic factors, such as tariffs and government incentive programs

Of course, such events as the acquisition or divestiture of facilities will also change the company's production resource.

Major modifications in production capability, such as building a new plant, adopting a new production technology or even substantially expanding an existing facility, normally do not happen very often. In a mature business unit, five or ten years or more may pass without such a fundamental change. However, during this period, numerous smaller changes do occur.

In the shorter term the transfer of production from one plant to another and changes in production methods are stimulated and influenced by such factors as:

• the growth or decline in sales volume of particular products
• line extensions, deletions and the development of new products
• product design changes, including packaging modifications, size changes and the use of new materials

• improvements in manufacturing processes and equipment
• increases or decreases in factor costs

The following four examples all illustrate the way numerous economic, technological, political and demographic factors interact to establish and then inevitably to change a company's production activities.

EXAMPLE 1: COST FACTORS RESULT IN TWO BLENDING PLANTS

A large Canadian oil company distributes lubricating oil and other "specialty" products to more than 200,000 destinations across both urban and rural Canada. Lube oils are made from crude petroleum. The crude is refined into base oils which are blended (with additives) at a lube blending plant. The finished product is packaged and then makes its way to industrial and commercial customers and to the neighbourhood service station. The distribution channel can include a distribution centre, a regional warehouse and a local distribution agent.

The company has two main sources of crude oil. Most domestic crude comes from Alberta; most imported crude enters Canada from the east. The company operates a number of refineries, the two largest of which are in Ontario and Alberta.

The cost of distributing a gallon of packaged lubricating oil across the country exceeds the cost of blending and packaging by as much as 100%. As a result the company has built two blending plants, one in the East and one in the West. Each serves as the source of finished product for its half of the country.

As is not uncommon in such situations, only one of the plants produces the full product line. The other blends only the higher-volume products, sourcing the remaining ones from the full-product-line plant in bulk form for packaging.

EXAMPLE 2: TWO COMPANIES CONSOLIDATE PRODUCTION TO LOWER COSTS

As part of a diversification program a large conglomerate acquired two confectionery companies. One produced premium-quality boxed chocolates which it sold through its own chain of specialty retail shops. There were about 150 shops altogether. Production was in small batches and was labour-intensive.

The second company made bars and boxed chocolates of standard quality which were distributed through food brokers and retailers. Production in this plant was somewhat more automated, but its packaging equipment was relatively slow.

Both companies required more chocolate-making capacity to permit growth. A key step in making chocolate is the grinding of cocoa butter and roasted cocoa beans with other additives. Grinding is done in "conches"; each batch of 500 pounds requires from 24 to 36 hours to process. A conche costs about $500,000.

Since chocolate candy is substantially more costly per pound to manufacture than to distribute, the production activities of these two companies were consolidated into one large new facility. The plant had modern equipment (including four conches) and was highly automated. Both direct and overhead production costs were reduced as a result.

EXAMPLE 3: DISTRIBUTING SUB-ASSEMBLIES AROUND THE WORLD

A Scandinavian company manufactures large drilling machines which are used in rock blasting for mining and road construction. The company has led its industry in the development of hydraulic drilling equipment. Its market is world-wide.

There are as many as 4,000 parts in one machine. Most of these parts are manufactured in the Scandinavian plant or bought centrally. However, only machines that are sold in Scandinavia are assembled there. In all other cases, sub-assemblies are shipped to subsidiary companies for final assembly in plants located much closer to the ultimate customer.

The U.S. assembly plant is located in Denver. There is a plant in Canada, one in Germany, one in Australia and several others around the world. Producing parts and components centrally allows the parent company to realize economies of scale. Raw materials can be bought less expensively in larger quantities; longer production runs keep unit costs low. Assembling the finished machines in their final markets also has a number of advantages. The machines can be more easily customized as required and, since component inventories are held in the assembly plants, delivery lead times can be relatively short.

EXAMPLE 4: INCREASED VOLUME LEADS TO NEW TECHNOLOGY

A biologicals company sells a medical vaccine in two package sizes — 10-dose glass vials and 1-dose glass ampoules. Production of the bulk vaccine is a highly scientific process. Filling and packaging is more routine, but it still requires sterile conditions and careful temperature and lot control.

The company processed vials quite efficiently. They could take a lot of 30,000 vials (300,000 doses) through filling, stoppering, examining, labelling and packaging in one day on an automated line with a crew of 14 operators. However, they were less efficient with ampoules. The operations involved in finishing ampoules were filling and sealing, leak testing, examining, labelling and packaging. Each operation was manual, or semi-automated at best, and was done at a separate work station. Ampoules were carried between work stations in plastic tubs. It would take six people seven full working days to finish a lot of 200,000 ampoules — only 200,000 doses.

One dose of the vaccine packaged in ampoules required four and a half times the finishing labour of one dose packaged in vials. Scale was the reason for the difference. Many millions of vials were processed each year, whereas ampoules were run only once every two months. Since volume was low, the investment in better ampoule equipment could not be justified.

A major customer, who in the past had bought this vaccine only in 10-dose vials, decided to switch mostly to ampoules. Although the price of a dose would be higher, there would be savings in the long run by eliminating wastage.

The impact on the company's ampoule operation was significant. They would now be running three lots each month — a sixfold increase in volume. Total labour devoted to finishing ampoules would increase from one to six person-years. An investment in new technology could now be justified. New examining and labelling equipment was purchased and brought on stream. The equipment paid for itself in less than two years. The time to finish ampoules was reduced from seven to three days, and the labour bill was cut in half.

Each of these brief examples illustrates the logic of how a company's production activities are established and evolve over time. The driving forces are demographic and economic. The resulting decisions shape the company's physical plant and define the corporate production resource. As we shall discuss, good production planning is an important element in the effective utilization of this resource.

THE JOB OF PRODUCTION PLANNING

Production planning is an ongoing challenge and a sizeable responsibility in any production setting. The planner has a direct influence on several key aspects of the business, including:

- the availability of finished product and hence the ability of the business to meet its commitments and service its customers
- the efficiency of production and hence profit

- the level of the company's investment in inventory and thus its return on capital

Developing the production plan or schedule is the production planner's primary task. The schedule establishes the work to be done in the plant. It specifies the timing and quantity of each product to be made. In some cases the schedule also selects the production equipment to be used and designates the particular workers for the job.

But modern production planning goes beyond merely scheduling production to helping the company to operate the schedule. In many companies, production planners play an expanded role which can include:

- determining materials and supplies requirements to be purchased
- developing production staff projections
- co-ordinating special projects, such as trial production runs for new products
- undertaking cost studies and evaluations

There are two main factors which create the need for the planning activity. The first is that the natural rhythms of sales and of production are quite different and are often in fundamental conflict.

Sales is usually an unruly process. Its timing is erratic and its quantities are irregular. A large order that is expected today may not arrive for weeks, or may not arrive at all. One product catches fire while another goes down in flames. And, along with short-term variations in sales, there are often seasonal buying patterns to contend with. Whether caused by the whim of the customer, the skill (or ineptitude) of the competition, the vagaries of nature or the sheer perversity of the sales force, one can rely on the stable disorder of sales.

But disorder is the bane of production. Lead times are required in any plant if changes are to be made. Procedures must be established and refined. Materials must be assembled. Equipment must be set up. The work-force must be readied. And all of these resources must be steadily utilized, without undue delays or interruptions. For the sake of cost efficiency and product quality, production must be shielded from the relative chaos of the marketplace.

Except in pure make-to-order situations, the finished goods inventory provides the buffer between sales and production. The job of production planning is to (1) put product into inventory to meet the needs of sales, while (2) following operating guidelines designed to keep customer service acceptably high and the inventory investment acceptably low and (3) using production schedules that allow efficiency on the plant floor. Thus the production planning department is a delicate point of contact between the selling activity and the production activity, with the ongoing job of finding practical compromises between conflicting needs and responsibilities.

The second main factor that creates the need for production planning is really an outgrowth of the first. It is the need for efficient utilization of production resources. The production plant must strike an overall balance between materials costs, labour costs and inventory costs. As we describe in later sections, this often requires a three-stage planning process.

One of the more interesting examples which illustrates the often intricate nature of production planning occurs in the food processing industry. It is the fresh-pack problem.

A food company operates a large production complex in the heart of fertile southwestern Ontario. Their line of about 500 items includes soups and juices, pickles and relishes, ketchup and other sauces and a number of fruit, meat and noodle products. They sell to both retail and institutional markets.

Production is organized into a number of units, each including batch-processing and packing-line operations. As many as 20 lines can be operated at once. At times, the work-force will grow to 1,000 plant employees.

The equipment in each unit may be combined in many different arrangements. Processing kettles and tanks will feed one packing line on one day and another line the next. This is one of the sources of scheduling complexity. Since equipment is shared among products, only certain combinations of products and package sizes can be run at the same time.

Some of the products are subject to seasonal selling patterns. For example, relishes and barbecue sauces have their highest sales during the spring and summer outdoor cooking season. Certain mixed pickles are most popular in the fall and winter holiday time. However, the company must also contend with another kind of seasonal pattern — the crop cycle. Fresh domestic produce is available only in the July–September period.

Every product group contains important "fresh-pack" items which can only be produced in season. Tomato products are a good example. Many products can be made from concentrated tomato solids or tomato paste. These products can be packaged all year round. A number of products, however, must be produced from fresh tomatoes. The year's supply of these products must be packed in August and September. Thus there is a six-to-eight-week period at the end of the summer when virtually all of the productive capacity in the plant has to be devoted to processing fresh produce.

In the weeks leading up to the fresh produce season, enough of the other products must be put into inventory to meet sales through the summer and into the early fall. During the fresh-pack period the year's supply of all fresh produce items must be produced. (This incidentally puts quite a premium on accurate sales forecasting.) And when the plant comes free again it must move quickly into production of those items with sales that have been higher than expected. Careful production planning is vital.

We have identified the major objectives of the production planning function and discussed the factors that shape the job. We shall now examine the typical tasks of production planning. For most companies that make to stock there are three distinct planning stages:

• the annual plan
• the provisional rolling plan
• the firm schedule

We shall discuss these activities in the following sections.

THE ANNUAL PLAN

The annual plan is normally done several months before the start of the fiscal year. It is often done as part of the corporate planning cycle, forming an important input to the budgeting process.

The annual production plan accomplishes several purposes. It provides a logical basis for budgeting both within the production department and in related operating departments such as purchasing. Equally important, annual planning allows the company to identify and resolve cost and operating trade-off opportunities.

The annual plan begins with a sales forecast — a detailed forecast of each item to be sold, in units by period (often by month) over the coming year. Working from the sales forecast, the planners create not only a production plan but also an input plan and an inventory plan.

The production plan specifies when the company's various products are going to be produced, and with what equipment. The plan thus determines how the plant's productive capacity will be utilized over the coming year. The input plan specifies the levels and timing of labour and raw materials needed to accomplish the production plan. And the inventory plan indicates the resulting inventory levels throughout the year in raw, in-process and finished form.

It is worth emphasizing that the production plan, the input plan and the inventory plan are not devised independently. All three are drawn up together. This allows the planners to confront and explicitly resolve any number of operating trade-off decisions. For example, decisions can be made about the allocation of raw materials storage areas to achieve the best balance of materials inventory investment against their purchase cost. Also, as is quite common in seasonal business, trade-offs can be made between the costs of carrying finished inventories and the costs of changing the rate of production. In this way the company creates an overall operating plan for the year — an integrated statement of how it will service its customers, with resulting operating budgets.

The annual production plan is normally worked at the level of the product group. The planner uses aggregate quantities and average costs. (In fact, this kind of planning is often referred to in the literature of operations management as "aggregate planning.") Although it is beyond the scope of this book to delve too deeply into the methodology of annual planning, we do present the following example to illustrate the general approach.

Assume that a company operates a production line that is devoted to three products. The sales forecast for these products is given in Table 5.1. Assume as well that the production rates differ for the three products. The first comes off the line at 1,500 units per hour, the second at 1,800 units per hour and the third at 900 units per hour.

For the purpose of this illustration, let us establish some production and inventory policies:

• We want to avoid an out-of-stock position.
• If a second shift is required, we must bring it on for at least three months at a time.
• We will carry a safety stock for each product to guard against error or unforeseen circumstances, with the quantities set as follows: Product 1 — 50,000 units; Product 2 — 20,000 units; Product 3 — 5,000 units.

Our objective is to devise an annual production plan for this product group. We begin by calculating the production time required to meet the forecast sales. For example, in January we expect to sell 90,000 units of Product 1, 54,000 units of Product 2 and 9,000 units of Product 3. We can calculate the production line would have to operate for 100 hours to manufacture these quantities. In Table 5.2 the sales forecast is expressed in production line hours for each month of the year.

We next determine the amount of production line time that is available. Table 5.3 shows the number of line hours available each month for a one- and a two-shift operation. In preparing Table 5.3 we have of course taken note of any statutory holidays that will occur in the year, and of the two-week plant shutdown at the beginning of June.

We will now begin to develop an annual plan. Let us first determine what would happen if we began the year with no inventory and operated

TABLE 5.1

UNIT SALES FORECASTS (IN 000 UNITS)

	JAN.	FEB.	MAR.	APR.	MAY	JUNE	JULY	AUG.	SEPT.	OCT.	NOV.	DEC.
Product 1	90	105	120	90	210	270	300	300	150	105	75	60
Product 2	54	63	63	72	45	36	90	18	36	45	45	54
Product 3	9	13½	13½	27	13½	18	27	9	27	18	18	18

TABLE 5.2

SALES FORECAST EXPRESSED IN LINE HOURS

	JAN.	FEB.	MAR.	APR.	MAY	JUNE	JULY	AUG.	SEPT.	OCT.	NOV.	DEC.	TOTAL
Product 1	60	70	80	60	140	180	200	200	100	70	50	40	1,250
Product 2	30	35	35	40	25	20	50	10	20	25	25	30	345
Product 3	10	15	15	30	15	20	30	10	30	20	20	20	235
TOTAL	100	120	130	130	180	220	280	220	150	115	95	90	1,830

TABLE 5.3

PRODUCTION LINE HOURS AVAILABLE

	JAN.	FEB.	MAR.	APR.	MAY	JUNE	JULY	AUG.	SEPT.	OCT.	NOV.	DEC.	TOTAL
1 Shift	150	135	155	120	150	80	135	155	135	140	150	120	1,625
2 Shifts	300	270	310	240	300	160	270	310	270	280	300	240	3,250

TABLE 5.4
PLAN A (QUANTITIES IN LINE HOURS)

	OPENING INVENTORY	PRODUCTION	SALES	CLOSING INVENTORY
January	0	150	100	50
February	50	135	120	65
March	65	155	130	90
April	90	120	130	80
May	80	150	180	50
June	50	80	220	−90
July	−90	135	280	−235
August	−235	155	220	−300
September	−300	135	150	−315
October	−315	140	115	−290
November	−290	150	95	−235
December	−235	120	90	−205
TOTAL		1,625	1,830	

FIGURE 5.1

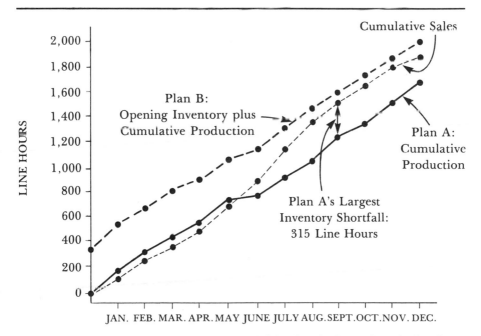

one full production shift all year long. This plan is shown in tabular form in Table 5.4 and graphically in Figure 5.1. Plan A is obviously unacceptable. We run out of stock in June and never recover. Of course, we should have expected this kind of result, because total forecast sales of 1,830 line hours exceeds the line's one-shift capacity of 1,625 hours.

But we could operate a plan with only one production shift all year if we were to start the year with enough inventory. We must start with enough to remedy the largest inventory shortfall in Plan A (this was 315 line hours) and also enough to cover our safety stock policy (which, we can calculate, requires an additional 50 line hours). Thus we must begin the year with an inventory equivalent to 365 line hours of production. Hence, we arrive at Plan B, as shown in Table 5.5 and Figure 5.1.

Plan B is workable, falling within our policy guidelines. However, it appears to be a costly way to operate, for inventories are high. We have calculated that the average inventory level during the year is equivalent to 258 line hours of production — about two months' supply. We can express this in dollars by using the value (at cost) of production. Assume one unit of each of the three products is worth, respectively, $2.00, $2.60 and $4.00. Then we can calculate that an average hour of production has a value of $3,400.[1] This means that the average inventory level for Plan B is nearly $880,000.

TABLE 5.5
PLAN B (QUANTITIES IN LINE HOURS)

	OPENING INVENTORY	PRODUCTION	SALES	CLOSING INVENTORY
January	365	150	100	415
February	415	135	120	430
March	430	155	130	455
April	455	120	130	445
May	445	150	180	415
June	415	80	220	275
July	275	135	280	130
August	130	155	220	65
September	65	135	150	50
October	50	140	115	75
November	75	150	95	130
December	130	120	90	160
TOTAL		1,625	1,830	

Note: Average Inventory = 258 Line Hours = $878,400

---

[1] The year's output will be about 68% Product 1, 19% Product 2 and 13% Product 3. These factors are used in averaging the value of one hour's output as follows:
(.68 × 1,500 × 2.00 + .19 × 1,800 × 2.60 + .13 × 900 × 4.00) = $3,400.

TABLE 5.6
PLAN C (QUANTITIES IN LINE HOURS)

	OPENING INVENTORY	PRODUCTION	SALES	CLOSING INVENTORY
January	70	150	100	120
February	120	135	120	135
March	135	155	130	160
April	160	120	130	150
May	150	150	180	210
June	120	160	220	60
July	60	270	280	50
August	50	310	220	140
September	140	135	150	125
October	125	140	115	150
November	150	150	95	205
December	205	120	90	235
TOTAL		1,995	1,830	

Note: Average Inventory = 130 Line Hours = $444,700

Let us try to improve on Plan B by operating a second shift in June, July and August. This will permit us to open the year with less inventory. Plan C, shown in Table 5.6 and Figure 5.2, is also a workable plan. It is quite likely preferable to Plan B, for in Plan C the average inventory level is about $430,000 lower. Assuming an inventory carrying cost as low as 20%, Plan C offers an inventory cost saving of almost $90,000 over Plan B.

There would, however, be added costs to operate the two-shift production program. Unless they could be transferred from elsewhere in the plant, extra workers would have to be hired in June and laid off in September. There could be training costs for the new employees, and extra supervision would be required for the second shift. It is also possible that the second shift would not be as productive as the regular shift, at least during the first few weeks. Product quality might even be lower with the new production crew.

To complete the annual plan for this group of products would involve examining a number of variants of the two plans we have so far. One variation, for example, might be to use a little carefully placed overtime to further reduce inventories. Also, producing at less than full capacity in the last quarter might be a worthwhile option. Other possibilities exist as well.

FIGURE 5.2

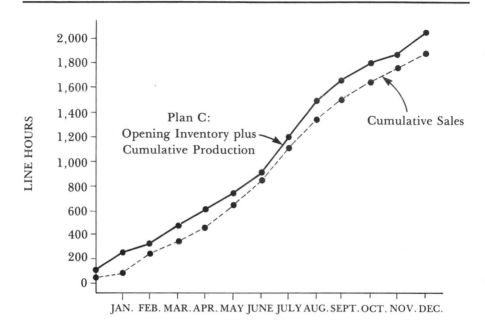

The ultimate selection of how to operate this product group would rest on a careful evaluation of the profitability and other operating consequences of the candidate plans.

We have seen an example of annual planning for one product group. In practice it is necessary to go through the same procedure for every major product group. The final step is to assess the combination of the various production programs with their different timings and make whatever compromises may be necessary. The end result is an integrated operating plan, consistent with policy guidelines, within which trade-off opportunities have been examined and resolved for acceptable cost levels and adequate service to customers.

If, as the year unfolds, actual sales were to correspond exactly to the forecast, and there were no hitches in production, then the job of production planning would be all but complete, and it would only be necessary to issue production orders as guided by the annual plan. Of course, this is never the case. The next section looks at the next two stages of production planning.

DETAILED PLANNING AND SCHEDULING

The annual plan is useful in getting the major cost and service trade-offs right. Now come the tasks of deciding in complete detail what to produce, how much and when, and of orchestrating all the required materials to be available when needed.

Many make-to-stock companies approach this detailed planning in two stages. First, a "rolling" production plan is developed to cover, say, a 4-to-6-month period. The plan covers each end-item that is produced, but it is not a schedule. It typically does not specify the plant equipment that will be used. Plant capacity is checked, but only approximately.

This kind of plan serves several important purposes:

- It provides the basis for buying and releasing materials.
- It alerts other operating departments when specific items will be produced — items that may require special warehousing, handling or transportation.
- It permits the smoothing of production peaks and valleys.
- It permits work-force planning — particularly the timing of adding and removing second and third shifts.

This plan is normally revised once each month. The first month is dropped, the remaining months are revised in light of events, and a new month is added. (It is this method of revision that results in the term "rolling plan.")

The final stage of production planning is the development of a firm production schedule. The schedule typically covers one to three weeks, is revised each week and is issued several days ahead of the new week. As much of this final work plan as possible is "frozen" when it is issued. It is not changed except for truly unavoidable occurrences on the plant floor.

This combination of a less detailed, tentative plan covering a number of months and a fully detailed firm work plan for the immediate short term has proven to be an effective way to organize operations in many diverse production settings.

We have referred earlier to the sometimes intricate nature of detailed plant scheduling. The following example illustrates what can be involved.

A company assembles a line of six home appliances on two production lines. Table 5.7 shows the current inventory levels, the desired safety stock levels and the shipment forecast in units for the coming eight weeks. Table 5.8 shows the one-shift weekly production rates on each line and also indicates the economic run lengths for the products.

Let us assume that the annual plan for this product group calls for each line to operate one full shift during this period of the year. No significant inventory build-up is planned, nor is any appreciable use of overtime.

Assume finally that a particular raw material used in Products B and F will not be available from the supplier until the beginning of Week 3.

TABLE 5.7
PRODUCT FORECAST AND INVENTORY LEVELS

PRODUCT	CURRENT INVENTORY	SAFETY STOCK	WEEKLY UNIT FORECAST								TOTAL
			1	2	3	4	5	6	7	8	
A	120	100	60	70	40	70	50	40	30	40	400
B	80	100	40	50	50	80	50	30	40	30	370
C	90	50	20	10	20	20	10	10	20	20	130
D	40	50	10	20	10	10	20	10	10	20	120
E	30	50	20	20	10	10	20	10	10	20	120
F	80	50	20	20	10	20	10	20	20	20	140
		TOTALS	170	190	140	210	160	120	130	150	

TABLE 5.8
PRODUCTION RATES

	LINE 1		LINE 2	
PRODUCT	WEEKLY* PRODUCTION	ECONOMIC** RUN LENGTH	WEEKLY* PRODUCTION	ECONOMIC** RUN LENGTH
A	100	2	60	2
B	120	1	80	2
C	90	1	60	2
D	120	1	80	2
E	80	2	50	2
F	60	2	40	2

* Units   ** Weeks

TABLE 5.9
RUN-OUT DATES

PRODUCT	HITS SAFETY STOCK IN WEEK	RUNS OUT IN WEEK
A	1	2
B	0	2
C	3	6
D	0	4
E	0	2
F	2	6

TABLE 5.10
THE PRODUCTION SCHEDULE

WEEK	LINE 1 PRODUCT	LINE 1 QUANTITY	LINE 2 PRODUCT	LINE 2 QUANTITY
1	A	100	E	50
2	A	100	E	50
3	B	120	D	80
4	B	120	F	40
5	E	80	A	60
6	C	90	F	40
7	B	120	A	60
8	F	60	A	60

A production schedule is required for these products over the coming eight weeks. Our criteria for scheduling are as follows. We want to:

- meet forecast shipments
- keep inventory levels at or above safety stocks
- schedule economic runs on the assembly lines
- achieve good utilization in the plant

A useful starting point is to determine when the current inventory for each product will fall below its safety stock level and when it will run out altogether. This information is shown in Table 5.9. Clearly Products A, B and E are high on the priority list. A production schedule for these products is shown in Table 5.10. It was developed by trial and error. The resulting inventory levels are shown in Table 5.11.

The schedule does not meet our criteria perfectly:

TABLE 5.11
PLANNED INVENTORY LEVELS

| WEEK | PRODUCT | | | | | |
	A	B	C	D	E	F
0	120	80	90	40	30	80
1	160	40	70	30	50	60
2	190	−10	60	10	70	40
3	150	60	40	80	60	30
4	80	100	20	70	50	50
5	90	50	10	50	110	40
6	50	20	90	40	100	60
7	80	100	20	30	90	40
8	100	70	50	10	70	80

- Product B goes out of stock in Week 2 because material is unavailable.
- In several cases assembly run lengths are shorter than desired: for example, in Week 5, Product A is set up for only one week on Line 2.
- The inventory for several of the products does fall below its safety stock level: for example, Product C in Weeks 3, 4 and 5.

These deficiencies could be addressed in a number of ways. It may be possible to expedite the arrival of the raw material needed for Product B, to renegotiate several shipping dates or to schedule some overtime work. Whether to accept the current schedule or not depends, of course, on relative business priorities.

CURRENT TRENDS IN PRODUCTION PLANNING

JUST-IN-TIME PRODUCTION

The last five years has seen a "back-to-basics" revival sweep across the North American production community. This trend has been called by many names (zero inventory, continuous flow manufacturing, material as needed), but its most common name is just-in-time production (JIT).

JIT is the North American adaptation of the manufacturing techniques that have given Japanese companies like Toyota their reputation for manufacturing excellence. Not simply an inventory project by any means, JIT can be a wide-ranging effort to eliminate waste of all kinds, improve productivity and simplify the production process. Many of the companies that have adopted the JIT approach have found the changes fundamental, the impacts profound and the benefits surprisingly large.

JIT can involve many different kinds of changes to the production process. One is the reduction of production run lengths. This serves to increase flexibility and responsiveness, decrease inventory levels and lead times and reduce the impact of sales forecasting errors. In order to reduce run lengths some reduction in set-up times and costs is often achieved.

Other common JIT production techniques include specializing equipment to a smaller number of products, setting up dedicated flow lines and work cells, synchronizing schedules throughout the plant, producing mixed models on one assembly line and fixing the daily rate of production for relatively long periods of time.

The impact of JIT on production planning in many companies as of this writing has been relatively small. This is because in most companies the JIT approach has only reached the pilot project stage. In the areas that have been tackled, the results have been, in general, extremely good. But for most companies the journey has just begun.

The potential impact on production planning of JIT is large. Each successful JIT initiative is a step towards speed and simplicity. Each step makes the task of planning and control a little easier and more straightforward.

MRP AND RELATED SYSTEMS

The use of computers to aid in production planning and control has become commonplace. Rare is a production shop, however small, that does not benefit from modern information technology.

Perhaps the single most common application is materials requirements planning (MRP). This is a way of calculating the materials that are required to support a given production plan. At the core of the MRP system is the calculation of time-phased net requirements information. The time phasing looks into the future period by period, while netting takes into account all on-hand and on-order quantities.

Time-phased net requirements information helps materials planners more effectively choose the timing and quantities of materials to order from suppliers. This can lead to sizeable reductions in materials inventory levels — the single largest benefit companies have derived from such systems.

Modern manufacturing planning and control systems have built fully integrated suites of programs around the core of the materials requirements planning application. Called MRP II systems, these programs link together the various planning activities in the company. Particularly relevant to production planning are the modules which aid in capacity planning, shop floor reporting, costing and purchasing.

As of this writing MRP II systems have the reputation of being difficult to develop and install and, therefore, risky — just like simple MRP systems 10 to 15 years ago. No doubt several years hence we will consider MRP II simply routine.

CHAPTER 6

Inventory Management

INTRODUCTION

Inventory is the common thread that ties all logistics activities together. Stocking and distribution policies ultimately determine the level of service provided to customers. Replenishment decisions affect the purchasing department's workload. Requirements for warehouse space are a function of the policies used to control reordering, and transportation costs are affected by the way in which inventories are ordered and subsequently distributed to branch warehouses.

Inventory management practices dramatically affect the bottom-line profitability of any company involved in the manufacturing and distribution of goods. Implementation of procedures which allow customer service objectives to be met with lower inventories will result in significant cost savings. A modest 10% improvement in inventory performance, for example, on an inventory of $10 million, will result in an inventory reduction of $1 million, representing annual savings of $100,000 to $200,000 through reduced costs to carry the inventory.

In this chapter, we discuss the different types of inventory and present several practical inventory management techniques.

TYPES OF INVENTORY

Inventory can be defined, in the broadest sense, as the items a company carries in stock to satisfy the future demand for them. Inventory can be further classified into the following categories:

- manufacturing inventories
  - raw materials
  - work-in-process
- distribution inventories
  - finished goods
  - maintenance spare parts items
  - supplies

Manufacturing and distribution inventories are quite different in the way they should be managed.

MANUFACTURING INVENTORIES

The raw materials inventories of a manufacturing company consist of the items which have not yet been processed by the company. They are still in their original form. These raw materials are used in the production process. As soon as raw materials enter the production process, they become work-in-process inventory. They will continue to be classified as work-in-process until the final manufacturing operations and quality checks are completed and the finished items are ready for sale.

The length of time items are considered as work-in-process depends on the nature of the manufacturing operation. In a food processing company, for example, raw materials may be transformed into finished goods in a matter of minutes. In an automobile manufacturing plant, it may be several days or weeks before the steel is manufactured into the car body, the body is attached to the chassis, and the completed car is ready for sale. Manufacturing inventories must be managed to ensure that the materials needed during the production process are available when required. Shortages of materials can cause stops in production, unplanned change-overs or costly expediting to obtain the required items. Manufacturing inventories (i.e., raw materials and work-in-process) have historically been controlled using reorder points. Over the past several years it has become apparent that a technique called manufacturing resource planning (MRP) is more effective. MRP is discussed later in this chapter.

DISTRIBUTION INVENTORIES

Finished goods inventories consist of items which are ready for sale to customers. These items may have been purchased from outside the organization or manufactured at a company plant. An example of a finished goods item is a car sold by automobile dealers. Demand for finished goods items is usually considered independent — in other words, it is a function of factors outside the company's direct control.

Maintenance inventories are another type of distribution inventory and consist of the spare parts necessary to repair plant equipment. Maintenance items are usually subject to very sporadic demand, but must be inventoried in case a critical part fails. A shortage could result in machine downtime and, in some cases, the interruption of an entire production process. The demand for maintenance inventories occurs whenever a part fails and needs to be repaired. Demand also occurs as the result of planned maintenance programs. This type of demand is often known several weeks or months in advance.

Supplies inventories are yet another form of distribution inventory and comprise items which are normally consumed in the day-to-day operation of a business. Examples of supplies items include oils, lubricants and computer forms.

Distribution inventories are most commonly managed using some form of reorder points. A technique called distribution requirements planning (discussed in Chapter 10) is becoming more prevalent for managing the distribution inventories of companies with more than one warehouse.

WHY DO INVENTORIES EXIST?

The high cost of carrying inventory suggests that inventory levels should be kept as low as possible. There are, however, four main reasons why inventories exist, and why they are necessary to support the day-to-day operation of any manufacturing or distribution company: fluctuation in supply and demand, anticipation of future events, large lot-sizes, and goods in transit.

FLUCTUATION INVENTORIES

Companies maintain inventories because demand and supply cannot always be predicted. The demand for a particular item, for example, may average 200 units per week, but may occasionally rise as high as 350 in a particular week. By carrying an inventory of the items, it is possible to reduce the risk of running out of stock when demand is higher than normal.

The supply of items is also usually subject to some uncertainty. Supply of finished goods from a company plant could be interrupted because of machine downtime or a shortage of parts. Orders for finished goods from suppliers may be delayed because of problems experienced by them, or delays in transportation. Additional inventory offers protection against these unexpected changes in supply.

ANTICIPATION INVENTORIES

Many companies carry extra inventory during certain times of the year in anticipation of future events. Demand in a peak sales period, for example, may far exceed the quantity that can be produced during the period. Inventory must be built up so that enough is available when demand exceeds the rate at which goods can be produced. Examples of anticipation inventories include the practice of building up inventories prior to sales promotions and prior to plant shutdowns. One manufacturer of batteries in Canada builds inventories for the first nine months of each year in order to meet sales commitments in the last three months.

LOT-SIZE INVENTORIES

Inventories often result from lot-sizes which exceed the amounts immediately required. An item, for example, may have to be purchased in quantities of 100, even though demand is only 15 units per month. Examples of situations which cause lot-size inventories include:

• minimum purchase or manufacturing order quantities
• volume discounts (which may make it worthwhile to accept lot-size inventories in return for lower purchase costs)

Industry is focusing a great deal of effort on finding ways to reduce lot-size inventories. Improvements to manufacturing methods which result in easier and faster change-overs and set-ups make it possible to reduce minimum run quantities. These reductions offer immediate savings in the lot-size inventories of low-volume items.

TRANSPORTATION INVENTORIES

The fourth type of inventory is the transportation inventory that occurs when goods are shipped from one location to another. When these items are in transit they are not immediately available for use. The size of transportation inventories is a function of the time it takes to move goods between locations. Longer distances and slower modes of transport obviously increase the size of inventories in transit.

THE CONFLICTING OBJECTIVES OF INVENTORY MANAGEMENT

The primary objectives in managing inventory levels are to:

• maximize customer service levels
• minimize inventory levels
• minimize the costs of buying goods from outside suppliers

- maximize production efficiency
- maximize transportation efficiency

Unfortunately, these objectives conflict with each other. Customer service, for example, can easily be improved by carrying additional inventory, but this violates our objective of minimizing inventory levels. Inventory levels can be minimized by producing goods in small quantities, but this may violate our objective of maximizing production efficiency. The cost of buying goods from outside suppliers can be minimized by buying in large quantities to obtain volume discounts, but this violates our objective of minimizing inventory levels. Inventories at branch warehouses can be minimized by sending small replenishment quantities frequently, but this violates our objective of maximizing transportation efficiency.

Inventory managers often get little support (or understanding) from others in the organization. Salespeople typically expect a large inventory of every item just in case an order comes in. Financial managers seem to focus only on the cost of carrying inventory and see inventories as a drain on the financial resources of the business. Plant managers, whose own performance is usually based on manufacturing costs, want long production runs to keep costs down.

It's difficult to sort through these conflicting objectives to determine the policies that maximize service while minimizing total costs. Effective inventory management makes it possible to reduce inventories while maintaining the same level of service. Alternatively, current overall inventory levels can be used to deliver a substantially higher level of customer service.

THE COST OF INVENTORY

The need to manage inventories is driven by the fact that inventory costs money. The cost of carrying inventory is composed of the following elements:

- Capital. The cost associated with tying up money in inventory that could be spent elsewhere or invested at market rates.
- Storage. The cost of providing storage facilities, comprising labour costs, equipment costs and building costs.
- Deterioration. The cost of items which are no longer saleable because of physical deterioration.
- Shelf-life. The cost of items no longer saleable because shelf life has been exceeded.
- Obsolescence. The cost of items no longer saleable because they have been replaced by other items.

• Insurance. The cost of insurance to protect against loss of inventory through fire or theft.

The cost of carrying inventory depends on the nature of the business and management policies regarding the return on investment expected from short-term investments. Although there are no specific industry standards, most companies estimate that inventory carrying costs are between 10% and 40% of the value of the inventory. In the absence of specific company policies, use a figure between 15% and 18% as a guideline for evaluating the cost of inventory.

INVENTORY MANAGEMENT TECHNIQUES: REORDER POINTS AND ORDER QUANTITIES

There are two basic decisions in inventory management: determining when to order additional stock and determining the quantity that should be ordered whenever an order is placed. A variety of techniques has been developed to address these two issues. The most useful and practical of these are described below.

REORDER POINTS

Reorder points are the simplest and most commonly used method for controlling inventories. Additional stock of an item is ordered whenever the inventory level drops below the reorder point set for that item. There are two types of reorder points: continuous review and periodic review. The difference between the two types is the frequency with which inventory balances are reviewed and compared against the reorder points and orders placed with suppliers.

CONTINUOUS-REVIEW REORDER POINTS
Under a continuous-review approach, inventory levels are monitored on a transaction-by-transaction basis. Orders for replenishment are placed as soon as the on-hand plus the on-order balance for any item falls below the reorder point. Continuous-review systems can be used in even the smallest company. Inventory record cards (see Figure 6.1) are updated with every stock issue and receipt. Reorder points, recorded on each card, are reviewed each time a transaction is posted to the card. Orders are placed whenever the on-hand plus on-order quantity for an item is below the reorder point. Manual "two-bin" systems have also been used as a form of continuous review, usually to control high-volume, low-value parts. Each such part is stocked in two bins. The quantity in one of the bins (Bin 2) is equal to the reorder point. Issues are made from Bin 1. When Bin 1 is

FIGURE 6.1
SAMPLE MANUAL STOCK RECORD CARD

Lead Time: 3 weeks   Order Quantity: 250   Reorder Point: 350

Date	Purchase PO #	Purchase Quantity	Receipts PO #	Receipts Quantity	Quantity On Order	Issues Invoice #	Issues Quantity	On Hand Balance
1/2/87						1294	25	400
1/5/87						1303	37	363
1/7/87	4104	250			250	1323	23	340
1/9/87						1402	41	299
1/16/87						1473	97	202
1/19/87						1501	45	157
1/22/87	4205	250			500	1573	63	94
1/26/87						1592	23	71
1/29/87						1604	37	34
1/30/87			4104	250	250			284
2/2/87						1632	21	263

emptied, the reorder point has been reached and an order is placed. Issues are made from Bin 2 until the replenishment quantity is received.

Continuous-review reorder point systems are usually computerized. The basic logic is the same as that used with manual cards, but computerization offers several benefits:

• Less clerical effort is required to keep inventory records up to date.
• There is less chance of mathematical posting errors.
• All inventory items can be scanned to identify items or groups of items which need to be reordered.

Significant reductions in the cost of computerization have made it possible for even small companies to computerize their inventory function. Microcomputer packages costing less than $1,000 can handle inventories of 2,000–3,000 items.

To prevent a stock-out from occurring, reorder points must be at least as large as the demand from the time the need to order is recognized to the point when the items are received and available for use. Since future demand is rarely known with certainty, reorder points are most often calculated using average demand and average lead times. Additional stock, called "safety stock," is carried in case the actual demand during the replenishment cycle exceeds the expected normal demand.

> Reorder Point = Average Demand during
> Normal Lead Time + Safety Stock

> Example: average demand = 100 units/month
>
> replenishment lead time = 2 months
>
> safety stock = 50 units
>
> Reorder Point = 100(2) + 50
>
> = 250

This example is shown graphically in Figure 6.2.

With this type of reorder point system, stock-outs will occur whenever the actual demand during the actual lead time exceeds the reorder point. This may be the result of:

• greater than normal demand over the lead time
• a longer than normal lead time
• both of the above

The level of service provided to customers will depend on the quantity of safety stock carried for each item. A method for calculating safety stock quantities is covered later in this chapter.

FIGURE 6.2
EXAMPLE OF A CONTINUOUS-REVIEW REORDER POINT

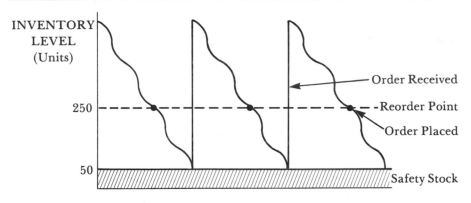

PERIODIC-REVIEW REORDER POINTS

Under a periodic-review approach, inventory balances are reviewed at regular intervals (e.g., weekly or monthly). Orders are placed for any items where the on-hand balance plus on-order balance is below the reorder point, at the time when balances are reviewed.

Periodic-review systems are most often used when:

• It is too expensive or impractical to update inventory records as each issue or receipt occurs.
• Suppliers' ordering policies dictate that orders can be placed only according to a pre-set schedule.
• Specific ordering days enable manufacturers to plan production and distribution to ensure the products arrive at the customer's facilities on specific days, e.g., the grocery industry, where a buyer will place an order with a supplier every Monday for delivery the following Monday.

Many distributors are still faced with rigid rules for ordering from their own or outside manufacturing facilities. Many companies work on a one-, two- or three-month cycle in which orders must be placed by a specified cut-off date each month. Once the cut-off has passed, orders cannot be placed until the next month.

Reorder points for periodic-review systems must cover the demand during the lead time plus the demand during the review period. This can be best illustrated by a simple example:

Example: Average demand = 100 units/month
         Replenishment lead time = 2 months
                    Safety stock = 50 units
                    Review cycle = monthly

The standard reorder point formula gives a reorder point of 250 units. But what happens if the balance is 260 units when the inventory is reviewed?

Assuming that demand is exactly as expected (i.e., 100 units/month):

- After one month the inventory will be 160 units, and an order is placed to arrive in two months.
- After two months, the inventory will be 60 units, and an order will be received at the end of the next month.
- Therefore, a stock-out will occur during the third week of the third month.

The stock-out occurs because the reorder point of 250 ignores the fact that it can take as long as a month to react to the fact that a reorder point has been reached.

CALCULATION OF PERIODIC-REVIEW REORDER POINTS
Reorder points for periodic-review items should be calculated as follows:

Reorder Point (periodic review) = Average Demand
during Normal Lead Time

+

Average Demand during Review Cycle

+

Safety Stock

Using this formula, the reorder point will be 350 units (200 + 100 + 50). A graph of projected inventory levels is shown in Figure 6.3.

FIGURE 6.3
EXAMPLE OF A PERIODIC-REVIEW REORDER POINT

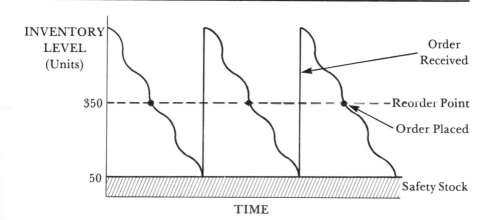

Stock-outs will occur if the actual demand during the lead time and review period is higher than the reorder point. This can be the result of:

• greater than normal demand over the lead time *and* review period
• a longer than normal lead time or review period
• both of the above

Safety stock for periodic-review items has to cover fluctuations in demand and supply that can occur over both the procurement lead time and the review period. This means that larger safety stocks (and higher average inventories) are necessary with periodic-review systems. It also follows that more safety stock is required for longer review cycles.

SAFETY STOCK

Reorder point systems assume that safety stock is carried to offer protection against unforeseen fluctuations in supply and demand. Safety stocks can be calculated using rough rules of thumb, or more scientifically using the laws of probability and statistics.

RULE-OF-THUMB APPROACHES FOR CALCULATING SAFETY STOCK

Rule-of-thumb approaches are usually based on some guideline like "safety stock is five days' demand" or "safety stock is equal to the forecast for the next month." While easy to implement, this type of approach inevitably results in too much inventory for some items and not enough for others.

An example of what can happen if safety stocks are calculated using rough guidelines is shown in Table 6.1. The average demand is 100 units per month for both items, so safety stock, set at one week, is 25 units for each item. Reorder points (assuming continuous review) are 125 for both items.

The service levels we will actually achieve will be dramatically different for Items 1 and 2. Inventory of Item 1 will never fall below 19 units. A stock-out will occur for Item 2, however, if the reorder point is reached near the end of either the third or the fifth month. The use of the same rule for calculating safety stock results in too much inventory for Item 1 and not enough for Item 2.

The reason for this should be fairly obvious. Demand for Item 1 is very predictable and never varies from the average (which was used to calculate the reorder point) by more than six units. Demand for Item 2, on the other hand, is less predictable and is as much as 43 units above the average. Clearly, a more appropriate way to calculate safety stocks would take account of the predictability of demand for each item.

TABLE 6.1
COMPARISON OF BASIC METHODS FOR TWO ITEMS

MONTH	DEMAND FOR ITEM 1	DEMAND FOR ITEM 2
1	98	110
2	97	73
3	106	67
4	102	143
5	97	77
6	100	130
	600	600
Average Demand per Month	100	100
Safety Stock	25	25
Reorder Point	125	125

Lead Time = 1 Month
Safety Stock = 1 Week

THE SCIENTIFIC APPROACH TO CALCULATING SAFETY STOCK

The scientific approach to calculating safety stock is based on the assumption that safety stocks are necessary because demand (and supply) may differ from what is expected to happen. The degree to which demand and supply have been unpredictable in the past is used to calculate appropriate safety stock levels for the future.

If inventories are controlled, using a reorder point approach, a stock-out can occur only if the demand during the lead time and review time exceeds the reorder point for the item. Suppose, for example, that an item has a reorder point of 200 units. Assume that the inventory level has just fallen to 200 units as the result of a sale, and that an order for replenishment is placed. If the actual demand during the lead time is only 100 units, there will still be 100 units on hand when the replenishment order is received. If the demand during the lead time is 200 units, the inventory level will just reach zero when the next order is received. The only way in which a stock-out can occur (assuming the order is received within the normal lead time) is if demand during the lead time exceeds the reorder point of 200 units.

The statistical approach for calculating inventories involves determining the probability that demand during the lead time will exceed a given value. We'll use the example we began in Table 6.1 to illustrate the concepts involved. The figures are reproduced in Table 6.2. The predict-

TABLE 6.2
CALCULATION OF FORECAST ERROR

MONTH	DEMAND FOR ITEM 1	FORECAST FOR ITEM 1	FORECAST ERROR	DEMAND FOR ITEM 2	FORECAST FOR ITEM 2	FORECAST ERROR
1	98	100	−2	110	100	10
2	97	100	−3	73	100	−27
3	106	100	6	67	100	−33
4	102	100	2	143	100	43
5	97	100	−3	77	100	−23
6	100	100	0	130	100	30
	600		0	600		0

ability of the demand is approximated by calculating the standard deviation of the forecast errors. The mathematical formula for estimating the standard deviation is:

$$SD = \sqrt{\frac{\Sigma (X_i - \bar{x})^2}{N}}$$

SD = standard deviation

X_i = forecast error for period i

$\bar{x}$ = average forecast error

N = number of months used to calculate the standard deviation

Since many forecasts are based on the average historical sales over a period of time, the average forecast error will be zero; the formula can be simplified to:

$$SD = \sqrt{\frac{\Sigma (X_i)^2}{N}}$$

You can see from the formula that the standard deviation is related to the size of the forecast errors.

The estimates of the standard deviation of forecast errors for Items 1 and 2 are:

$$Item\ 1\ SD = \sqrt{\frac{(-2)^2 + (-3)^2 + (6)^2 + (2)^2 + (-3)^2 + (0)^2}{6}}$$

$$= 3.2$$

$$Item\ 2\ SD = \sqrt{\frac{(10)^2 + (-27)^2 + (-33)^2 + (43)^2 + (-23)^2 + (30)^2}{6}}$$

$$= 29.4$$

The standard deviations we have calculated are essentially a measure of the accuracy of our forecasts for Items 1 and 2. Statistical safety stocks are calculated, based on the assumption that demand and forecast errors during the lead time follow the normal probability distribution. We'll take a brief look at the normal probability curve before reviewing how safety stocks are calculated.

THE NORMAL PROBABILITY DISTRIBUTION

Modern life is filled with the need to estimate the probability of certain events occurring. While many of us don't realize it in a formal way, we are continuously estimating and re-estimating the probability of several different situations. Examples include:

- the probability of it raining tomorrow
- the likelihood of the stock market going up or down
- the chance of interest rates rising or falling
- the probability of winning one lottery versus another

We are constantly bombarded by statements of probability. "A 60% chance of rain tomorrow" and "You can't win without a ticket" are just two examples.

In studying several different types of situations, statisticians have found that a probability distribution called the *normal distribution* is particularly useful for estimating the probability with which events will occur. The normal probability curve (or bell curve) has been used to represent the probability of hundreds of situations, including:

- individuals achieving certain scores on IQ tests
- students obtaining specific scores on tests and examinations

The area under the normal curve (see Figure 6.4) represents the probability of events occurring. An examination of the shape of the normal curve reveals the assumptions implicit in its use:

- Events closer to the average are more likely to occur (i.e., they have a higher probability) than those further away from the average.
- The probability of events occurring which are above the average is exactly the same as the probability of events which are lower than the average (i.e., the curve is symmetrical about the average).
- The curve extends to infinity in both directions. This means that there is some probability of any value occurring, but the probability gets smaller and smaller as you move further and further away from the average.

FIGURE 6.4
THE NORMAL PROBABILITY DISTRIBUTION

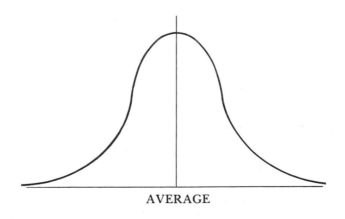

AVERAGE

We can review each of these assumptions using the example of a class's results on an examination. If we assume that exam results are normally distributed with an average mark of 60, the three assumptions outlined above can be interpreted as follows:

- Exam scores are more likely to be close to 60 than significantly higher or lower than 60.
- The probability of students scoring higher than 60 is exactly the same as that of students scoring lower than 60.
- Student scores can have any value. However, the probability of achieving a given score gets smaller and smaller the more different the score is from the average of 60. In this case, the normal curve is essentially cut off at 0 and 100, since students can't score less than 0 or higher than 100. One of the assumptions in using the normal curve to model the probability of exam scores would be that the error in cutting off the "tails" of the distribution would not be significant.

One of the unique properties of the normal probability distribution is that estimates of the average and standard deviation are all that are required to uniquely determine the probabilities of events occurring. Assuming that the values of an event are normally distributed:

- The probability of a value within plus or minus one standard deviation of the average is 68%.
- The probability of a value within plus or minus two standard deviations of the average is 95%.
- The probability of a value within plus or minus three standard deviations of the average is 99.8%.

These probabilities are shown graphically in Figure 6.5.

The scientific calculation of safety stocks is based on the assumption that demand and forecast errors are normally distributed.

USING THE NORMAL PROBABILITY DISTRIBUTION TO CALCULATE SAFETY STOCK LEVELS

The statistical calculation of safety stocks is based on the assumption that forecast errors can be approximated using the normal distribution. The assumptions we have to make to use the normal probability distribution are as outlined below.

- Forecast errors are more likely (i.e., have a higher probability) to be close to zero than to be either higher or lower than zero.
- The probability of forecast errors being greater than zero (i.e., actual demand exceeds forecast) is equal to the probability of forecast errors being less than

FIGURE 6.5
THE NORMAL PROBABILITY DISTRIBUTION

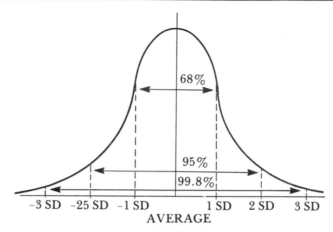

NUMBER OF STANDARD DEVIATIONS

zero (i.e., forecast exceeds actual demand). This is shown in Figure 6.4 by the symmetry of the curves around the forecast error of zero.

• In theory, infinitely large positive or negative forecast errors can occur. The probability of such large forecast errors gets smaller and smaller for larger and larger positive or negative forecast errors.

One of the unique properties of the normal curve pointed out in the previous section is that estimates of the average and the standard deviation are all that are required to uniquely specify the shape of the normal curve. In other words, estimates of the average forecast error and the standard deviation of forecast error are sufficient to determine the probabilities of different forecast errors occurring. The probability of specific ranges of forecast errors occurring can be related to the average and standard deviation.

The average forecast error will be zero or close to zero if the forecasts are unbiased. By unbiased, we mean that the probability of demand exceeding the forecast is the same as the probability of the forecast exceeding the demand. The standard deviation of forecast errors can be computed, using the formula shown on page 125.

Normal probability curves for the forecast errors of Items 1 and 2 are shown in Figure 6.6. You will see that the probability curves for both items are centred about an average value of zero. Item 1 has a small standard deviation of forecast error, which means a high probability that forecast errors will be very close to zero. Item 2 has a large standard deviation of forecast error, which means a much lower probability that forecast errors will be close to zero. If you remember that the area under the curve represents probability, you can see that there is a much higher

FIGURE 6.6
PROBABILITY OF FORECAST ERRORS

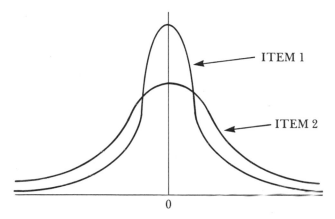

probability that the forecast error for Item 2 will exceed that of Item 1.

In the previous section, we outlined the probabilities related to the normal curve. If we use these probabilities in terms of inventory management, we get the relationship outlined in Table 6.3. Using statistical analysis, we can estimate that the forecast for Item 1 will be within 6 units of the actual demand 95% of the time. The forecast error for Item 2 is less predictable (i.e., a higher standard deviation). The forecast for Item 2 will be within 59 units of the actual demand 95% of the time.

The probabilities in Table 6.3 are based on the forecast being either higher or lower than actual demand. Earlier in this chapter, however, we indicated that a stock-out can occur only if the actual demand exceeds the forecast. If the forecast exceeds the actual demand, a stock-out will not occur. What we are really interested in from an inventory management point of view is the probability of forecast error exceeding actual demand by more than some specified quantity. This isn't very difficult, because the normal curve is symmetrical.

TABLE 6.3
PROBABILITY OF FORECAST ERRORS

| | FORECAST ERROR | |
	ITEM 1	ITEM 2
Standard Deviation	3.2	29.4
68% probability	− 3.2 to 3.2	− 29.4 to 29.4
95% probability	− 6.4 to 6.4	− 58.8 to 58.8
99.8% probability	− 9.6 to 9.6	− 88.2 to 88.2

- Probability that forecast error exceeds one standard deviation is 15.9%.
- Probability that forecast error exceeds two standard deviations is 2.3%.
- Probability that forecast error exceeds three standard deviations is .2%.

Using our example of Item 1 and Item 2, we can see the effect that forecast accuracy has on safety stock. We'll assume that we want a 98% level of service. Since the probability that forecast error exceeds two standard deviations is 2.3%, it follows that the probability of not having a stock-out is approximately 98%. For a 98% level of service, then, the safety stock we need to carry for each item is equal to two standard deviations of forecast error for each item (see Table 6.4). The reorder points are calculated by adding the forecast of demand during the lead time (100 units) to the safety stock required for a 98% level of service. You can see that our inability to forecast demand for Item 2 very accurately means that we have to carry a much larger quantity of safety stock to achieve the same level of service.

The safety stock and reorder point required for any item can be calculated using the values in Table 6.5 and the formulae below.

Continuous-Review Reorder Point:

Safety Stock = Safety Factor × Standard Deviation of Forecast
Errors during Lead Time

Reorder Point = Forecast of Demand during Lead Time +
Safety Stock

Periodic-Review Reorder Point:

Safety Stock = Safety Factor × Standard Deviation of Forecast
Errors during Lead Time and Review Time

Reorder Point = Forecast of Demand during Lead Time and
Review Time + Safety Stock

TABLE 6.4
SAFETY STOCK AND REORDER POINT FOR 98% LEVEL OF SERVICE

ITEM	STANDARD DEVIATION OF FORECAST ERROR	SAFETY STOCK FOR 98% SERVICE	REORDER POINT
Item 1	3.2	6.4	107
Item 2	29.4	58.8	159

TABLE 6.5
SAFETY FACTORS FOR SPECIFIC LEVELS OF SERVICE

NO. OF STANDARD DEVIATIONS (SAFETY FACTOR)	PROBABILITY OF STOCK-OUT	CUSTOMER SERVICE LEVEL (%)
0.0	.500	50.0
0.1	.460	54.0
0.2	.421	57.8
0.3	.382	61.8
0.4	.345	65.5
0.5	.309	69.1
0.6	.274	72.6
0.7	.242	75.7
0.8	.212	78.7
0.9	.184	81.6
1.0	.159	84.1
1.1	.136	86.4
1.2	.115	88.5
1.3	.097	90.3
1.4	.081	91.9
1.5	.067	93.3
1.6	.055	94.5
1.7	.045	95.4
1.8	.036	96.3
1.9	.029	97.1
2.0	.023	97.7
2.1	.018	98.2
2.2	.014	98.6
2.3	.011	98.9
2.4	.008	99.2
2.5	.006	99.4
2.6	.005	99.5
2.7	.004	99.6
2.8	.003	99.7
2.9	.002	99.8
3.0	.002	99.8

The figures in Table 6.5 demonstrate the relationship between safety stock and customer service.

- A 50% level of service can be obtained with no safety stock at all, since the forecast of demand during the lead time will be higher than actual demand 50% of the time.
- The addition of larger quantities of safety stock will always raise the level of service, but at a slower rate.

- Safety stock equal to one standard deviation will raise the service level from 50% to 84%.
- Additional safety stock, equal to one more standard deviation, will also raise the level of service, but to a lesser degree (84% to 98%).
- The addition of one more standard deviation of safety stock will again raise the service level, but only from 98% to 99.8%.
- Theoretically, an infinite amount of safety stock is required to guarantee a 100% level of service.

The relationship between safety stock and customer service is shown in Figure 6.7.

FIGURE 6.7
RELATIONSHIP BETWEEN SAFETY STOCK
AND CUSTOMER SERVICE

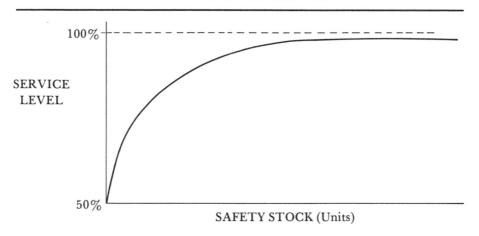

LEAD TIME DIFFERENT FROM FORECAST PERIODS

The statistical formula for calculating safety stocks is based on the standard deviation of forecast errors during the lead time (or lead time and review time) to obtain additional items. Few companies, however, measure demand relative to the lead time or the lead time plus the review period. The reasons are fairly obvious:

- It would entail different measurement periods for items with different lead times and review periods.
- Most companies track sales or demand activity in fixed time buckets, usually a month in duration. Records of monthly sales or demand are most common because of the need to provide monthly data for accounting purposes.

Clearly, the statistical formula has to be modified if the lead time (or lead time plus review period) differs from the periods over which forecast accuracy is measured. If the lead time for a continuous-review item is two months, we need to base our safety on the forecast error we can expect over the two months. Expected forecast error over one month is not a particularly relevant figure.

The usual approach is to calculate the safety stock using the following formula:

$$\text{Adjusted Safety Stock} = \begin{array}{c}\text{Safety Stock}\\ \text{(Based on}\\ \text{reporting period)}\end{array} \times \sqrt{\frac{\text{Lead Time Period}}{\text{Reporting Time}}}$$

If, for example, we determine that we need 50 units of safety stock for an item, using monthly data, and the item has a two-month lead time, the revised safety stock would be:

$$\text{Revised Safety Stock} = 50 \times \sqrt{\frac{2}{1}}$$

$$= 71 \text{ units}$$

If the lead time was half a month, the revised safety stock would be:

$$\text{Revised Safety Stock} = 50 \times \sqrt{\frac{.5}{1}}$$

$$= 35 \text{ units}$$

The effect of the formula is to adjust the computed safety stock, but by less than a pro-rated amount. The reason for this is that it is unlikely that two or more extremes in forecast error will occur in sequence. If we need 50 units of safety stock to cover forecast error over a one-month period, it is unlikely that we will have errors in two consecutive months of 50 units each. Positive errors in one period should tend to cancel out negative errors in other periods. The square root sign in the formula results in a less than proportionate increase or decrease in safety stock since the lead time (or lead time plus reviewed period) differs from the period over which forecast accuracy is measured.

THE MEANING OF SERVICE

In the chapter on customer service, we identified a number of possible measures of customer service, such as:

- % line fill
- % order fill
- % dollar fill

A frequently asked question is, "What type of service level is used to calculate safety stocks?" The answer is, "None of the above."

The statistical calculation of safety stock described in this chapter is based on the probability or likelihood of running out of stock over the lead time to resupply. If reorder points are used to control ordering decisions, the number of times you can run out of stock is equal to the number of times an item is ordered. If, for example, an item is ordered in quantities of 1,000 and demand averages 1,000 units per year, orders will be placed once a year. There will be only one opportunity each year for a stock-out to occur. If demand for the item was 1,000 units per month, there would be 12 chances of a stock-out during the year.

Safety stock calculated based on a 95% level of service will result in an average of five stockouts for every 100 replenishment cycles. The degree to which the order frequency affects the service provided to customers can be demonstrated using the example in the previous paragraph. If demand is 1,000 units per year, we can expect a stock-out five times over the next 100 years. If demand is 1,000 units per month, we can expect five stock-outs over the next 100 months (8.3 years).

The relationship between service and ordering frequency suggests that safety stocks should be calculated based on the number of times you are willing to be out of stock each year. The ordering frequency can then be used to determine the appropriate service percentage to use to calculate the safety stock quantity.

$$\text{Desired Service Level} = 100 \times \left(1 - \frac{\text{Acceptable Number of Stock-outs/Year}}{\text{Number of Order Cycles}}\right)$$

TABLE 6.6
EXAMPLE OF SERVICE LEVEL CALCULATION

ACCEPTABLE NUMBER OF STOCK-OUTS PER YEAR	NUMBER OF ORDER CYCLES PER YEAR	DESIRED SERVICE LEVEL (%)
1	2	50
1	6	83
1	12	92
1	24	96
1	52	98

ORDER QUANTITIES

Once the need to order is determined, using reorder points or by other techniques outlined later in this chapter, a planner still has to determine the size of the replenishment order — the order quantity. This decision essentially involves a trade-off between the costs of ordering and the costs to carry inventory.

ORDERING COSTS

The cost of placing orders with suppliers is composed of a portion of the salaries and wages of:

- inventory managers
- purchasing staff
- expediters
- receivers
- accounts payable staff

The work-load of these individuals is related to the number of orders placed with suppliers. Telephone and telex charges and the cost of purchase order forms are also related to the purchasing activity. Total ordering costs probably follow a step function pattern. A specific complement of staff can likely handle a wide range of purchasing activity. One inventory manager, one purchasing agent, one receiver and one accounts payable clerk, for example, may be able to handle 1,000 purchases per year. A larger volume of purchases may require additional staff. This is shown in Figure 6.8.

FIGURE 6.8
TOTAL PURCHASING-RELATED COSTS

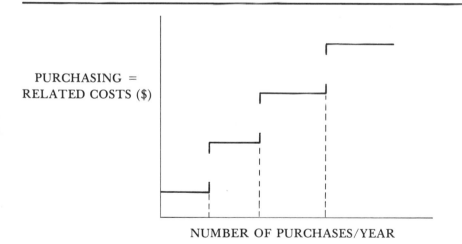

PURCHASING =
RELATED COSTS ($)

NUMBER OF PURCHASES/YEAR

The cost of placing one purchase order is usually estimated by dividing the total purchasing-related costs by the average number of purchase orders issued over the corresponding period of time. While the cost will vary by company and type of industry, most organizations use a figure between $30 and $100 per order as an approximation.

The ordering costs per unit ordered decrease as larger and larger quantities are purchased at the same time. The cost of placing each order is essentially spread over a larger number of units. Table 6.7 and Figure 6.9 demonstrate this.

TABLE 6.7
ORDERING COSTS

Cost to Order: $50
Annual Demand: 1,000 Units

ORDER QUANTITY (UNITS)	ORDERS/YEAR	ORDERING COST/YEAR ($)
1	1,000	50,000
10	100	5,000
25	40	2,000
50	20	1,000
75	13.3	667
100	10	500
•	•	•
•	•	•
•	•	•
1,000	1	50

FIGURE 6.9
ANNUAL ORDERING COSTS VERSUS QUANTITY ORDERED

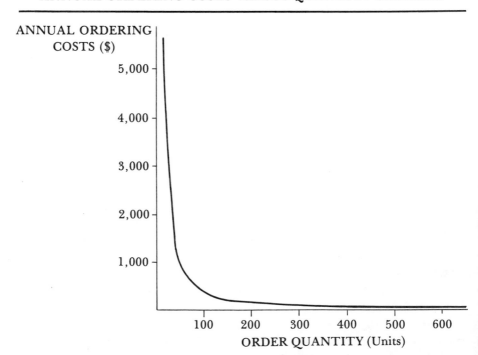

INVENTORY CARRYING COSTS

Order quantities have a direct effect on average inventory levels. In fact, if we assume that demand is at a fairly constant rate over time, the average inventory level will be one-half of the order quantity, plus the safety stock carried to protect against fluctuations in supply and demand. Inventory carrying costs are usually expressed as a percentage of the purchase or manufactured costs. Larger order quantities will result in larger average inventories and higher carrying costs. Carrying costs which correspond to the order quantities shown in Table 6.7 are shown in Table 6.8 and Figure 6.10.

TABLE 6.8
INVENTORY CARRYING COSTS

Inventory Carrying Cost Rate	.10		
Unit Cost	$100.00		

ORDER QUANTITY	AVERAGE INVENTORY (UNITS)	AVERAGE INVENTORY ($)	CARRYING COST ($)
1	.5	50	5
10	5.0	500	50
25	12.5	1,250	125
50	25.0	2,500	250
75	37.5	3,750	375
100	50.0	5,000	500
•	•	•	—
•	•	•	—
•	•	•	—
1,000	500.0	50,000	5,000

TOTAL ORDERING AND CARRYING COSTS

Ordering in larger quantities will reduce the annual costs of ordering, but will result in large inventories and high inventory carrying costs. Smaller order quantities will keep inventory costs down, but will increase the cost of ordering. Rather than minimizing the cost of either ordering or carrying inventory, we need to minimize the total of these two sets of costs. Adding the ordering and carrying costs together produces the U-shaped curve shown in Figure 6.11. The cost data are summarized in Table 6.9. The lowest point on the total cost curve is the order quantity where ordering costs are equal to the carrying costs. This will always be the case, regardless of the demand, unit cost, carrying cost rate or ordering cost.

FIGURE 6.10
INVENTORY CARRYING COSTS

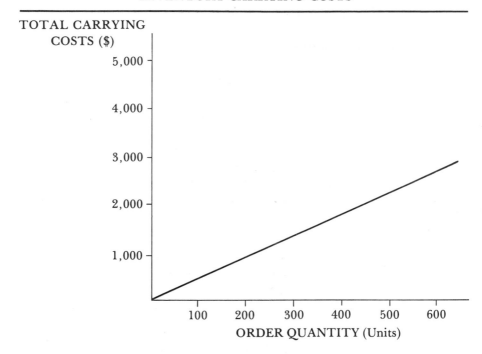

TABLE 6.9
TOTAL ORDERING AND CARRYING COSTS

Cost to Order: $50
Annual Demand: 1,000 units
Inventory Carrying Cost Rate: .10
Unit Cost: $100

ORDER QUANTITY (UNITS)	ORDERING COSTS/YEAR ($)	INVENTORY CARRYING COSTS/YEAR ($)	TOTAL COSTS ($)
1	50,000	5	50,005
10	5,000	50	5,050
25	2,000	125	2,125
50	1,000	250	1,250
75	667	375	1,042
100	500	500	1,000
•	•	•	•
•	•	•	•
•	•	•	•
1,000	50	5,000	5,050

FIGURE 6.11
TOTAL ORDERING AND CARRYING COSTS

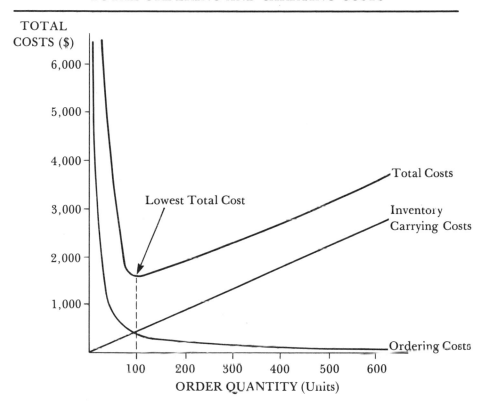

The order quantity that gives the lowest total cost is called the economic order quantity (EOQ). The EOQ can be calculated for any item, using the following simple formula.

$$EOQ = \sqrt{\frac{2 * A * S}{I * C}}$$

A = Annual Demand (in units)

S = Set up or Purchase Cost ($)

I = Inventory Carrying Cost Rate (as a decimal)

C = Purchase Cost ($)/Unit

Using the formula for the data shown in Table 6.9, we get an EOQ of 100 units.

$$EOQ = \sqrt{\frac{2 * 1,000 * 50}{.1 * 100}}$$

$$= \sqrt{10,000}$$

$$= 100$$

To verify that EOQ of 100 units gives the lowest total cost, we calculated the total costs for order quantities of 99, 100 and 101 units. The total costs are shown in Table 6.10.

PRACTICAL USE OF THE ECONOMIC ORDER QUANTITY (EOQ) FORMULA

The basic EOQ formula, described in the previous section, can be used to calculate the order quantity that minimizes the total costs of ordering and carrying inventory. Application of the EOQ formula in industry, however, is limited because of the assumptions used to develop it.

- Demand is assumed to occur at a constant rate over time. While this may be a good approximation for most items, it can be misleading for items which really have lumpy or sporadic demand.
- The basic EOQ formula is based on the assumption that orders are received instantaneously (i.e., in one receipt) exactly one lead time after an order is placed. In some situations, the quantity ordered may be delivered over a period of time. A special EOQ formula has been developed to handle situations involving non-instantaneous receipt (NIR).

$$EOQ(NIR) = \sqrt{\frac{2RS}{IC\,(P\text{-}D)}}$$

R = Annual Demand (in units)

S = Annual Ordering Cost ($)

I = Inventory Carrying Cost Rate (decimal)

C = Purchase Cost ($/unit)

D = Rate of Demand

P = Rate of Receipt

- The basic EOQ formula was developed based on the assumption that ordering costs are directly dependent on the number of orders placed. While the two factors are obviously related, we expect that one additional order does not really result in measurable extra costs to a company. In fact, it may be possible to place several hundred additional orders each year before the increased work-load requires the hiring of additional staff.
- Inventory carrying costs are assumed to be directly related to average inventory levels. While larger inventories do mean a greater capital investment, other components of inventory carrying costs, such as warehouse space and labour, are probably affected only by large changes in inventories.
- While it seems obvious that there is some cost incurred when orders are placed and some cost associated with carrying inventory, it is very difficult to deter-

TABLE 6.10

COMPARISON OF EOQ AND OTHER ORDER QUANTITIES

Cost to Order: $50
Annual Demand: 1,000 units
Inventory Carrying Cost Rate: .10
Unit Cost: $100

ORDER QUANTITY (UNITS)	ORDERS PER YEAR	ORDERING COST PER YEAR	AVERAGE INVENTORY (UNITS)	AVERAGE INVENTORY ($)	CARRYING COST ($)	TOTAL COSTS ($)
99	10.101	505.05	49.5	4,950	495	1,000.05
100	10.000	500.00	50.0	5,000	500	1,000.00
101	9.901	495.05	50.5	5,050	505	1,000.05

mine what these values should be. In fact, the true values are probably different for different types of items and purchasing methods.

A number of authors discount the value of the EOQ formula because of the limiting assumptions on which it is based. In our opinion, the EOQ formula can serve as a rough guideline for evaluating the order quantities used by a company. Although the assumptions behind the formula are simplistic, the total cost curve (Figure 6.11) is fairly flat near the minimum point; order quantities close to the EOQ are "almost economic." Ordering 75 units of an item which comes in packs of 75 units, when the EOQ is 100 units, is not much of a concern. If the EOQ, on the other hand, is 675 units, it would make sense to review the order quantity and see if the item should be ordered in larger quantities.

The EOQ may give you a good idea of a reasonable order quantity. There are a number of other factors, though, which also need to be taken into consideration.

MINIMUM PURCHASE OR PRODUCTION QUANTITIES

The most obvious factors which affect the size of an order quantity are constraints imposed by your suppliers. Orders may be subject to a minimum number of units. These minimums may be:

• The smallest quantity the vendor is willing to sell.
• The quantity produced in one production run.

These minimums will rarely affect ordering decisions on high-volume items. They may, however, represent several months or years of demand for items with low turnover.

EFFICIENT MATERIALS-HANDLING QUANTITIES

Ordering decisions should take account of the quantity which is most efficient from a materials-handling point of view. If an item is stacked 200 to a pallet, you should try to order in multiples or 200 units, unless even 200 represents too much inventory. Any economy from an inventory point of view in ordering, say, 360 units instead of 400 will be more than offset by the time it takes the receiving department to move the 160 cases by hand.

DEMAND DURING THE ORDER CYCLE

The quantity you order must be at least as large as the demand you can expect over the period of time until you can place the next order. This period could be as short as one day if a continuous reorder point system is used. It could, however, be much longer. Some companies supplied by their own factories can place orders only on a monthly basis. The order quantity then must be at least as large as the demand expected to occur over the next month.

Another example is the replenishment of branch warehouses. If branches are replenished according to a fixed schedule, the replenishment quantities must be at least as large as the demand expected over the next cycle.

The cycles we are talking about here are the cycles which determine the frequency with which orders can be placed. They have absolutely nothing to do with replenishment lead time. This important point escaped virtually all of the inventory planners in a major department of the Canadian government. Faced with long lead times (usually exceeding one year), almost all planners felt that order quantities had to be at least as large as demand during the lead time. Most planners typically ordered several years' demand of each item. Careful analysis of the situation showed that orders could be placed as frequently as once a month. More frequent ordering of smaller quantities has a tremendous effect on overall inventory levels. Inventory reductions of several million dollars were possible as the result of "pipelining" future orders.

PURCHASE VOLUME DISCOUNTS

Outside suppliers often offer financial incentives if you increase the size of your order. These incentives may be offered in different forms:

- on a unit basis, for individual items
- on a unit basis, for the total order
- on a dollar basis, for the value of the total order

In evaluating volume discounts, you have to remember that there is a significant cost to holding inventory and that order quantities are directly related to inventory levels. By offering volume discounts, suppliers are encouraging you to make a greater investment in inventory. The purchase cost savings you receive in return for buying larger quantities have to be weighed very carefully against the cost of carrying the additional inventory.

Price discounts can be evaluated by following the three steps outlined below.

1. Calculate the EOQ for each cost price.
2. Eliminate infeasible solutions (i.e., the EOQ is less than the quantity which must be ordered to receive the discount).
3. Calculate the total costs for each feasible option.

Consider an item with annual usage of 12,000 units. Assume that the cost to place an order is $30 and the carrying cost rate is 20%. The item costs $21.50 each, $21.00 if you buy at least 1,000 at a time and $20.00 if you buy 10,000 units or more.

The EOQs for each cost are:

- 409 units, if price is $21.50
- 414 units, if price is $21.00
- 424 units, if price is $20.00

Only the first one of these is feasible, since 1,000 units have to be ordered to get the $21.00 price and 10,000 units are required to get the $20.00 price. The strategies to evaluate them are:

- 409 units @ $21.50 each
- 1,000 units @ $21.00 each
- 10,000 units @ $20.00 each

These strategies are evaluated in Table 6.11.

The most economical option is to order 1,000 units at a price of $21.00 each. This will save $5,298.00 each year relative to the EOQ of 409 units. Buying 10,000 units at a time to achieve the vendor's "best" price will cost $5,576.00 a year more.

THE BEST ORDER QUANTITY
The best order quantity is the smallest quantity that:

- Meets vendor or production minimums.
- Takes account of effective shipping and materials-handling quantities.
- Is sufficient to cover demand over the cycle until the next replenishment can be received.

Keeping order quantities as small as possible will have a dramatic effect on inventory levels. The flip side to small order quantities, of course, is that purchasing activity increases. This is most significant for high-volume items where the minimum may be only a few days' stock. The most effective approach for these items is to adjust the purchasing technique to address the problem. Using blanket orders or systems contracting makes it feasible to place a large number of orders (essentially call-offs against contracts) and thus keep inventories low without placing an undue work-load on your purchasing department.

OTHER INVENTORY MANAGEMENT TECHNIQUES

The reorder point techniques described earlier in this chapter are the methods which most distributors use to control their inventories. There are a number of other techniques, however, which merit discussion. Some of them are just special types of reorder points. Others, such as manufacturing resource planning (MRP) and distribution resource planning (DRP; covered in Chapter 10), are quite different.

TABLE 6.11

EVALUATION OF QUANTITY DISCOUNT POLICIES

ORDER QUANTITY (UNITS)	ANNUAL COST TO PURCHASE ($)	ANNUAL NUMBER OF ORDERS	ANNUAL ORDER COST ($)	AVERAGE INVENTORY (UNITS)	AVERAGE INVENTORY ($)	ANNUAL CARRYING COST ($)	TOTAL COST PER YEAR ($)
409	258,000	29.3	879	204.5	4,896.75	879.35	259,758
1,000	252,000	12.0	360	500	10,500.00	2,100.00	254,460
10,000	240,000	1.2	36	5,000	100,000.00	20,000.00	260,036

MIN/MAX OR (s, S) POLICIES

This technique is a special form of periodic-review reorder point. The small "s" value is the reorder point. If the inventory balance plus the quantity on order is below this value when the inventory is reviewed, an order is placed. The order quantity is the quantity necessary to bring the quantity on hand plus on order up to the large "S" (maximum) value. This method is similar to the periodic-review reorder point method. The small "s" value can be calculated in the same manner as the periodic review reorder point. The order quantity, however, is not a fixed quantity. It will depend on the inventory level at the time the balance is reviewed. Most companies set the maximum at the largest quantity they ever want to have in inventory. Alternatively, the maximum could be calculated as the minimum-plus-one order quantity.

TABLE 6.12
EXAMPLE OF (50,200) POLICY

QUANTITY ON HAND & ON ORDER WHEN BALANCE REVIEWED	ORDER QUANTITY
100	0
75	0
50	0
25	175
0	200

TIME-PHASED ORDER POINTS

Reorder points should be calculated by adding the projected demand during the lead time to the quantity of safety stock required to meet the desired level of service. Most companies, however, use average demand (instead of forecast demand) to calculate reorder points. The chief reason for this is that the use of forecast values would mean that reorder points would change with each change to the forecasts. Most companies which use reorder points set the trigger levels based on average sales, and revise them infrequently, perhaps only once each year.

Reorder points based on average demand cannot effectively take account of projected changes in sales activity. Situations which cause changes in demand (e.g., promotions, trends) or supply (e.g., planned plant shutdowns) cannot be addressed.

The time-phased order point technique plans the ordering of items based on the projected timing of future demand. Orders are scheduled to be received in the period when the inventory balance is expected to fall below safety stock. Orders are placed, taking account of when receipts are required and the product lead time. An example of the time-phased technique is shown in Table 6.13.

The projected on-hand balances are calculated by starting with the opening inventory balance of 160 units and then subtracting the forecast for each week. With an opening balance of 160 units and a forecast of 40 units in Week 1, we expect an inventory balance of 120 units at the end of the week. The inventory at the end of Weeks 2 and 3 should be 80 and 30 units. A receipt of 200 units is due in at the beginning of Week 4, so the balance at the end of Week 4 will be 170 units (30 + 200 − 60). The projected inventory balances at the end of Weeks 5, 6 and 7 are expected to be 120, 70 and 20. At the end of Week 8, we would expect to have a stock-out of 40 units. Since this is obviously below the safety stock level of 10, we need to schedule the receipt of additional stock for the beginning of Week 8. With a lead time of 4 weeks, this order must be placed at the beginning of Week 4.

The time-phased order point technique gives planners better information than that provided by simple reorder points. Reorder point methods are good for determining when orders need to be placed if supply and demand are fairly constant. They are not as good if these parameters are changing. While reorder point methods can be used to determine when to release orders, they don't help a planner to determine which orders need to be expedited or delayed to keep supply in line with demand. Two examples will help to clarify these points.

For the example we used in Table 6.13, assume the demand in Week 1 was actually 80 units instead of the forecast of 40 units. The inventory balance at the end of Week 1 was then 80 units (160 − 80). At the end of Week 1, we project that the balance at the end of Week 2 will be 40 units. With forecast demand of 50 in Week 3, we expect a stock-out of 10 units to occur. You can see from the schedule in Table 6.14 that additional inventory does not need to be ordered. (If it is, it won't be received until the beginning of Week 6, because the lead time is four weeks.) The only way to avoid the stock-out we expect to occur in Week 3 is to try to expedite the order for 200 units that has already been placed and which is due in the beginning of Week 4. If we can get the shipment a week or two early, we can probably avoid the stock-out.

Continuing with the same example, assume that demand in Week 1 was actually zero. The inventory at the end of Week 1 is then 160 units. As shown in Table 6.15, the projected inventory balance at the end of Week 2 is 120, and at the end of Week 3 it is 70. The projected balance at

TABLE 6.13
TIME-PHASED ORDER POINTS

Lead Time: 4 weeks
Safety Stock: 10 units
Order Quantity: 200 units
On-Hand Quantity: 160 units
Order Scheduled for Receipt in Week 4

Week	1	2	3	4	5	6	7	8	9	10
Forecast	40	40	50	60	50	50	50	60	60	40
On Hand	120	80	30	170	120	70	20	160	100	60
Due In				200						
Scheduled Receipts								200		
Planned Orders				200						

TABLE 6.14
TIME-PHASED ORDER POINT (DEMAND HIGHER THAN FORECAST)

Lead Time: 4 weeks
Safety Stock: 10 units
Order Quantity: 200 units
On-Hand Quantity: 80 units
Order Scheduled for Receipt in Week 4

Week	2	3	4	5	6	7	8	9	10	11
Forecast	40	50	60	50	50	50	60	60	40	40
On Hand	40	−10	130	80	30	180	120	60	20	180
Due In			200							
Scheduled Receipts						200				200
Planned Orders		200				200				

TABLE 6.15
TIME-PHASED ORDER POINT (DEMAND LESS THAN FORECAST)

Lead Time: 4 weeks
Safety Stock: 10 units
Order Quantity: 200 units
On-Hand Quantity: 160 units
Order Scheduled for Receipt in Week 4

Week	2	3	4	5	6	7	8	9	10	11
Forecast	40	50	60	50	50	50	60	60	40	40
On Hand	120	70	210	160	110	60	200	140	100	60
Due In			200							
Scheduled Receipts							200			
Planned Orders			200							

the end of Week 4 would be 10 units. Since this is not below our safety stock level of 10, we don't need to receive the order for 200 units until Week 5. We can minimize inventory and still meet our service objectives by delaying receipt of the order (if possible) until the end of Week 4.

As a final example of the benefits of using time-phased order points, we'll use the same data shown originally in Table 6.13. Assume that your supplier for this item closes its order desk for a two-week period over the Christmas holidays. No orders can be placed in Weeks 3 or 4. The schedule shown in Table 6.16 shows that 200 units are needed at the beginning of Week 8. With a four-week lead time, we would normally place the order at the beginning of Week 4. Since the supplier's order desk is closed during Weeks 3 and 4, we will have to place the order in Week 2, and request delivery in Week 8. If we use reorder points, we will identify the need to order some time in Week 3 or 4. By then it's too late to order the items and receive them in time.

Time-phased order points are a very effective way of controlling inventory levels. Particular advantages of using this technique are:

- a much-improved understanding of what is likely to happen (e.g., when orders will be received, when stock-outs may occur)
- detection of scheduled orders which need to be expedited because demand has exceeded the forecast
- detection of situations where scheduled orders can be delayed without affecting customer service
- the ability to take account of unusual situations:
  - plant shut-downs
  - fixed production cycles
  - strikes
  - promotions

While this technique is very effective for controlling inventories, it does require a greater degree of planner involvement. The technique generates better information for planners to use. Planners, however, must be trained to use the additional information effectively.

A simple scheduling form for time-phased order points is shown in Figure 6.12. While this form was used to control inventories manually, the approach can be computerized quite easily. The heavy vertical lines are used to indicate the break between historical and planning data. Columns to the left of the line contain historical data (e.g., actual sales, timing of orders placed on suppliers, timing of actual receipts). Columns to the right of the line contain planning data (e.g., forecast demand, projected timing of scheduled orders and receipts).

The form is designed so that planners can monitor actual demand against the forecasts. Actual lead times can be determined by comparing

TABLE 6.16
TIME-PHASED ORDER POINT (PLANT SHUT-DOWN)

Lead Time: 4 weeks
Safety Stock: 10 units
Order Quantity: 200 units
On-Hand Quantity: 160 units
Order Scheduled for Receipt in Week 4

Week	1	2	3	4	5	6	7	8	9	10
Forecast	40	40	50	60	50	50	50	60	60	40
On Hand	120	80	30	170	120	70	20	160	100	60
Due In				200						
Scheduled Receipts								200		
Planned Orders		200								

FIGURE 6.12
TIME-PHASED ORDER POINTS—PLANNING WORKSHEET

ITEM #: 123975   DESC: WIDGET   MPOQ: 27,000   PALLET QTY: 3,264   TARGET MIN: 211,958

DATE: DEC. 31
INVENTORY: 630,000
PROJ M/E INVTY: 630,000

	JAN	FEB	MAR	APR	MAY	JUNE	JULY	AUG	SEPT	OCT	NOV	DEC
FORECAST/SALES	215,359	195,555	188,129	175,752	212,883	178,227	165,850	225,260	193,080	299,522	222,784	202,982
BACK ORDER												
INVENTORY	414,641	219,086	30,957									
RECEIPTS			189,000									
M/E INVENTORY	414,641	219,086	219,957									
PRODUCTION			189,000									

DATE: JAN. 30
INVENTORY: 417,370
PROJ M/E INVTY: 417,370

	JAN	FEB	MAR	APR	MAY	JUNE	JULY	AUG	SEPT	OCT	NOV	DEC
FORECAST/SALES	212,630	195,555	188,129	175,752								
BACK ORDER												
INVENTORY	417,370	221,815	33,686	46,934								
RECEIPTS			189,000	189,000								
M/E INVENTORY	417,370	221,815	222,686	235,934								
PRODUCTION			189,000	189,000								

DATE: FEB. 28
INVENTORY: 258,508
PROJ M/E INVTY: 258,508

	JAN	FEB	MAR	APR	MAY	JUNE	JULY	AUG	SEPT	OCT	NOV	DEC
FORECAST/SALES	212,630	158,862	188,129	175,752	212,883							
BACK ORDER												
INVENTORY	417,370	258,508	70,379	83,627	59,744							
RECEIPTS			189,000	189,000	162,000							
M/E INVENTORY	417,370	258,508	259,379	272,627	221,744							
PRODUCTION			189,000	189,000	162,000							

(continued)

FIGURE 6.12 continued

ITEM #: DESC: MPOQ: PALLET QTY: TARGET MIN:

DATE: MAR 30
INVENTORY: 264,077
PROJ M/E INVTY: 264,077

	JAN	FEB	MAR	APR	MAY	JUNE	JULY	AUG	SEPT	OCT	NOV	DEC
FORECAST/SALES	212,630	158,862	183,431	175,752	212,883	178,227						
BACK ORDER												
INVENTORY				88,325	64,442	48,215						
RECEIPTS			189,000	189,000	162,000	189,000						
M/E INVENTORY	417,370	258,508	264,077	277,325	226,442	237,215						
PRODUCTION				189,000	162,000	189,000						

DATE: APR 30
INVENTORY: 320,071
PROJ M/E INVTY: 320,071

	JAN	FEB	MAR	APR	MAY	JUNE	JULY	AUG	SEPT	OCT	NOV	DEC
FORECAST/SALES	212,630	158,862	183,431	133,006	212,883	178,227	165,850					
BACK ORDER												
INVENTORY					107,88	90,961	114,111					
RECEIPTS				189,000	162,000	189,000	109,000					
M/E INVENTORY	417,370	258,508	264,077	320,071	269,188	279,961	222,111					
PRODUCTION					162,000	189,000	108,700					

DATE: MAY 30
INVENTORY: 328,297
PROJ M/E INVTY:

	JAN	FEB	MAR	APR	MAY	JUNE	JULY	AUG	SEPT	OCT	NOV	DEC
FORECAST/SALES	212,630	158,862	183,431	133,006	153,774	178,227	165,850	225,260				
BACK ORDER												
INVENTORY							173,220	55,960				
RECEIPTS				189,000	162,000	189,000	108,000	162,000				
M/E INVENTORY	417,370	258,508	264,077	320,071	328,297	339,070	281,220	217,960				
PRODUCTION					189,000	189,000	108,000	162,000				

order release data to receipt data. The form contains a complete record of what has happened and what is expected to happen for a particular item. In effect, it documents planner performance. Managers can review the forms (or computer records) and evaluate the decisions made by inventory planners.

Introduction of the time-phased order point technique has allowed many organizations to achieve substantial inventory reductions while maintaining or improving customer service levels. Inventory reductions of 15%–25% are not unusual. The time-phased order point technique can also be used to control the distribution of finished items to branch warehouses (see Chapter 10).

MANUFACTURING RESOURCE PLANNING (MRP)

The techniques we have discussed so far are appropriate for the management of finished goods inventories. They are not generally appropriate for managing the inventories of raw materials and sub-assemblies used in a manufacturing operation. Many manufacturing companies, however, continue to use reorder point techniques in spite of their significant limitations. In this section, we'll briefly review why reorder points don't work well in a manufacturing environment and outline the basic concepts of manufacturing resource planning (MRP).

Reorder point techniques and safety stock calculations are based on the assumption that the demand for any item is independent of the demand for any other item. While this assumption generally holds true for finished goods inventories, it doesn't apply to materials or components used to manufacture other items. Consider the example shown in Figure 6.13. Item A, a finished item, is sold to customers. It is manufactured from three components, A1, A2 and A3. Each of these components is, in turn, manufactured from three other items.

Let's assume, for the moment, that the inventories of all nine raw materials are controlled using reorder points. We'll also assume that the reorder points were calculated based on a 95% level of service. The probability of the three raw materials necessary to produce any one of the components being in inventory at the same time is 85.7% (.95 × .95 × .95). The probability of being able to produce all three components (i.e., all nine raw materials in inventory) at the same time is only 63%. Thus, even with a 95% level of service on each of the raw materials, we will only be able to manufacture the end-item 63% of the time.

It should be fairly obvious that the demand for the nine raw materials is dependent on the demand for the end-item. The inventory of the nine

FIGURE 6.13
BILL OF MATERIALS

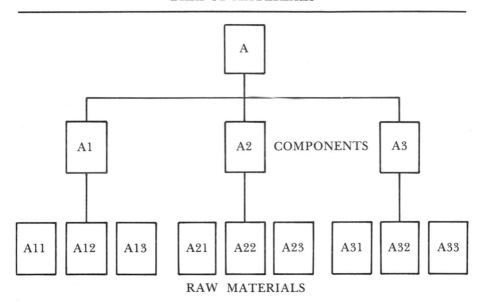

RAW MATERIALS

raw materials must be controlled so that all of them are available to meet manufacturing schedules.

The future demand for Item A determines the requirements for all of the raw materials and components used to manufacture it. Table 6.17 shows the production schedule for Item A. A manufacturing bill of materials for Item A is shown in Table 6.18. The bill of materials shows the quantity of raw materials needed to manufacture each component, and the number of components required to assemble one unit of Item A. Item A, for example, is assembled from one unit of A1, two units of A2 and two units of A3. A1, in turn, is manufactured from two units of A11, one unit of A12 and four units of A13. The bill of materials (see Table 6.18) can be used to determine the gross requirements necessary to meet the production schedule (see Table 6.17) for Item A.

As shown in Table 6.19, production of 500 units in Week 3 will require 500 units of component A1, 1,000 units of A2 and 1,000 units of A3. Production of 100 units in Week 6 will require 100, 200 and 200 units of com-

TABLE 6.17
PRODUCTION SCHEDULE FOR ITEM A

Week	1	2	3	4	5	6	7	8
Production Quantity	0	0	500	0	0	100	0	0

TABLE 6.18
BILL OF MATERIALS FOR ITEM A

ITEM A COMPONENT	RAW MATERIAL	QUANTITY
A1		1
	A11	2
	A12	1
	A13	4
A2		2
	A21	1
	A22	1
	A23	1
A3		2
	A31	1
	A32	2
	A33	10

ponents A1, A2 and A3 respectively. The net requirements for each component can be determined by taking account of the current inventory status. A convenient way to do this is to use a schedule like the one we used for time-phased order points.

Table 6.20 shows that we require 1,000 units in Week 3 to manufacture the 500 units of Item A. Since there are 400 units on hand and no demand before Week 3, we can see that additional inventory of component A2 is required in Week 3. With a manufacturing lead time of one week, assembly of additional A2 components must be scheduled for Week 2.

The net requirements for the parts used to manufacture A2 can be determined in a similar manner. The net requirements for part A21 are shown in Table 6.21. Orders need to be placed in Weeks 1 and 4. Table 6.22 illustrates that the demand for part A21 is, in fact, dependent on the demand for Item A.

The logic we have used to calculate the net requirements for all raw materials and components is called materials requirements planning. This logic is the foundation upon which manufacturing resource planning (MRP) is built. While materials requirements planning is a specific technique, MRP is more of a philosophy for the operation of a manufacturing organization.

Using MRP, companies first develop a business plan. This plan, which often covers a three- to five-year time frame, addresses issues such as:

• changes to business goals and objectives
• opportunities for new product development and introduction

TABLE 6.19
GROSS REQUIREMENTS

WEEK		1	2	3	4	5	6	7	8
PRODUCTION QUANTITY (ITEM A)		0	0	500	0	0	100	0	0
COMPONENT/ RAW MATERIAL	QUANTITY REQUIRED								
A1	1			500			100		
A11	2			1,000			200		
A12	1			500			100		
A13	4			2,000			400		
A2	2			1,000			200		
A21	1			1,000			200		
A22	1			1,000			200		
A23	1			1,000			200		
A3	2			1,000			200		
A31	1			1,000			200		
A32	2			2,000			400		
A33	10			10,000			2,000		

TABLE 6.20
GROSS AND NET REQUIREMENTS FOR COMPONENT A2

Manufacturing Lead Time: 1 week
Production Lot-Size: 700
On Hand: 400 units

Week	1	2	3	4	5	6	7	8
Gross Requirements	0	0	1,000	0	0	200	0	0
On Hand	400	400	100	100	100	600	600	600
Planned Receipts			700			700		
Planned Orders		700			700			

TABLE 6.21
NET REQUIREMENTS FOR PART A21

Procurement Lead Time: 1 week
Order Quantity: 1,000 units
On Hand: 300 units

Week	1	2	3	4	5	6	7	8
Gross Requirements	0	700	0	0	700	0	0	0
On Hand	300	600	600	600	900	900	900	900
Planned Receipts		1,000			1,000			
Planned Orders	1,000			1,000				

• changes to manufacturing methods and implementation of new technologies
• adjustments to manufacturing capacities
• high-level sales and profit projections

Long-term business plans are used to develop short-term operating plans, usually for the next three months to one year. These operating plans generally take account of:

• short-term sales projections
• desired inventory levels
• manufacturing capacities

Master production schedules are then developed to meet the desired inventory levels of finished goods items. These schedules show the intended production of each end-item over the planning horizon. Materials

TABLE 6.22
DEPENDENT DEMAND

Week	1	2	3	4	5	6	7	8
Production Quantity, Item A	0	0	500	0	0	100	0	0
COMPONENT A2 (2 PER ITEM A)								
Gross Requirements	0	0	1,000	0	0	200	0	0
On Hand	400	400	100	100	100	600	600	600
Planned Receipts			700			700		
Planned Orders		700			700			
PART A21 (1 PER COMPONENT A2)								
Gross Requirements	0	700	0	0	700	0	0	0
On Hand	300	600	600	600	900	900	900	900
Planned Receipts		1,000			1,000			
Planned Orders	1,000			1,000				

Orders on Suppliers

requirements planning logic is used to determine manufacturing and purchasing requirements. Once the preliminary schedules have been determined, the total requirements for meeting the planned manufacturing activity are calculated. Manufacturing plans are adjusted or capacity increased, as necessary, to ensure that the plan is achievable. Control of activities on the shop floor is based on the dates when specific operations have to be completed in order to meet subsequent manufacturing commitments.

A schematic of the MRP planning activity is shown in Figure 6.14. This figure illustrates two important feedback loops. The capacity required to produce the master schedule is checked. If the capacity required exceeds the capacity available, either the plan is changed or capacity is increased (e.g., using overtime, extra staff, etc.). Shop floor

FIGURE 6.14
MANUFACTURING RESOURCE PLANNING (MRP)

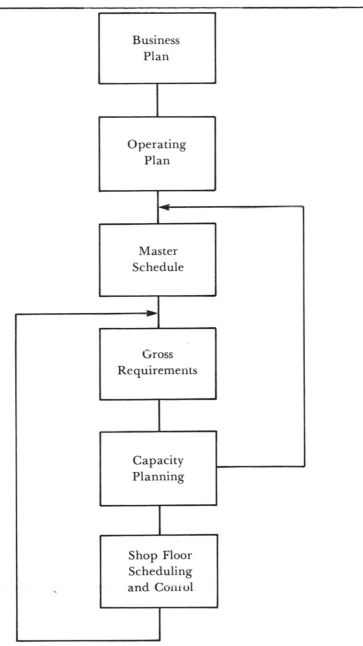

activities are monitored closely, so that manufacturing priorities are set based on what is needed and, more importantly, when it is needed.

The MRP concept is simple to understand. Implementation of MRP, however, has proven to be a major task for the organizations which have attempted it. Factors that make implementation difficult are outlined below.

- MRP touches virtually all functions in an organization, creating a need for a substantial amount of education and training.
- MRP requires a high degree of data integrity. Inventory records, bills of materials, product routings and shop floor data are all used to develop plans and set priorities. Errors in any of this base data will result in less than optimal plans.
- MRP is a new and different concept. Reliance, even to a small extent, on the methods used to control manufacturing operations in the past will seriously affect the success of an MRP implementation. If more than one planning system is used, employees will never be sure which one they should believe.

One success factor noticeably absent from this list is computer software. Good software with an adequate degree of functionality is, of course, a requirement for success in all but the smallest of applications. Software is rarely, however, the limiting factor. Organizations with basic software and a good understanding of MRP are far more likely to succeed than those who ignore the importance of the issues outlined above, no matter how sophisticated the software they are using.

MAINTENANCE INVENTORIES

Maintenance inventories consist of the spare parts and supplies necessary to keep plant and operating equipment in good repair. Organizations in the resource sector (e.g., mining, petroleum exploration) and the transportation sector (e.g., public transit, airlines) carry large inventories of maintenance items. These items are stocked essentially for two reasons:

- repair in emergency situations when other components fail
- use during routine servicing or as part of planned maintenance programs

Maintenance inventories are typically divided into insurance spares and operating supplies. Inventories of these items are most often controlled using basic reorder points. Reorder points for critical items are usually set very high because a shortage will mean that a piece of equipment or an entire production line will sit idle until a spare is obtained. Reorder points for other items are usually set based on historical usage patterns.

Control of maintenance inventories can be improved by using the time-phased reorder point method. A significant proportion of maintenance activities are planned. Maintenance planners usually schedule maintenance programs several weeks or months in advance, based on machine activity, utilization and recommended service intervals. The planned service programs usually have a pre-set list of parts which are required to complete the maintenance program. The time-phased order point technique can be used to schedule receipt of the maintenance items just prior to the start of the maintenance program.

INVENTORY DEPLOYMENT TO BRANCH WAREHOUSES

Design of the best distribution network involves an evaluation of the trade-offs between the following factors:

* inventory levels
* transportation costs
* warehousing costs
* customer service (i.e., delivery time frame)

These trade-offs are covered in some detail in Chapter 12.

BRANCH INVENTORY LEVELS

From an inventory point of view, more warehouses means more inventory. Safety stock will have to be carried at each branch location to protect against fluctuations in demand at each branch. Sales fluctuations at the branches will be more significant than those at one central warehouse, which means that additional safety stock will have to be carried. A general guideline for the relationship between the number of branches and inventory levels is:

Total
Inventory Required = Central Inventory × Number of Branches

BRANCH STOCKING POLICIES

The relationship between the number of branches and inventory levels makes it desirable to limit the number of items carried in branch warehouses. This will help to reduce:

* total safety stocks
* warehouse costs at the branches

High-volume items should be stocked at branches in order to meet the delivery time-frame required by customers. Low-volume items, in general, should be carried only at the main warehouse or, in a large network, at main regional distribution centres.

Branch inventories can be controlled at the branch level (i.e., a pull system) or at the main central location (i.e., a push system). While branch inventories have historically been controlled at the branch level, there is growing awareness of the advantages offered by centralized control.

- More highly trained inventory managers can be employed at a central site. Individuals controlling replenishment at the branch level often lack inventory management training.
- Greater control over branch inventory levels. Many companies using a decentralized approach have difficulty keeping track of inventories out at the branches. Branch inventories are often controlled by branch managers who are not held accountable for inventory levels.
- Greater control over inventory allocation when supply is limited. Allocation decisions can be based on some sort of "fair share" basis between branches, or on the advice of marketing and sales management, who are usually centrally located.

The distribution resource planning technique gives central inventory planners the data they need to effectively control the distribution of inventories to branch locations.

ABC INVENTORY MANAGEMENT

A general rule which seems to apply to almost all situations is that a small percentage of items or activities account for a disproportionately high share of the total activities. A small number of customers, for example, usually accounts for a large percentage of company sales. A small number of items may represent a large proportion of total sales. An example of the typical relationship between the number of items in inventory and the demand they account for is shown in Figure 6.15.

FINISHED GOODS INVENTORIES

In most manufacturing and distribution companies, about 20-30% of the finished items account for 75%-80% of the total sales volume. The ABC inventory management concept is based on the premise that the degree of effort placed on the control of inventory levels should reflect the degree of importance of individual items. An item which accounts for 5% of the total sales volume should be controlled differently than an item which accounts for only .01%.

Inventories are normally stratified into three categories called "A," "B" and "C." "A" items are high-dollar-volume items that account for 75%-80% of total sales. "B" items are those which account for 10%-15% of total sales. "C" items account for the remaining 5%-15%. An optional fourth class consists of items with no recent sales and items which are obsolete or planned for delisting.

The stratification can be based on:

- historical sales volume (units)
- historical sales volume (dollars)
- projected volume (units)

FIGURE 6.15
PERCENT OF SALES ACCOUNTED FOR BY INDIVIDUAL ITEMS

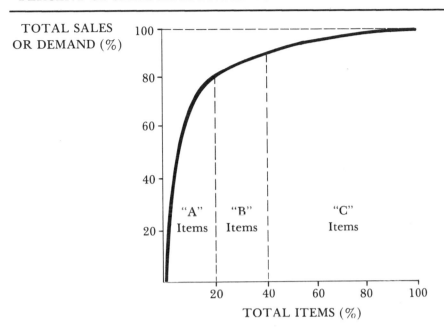

- projected volume (dollars)
- profit contribution

ABC stratification for finished goods items is usually based on historical dollar sales volume.

The ABC categories can be used as a basis for selecting forecasting techniques, selecting inventory control techniques, setting inventory parameters and monitoring performance. Examples of typical policies are shown in Table 6.23.

MAINTENANCE INVENTORIES
Maintenance inventories can also be controlled using ABC concepts. ABC categories should be based, however, not on dollar sales volume, but on quantity usage and on the severity of the implications of being out of stock. Different policies are clearly required for items where stock-outs will result in costly machine or equipment downtime.

MANUFACTURING INVENTORIES
The ABC concept is not particularly relevant for controlling manufacturing inventories. Although some items will have a higher usage rate than other items, they all must be available when needed to meet manufacturing schedules.

TABLE 6.23
**SELECTION OF TECHNIQUES/PARAMETERS BASED ON
THE ABC CLASSIFICATION**

	CLASS A	CLASS B	CLASS C
Forecasting Method	Sophisticated analysis using trend and seasonality factors with marketing involvement	Basic techniques such as moving averages or exponential smoothing	Basic techniques such as moving averages or exponential smoothing
Inventory Management Technique	Time-phased order point, or Distribution Resource Planning (DRP)	Continuous-review reorder points	Periodic-review reorder points
Customer Service Targets	98%	95%	85%
Performance Monitoring	Continuous	Monthly	Quarterly

Application of the ABC concept in the manufacturing environment is usually limited to the control of finished goods items. Since companies using MRP must have a very high degree of inventory record accuracy, ABC concepts may be applied to monitor the degree of record accuracy (i.e., 98% target for "A" items, 95% for "B" items, 90% for "C" items). These classifications should be based on volume, not dollar usage.

DATA INTEGRITY

All inventory decisions are based on data collected as a result of daily operations. Lead times are used to calculate reorder points. Forecasts or historical demand may be used to calculate order quantities, reorder points and safety stocks. Estimates of ordering costs and carrying costs are used to determine appropriate order quantities.

It is obvious that the quality of inventory decisions depends on the accuracy of the data used to make these decisions. No decision rules, no matter how sophisticated, can turn bad data into good results. This basic point is all too often forgotten in companies' searches for the best system or approach. Even today, most of the inventory management software packages offer little in the way of tools to monitor data integrity. Custom-designed procedures and reports are often required to close the loop and ensure that planners are working with accurate data.

CONCLUSION

Inventory management is only one of several logistics activities, yet it attracts the most attention because it is so closely related to the other activities (warehousing, transportation and customer service). The techniques described in this chapter, if matched to the right application, will help you to minimize inventories while supporting the other goals of your organization.

CHAPTER 7

Warehousing

INTRODUCTION

Comprehensive coverage of the topic of warehousing should, and does, fill entire books. Necessarily, as a single chapter in this book, it will serve as an overview of the warehousing function, its design and its operation. References will guide the reader to other sources for in-depth discussions.

In a distribution network, a warehouse may serve any of the following needs:

1. It may hold inventory that is used to balance the variation between production schedules and demand. For this purpose, the warehouse is usually located near the point of manufacture and may be characterized by the flow of full pallets in and full pallets out assuming that product size and volume warrant pallet-sized loads. A warehouse serving only this function may have demands for monthly to quarterly replenishment of stock to the next level of distribution.

2. A warehouse may be used to accumulate products from various points of manufacture within a single firm, or from several firms, for combined shipment to common customers. Such a warehouse may be located central to either the production locations or the customer base. Product movement may be typified by full pallets in and full cases out. The facility is typically responding to regular weekly or monthly orders.

3. Warehouses may be distributed in the field in order to shorten transportation distances to permit rapid response to customer demand. Frequently, single items are picked, and the same item may be shipped to the customer every day.

Figure 7.1 illustrates warehouses performing these functions in a total

FIGURE 7.1
WAREHOUSE ROLES WITHIN THE DISTRIBUTION NETWORK

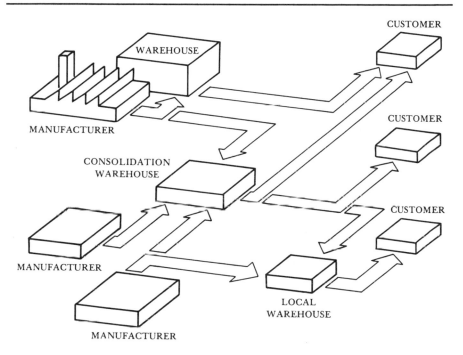

distribution network. Unfortunately, in many of today's networks, a single item will pass in and out of a warehouse serving each of these functions between the point of manufacture and the customer. It is certainly desirable to combine two or more functions in the same warehousing operation, when feasible. Current changes in the availability and cost of transportation options has made combination possible for many products. In particular, small high-value items with unpredictable demand are frequently shipped world-wide from a single source using overnight delivery services.

The design of an individual warehouse, its materials-handling equipment and its control system depend on which of the basic functions are being performed and the characteristics of the products that are being handled.

The warehouse design process described in this chapter will be devoted to planning the material flow and storage and the resulting requirements for building size, shape and height. A good discussion of building construction may be found in the "Facilities" chapter of the *Distribution Handbook* (Robertson and House, 1985).

The objective of warehouse design is to develop an effective combination of people, space and equipment to meet the projected storage and throughput requirements of the facility. The general design process will follow these steps:

1. Identify the functions within the warehouse.
2. Gather data and make projections to define the requirements for each function.
3. Develop alternative methods for satisfying the requirements of each function.
4. Combine functional alternatives into a single materials-flow system. This step must be repeated to generate several total system designs to compare with one another.
5. Select the total system that meets the projected requirements at the lowest annualized cost.

An overriding and integrating function is the control system that keeps track of inventory and directs and tracks all activity in the warehouse. Various combinations of alternatives for each function will require different levels and sophistication of control. Controls have become not only the most important part of any warehouse design, but also in many cases the most costly. A section later in this chapter will discuss control system considerations in more detail.

In Step 5, it is important to test the "best" system for its sensitivity to change in the requirements. For this purpose, it is useful to think of the requirements in terms of a range rather than a single projected value. This is also the appropriate time to consider the risk associated with each alternative. A perfect technical plan may experience difficulties in one or more of the following areas:

• cost overruns
• installation and start-up delays
• operator or management resistance
• inflexibility to requirements changes

A preferred alternative may have a slightly higher theoretical cost, but a much greater probability of successful implementation.

The balance of the chapter will follow the sequence of the preceding design steps.

FUNCTIONS WITHIN THE WAREHOUSE

Although it is easy to think of a warehouse as being dominated by product storage, there are many activities that occur as part of the process of getting material into and out of the warehouse. The following list includes the activities found in most warehouses. These tasks, or functions, are also indicated on a flow line in Figure 7.2 to make it easier to visualize them in actual operation.

FIGURE 7.2
BASIC WAREHOUSING FUNCTIONS

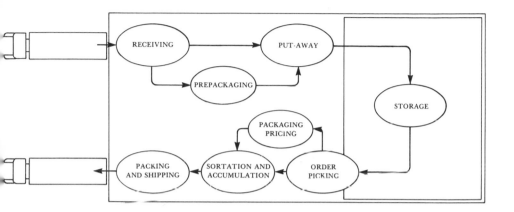

1. Receiving
2. Prepackaging (optional)
3. Put-away
4. Storage
5. Order picking
6. Packaging and/or Pricing (optional)
7. Sortation and/or Accumulation
8. Packing and Shipping

The functions may be defined briefly as follows:

1. *Receiving* is that activity concerned with the orderly receipt of all materials coming into the warehouse, the necessary activities to assure that the quantity and quality of such materials are as ordered and the disbursement to storage or to other organizational functions requiring them.
2. *Prepackaging* is performed in a warehouse when products are received in bulk from a supplier and subsequently packaged singly, in merchandisable quantities or in combinations with other parts to form kits or assortments. An entire receipt of merchandise may be processed at once, or a portion may be held in bulk form to be done later. This may be done when packaging greatly increases the storage-cube requirements or when a part is common to several kits or assortments.
3. *Put-away* is the act of placing merchandise in storage. It includes both a transportation and a placement component.
4. *Storage* is the physical containment of merchandise while it is awaiting a demand. The form of storage will depend on the size and quantity of the items

in inventory and the handling characteristics of the product or its container.

5. *Order picking* is the process of removing items from storage to meet a specific demand. It represents the basic service that the warehouse provides for the customer and is the function around which most warehouse designs are based.

6. *Packaging and/or pricing* may be done as an optional step after the picking process. As in the prepackaging function, individual items or assortments are boxed for more convenient use. Waiting until after picking to perform these functions has the advantage of providing more flexibility in the use of on-hand inventory. Individual items are available for use in any of the packaging configurations right up to the time of need. Pricing is current at the time of sale. Prepricing at manufacture or receipt into the warehouse inevitably leads to some repricing activity as price lists are changed while merchandise sits in inventory. Picking tickets and price stickers are sometimes combined into a single document.

7. *Sortation* of batch picks into individual orders and *accumulation* of distributed picks into orders must be done when an order has more than one item and the accumulation is not done as the picks are made. Figure 7.3

FIGURE 7.3
DISTRIBUTION OF PICK FREQUENCY
(Percentage of Part Numbers)

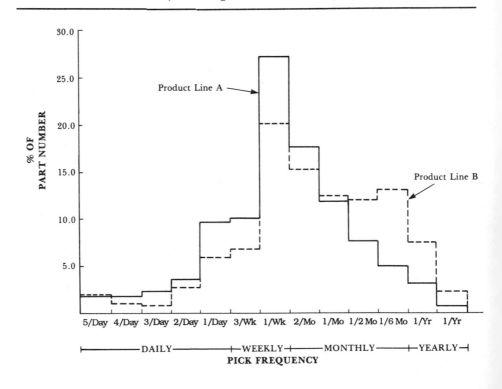

illustrates the concepts of sorting or accumulating after picking from storage.

8. *Packing and shipping* may include the following tasks:
   - checking orders for completeness
   - packaging of merchandise in an appropriate shipping container
   - preparation of shipping documents, including packing list, address label and bill of lading
   - weighing of order to determine shipping charges
   - accumulation of orders by outbound carrier
   - loading trucks (in many instances, this is a carrier's responsibility)

DATA REQUIREMENTS FOR SYSTEM DESIGN AND EQUIPMENT SELECTION

In order to design and evaluate a proposed warehouse system, we must understand clearly the nature of the task — *as described with numbers*. Since the warehouse is to be designed to handle future business, it is important to use historical data only as a guide in projecting future requirements, and not as an accurate description of the problem itself.

A word of caution: averages are seldom of much help in system design. One should be more interested in the range and distribution of values. Also, since a major design task for the warehouse involves the order cumulation process, it is important to understand not only the data regarding individual items (stock-keeping units, or SKUs) but also how they must be combined to form orders.

Below is a list of the most important data that must be collected. Figure 7.4 and Tables 7.1 and 7.2 illustrate typical summaries of some of that data.

Receiving Data
- Arrival time and dock time for carriers
- Number of items per carrier
- Physical handling units
- Frequency of receiving individual items

Storage Data
- Minimum and maximum quantity on hand per item
- Receiving and issuing quantities
- Handling units
- Cube per item

Order Data
- Number of orders
- Number of lines per order
- Number of pieces per order
- Frequency of picks per item

FIGURE 7.4

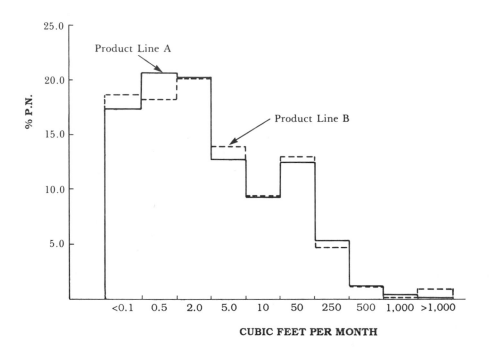

CUBIC FEET PER MONTH

BASIC WAREHOUSING EQUIPMENT

Before developing any physical system design to meet the prescribed requirements, it is most important to have a familiarity with the alternative equipment that is available. One of the biggest mistakes made in system design is the consideration of only *one* alternative to the current methods. It may, in fact, be superior to today's operation, but perhaps not nearly as good or as cost-effective as some alternatives that were *not* considered.

Selection of the appropriate equipment for use in the warehouse is a function of the throughput and storage requirements. However, complete evaluation of some types of equipment may require additional data or further detail in the basic data already collected. This section describes equipment in the following categories:

• Conventional Pallet-Storage Equipment
• Automated Pallet Storage-and-Retrieval Systems (AS/RS)

TABLE 7.1
STORAGE REQUIREMENTS

PALLET STORAGE

1 Mo. Storage Cube	No. SKUs	2-Month Inv. Pallet Storage	
		@ 20 Cu. Ft. (70% Util.)	@ 25 Cu. Ft. (85% Util.)
>1,000	4	480	384
500–1,000	11	800	660
250–500	37	1,400	1,110
50–250	177	2,635	2,124
10–50	432	1,296	1,296
	661	6,611	5,574

SHELF STOCK

1 Mo. Cube	No. SKU	Shelf Length per SKU	2-Month Inv. Total Shelf Length for Group
5–10	321	4'	1,284
2–5	437	2'	874
.5–2	693	1'	693
	1,451	For 50" Decked Rack =	2,851
		For 24" Bin Shelving × 1.5 =	4,276

SMALL-PARTS STORAGE

Monthly Cube	Number SKU	SKU per Tote	Number Totes	2-Month Inv. Rack Bays at 7' High
.25–.5	336	1	336	16
.125–.25	256	2	128	6
>.125	688	4	172	8
	1,280		636	30

- Case and small-item storage
- Conveyors and transportation

CONVENTIONAL PALLET-STORAGE EQUIPMENT

In recent years our emphasis in planning has been focused on the development of integrated manufacturing and distribution systems. Many of these have involved highly automated handling and storage systems. The controls necessary for the integrated system to be effective

TABLE 7.2

LINE ITEMS PER ORDER

LINE ITEMS/ ORDER	ORDER CUBE							TOTAL NO. ORDERS	% TOTAL NO. ORDERS	TOTAL STORAGE CUBE FOR LI/ORDER	% TOTAL STOR. CUBE	AVG. TOTAL CUBE
	≤1.0	1–2.0	2–5.0	5–10.0	10–20.0	20–46.0	>46.0					
1	43,796	3,827	4,107	1,760	607	251	109	54,457	47	64,494.63	15	1.18
2–5	24,486	6,018	6,766	3,665	2,224	635	248	44,042	38	133,371.45	32	3.03
6–10	1,978	1,570	2,406	1,513	1,321	599	187	9,574	8	71,043.55	17	7.42
11–25	409	625	1,531	1,514	1,353	953	351	6,736	6	90,595.06	22	13.45
26–50	7	22	170	235	355	399	206	1,394	1	40,298.83	10	28.91
51–75	0	0	1	10	27	52	67	157	—	10,249.66	2	65.28
76–100	0	0	0	0	10	5	22	37	—	3,045.58	1	82.31
>100	0	0	0	1	1	4	26	32	—	3,733.01	1	116.66
Total Orders	70,676	12,062	14,981	8,698	5,898	2,898	1,216	116,429	100	416,771.77	100	—
% of Total Orders	60	10	13	8	5	3	1	100				
Total Stor. Cube	18,396.49	17,451.33	48,918.11	63,286.31	82,513.22	84,111.49	104,094.82	416,771.77				
% of Total Stor. Cube	4	4	12	15	20	20	25	100				
Avg. Stor. Cube	.26	1.45	3.27	7.28	13.99	29.02	83.96					

were "built-in" as a part of the materials-handling equipment package. Many installations have been justified primarily on the basis of the improvement in controls.

The great benefits of better control made it logical to apply the same philosophy to less-automated methods of material movement and storage. It is now commonplace to see conventional trucks and racks employed as a vital part of a sophisticated system. The control systems, coupled with more advanced planning methods, have given new life to existing equipment and space.

The benefits of considering lift-truck storage as an alternative to automated storage include:

• lower initial equipment cost
• lower cost increments of expansion for both storage and throughput
• possible use of existing space
• more flexibility in long-term use of space
• faster to implement
• less start-up risk

This section summarizes the various configurations of storage mode, storage-and-retrieval method and considerations in determining which are most appropriate for a particular application.

ALTERNATIVE STORAGE MODES

The unit loads themselves may be held in a variety of configurations while in storage. They are listed and described below and illustrated in Figure 7.5.

SELECTIVE PALLET RACK

The most universal of storage modes, selective pallet rack provides access to each load stored. When a pallet space is created by the removal of a load, it is immediately available for another. Loads do not need to be stackable and may be of varying heights and widths. In instances where the load depth is highly variable, it may be necessary to provide load supports or decking.

Selective pallet rack might be considered as the "bench-mark" storage mode, against which other systems may be compared for advantages and disadvantages. Most storage systems benefit from the use of at least some selective pallet rack for SKUs whose storage requirement is less than six pallet loads.

BLOCK STACKING

Block stacking refers to unit loads that are capable of being stacked on top of each other. Depending on the type of load, the stacks may be from two high up to an acceptable safe limit. This storage mode is particularly

FIGURE 7.5
UNIT-LOAD STORAGE MODES

SELECTIVE PALLET

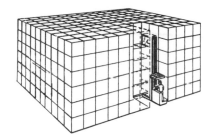

BLOCK STACKING

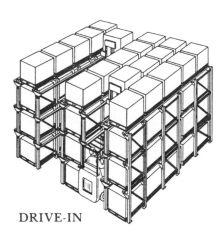

DRIVE-IN

DRIVE-THROUGH

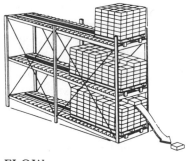

FLOW

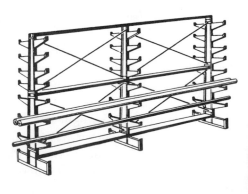

CANTILEVER

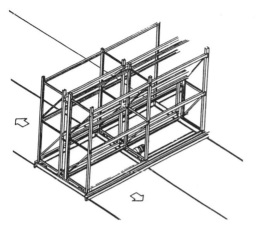

STACKING

MOVABLE

DOUBLE-DEEP

useful when there are multiple pallets per SKU and when inventory is turned in large increments, i.e., several loads of the same SKU are received or withdrawn at one time. A phenomenon referred to as honeycombing occurs as loads are removed from a storage lane. Empty pallet spaces are created which cannot be utilized effectively until the entire lane has been emptied. Therefore, in order to maintain high utilization of the available storage positions, lane depth (number of loads stored from the aisle) must be carefully determined based on the number of loads per SKU. Because no investment in racks is required, block stacking is easy to implement and allows flexibility with floor space. It is commonly used in leased space.

DRIVE-IN RACK

Drive-in racks are principally used to attain maximum utilization of space for pallet storage. They allow a lift truck to drive in to the rack several pallet positions and store or retrieve a pallet. This is possible because the pack consists of upright columns that have horizontal rails to support pallets at a height above that of the lift truck. This construction permits a second or even third level of pallet storage, with each level being supported independently of the other. Considerations for using drive-in rack include the rack cost, pallets per SKU, the space for the rack, the load clearance and possibly the time required to load and unload the pallet.

DRIVE-THROUGH RACK
Drive-through rack is merely drive-in rack that is accessible from both sides of the rack. It is for staging loads in a flow-through fashion, in which a pallet is loaded at one end and retrieved at the other end. The same considerations for drive-in rack apply to drive-through rack.

FLOW RACK
Functionally, flow rack is used like drive-through rack, but loads are conveyed from one end to the other. They provide for another item to move in a forward position when the front item is removed from storage. The main purpose of the flow rack is to provide a rapid method of order picking, therefore it is used when there is high throughput and rapid turnover of inventory.

CANTILEVER RACK
The load-bearing arms of a cantilever rack are supported at one end, as the name implies. The racks consist of a row of single upright columns, spaced several feet apart, with arms extending from one or both sides of the uprights to form supports for storage. The important advantage of cantilever racks is that they provide long unobstructed storage shelves with no uprights to restrict the use of horizontal space. The arms can be covered with decking of wood, or metal or can be used without decking. They are very efficient for items of long configuration such as sofas, rugs, rod, bar, pipe and sheets of metal or wood.

MOVABLE RACK
Movable racks have an arrangement of wheels and rails or some other mobile mechanics that permits an entire row of racks to move away from the adjacent row. The principle on which movable rack is based is that aisles are only useful when they are being used; the rest of the time they are wasting good space. Usually there are several rows of racks in a movable system. Access between rows is made possible by moving the adjacent row and creating an aisle. When the order packing or restocking function is completed the racks are bunched together again. These type of racks are useful when space is very valuable and inventory turnover is low.

DOUBLE-DEEP RACK

Double-deep racks are merely selective racks that are two pallet positions deep. The advantage of the double-deep feature is that fewer aisles are needed; this results in a more efficient use of floor space. In most cases a 50% aisle-space saving is achieved over selective rack. Double-deep racks are used where the storage requirement for an SKU is six pallets or greater and when product is received and picked frequently in multiples of two pallets. Since pallets are two deep, a double-reach fork-lift is necessary.

STACKING RACK

Stacking racks are portable and enable the user to stack material, usually in pallet-sized loads, one on top of the other, thus increasing mobility and using floor space more efficiently. Portable racks can be either frames that are attached to standard wooden pallets or self-contained steel units made up of decks and posts. When not in use their racks can be disassembled and stored in a minimum of space.

STORAGE-AND-RETRIEVAL VEHICLES

When all of the specialty vehicles are considered, there is a nearly limitless variety of storage-and-retrieval trucks. This discussion will be limited to only those that are most commonly used. These are illustrated in Figure 7.6.

COUNTERBALANCED LIFT TRUCK   Just as selective pallet rack is the benchmark storage mode, the counterbalanced truck may be considered the benchmark storage-and-retrieval vehicle. For use in block stacking, drive-in and drive-through rack and floor racks, the operating aisles normally provided are suitable for counterbalanced trucks. However, in selective rack systems, a counterbalanced truck will require aisles that are 50%–100% wider than those required by other vehicle alternatives.

The counterbalanced truck may be gas- or battery-powered. Besides forks, other attachments are used to lift unique load configurations. Counterbalanced trucks are available with operating capacities up to 100,000 lbs.

The relatively low cost and flexibility of counterbalanced trucks are their main advantages.

Because counterbalanced trucks must make a turn within the aisle to face a load for pick-up, the aisle required to operate must be wider than required for some other lift-truck alternatives. The height limitation is generally around 25 feet. A counterbalanced truck cannot be used to store double-deep.

WALKIE STACKER (OR WALKIE LIFT)   In the hierarchy of pallet-handling equipment, the walkie lift might be considered to fall between a pallet jack and a counterbalanced truck.

FIGURE 7.6
STORAGE-AND-RETRIEVAL VEHICLES

COUNTERBALANCED

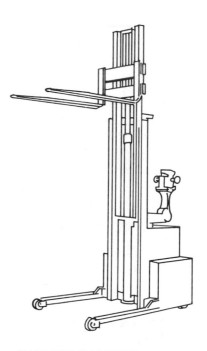

WALKIE STACKER

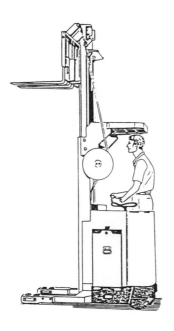

STRADDLE

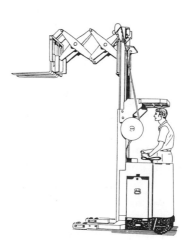

REACH

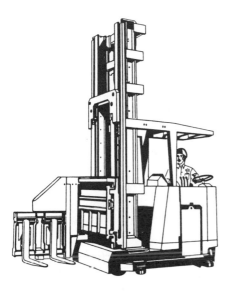

TURRET

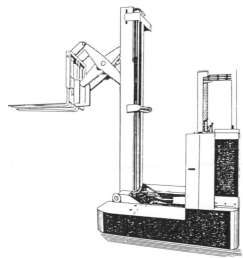

S/R T

SIDE LOADER

The walkie lift allows a pallet to be lifted, stacked and transported short distances. The operator steers from a walking position behind the vehicle.

In a situation where there is low throughput, short travel distances and low vertical storage height, and a low-cost solution is desired, the walkie lift may be appropriate.

STRADDLE TRUCK A straddle truck is most often used in warehouses, where aisle space is at a premium. The principle is to provide stability in the truck using outriggers instead of counterbalanced weight.

When a straddle truck is used to access rack, the outriggers are driven into the rack. It is necessary to support the ground-level load on rack beams or use wing-type pallets in rack serviced by straddle trucks.

NARROW-AISLE REACH TRUCK The next generation of narrow-aisle trucks, the reach truck, was obtained by shortening the outriggers on the straddle truck and providing a "reach" capability. Two basic designs are available: mast-reach design and form-reach design. The mast-reach design consists of a set of tracks along the outriggers that support the mast. The fork-reach design consists of a pantograph or scissors device mounted on the mast.

The double-deep reach truck, a variation of the fork-reach design, allows the forks to be extended to a depth that permits loads to be stored two deep.

NARROW-AISLE TURRET TRUCKS (TURRET, SWINGMAST AND SHUTTLE TRUCKS) Turret trucks, swingmasts and shuttle trucks are members of the modern family of designs which do not require the vehicle to make a turn within the aisle to store or retrieve a pallet. Rather, the load is lifted by forks which swing on the mast, by a mast which swings from the vehicle or by a shuttle fork mechanism.

Generally, these types of trucks provide access to load positions at heights up to 40 feet, which provides the opportunity to increase storage density where floor space is limited. They can also run in aisles 5 or 6 feet wide, further increasing density.

Narrow-aisle side-reach trucks generally have good manoeuvrability outside the aisle, and some of the designs with telescoping masts may be driven into a shipping trailer.

As with all non-man-up vehicles which are capable of operating above 25 feet, operator visibility is impaired. Operator training becomes more crucial as cost and sophistication of equipment go up.

Typically, when systems which incorporate narrow-aisle, high-vertical-height-type equipment are designed, they are designed for new facilities. Most existing facilities over ten years old will not have a high enough ceiling or level enough floors to take advantage of the capabilities of modern narrow-aisle equipment.

Since narrow-aisle side-reach trucks do not turn in the aisle, the vehicle may be wire-guided or the aisles may be rail-guided, allowing greater speed and safety in the aisle and reducing the chances of damage to the vehicle or rack.

VERY NARROW AISLE STORAGE/RETRIEVAL TRUCK (S/R TRUCK) The VNA S/R truck is similar to the turret truck, except that the operator's cab is lifted with the load.

The VNA S/R truck evolved from the S/R machine used in automated storage-and-retrieval systems. Unlike the S/R machine, the VNA S/R truck is not captive to an aisle, but may leave one aisle and enter another. Present models available are somewhat clumsy outside the aisle, but operate within the aisle at a high throughput rate.

The design of a storage-and-retrieval system using a VNA S/R truck usually begins with the vehicle itself. Some typical characteristics of such a system are five- to-seven-foot-wide aisles, rack storage up to 60 vertical feet, a rack-supported building, a constant electrical power source to the vehicle provided through a suspended track above each aisle, an enclosed operator's cab which may be air-conditioned or heated and single or double-deep storage.

The more sophisticated of these trucks are able to travel both horizontally and vertically simultaneously to a load position. There may be an interactive computer terminal in the operator's cab. It is customary for designs incorporating VNA S/R trucks to include pick-up/delivery points at the end of the aisle to interface with another type of transportation device. The disadvantages of such a system are the lack of flexibility, the high capital commitment and high dimensional tolerance in the rack.

SIDELOADER VEHICLE   The sideloader vehicle loads and unloads from its side. There are two design types: the entire mast moves on a set of tracks transversely across the vehicle, or the forks project from a fixed mast on a pantograph.

Aisle width requirements are less than for straddle trucks and reach trucks. A typical aisle would be 6½ feet wide, rail- or wire-guided. Sideloaders can generally access loads up to 30 feet high.

The sideloader truck must enter the correct end of the aisle to access a particular location, which adds an additional burden to routing the truck.

A variety of load types can be handled using a sideloader. The vehicle's configuration lends itself particularly to storing long loads in cantilever rack.

Typical pallet rack dimensions are shown in Figure 7.7. A comparison of aisle widths between load faces is illustrated in Figure 7.8.

AUTOMATED PALLET STORAGE-AND-RETRIEVAL SYSTEMS (AS/RS)

A typical AS/RS system consists of narrowly spaced selective pallet rack with 1,000–3,000-pound loads supported on rails similar to those in drive-in racks. Rack structures are typically 60–100 feet high and 300–500 feet long.

In most systems, loads are stored one pallet deep. However, when requirements call for high levels of storage and low throughput, double-deep racks may be used.

FIGURE 7.7
TYPICAL PALLET RACK DIMENSIONS

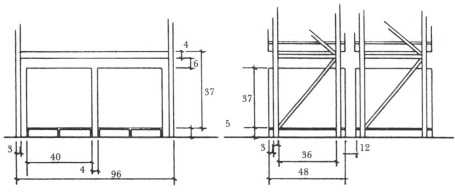

Note: All dimensions are in inches

FIGURE 7.8
COMPARISON OF AISLE WIDTHS BETWEEN LOAD FACES

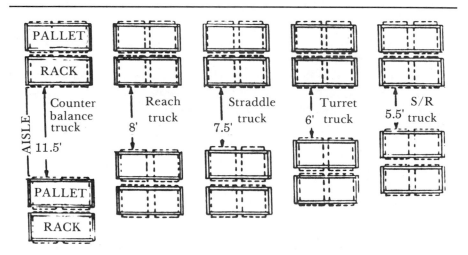

The racks may be installed within a free-standing building, or they may be erected on a foundation slab and the roof and siding mounted directly to them.

Pallet loads are stored and retrieved by rigid-masted vehicles riding on floor-mounted rails and guided by upper rails at the top of the rack or at the ceiling. The vehicle usually receives its power and communication via a conductor in the upper guide-rail. One machine is normally dedicated and captive to each storage aisle in the system.

Although the throughput capacity of a vehicle is dependent on the height and length of the system and on the storage locations assigned to each load, a range for planning purposes may be 15–20 dual-command transactions per hour. A dual command consists of storing an inbound load and retrieving an outbound load from the same aisle.

Since the storage-and-retrieval machines are captive to the system, loads must be delivered to and taken away from the end of the rack structure. This may be accomplished with one of the following methods:

1. Loads may be delivered to a queuing position with a conventional lift truck. A shuttle device is normally used to transfer the load into pick-up position for the S/R machine.
2. An automated guided vehicle may deposit a load directly onto the pick-up position and retrieve one from the output position.
3. A conveyor may be used to transport loads to inbound and outbound spurs for each storage aisle.

A typical system with a conveyor "front-end" is shown in Figure 7.9.

Automated storage systems have a significantly higher capital cost than conventional ones. Justification based on labour savings alone is rare. Occasionally, in a round-the-clock operation where high labour rates prevail, the savings may be sufficient. It is more common to find them installed where additional considerations are present — for example, a shortage of space that can be resolved only with the high density of an automated system, or an unusual environmental requirement such as security or temperature control that can best be met by a completely enclosed system.

FIGURE 7.9
TYPICAL AS/RS CONFIGURATION

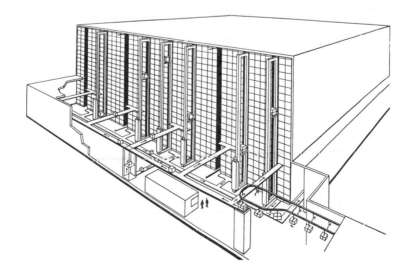

CASE AND SMALL-ITEM STORAGE

Cases and less-than-case quantities may be stored using the same equipment. However, very small items or quantities are likely to be containerized in standard tote boxes and sub-containers which, in turn, may be handled like cases. The number of cases for each item (SKU) or the size of the inventory will usually determine the appropriate storage mode. In order of simplest to most mechanized, the most common storage modes are:

- *Steel Shelving*. Normally 7 feet tall for access by walking, shelving may be erected more than 20 feet high and accessed by order picking truck or operator-aboard machine. See Figure 7.10.

   Mezzanine walkways may be supported by shelving to create multi-level storage.
- *Deck Rack*. Standard pallet rack may be fitted with metal or wooden decking for hand stacking of cases. When used this way, single-rack rows will permit access from either side of the rack, reducing the operator's reach to place or retrieve cases. Upper levels may be used for full-pallet storage.

FIGURE 7.10
STEEL SHELVING WITH ORDER PICKING TRUCK

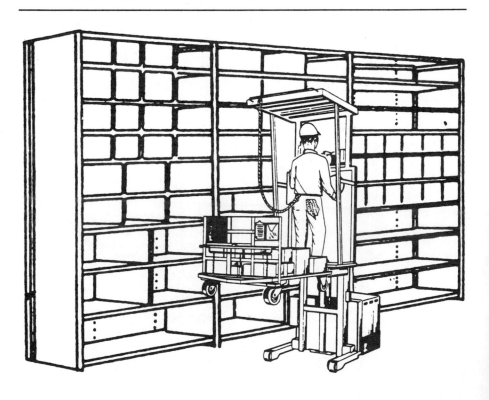

FIGURE 7.11
DECKED PALLET RACK WITH FULL-PLANT STORAGE ABOVE

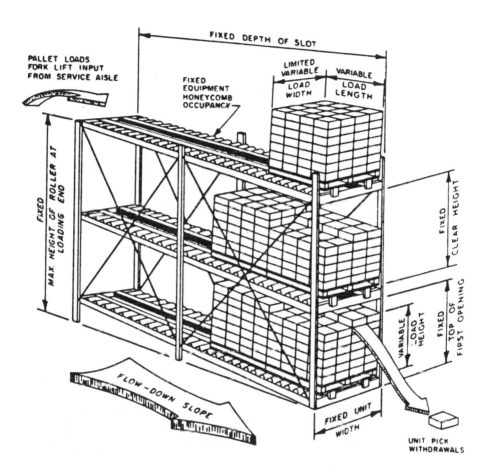

- *Flow Rack*. Although normally used for forward picking, carton flow rack may provide a substantial amount of primary storage. With an entire lane dedicated to a single product, careful planning is required to prevent a high incidence of partial or nearly empty lanes.

    The flow-through concept permits restocking without interfering with picking activity at the front of the rack. Figure 7.11 illustrates case picking from a pallet flow rack.
- *Drawer Units*. For very small parts, shallow storage drawers offer high density, easy access and security. They may be combined with steel shelving in a single aisle to provide a variety of storage-slot sizes in the same zone.
- *Horizontal Carousel*. Individual wire-framed bins with adjustable shelves are suspended on a narrow conveyor loop. The conveyor rotates the bins to a pick-

ing location at the end of the unit. Both cartons and tote boxes are stored on the shelves. In manually operated systems, an order picker may be served by two or more carousels so that while one unit is stationary during the picking transaction, the other may be rotating to bring the next bins forward. Even simple controllers will accept a batch of pick requests and resequence them to minimize carousel movement. See Figure 7.12.

More complex control systems maintain inventory balances and interface with host systems. Fully automated systems include inserter/extracters to remove and replace tote boxes. In those systems, picking is done at a remote station where totes are delivered by conveyor.

- *Vertical Carousels.* Long trays suspended from their ends revolve vertically to provide high storage density and to present parts at a convenient working height for the picker. Operation is similar to the horizontal carousel.
- *Mini-Load.* A bin storage system that looks and operates like a scaled-down pallet AS/RS. (See Figure 7.13.) Bins are usually 24 inches wide and 48 inches long. Heights vary from 3 inches to 12 inches. Systems typically are 20 to 40 feet high and 50 to 100 feet long, providing as many as 5,000 bins in a single aisle. Since throughput is limited to about one bin retrieval and storage per minute by the single crane in the aisle, the system finds its best application is environments where many SKUs are accessed infrequently.

FIGURE 7.12
CAROUSEL STORAGE AND PICKING

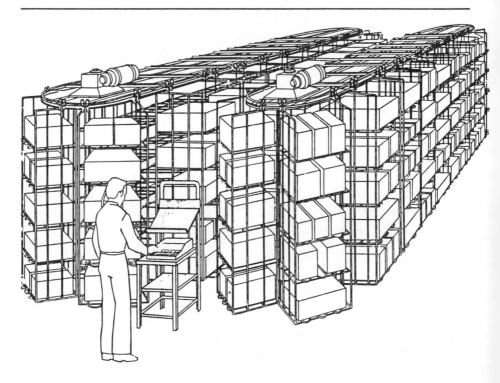

FIGURE 7.13
MINI-LOAD STORAGE SYSTEM WITH END-OF-AISLE PICKING

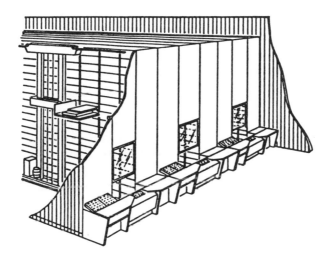

CONVEYORS AND TRANSPORTATION

In many warehousing environments, the primary method for horizontal travel within the facility is via lift trucks. They work particularly well when the operation requires mostly pallet-load handling and distances are short. In other operations, smaller load size (cases and tote boxes) or long distances or both make lift-truck transport impractical or expensive.

CASE AND TOTE-BOX TRANSPORT

In cases and tote boxes, a variety of conveyors are available. In addition to these, cases may be accumulated on a pallet or cart and treated as a unit load for transport. The simple picking and sortation system in Figure 7.14 employs several of the types of case conveyor described below.

GRAVITY ROLLER CONVEYOR Unpowered rollers (or wheels) set in a frame may be installed level or with a slight slope. In the illustration, the conveyor is set level, where it is used to make it easier for the order picker to move the case or tote along the pick line as he or she selects items from the forward storage area.

At the accumulation area, the gravity conveyors are set with a slight pitch to permit diverted totes and cases to flow to the packing and shipping end of lanes. The pitch must be sufficient to permit the cases to clear

FIGURE 7.14
SIMPLE ORDER-PICKING SYSTEM USING SEVERAL TYPES OF CONVEYOR

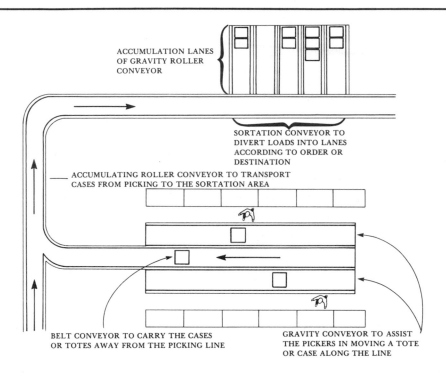

ACCUMULATION LANES OF GRAVITY ROLLER CONVEYOR

SORTATION CONVEYOR TO DIVERT LOADS INTO LANES ACCORDING TO ORDER OR DESTINATION

ACCUMULATING ROLLER CONVEYOR TO TRANSPORT CASES FROM PICKING TO THE SORTATION AREA

BELT CONVEYOR TO CARRY THE CASES OR TOTES AWAY FROM THE PICKING LINE

GRAVITY CONVEYOR TO ASSIST THE PICKERS IN MOVING A TOTE OR CASE ALONG THE LINE

the divert, but not so great as to allow heavier loads to gain speed and crush or knock off lighter loads in front of them.

BELT CONVEYOR A wide belt powered by a drive pulley and supported by either a steel "slider bed" or rollers is often used to carry loads quickly away from the pickers. Belt conveyors are quieter than powered-roller conveyors, providing a more comfortable environment for the pickers.

Belt conveyors may also be inclined to accommodate elevation changes. The angle of the incline depends on the centre of gravity of the loads and the friction characteristics of their bottoms.

ACCUMULATING ROLLER CONVEYOR When cases cannot flow continuously, or when gaps need to be created to permit merging of lanes or separation for sortation, roller conveyors with the capability to permit loads to accumulate behind one another are used. The rollers may be powered by a narrow belt or cable running below them with gentle pressure applied by supporting idler rollers or by small individual drive belts that connect each roller to a central driveshaft.

Accumulation may be provided by simply permitting rollers or drive pulleys to continue turning beneath loads that have been stopped. This is possible when the loads are light and the expected accumulation time is short. Obviously, the rollers' attempt to propel the loads creates "line pressure" of loads on one another. This pressure may cause loads to jump from the conveyor or make it difficult to release them in an orderly manner.

The most complex method is zero pressure accumulation, in which power is selectively removed from zones of the conveyor. Through a lever action, the weight of the load in one zone relieves the drive pressure from the rollers in the preceding zone, preventing one load from contacting another. This conveyor is more expensive to purchase and to maintain and consequently should be applied only where requirements dictate.

In Figure 7.14 an accumulation conveyor is provided between the belt conveyor take-away from the pickers and the sortation section. One place that accumulation is usually required is just prior to sortation, where loads must be released singularly to provide space for accurate diverting.

SORTATION CONVEYOR   When loads need to be diverted from a continuous stream into various lanes by order or destination, one of several types of sortation conveyors is used.

The simplest, but perhaps slowest, sortation is accomplished using divert arms that swing into position diagonally across a belt conveyor. The moving belt pushes the load against the arm and into a position which causes the load to slide off to one side.

Right-angle diverts may be accomplished by using a powered roller conveyor with pop-up wheels or belts that lift the load from the transport rollers and convey it, perpendicular to the direction of flow, into a spur. Additionally, pushers or pulleys may be used to intercept a load at the desired divert point and slide it sideways off the powered conveyor.

Very fast (up to 120/minute) sortation is provided by tilting trays mounted on a chain conveyor or by cam-actuated slides mounted on a roller flight conveyor.

In order for any of the sortation systems to operate, the action of the diverter must be synchronized with the presence of a load. This is done at an induction point where the divert destination of each load is communicated to the conveyor control system either by manually keyed entry or by automatically reading a code affixed to the load.

TROLLEY CONVEYORS   The most common use of the overhead trolley conveyor in a warehouse is for the return of empty tote boxes from sortation back to the picking line, where they are refilled.

PALLET-LOAD TRANSPORT

As mentioned earlier, when travel distances are long, it is expensive to use lift trucks to move the loads. The most common alternatives are listed below.

TRACTOR-TRAILER TRAINS When many loads need to be moved to the same destination — either a storage zone in the warehouse or the shipping dock — they may be placed on trailers and towed as a train with an industrial tractor. As many as 15 or 20 loads may be transported in a single trip. This is an alternative that lacks the excitement of automation, but is difficult to match for economy.

IN-FLOOR TOWLINES A continuously moving chain running in a shallow slot in the floor can pull carts via a tow pin dropped through the slot and engaged by a pusher dog on the conveyor. Cars are normally placed on the path by operators and programmed to stop or divert at a specified destination. These systems have very high throughput capacity but limited flexibility.

AUTOMATED GUIDED VEHICLES Battery-powered vehicles may carry or tow loads, following an optical or buried wire path. Sophisticated control systems permit complicated routing of the vehicles, dispatching and call-in capabilities and automatic loading and unloading. Capital costs are relatively high and generally proportional to the control system's complexity.

POWERED ROLLER CONVEYOR For pallet-sized loads, a roller conveyor is seldom used for long-distance transport. It is most often applied when accumulation and sortation are necessary: for example, as the input and output of an automated storage system. They may also be used to convey loads through various processes such as receiving, packing or stretch-wrapping.

STOCK-LOCATION SYSTEMS AND CONTROL

There are a number of ways to assign the space provided in racks, shelving, bins and drawers for the storage of material. Each assignment system provides a different combination of cube utilization, throughput or productivity and control. In general, the following objectives apply to stock-location planning:

1. Good space utilization
2. Facilitating placement into storage
3. Facilitating efficient and accurate order picking
4. Matching control-system capability
5. Flexibility to accept change

In many instances where limited control system capability exists or when absolute simplicity of controls is necessary, merchandise may be stored in part-number sequence, grouped by product line or manufacturer. This system is easy to implement and to learn, but when applied strictly it compromises both cube utilization and productivity. It is usually difficult to add part numbers or to increase the inventory of selected items.

Other location systems include some combination of random assignment and zoning.

When an individual part number can be put away in any available storage slot, it is subject to random location assignment. Storage slots may be classified by size, so that there can be a closer match between the cube of the item to be stored and the available locations.

There are two types of randomized storage: (1) true randomized storage, in which all locations have an equally likely chance of having product stored in them, and (2) closest-available-slot (CAS). Outgoing items may be picked automatically on a first-in-first-out (FIFO) basis, or they may be selected based on the opportunity to complete the pick from a single location. Yet another option is to select based on an opportunity to empty partially filled locations to make them available for the storage of new items. The CAS type of randomized storage is the most common in today's industrial environment. If the storage levels remain fairly constant and at a high level of utilization, there is little difference between the two types of randomized storage. However, if utilization is low and inventory levels vary, the CAS method of randomized storage will increase throughput in the system.

Dedicated storage based on activity will maximize throughput at the expense of storage space utilization. Conversely, randomized storage will optimize storage space but reduce throughput of the system. Studies have shown that dedicated storage can yield savings in increased throughput of 15% to 50% over pure or true randomized storage. Additionally, studies have shown that dedicated storage can require from 20% to 60% more storage slots than are required for random storage. Thus, the selection of the appropriate storage location assignment method depends on the importance given to space versus throughput levels.

Figures 7.15 and 7.16 illustrate possible location assignment methods to balance space utilization and throughput.

When items are often used or sold together they may be co-located to increase picking productivity. With locations next to or close to one another, travel time is reduced. In automated-bin storage systems, several picks may be made with a single bin retrieval. With the exception of co-location, storage assignment in automated systems is more likely to be random in order to maximize the utilization of the expensive storage cube. Rapid horizontal and vertical travel combined with relatively slow

FIGURE 7.15
ASSIGNMENT OF BIN FACINGS FOR ACCESS BY
OPERATOR-ABOARD OR ORDER PICKING TRUCK.

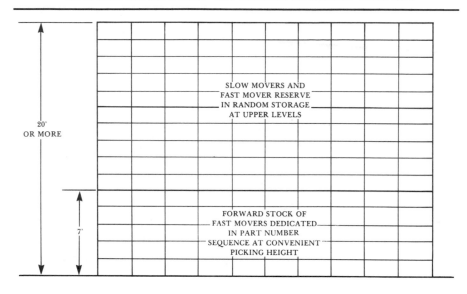

FIGURE 7.16
POSSIBLE USE OF DEDICATED, RANDOM AND ZONED STORAGE

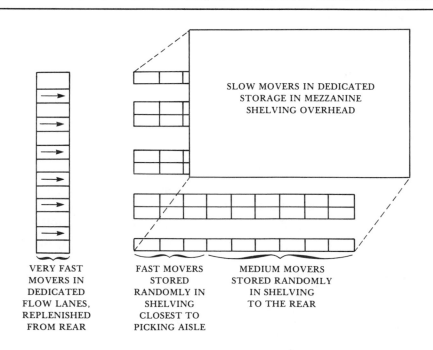

positioning and load transfer moves make total cycle times, and hence throughput, less dependent on optimized location assignment. The control systems typically associated with automated storage can accommodate random locations easily.

FORWARD-AND-RESERVE STORAGE

To reduce travel distances and expedite order selection, it is a common practice to create a forward picking area in which smaller quantities of each item are stored. The storage mode is one that provides easy access by the order picker. An example of an arrangement for forward-and-reserve storage is shown in Figure 7.17.

As indicated, a selection of small quantities (less than a full case) is picked from 20-foot-high shelving using an aisle-captive operator-aboard machine. All 5,000 items in the warehouse, except those that are physically too large, are represented in the shelving so that any small order may be picked complete from this single system. Orders for one or more full cases are selected at a picking platform served by two automated storage-and-retrieval machines. Replenishment for item picking is

FIGURE 7.17
BLOCK LAYOUT
ILLUSTRATING FORWARD-AND-RESERVE STORAGE

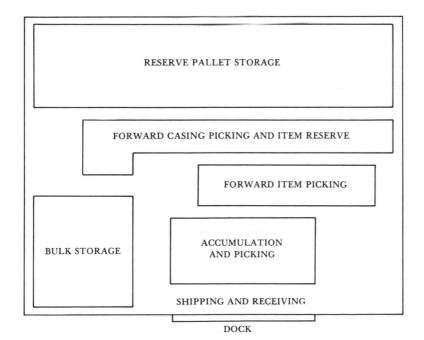

RESERVE PALLET STORAGE

FORWARD CASING PICKING AND ITEM RESERVE

FORWARD ITEM PICKING

BULK STORAGE

ACCUMULATION
AND PICKING

SHIPPING AND RECEIVING

DOCK

also made from this system. About 15% of the items are represented here. Orders for larger quantities are picked with a turret truck from the reserve storage area. When the order quantity is less than a full pallet but greater than half a pallet, the pallet is split at a picking station and the remainder becomes a replenishment load for the case-picking system.

The configuration of a forward/reserve system may be determined by the following steps:

1. Determine which items should be in the forward picking area. Because most inventories include many slow-moving items that have relatively small storage cube requirements, a forward picking area may include the entire inventory of each of the slow movers and only a representative quantity of the fast movers. Alternately, to provide the fastest possible picking, very slow-moving items may be stored elsewhere in the warehouse in a less accessible but higher-density storage mode.
2. Determine the *quantities* of each item to be stored in the forward picking area. As mentioned, slow movers may have their entire on-hand inventory located in the forward picking area. Storage allocation for other parts may be determined by either (1) an arbitrary allocation of space, as much as one case or one shelf, or (2) space for a quantity sufficient to satisfy the expected weekly or monthly demand.

    It is common to select for large quantities from reserve storage and smaller quantities from forward storage.
3. Size the total storage cube requirement for items in the forward picking area. Space planned for each item must be adequate for the expected receipt and/or replenishment quantity, not just for the average balance on-hand.
4. Identify alternative storage methods that are appropriate for the total forward picking cube and that meet the required throughput.
5. Determine the operating methods within each storage alternative in order to project personnel requirements. The description of the operating method must also include consideration of the storage location assignment (i.e., random, dedicated, zoned or a combination of these), because this will have a significant impact on picking productivity. It is also necessary to evaluate the opportunity for batch picking (picking multiple orders simultaneously).
6. Estimate the costs and savings for each alternative system described.

WAREHOUSE LAYOUT

The size of a warehouse is determined basically by the storage requirement, but the layout is determined by the materials flow. The specific functions in each warehouse and their relationships to one another will dictate the actual arrangement. The basic block layout in Figure 7.18 reinforces many of the principles listed below, which can serve as guides to begin a plan.

1. For most operations, place both the receiving and shipping docks on one wall and provide U-shaped flow within the warehouse.
   - Driveways and truck-turning space will be minimized.
   - Expansion possibilities will be increased.
   - Cross-docking of very fast-moving product is facilitated.
   - Some pallet storage and retrieval moves may be combined to minimize empty travel.
2. Place small parts close to the dock.
   - Activity and personnel requirement is usually high and the space requirement small.
3. Within the major storage areas, locate the fastest-moving products closest to the dock to shorten travel distances.
4. Link functions for straight-through flow to minimize time delays of getting product into and out of storage, to minimize staging space and to reduce materials-handling steps.

A radical alternative to the traditional "box" design of a warehouse is illustrated in Figure 7.19. It may be described as a collection of boxes, in which each box houses and is designed specifically for a single function. Receiving and shipping are located in typical truck-terminal construction. The high-rise storage system is a rack-supported structure. Bulk storage and picking are in a conventional building. This approach is advantageous when throughput levels are very high and the basic flow concept and use of the facility is expected to remain in place for a long time. This particular facility may be expanded easily without inter-

FIGURE 7.18
TYPICAL WAREHOUSE BLOCK LAYOUT

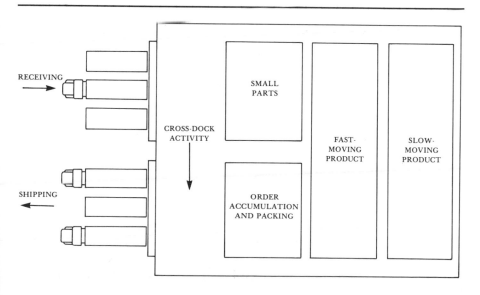

FIGURE 7.19
DISTRIBUTION CENTRE
WITH FUNCTIONAL BUILDING MODULES

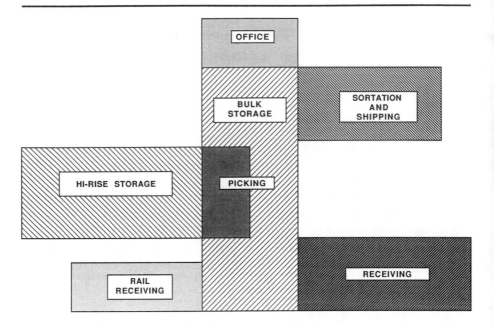

ruption of current activity. The shipping and receiving docks may be extended onto pre-graded land, and the high-rise storage may be expanded by simply adding more aisles on the open side.

CONTROL SYSTEMS

Warehouse efficiency and accuracy are largely a function of the control system used to direct and track activity. Figures 7.20 and 7.21 depict flow diagrams for typical warehouse control requirements.

RECEIVING CONTROL

The receiving function is primarily one of information processing rather than physical handling. Consequently, it is desirable to plan and concentrate the information-related tasks into as few steps as possible. Accomplishing this requires on-line accessibility to receiving information and real-time interaction with the data base.

Receiving tasks might be thought of as a series of questions to be answered regarding each item that crosses the dock. The basic questions, which should be built into a control system for each receipt, are listed below. "Yes" answers indicate straight-through flow with little cause for

FIGURE 7.20
RECEIVING SYSTEMS TRANSACTIONS

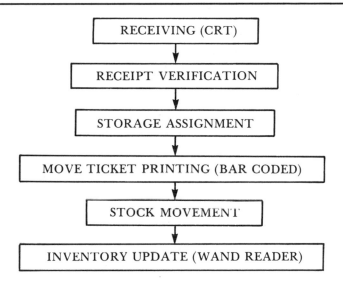

FIGURE 7.21
PICKING AND SHIPPING TRANSACTIONS

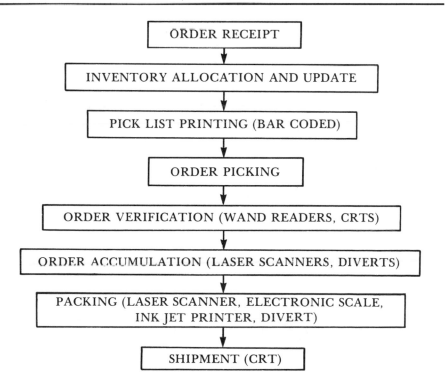

delay. A "no" answer requires resolution, or exception processing, and usually interruption of flow. It becomes obvious that the best improvements in receiving operations are a direct result of ensuring that the answers will be yes.

- Am I expecting a shipment from this company on or before this date?
- Do the cartons/pallets match the freight bill?
- Does the merchandise appear to be undamaged?
- Are the items on the packing slip included on open purchase orders?
- Do the items and quantities in the shipment match the packing list?
- Is the merchandise in good condition, and do the parts match the purchasing specifications?
- Is the merchandise received needed by production or a customer now, and what are the destinations?
- If it is not needed immediately, where should I store it?

PHYSICAL HANDLING AT RECEIVING   The information-processing requirements are used to generate a physical handling system. Each of the decision points should be reviewed to determine which ones can be performed at a single station. The consolidation of information-processing tasks into groups should be based on the following three principles:

1. Simplify the workplace
2. Utilize personnel
3. Minimize materials movement

A shortcoming of many receiving systems is the distance between the merchandise and the documentation required to perform the receiving functions. It is not uncommon to have the receipts spread out in a staging area while the first steps are undertaken. Excessive walking, waiting and locating are symptoms of a poor design (or, more likely, a non-design).

The most effective receiving systems use layout and handling equipment to permit material to *flow* through or past a receiving station. At this point, as many of the tasks as possible, including exception processing, should be done at one time.

Two major objectives must be achieved for this type of flow-through receiving to be possible:

1. Immediate availability of information
2. Capacity to handle peak demands

Solving the first problem usually speeds up the process so much that capacity is no longer a problem. Having information immediately available will eliminate wasted time by personnel searching for the information. Most of the delays in the receiving process result from lack of correction or of adequate information. Easy access to information will reduce the need for staging space as well.

Computerized data bases with on-line terminals would appear to be the logical solution. And indeed they are — when the computer is up, the response time is short and the data is all there. For years, large central mainframe computers have forced us to grow accustomed to batch processing of data and long response times — approaching, or even exceeding, a minute for a reply to a command. Data-processing system designers felt successful when they were able to consistently respond within three seconds. However, recent studies have indicated that *sub-second* responses provide a dramatic increase in productivity at computer terminal operations.

With today's computer costs falling, the problems of availability and response time are frequently addressed with a processor dedicated to the warehousing or even the receiving function. Data completeness and accuracy result from a truly integrated system design that requires that data relevant to receiving be in place in the files before purchase orders can be released.

Working in conjunction with computers, automatic identification systems also play a vital role in speeding data entry, maintaining system integrity and facilitating automatic operations. It is common for documents, containers and even individual parts to be labelled with a code.

ORDER PICKING AND SHIPPING CONTROL

Most of the general issues discussed in the section on receiving control apply to picking and shipping control as well. Particularly important are the concepts related to performing as many information-related tasks as possible at a single station. This is applicable when picking is done at the end of the aisle, as in mini-load or carousel systems, and for verification, packing and shipping functions.

As random storage systems become more common, in order to conserve space, it is mandatory to include the picking location along with the item and quantity to be picked. Since the same item may be stored in several locations, it is also necessary to include logic in the control system that maintains first-in, first-out product movement, if required, or that facilitates picking by directing the operator to a location with sufficient quantity to satisfy the pick. Other logic may attempt to clear out partially used locations to make space available for new merchandise.

Real-time receipt of orders and allocation of stock is now commonplace, and, for many operations, orders received today are shipped today.

Printing picking instructions in the same sequence as the merchandise appears in the storage system improves efficiency for in-aisle picking. Picks for several orders may be interspersed and separated by the operator as the picks are made so that one trip down the aisle will satisfy several orders.

Product cartons, picking lists and tote boxes are commonly identified with bar codes to facilitate tracking, sorting, accumulation and data entry.

Many software packages are available to manage warehouse operations. Selecting the right package requires careful matching of the specific needs of a particular physical and operation design and the features in the alternative packages. Most often, some modification of the package must be done or some customized input/output modules must be developed to make a package fit exactly. Obviously, the fewer changes, the better. Costs stay down and reliability remains high.

SUMMARY

Warehouse design is primarily a matter of using common sense to match requirements with available technologies. There are three important principles to remember:

1. Understand the problem, as described in numbers. Forecast ranges of activity for the future and test the design for sensitivity to these changes.
2. Be familiar with all of the alternatives for handling and storage. Do not limit the designs to only the most automated solutions.
3. Focus on reducing the elapsed clock time to perform tasks and not on minimizing warehouse labour. Efficient use of people will result from moving material quickly from receiving into storage and from storage back to the shipping dock.

REFERENCES

Apple, James M. *Material Handling Systems Design*. Ronald Press, 1972.
Apple, James M. *Plant Layout and Material Handling*. John Wiley and Sons, 1977.
Apple, James M. *Receiving Is Where It All Begins: Warehouse Distribution*. Irving-Cloud, March 1973.
Jenkins, Creed H. *Modern Warehouse Management*. New York: McGraw-Hill, 1968.
Material Handling Engineering, 1987 Handbook and Directory. Cleveland, Ohio: Penton Inc., 1987.
Modern Material Handling, 1987 Casebook Directory. Boston, MA: Cahners Publishing Co.

Modern Material Handling, 1987 Warehousing Guidebook. Boston, MA.: Cahners Publishing Co.

Muther, Richard. *Systematic Layout Planning*. Boston, MA: CBI Publishing Co., Inc., 1973.

Robertson, James F. (Editor-In-Chief), and James F. House (Associate Editor). *Distribution Handbook*. New York: The Free Press, 1985.

Warehousing Modernization and Layout Planning Guide. Department of the Navy, Naval Supply Systems Command, NAVSUP, Publication 529, December 1978.

Wenzel, Charles D. *Order Picking Systems for Automated Operations*. Presented to 1983 ITE/MHI Seminar, Philadelphia, PA.

White, John A., and Hugh D. Kinney. *Storage and Warehousing*, Handbook of Industrial Engineering. New York: John Wiley and Sons, 1982.

Woodson, Wesley E. *Human Factors Design Handbook*. New York: McGraw-Hill, 1981.

CHAPTER 8

Transportation

INTRODUCTION

Transport has played a major role in the growth and expansion of the society and economy of North America. The ability to transport goods effectively has been a major contribution to our high standard of living. The transport network required to run our society is vast.

- The demand for goods is widespread across the continent.
- Efficiencies gained through mass production have tended to centralize production.
- Raw materials are obtained from a few specific geographic regions.
- Imports and exports are channelled through a few major ports.

Transport links each of these point-to-point movements: from raw material sources to plants, from plants to warehouses and from warehouses to customers.

To support expansion, the governments of the day closely regulated the operation of transportation. These regulations attempted to allow enough vehicles on each route to service the demand, yet maintain the balance between healthy competition and overcapacity. Over the years, these regulations have gradually restricted competition and created artificially high costs. They are now being lifted. In 1980, the United States deregulated the transportation industry, removing restrictions on rate competition and entry to the industry. In December 1987, Canada passed legislation to reregulate the transportation industry as part of a gradual move to full deregulation.

This chapter is divided into six parts. The first part reviews modes of transport; the second, recent changes in regulations in the United States and Canada. Then freight rates are explained briefly, to assist readers who are not familiar with traffic operations. The next two parts deal with the responsibilities, problems and opportunities facing traffic managers and fleet operators. Finally, we present a transportation diagnostic which has been used successfully to reduce transportation costs for many companies in Canada and the United States.

MODES OF TRANSPORT

Shippers need transport service to move their commodities quickly, safely, consistently and at the lowest possible cost. The selection of a particular mode of transport depends on the trade-offs between these factors, which differ according to the characteristics of the commodity.

Road, rail, air, marine and pipeline are the five major modes competing for the freight business of the resource industries, manufacturers and distributors of goods in North America. Generally, the higher the capacity of the vehicle, the lower is the unit cost of transport. This is usually offset, however, by a slower transit speed and greater restriction on the available network.

Table 8.1 shows the comparative strengths of each of the five modes in satisfying customer needs for economy, speed, frequency, accessibility and reliability. The relative competitive advantages have resulted in each mode being positioned favourably in certain segments of the market as follows:

- Trucking is the only feasible mode for movement of goods of up to 40 tons for short distances.
- Rail is used for large-volume shipments of raw materials such as grain, oil and

TABLE 8.1
MODAL STRENGTHS

CHARAC-TERISTIC	TRANSPORT MODE				
	ROAD	RAIL	AIR	MARINE	PIPELINE
Cost/ton-mile	medium	low/ medium	high	low/ very low	very low
Speed (mph)	0–60	0–50	0–600	0–20	0–5
Frequency	very good	good	good	limited	continuous
Accessibility	extensive network	limited network	limited network	restricted network	dedicated network
Reliability	very good	good	very good	limited	very good

coal. Competition is from marine transport along the inland waterways and from trucking for short hauls.

- Air movement is dominant for high-value or high-urgency movements over 500 miles.
- Marine transport dominates the intercontinental and coastal market of large-volume shipments.
- Pipelines are used for the dedicated movement of fluids and gases, including local distribution.

The various modes work together in intermodalism (the transfer of freight from one mode to another during transit). The most appropriate mode is used for each leg of the journey. Until the advent of the container, intermodalism was costly. Goods had to be unloaded from one mode and loaded onto another. Anyone involved with the freight charged for their service, and some damaged the cargo or stole it. In the container system, however, goods are shipped door-to-door in a sealed container. The whole container is transferred from mode to mode.

Fortunately, container sizes have been internationally standardized. The ISO (International Standards Organization) container measures 8 feet by 8 feet by 10-, 20- or 40-foot lengths. These containers can be handled at almost all ports and railway container terminals across the world.

Each mode of transportation has characteristics which provide advantages to the shipper. The following pages describe the various modes.

ROAD TRANSPORT

Road transport is Canada's largest freight revenue earner. In 1984, the for-hire industry carried over 160,000,000 tonnes of goods, receiving revenues of more than $6.8 billion. In addition, private fleets carried more than 55,000,000 tonnes and incurred operating expenses of over $4 billion. More than 180,000 people were directly employed.

Road transport takes many different forms:

COMMON CARRIERS

Also known as for-hire carriers, common carriers operate commercial vehicles over the road for compensation, taking responsibility for loss and damage while goods are in their possession.

In a typical truck-load (TL) operation, the carrier moves a dedicated trailer-load of goods directly from the shipper's warehouse to the receiver's premises.

In contrast, the LTL (less than truck-load) operator picks up smaller shipments from a variety of clients using local pick-up and delivery vehicles. The shipments are sorted to common destinations in the LTL operator's terminal facility, cross-docked and loaded onto line haul vehicles for onward transportation to the destination terminal. Here the trailers are unloaded and the shipments are sorted to local delivery routes. It follows that the extra handling at the terminals greatly increases the costs per hundredweight of LTL shipments over those of TL shipments.

Certain carriers specialize. For example:

- Trimac Ltd. specializes in bulk transportation. Its licence covers most points in Canada.
- KwiKasair Ltd. (a division of Alltrans) and Excelerater (a division of Smith Transport) provide speedy scheduled delivery from Montreal and Toronto to the West (e.g., fourth-morning delivery from Toronto to Vancouver).
- Texport (a division of Alltrans) operates a fleet of vehicles designed to carry hanging garments such as suits, dresses and coats.

LOCAL CARTAGE

Local cartage firms pick up and deliver goods in a regional area for compensation. Shipment sizes may vary from a single parcel to truck-load quantities.

Typically, local cartage operators perform the following functions:

- Pick up shipments from a plant or branch warehouse and deliver them to local customers. Shipment sizes range from a single parcel to truck-load quantities.
- Interline with other transport modes.
- Provide dedicated trucks for certain shippers.
- Provide special equipment: trucks with hydraulic tailgates, trucks with booms, float trailers for carrying heavy equipment, etc.

Many smaller companies find local cartage less costly than operating private fleets. This is generally the case when there are large fluctuations in daily delivery volumes.

PARCEL AND COURIER SERVICES

Small-package freight is big business. Most companies dispatch regular small shipments (less than 100 lb.). These may be customer orders, back orders, internal company reports, documentation, etc.

Many common carriers are not equipped to handle this type of freight movement. Accordingly, they impose minimum charges to cover their costs. These charges are prohibitive for regular small-package shippers.

Over the last ten years, a whole new industry has sprung up to provide parcel and courier services. At one time, government postal services had a virtual monopoly on this operation. But inconsistent service led many shippers to look elsewhere. This opened the door for parcel and courier operators. The services offered by the major operators are listed in Table 8.2.

PRIVATE FLEETS

Private fleets are owned by the shipper and provide any or all of the

TABLE 8.2
SMALL-PACKAGE OPERATORS

United States Postal Service/Canada Post Corporation
- 4th class mail for delivery to any location
- Registered mail for proof of delivery
- Priority Post overnight premium service comparable to courier
- free delivery; pick-up for a fee
- exempt from liability for loss or damage
- cash in advance
- incentive rates available

Courier Services
- major national couriers are Federal Express, Gelco, Purolator
- delivery next day to most North American cities
- free pick-up and delivery
- lower-priority lower-cost surface service available
- credit terms available
- scheduled pick-up arrangements available
- contract rates available

Express Services
- major parcel services are United Parcel Service; Canpar
- slight premium to postal rates
- delivery in two days to most North American locations
- free pick-up and delivery
- credit terms available
- scheduled pick-up arrangements available
- contract rates available

Bus Parcel Express
- available on all intercity bus routes in North America
- terminal-to-terminal service
- same-day service within 400 miles
- premium rates

Messenger Services
- intracity two-hour service
- large number of small operators
- taxi provides the fastest and highest-cost service

---

previous services. Under current Canadian regulations, any firm can own its own vehicles. But these are restricted to the carriage of company-owned goods. This restriction has been eased up under reregulation. Private fleet operators can apply for carrier licences.

Most private fleets are engaged in local deliveries within an urban centre. With sufficient and consistent volume, private fleets can usually operate at lower costs than those charged by public carriers.

Private fleets are also engaged on some line-haul trips. However, many companies find that as distances increase, common carriers can provide a lower-cost service. Exceptions occur when companies can arrange regular shipments with backhauls.

Private fleets are usually justified by their ability to provide a planned transportation service at lower cost than public carriers. But several intangible benefits also arise from private fleet operations. These are:

- Timely deliveries. Delivery routes can be scheduled according to strict and orderly timetables.
- Responsive service. Special delivery requests and emergency orders can be delivered with greater flexibility than common carriers can provide.
- Low product damage. Trucks are loaded and unloaded by company personnel, thereby minimizing improper or multiple handling.
- Customer service. Company drivers call directly on customers. Properly directed, they can enhance the company's image.
- Advertising media. Trucks can be used as billboards. They offer a good opportunity to bring the company's name to the eyes of a large audience.

Companies which establish a private fleet operation take on additional managerial responsibilities. In effect, they set up their own internal carrier operation. This requires employees with the skills to route and schedule vehicles, control vehicle operating costs (maintenance, fuel, etc.) and supervise drivers. Issues concerning private fleet control are discussed in the "Fleet Management" section of this chapter.

CONTRACT CARRIERS
In a contract operation, the contractor or broker provides a company with exclusive use of trucks and drivers, for a predetermined fee. This service is often carried out by common carriers when the destination points are within their licensed servicing area. The company exercises control over truck routes and schedules. Driver discipline, truck ownership, fuelling, maintenance, repairs and replacements are the responsibility of the contractor. Thus the company is able to enjoy the intangible benefits of private carriage without many of the associated responsibilities.

A vehicle leasing/driver leasing arrangement is also referred to as a contract operation. Here, the company leases both trucks and drivers. To meet legal requirements in Canada, the trucks and drivers must be hired from distinct separate sources. Truck and driver leasing are discussed in more detail in the "Fleet Management" section of this chapter.

RAIL TRANSPORT

Rail transport provides quick, economical movement of bulk freight over long distances. This mode has been the backbone of North American transportation since the nineteenth century. It continues to provide a system for the economical movement of large shipments across the continent. The industry is dominated by eight large systems in North America — six in the U.S. and two in Canada. There are also many lesser lines providing local feeder services or in private hands for the movement of natural resources.

With competition from highway carriers, the railroads have been forced to adapt. As a result, rail services are available to handle a wide variety of freight commodities. Table 8.3 shows the Canadian freight carried by rail for 1985.

The major services are described in the next section.

TABLE 8.3
FREIGHT CARRIED ON CANADIAN RAILWAYS IN 1985

FREIGHT COMMODITY	CAR LOADS (THOUSANDS OF CARS)
Wheat	245
Other grain and grain products	169
Fresh fruits and vegetables	11
Other agricultural products	4
Animals and their products	10
Prepared food products	29
Iron ore and concentrates	426
Other metal ores and concentrates	143
Potash	109
Coal, sand, cement and other mine products	595
Lumber and plywood	193
Pulpwood	164
Other forest products	55
Iron and steel, primary and manufactured	93
Other metals, primary and manufactured	40
Motor vehicles and parts	149
Refined petroleum products	126
Chemicals and acids	124
Paper and paperboard	122
Other manufactures and miscellaneous	393
Piggyback traffic	399
Total car-loads	3,599
Non-car-loads (small-package freight) (thousands of tonnes)	33,435

Source: Statistics Canada.

RAILCARS FOR CAR-LOAD FREIGHT

Railcars (or boxcars) come in various sizes ranging from 3,500 cubic feet to 5,500 cubic feet. They are capable of carrying up to 85 tons.

For car-load shipments, the rail companies offer lower rates than road transport for many long-distance routes. This greatly benefits shippers who have rail spurs at origin and destination. Off-line shippers must take into account the extra cost of road transport to the rail terminal and subsequent handling into the railcar. This may eliminate any savings for off-line users.

UNIT TRAINS FOR BULK FREIGHT

Unit trains are made up of cars which all carry the same commodity. The economies of scale enable large-volume bulk traffic to be moved at low cost. Carrying between 3,000 and 15,000 tons of a single commodity, these trains run on a tightly scheduled, round-the-clock shuttle service. As an example, unit trains move iron ore pellets from the Sherman mine in Timigami to the Dofasco steel mill in Hamilton, some 335 miles. Three train sets of 35 100-ton cars run on a three-day cycle. Cars and motive units remain coupled at all times except for maintenance.

Unit trains usually return empty to prevent disruption of their time-table. CN, however, has started a dual-unit train. This carries potash headed overseas from Saskatchewan. At Vancouver, the cars are un-loaded, scrubbed clean and reloaded with phosphate rock for fertilizer plants in Alberta. Having unloaded in Alberta, they are again scrubbed clean and routed back to Saskatchewan mines for another load of potash.

PIGGYBACK FOR TRUCK-LOAD FREIGHT

Piggyback or TOFC (trailer-on-flatcar) combines the economies of long-distance rail movement with the flexibility of road transport. The piggy-back operation is quite simple:

- A tractor moves a highway trailer to a railway intermodal terminal.
- The trailer is loaded on a flatcar using either ramps, side crane or overhead crane.
- At the destination terminal, the trailer is unloaded from the flatcar in the same manner.
- A tractor hooks up and delivers the highway trailer to its local destination.

Common carriers, private fleets and the railways all use piggyback for long-distance freight movements. The rail company will supply trailers and even tractors to shunt the trailers between customer premises and the rail terminal. Alternatively, the rail company will handle a trailer owned or leased by the shipper. Rail service is ramp-to-ramp. Pick-up and delivery services may be arranged separately, using private fleet, highway carrier or railway tractors.

CONTAINER ON FLATCAR (COFC)

Rail plays a vital part in intermodalism, with connections to marine or major ports, and to roads at all major terminals. As with TOFC, the rail company will supply containers or move a customer container. The major railways have extensive container-car fleets and handling facilities and are equipped to make deliveries with special-purpose flatbed trailers.

POOL CARS FOR LCL FREIGHT

POOL CAR OPERATORS   Pool car operators (also referred to as freight forwarders) provide comprehensive service for LCL (less-than-car-load) shipments. They consolidate small shipments from various shippers into car-loads, arrange rail transport to destination terminals and distribute the shipments to their individual destinations. Usually, the freight forwarder issues a through-bill of lading and assumes complete responsibility for goods in transit. Additional services performed include: warehousing, terminal operations, container operations and customs clearance.

SHIPPERS' ASSOCIATIONS   Shippers' associations operate in a smiliar manner to pool car operators. They are, however, non-profit organizations whose members consolidate their shipments to gain the benefits of car-load freight rates from carriers (mainly railways in Canada).

AIR TRANSPORT

Air freight provides high-speed transport at high cost. Mail has been carried as freight on aircraft since the 1930s. However, except for emergencies and supplies for remote communities, it was not until the 1960s that airlines began to carry significant volumes of freight other than mail.

Since then, there has been an explosion in the demand for high-speed transport.

Cargo ton-miles flown by the major Canadian airlines increased from 20 million in 1957 to 298 million in 1970. The growth increased by more than 250% over the next fifteen years, to achieve 779 million cargo ton-miles in 1985.

The advent of ULDs (unit-load devices) has greatly increased air cargo productivity. ULD signifies any unitized freight from pallets to special containers (igloos), designed to fit the internal contours of the plane. ULDs increase aircraft cube utilization while reducing handling time. This latter element previously accounted for almost half of air-freight operating costs.

Air freight is regularly used for:

• High-value products. The products require less protection because handling is less rough. The reduced packaging costs and a reduction in the in-transit inventory can offset the increased transport cost.

- Perishable products. Because of the short shelf life of products such as strawberries and cherries, air freight is the only means of getting them to distant markets.
- Emergency products. Medical supplies and spare parts for repair of machinery are vital to save lives or to prevent large financial losses.
- Fashion items. Items which have a short sales life must be brought to market before the demand shifts to a newer version.
- Live animals. Race and show horses are often transported by air.

For each of these products, the benefits of fast delivery more than compensate for the increased cost of shipping by air.

AIR FREIGHT SERVICES

To satisfy a growing demand, the airlines have developed a wide range of services. These include:

- Point-to-point envelope and parcel delivery overnight — in competition with couriers.
- Airport-to-airport parcel service on scheduled flights.
- Air express of any size shipment for second-day delivery.
- Air freight of any size shipment to anywhere — pick-up and delivery extra.
- Reduced rates for container-loads.

AIR FREIGHT FORWARDERS

A large proportion of airline cargo is generated by freight forwarders. These "freight wholesalers" have been successful because they provide a total forwarding service at competitive rates. They consolidate LCL (less-than-container-load) shipments from several shippers and tender the unit-load to the airlines. This travels at lower rates than the shipments would individually. Part of the spread between the LCL rate and the unit-load rate is often passed back to shippers. In this way, air freight forwarders are able to offer the shipper lower rates than the airlines themselves. Additionally, the units move on a priority basis, since most forwarders pre-book space on specific flights.

The freight forwarders' expertise in routing and documentation is invaluable for international freight movement. Their transportation knowledge and international contacts enable them to find the optimum way of routing goods from door to door via several modes of transport. In the event of strikes or other obstacles, they can trace goods en route, reschedule them around the problem, use a different airline, avoid troubled airports, etc.

They are also familiar with complex international trade documents and procedures, including bills of lading, waybills, packing lists, export declarations, consular invoices, certificates (of inspection, origin or value) and banking services. Perhaps 80% of the forwarder's role is pushing paper around. Correct documentation saves shippers unnecessary delays and costs.

Additional services performed by freight forwarders can include:

• customs house brokerage
• cargo insurance arrangements
• financial transactions
• airport office and warehousing
• sufferance and bonded storage
• tariff and commodity interpretation to ensure goods travel at lowest rates
• preparation of duty drawbacks and sales and excise tax refunds
• pick-up and delivery service
• assistance with opening of letters of credit
• air freight packaging arrangements
• computerized tracking of goods in all stages of transport

MARINE TRANSPORT

Marine transport provides slow yet cheap freight movement. It is ideal for both domestic and international carriage of bulk commodities, such as oil, iron ore, coal and wheat. Container ships provide efficient overseas transport of manufactured goods.

Table 8.4 compares the shipment of freight in 1977 and 1985 through the 15 major ports. More than 60% of the volume was for trade with foreign points. The following sections discuss the nature of the North American industry.

INLAND WATERWAYS

In total, there are more than 26,000 miles of navigable inland waterways on the continent. There are two dominant waterways: the St. Lawrence Seaway and the Mississippi-Missouri river system. Between them, they give marine access to the heart of Canada and the United States, making shipping a viable alternative for most natural resources. Both have a long and interesting history and have contributed significantly to economic expansion.

The St. Lawrence Seaway extends through a network of lakes, canals and locks some 2,340 miles from the Atlantic Ocean to the head of Lake Superior at Thunder Bay. Ships sailing between these two points must travel through 20 locks and 16 separate lifts which elevate them more than 600 feet. Figure 8.1 shows the profile view. The canal is open for approximately 260 days per year, from April to December.

Modern lakers are 730 feet long by 75 feet wide and can be loaded to a draught of 26 feet. They can carry up to 30,000 tons of iron ore or 1,000,000 bushels of wheat.

TABLE 8.4
MARINE PORT ACTIVITY

| PORT | TOTAL CARGO HANDLED (MILLION TONNES) | | MAJOR COMMODITIES (>1 MILLION TONNES PER YEAR) | | | |
| | | | INTERNATIONAL | | DOMESTIC | |
	1977	1985	LOADED	UNLOADED	LOADED	UNLOADED
Vancouver	35.4	56.2	wheat, coal, sulphur, bulk cargo, lumber, potash, barley, containers	sand, gravel	general cargo, fuel oil	logs, sand, gravel
Sept-Îles	32.0	16.7	iron ore		iron ore	
Port Cartier	21.8	21.7	iron ore, wheat, corn	corn	iron ore	wheat
Thunder Bay	19.9	17.2	iron ore, bulk cargo		wheat, barley, iron ore	
Montreal	16.4	19.2	wheat, bulk containers	containers	fuel oil	wheat
Quebec	13.7	10.3	wheat	bulk cargo		wheat
Hamilton	12.1	10.3		coal		iron ore
Halifax	11.0	13.7	gypsum, containers	crude oil, containers	fuel oil	
Saint John	10.1	8.1	fuel oil	crude oil		
Sarnia	8.0	4.3		coal		
Port Hawkesbury	7.3	1.8		crude oil		

(continued overleaf)

TABLE 8.4 continued

| PORT | TOTAL CARGO HANDLED (MILLION TONNES) | | MAJOR COMMODITIES (>1 MILLION TONNES PER YEAR) | | | |
| | | | INTERNATIONAL | | DOMESTIC | |
	1977	1985	LOADED	UNLOADED	LOADED	UNLOADED
Baie Comeau	6.5	2.5			wheat	
Sault Ste. Marie	6.2	5.2		iron ore, coal		iron ore, coal
Sorel	5.7	2.9	wheat			titanium ore
Toronto	5.0	1.7				
EMERGING PORTS						
Prince Rupert		10.0	coal			
Nanticoke		8.7		coal		iron ore, coal

FIGURE 8.1

PROFILE VIEW OF THE GREAT LAKES AND ST. LAWRENCE SEAWAY

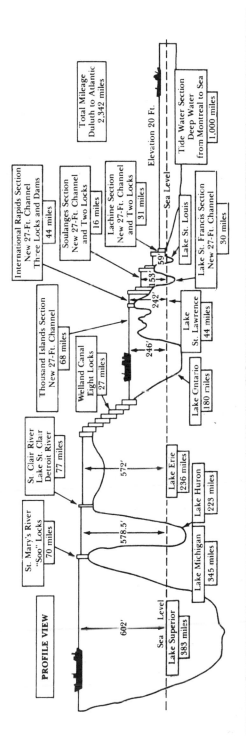

Source: St. Lawrence Seaway Authority.

Efficient marine transport is achieved by the two-way movement of goods. Grain is brought downstream from Thunder Bay to Montreal and Quebec. There it is discharged for trans-shipment aboard ocean vessels for export. The lakers are then loaded with iron ore at one of the nearby ports serving the rich fields of Quebec and Labrador. This cargo is delivered to Hamilton or to steel plants located on the shores of Lake Erie. Table 8.5 shows the commodities and tonnage moved along both the Montreal–Lake Ontario section and the Welland Canal.

The Mississippi–Missouri River is the third longest in the world at 3,860 miles. It serves the midwest states and flows into the Gulf of Mexico at New Orleans. Transport is dominated by barging of goods such as cement, chemicals and agricultural products.

CONTAINER PORTS

The elimination of cargo handling in intermodalism led to a major increase in container movement. In the 1960s, container facilities were built at all the major ocean ports and at selected ports on the Seaway. Container ships carrying up to 700 containers can be unloaded in a matter of hours, instead of days for the equivalent cargo of loose freight.

The benefits include speedier handling, less cost, less damage and less pilferage.

SUPERPORTS

Following the trend of the seventies to larger "superships," a number of major port developments were required. Accordingly, Port Hawkesbury

TABLE 8.5
**COMMODITIES AND TONNAGE CARRIED ON THE
ST. LAWRENCE SEAWAY**

| | MILLIONS OF SHORT TONS | | | |
| | MONTREAL–
LAKE ONTARIO | | WELLAND CANAL | |
COMMODITY	1977	1984	1977	1984
Grain*	22.8	22.8	24.1	27.3
Iron Ore	22.3	11.3	22.0	10.1
Coal	0.2	0.4	7.4	6.0
Other Bulk	9.6	11.7	12.0	8.4
General Cargo**	4.5	3.6	6.2	3.3

* Includes wheat, corn, rye, oats, barley, soybean, flaxseed, rapeseed, etc.
** Includes containers.

Source: The St. Lawrence Seaway Authority.

(Nova Scotia) and Lorneville (New Brunswick) were built to receive 130,000-ton crude-oil tankers. On the west coast, coal exports required the construction of a sophisticated superport at Prince Rupert to supplement the Roberts Bank Superport south of Vancouver.

When the demand for oil dropped in the 1980s, there was a corresponding decrease in the use of supertankers. Accordingly, the use of these ports has not expanded as expected. An upturn in the late eighties may see these facilities better utilized.

RO-RO FERRIES

On both coasts of Canada, ferries play a vital role in the movement of freight to large offshore islands. On the east coast, for example, CN Marine provides scheduled ferry service from Nova Scotia to Newfoundland. Ro-ro (roll-on roll-off) vessels are used to carry heavy road transport vehicles between ports. In the basic operation, trucks and cars drive onto the ferry, are transported across a stretch of water and drive off on the other side. For longer trips, the trailers are often staged at either end and are loaded and unloaded using a yard tractor — the marine version of "piggyback." The speed and elimination of either port handling or long-distance highway detours makes ro-ro ferry service very attractive.

OCEAN FREIGHT FORWARDERS

Ocean freight forwarders, also known as NVOCCs (non-vessel operating common carriers), perform the same small shipment service for ocean transport as air freight forwarders do for air. In fact, many freight forwarding companies handle both air and ocean freight. Additional services provided, such as customs brokerage, cargo insurance and documentation, are similar to those listed for air freight forwarders.

Freight forwarding companies range in size from one person and a telephone to international giants such as Schenker or Kuehne and Nagel, with branch offices in cities throughout the world. The one-person outfit often acts as an agent for shipping lines and does not get involved in the physical handling of cargo. The larger forwarders provide local cartage services and warehousing. They collect containers from the nearest railway terminal and stuff them with LCL shipments at their own warehouse facilities. These containers are then returned to the railway for onward transit to such locations as Vancouver, Saint John or Halifax. The container may then travel by water, rail and road transport before reaching the destination terminal. There the forwarder's representative destuffs the container and arranges delivery of the LCL shipments to their individual destination points.

PIPELINES

Pipelines are the most economical means of moving oil and natural gas over long distances. There is more that 320,000 miles of pipeline in North America. These pipelines now move about 25% of the commodity freight in North America, up from less than 10% at the end of World War II. The economic advantages of pipelines are:

- Continuous operation, unaffected by weather, strikes or traffic congestion.
- No empty backhaul costs.
- Only a handful of employees are needed to control the operation.
- Less susceptible to inflation, once built.
- Consumers need not hold inventory, but are generally assured of a ready supply.
- Round-the-clock operation without premium costs.
- Environmentally safer, quieter and less disruptive.

FREIGHT PIPELINES

Freight pipelines have been built to move such commodities as coal, limestone and iron ore over distances of several hundred miles. These second-generation pipelines are called slurry lines. In this system, a solid such as coal is crushed and mixed with a conveying liquid which is normally water. The slurry is then conveyed down the pipeline in a similar manner to a city's sewage system. At the destination point, the slurry is de-watered. Although Canada is considering the movement of coal and potash by slurry pipelines, the economics of this method are still uncertain.

Third-generation pipelines are already on the drawing board. These are referred to as capsule pipelines. They differ from slurry lines in that the solids are not mixed with the conveying medium (liquid or gas). Instead, they are packed to form rigid capsules, which are catapulted down the pipeline. This system eliminates the time and expense of watering and then de-watering the solids.

As long ago as 1965, Canadian scientists at the Alberta Research Council successfully conducted practical experiments. In one test, a 514-lb. capsule was conveyed more than 100 miles through a 20-inch crude oil line. The capsule averaged a speed of two miles per hour.

Although freight pipelines are technically feasible, their practical development has been almost non-existent in Canada. The reason for this is the current competitiveness of other modes. Transportation companies and shippers are reluctant to sink heavy investment into freight pipelines when unit trains can provide the service at equal, if not lower, cost.

THE REGULATION OF GOODS TRANSPORT

The 1980s have brought major changes to transport regulations. The Staggers Rail Act, the U.S. Motor Carrier Act, the U.S. Shipping Act and the Canadian "Freedom to Move" legislation [National Transportation Act (Bill C-18) and the Motor Vehicle Transport Act (Bill C-19)] were all designed to reduce government interference and promote free market forces.

The changes are intended to (1) spur competition, (2) encourage efficiency improvements and (3) reduce prices for the shippers, while retaining a vibrant and profitable industry.

With more than eight years of experience now documented in the United States, we are able to see the results. Trucking rates have fallen sharply as a result of ease of entry to all markets. In the deregulated sectors of the transport industry, operating efficiencies are being recorded. Larger, more fully integrated transport companies have emerged. These are able to provide higher-frequency service, greater capacity and more widespread networks.

The changes in Canadian regulations start with the agencies that control entry and ratemaking. Until recently, the Canadian Transport Commission was the arbitrator of disputes between shippers, carriers and the public. Its methods, which could include public hearings, were criticized as being time-consuming, costly and ill-suited to the resolution of private disputes on rates or service parameters. Under the new rules:

- The National Transportation Agency (NTA) will provide mediation services.
- Failing this, final offer arbitration will be binding on the parties.
- On request, the NTA will conduct investigations in the public interest, taking into account current policy.

The legislation also sets out time schedules for each of the steps which should see the majority of rulings made within 90 days. The result is a more streamlined process for resolving rate disputes.

TRUCKING

The responsibilities for regulation of the trucking industry are fragmented among federal, state or provincial and local authorities:

- for entry into business
- for operating authority
- for vehicle standards
- for operator licensing
- for road speed

- for vehicle licensing
- for vehicle weights and measures (see Table 8.6)
- for fuel tax payments
- for routing

Deregulation in the U.S. and Canada has addressed the business aspects of entry and operating authority. When restrictions were lifted in the U.S. in 1978, over 17,000 new companies came into existence by 1985, while the shake-out resulted in 6,500 failures. JB Hunt is one example of a success story born from deregulation. This company grew from 244 power units in 1980 to some 2,100 units in 1987. At the other extreme, McLean Trucking was unable to adjust and became a victim.

The major activities in the U.S. were centred in the truck-load segment. The number of operators in the less-than-truck-load segment remained relatively stable since the terminal networks required for load consolidation and breakdown could not be easily established. In fact the LTL business became more concentrated. The top ten truckers increased their share of revenues from 38% to nearly 60% between 1978 and 1986, while capturing approximately 90% of the profits. Not one new major LTL carrier has emerged to challenge this group since 1978.

These top ten carriers created extensive networks of consolidation centres with regional distribution links by merging or buying out regional companies. Their trunk line routes, managed through the use of sophisticated information systems for central dispatch, can operate at high load factors with resulting economies.

Shippers have benefited from these changes through reduced rates and improved service. While the U.S. GNP grew by 39.2% from 1980 to 1984, the national freight bill increased by only 28.1%.

Not all of the changes have been positive. In fact, many captive shippers and small shippers complain of continuing high rates. Small shippers typically receive 10% to 20% off published rates; larger shippers can command discounts of 40% to 50%.

In the U.S., deregulation resulted in higher average truck speeds, a higher average age of truck fleets and longer hours on the road for most drivers. Furthermore, pressures for more speed resulted in the federal government allowing speed limit maximums on interstate highways, which had been held at 55 mph for more than a decade, to be raised to 65 mph in 1987. Although these factors resulted in productivity gains for truck transport, they also lead to a less safe operation. The Canadian legislature has addressed this issue by negotiating with the provinces a uniform National Safety Code for trucking.

The major features of reregulation include:

- Applicants for operating licences need prove only fitness and not need (with a reverse onus test of public interest phased out over three to five years).
- All applicants must have an employee who has a Certificate of Competency attesting to his or her driving record and ability.
- All operators are subject to a National Safety Code.
- Licensing among the provinces is compatible.
- Rate regulation is eliminated.
- Confidential contracts are permitted.
- Collective ratemaking is not allowed.
- Acquisitions of more than 10% of the voting shares of any transportation company with assets or sales of more than $20 million are subject to review by the NTA.
- Extraprovincial tariff approval is eliminated.

Reregulation is not expected to have as drastic an impact on the trucking industry in Canada as deregulation had in the U.S. Adjustment by the industry started well in advance of the legislation. With only a few major freight corridors in Canada, competition on these routes has been fierce for many years. In addition, over the last few years, a large number of mergers and acquisitions occurred, bringing about more efficient operations. Very few larger shippers were paying tariff rates, having negotiated significant discounts through guarantees of volume and exclusivity.

However, further changes are expected. There will be a reduced regulatory burden on the carriers. The big American firms can be expected to enter the Canadian market in a signficant way, particularly to capture the transborder traffic into Ontario and Quebec. Domestic markets will be less affected by the U.S. invasion, but a greater number of small firms will emerge, and the number of failures, mergers and acquisitions will far surpass recent levels.

Recent changes in customs procedures will eventually affect the cost and time necessary to cross the border between Canada and the United States. The U.S. has recently imposed a user fee which will cause delays while the money changes hands. However, the new Canadian Customs Act of November 1986 has streamlined the customs rules and should thus reduce confusion. It has reduced the number of sections from 290 to 169 by modernizing the interpretations and making official those practices which had developed over the years:

- The owner and importer have joint liability for duty.
- Customs may make appraisals for duty.
- Confidentiality of information is extended to all documents.
- Licensing of customs brokers has been delegated to their national association.

- Rebates are allowed for loss, damage or clerical error.
- Appeals must be made within 90 days.
- Release procedures have been simplified.

Furthermore, an on-line computer record of performance (the Customs Automated Data Exchange System) will be kept to reduce the amount of time spent in customs dealings. Customs brokers will have access to the system through their own terminals, thus allowing electronic data exchange. It is forecast that by 1991 60% of transactions will be made through the system.

RAILWAYS

Between 1978 and 1986, the 13 large rail freight carriers in the U.S. shrank in number to six larger regional rail systems. These six railroads increased their share of the total rail industry freight revenues from 56% to 88%, while capturing 93% of the profits. There is now a fear that this rationalization of the industry may in fact reduce competition and send prices in the opposite direction from that originally intended by the legislators.

In Canada there are only two major railways, Canadian National and Canadian Pacific. The early indications are that price competition will become a reality after reregulation, as both railways serve the largest industrial corridors in the country. The legislation:

- increases access to the competitor's tracks for up to 30 kilometres from an interchange point
- allows terminal agreements for up to 50 kilometres with agreed rates (subject to arbitration at the request of the shipper)
- restricts the joint rate-fixing of earlier years
- allows railways to enter into private contracts with individual shippers for all traffic at agreed rates without reference to published tariffs
- allows volume rebates, which were previously outlawed
- requires compensatory pricing of each movement on standard accounting principles
- creates the National Transportation Agency as a watchdog while eliminating the Canadian Transportation Commission, which had rate approval authority
- broadens the scope of action in the abandonment of branch lines and streamlines the process

The confidential contract, volume rebate and restrictions on collective bargaining were the key features of the Staggers Act of 1980, which deregulated the U.S. railroads. The Canadian legislation will therefore put Canadian lines on an equal footing when competing for cross-border traffic.

AIR FREIGHT

Deregulation of airlines in the U.S. has seen the introduction of unrestricted discounters for passenger travel and the addition of a number of new players in the freight markets. But the merger of People Express with Texas Air has meant the demise of this segment (People is the only new entrant to have achieved more than a 1% share of the passenger market).

It is still possible to enter the market with a simple fitness test, but the resource requirements are so large that, until rates rise from their current competitive low, new companies are not likely to emerge.

Air freight continues to show large annual increases, and more freight-dedicated services continue to be introduced. Over the 1978–87 period there was a concentration of market among six carriers who competed in both passenger and freight. It is estimated that by 1990, these airlines will control over 90% of the total air transportation business. Air transport of courier parcels will be the one area where they will not dominate.

It is more difficult to differentiate the effects of deregulation on the cost of air freight, since the growth has been so substantial. Economies of scale will have been the major reason for decreases in rates over this period.

In Canada, reregulation of the airlines has not been as significant as in other modes. It was effectively implemented two years earlier when price regulation rules were relaxed. Furthermore, access to the north continues to be heavily regulated.

The key changes include:

- entry based on a "fit, willing and able" test
- removal of limits on the scope of service
- 60 days' notice of route changes
- unrestricted route access
- absence of tariff approval
- confidential contracts

There has already been a major shake-out of the industry. The "regional" airline no longer exists, and with the merger of PWA and CP Air in early 1987 the markets are dominated by the two national carriers. However, the rules have allowed Wardair to emerge as a scheduled and freight carrier, perhaps proving the effectiveness of the changes. A large number of smaller operators flying smaller turboprop aircraft on higher frequencies have entered the market on shorter routes.

Combined with the volume efficiencies, it is clear that shippers can look forward to lower air rates. These will make air freight more and more competitive.

MARINE

The marine mode was not deregulated in the U.S. until the U.S. Shipping Act of 1984. Both this Act and its Canadian counterpart, the revised Shipping Conference Exemption Act, have undermined the operations of "Conferences." These acts allow for individual confidential contracts and independent action by members. Reduced rates for many larger shippers have resulted. The legislation has been warmly received by the shippers and condemned by the Conferences.

PIPELINE

Deregulation of pipelines has effectively unbundled the commodity cost from the transmission cost. Thus consumers are able to negotiate with producers for the supply of natural gas, then contract separately for the transmission of the product to the point of consumption. For large energy users, the savings to be realized are significant.

TRANSPORTATION OF DANGEROUS GOODS

Another area of regulation concerns the movement of goods and commodities which pose a hazard to life, health, property or the environment. The Transportation of Dangerous Goods Act (DGA) was passed into Canadian law in July 1980. Since that time there have been numerous regulations added, primarily in the details of the implementation process.

Dangerous goods are categorized into classes as follows:

- Class 1 — explosives, including explosives within the meaning of the Explosives Act.
- Class 2 — gases: compressed, deeply refrigerated, liquefied or dissolved under pressure.
- Class 3 — flammable and combustible liquids.
- Class 4 — flammable solids, substances liable to spontaneous combustion, substances that on contact with water emit flammable gases.
- Class 5 — oxidizing substances, organic peroxides.
- Class 6 — poisonous (toxic) and infectious substances.
- Class 7 — radioactive materials and prescribed substances within the meaning of the Atomic Energy Control Act.
- Class 8 — corrosives.
- Class 9 — miscellaneous products, substances or organisms considered by the governor-in-council to be dangerous to life, health, property or the environment when handled, offered for transport or transported and prescribed to be included in this class.

It is the responsibility of the shipper and the carrier to stay abreast of these regulations and to ensure that their employees are aware of packaging and placarding requirements. Be aware that certain jurisdictions have limited the movement of some dangerous goods by road to specific routes.

FREIGHT RATES

This section is designed to introduce non-traffic personnel to the various types of freight rates. Examples are presented to illustrate the basic methods of determining freight costs.

RATE STRUCTURES

The primary rate structures are (a) class rates, (b) commodity rates and (c) freight all kinds (FAK) rates.

CLASS RATES

All products have been classified as to density and handling characteristics for the purpose of freight pricing. Similarly, classified products all have a similar rating, a lower rating resulting in a lower cost per hundredweight.

As an example, lead ingots are rated at Class 45. The rate between two locations may be $1.50/cwt. At the other extreme, styrofoam cooling boxes are rated at Class 85. The rate between the same two locations would be in the region of $6.00/cwt.

COMMODITY RATES

For regular movement of specific products between two points, special commodity rates may be established. Rates are often lower than the equivalent class rate.

FAK RATES

FAK rates are used to cover shipments of mixed products and commodities. Rather than charge for each commodity individually, an average rate is applied to the total shipment. This reduces the effort to classify each commodity separately. Accordingly, FAK rates are usually lower than class rates.

DETENTION AND DEMURRAGE

Carriers will allow a receiver a certain amount of time to unload a trailer, railcar or container. After the agreed time, a fee will be levied for demurrage of the equipment. On occasion, during peak periods, shippers will use the equipment as temporary storage, absorbing the cost as an alternative to public warehousing. Railways generally allow 48 hours before charging demurrage, while trucking firms may allow only a few hours. However, accounting of these charges is not precise, and the occasional lapse may not be assessed any charges.

TABLE 8.6
CARRIER RATES
(FROZEN FOOD — RATES DOOR TO DOOR)

Toronto to:

MINIMUM SHIPMENTS (lb.)
(Rates expressed in dollars per shipment)

	Up to 50	51–100	101–150	151–200	201–251	251–300	301–350	351–400	400–499
Montreal	21.40	27.30	44.40	52.20	60.30	68.60	76.50	84.80	96.60
Ottawa	20.50	25.90	36.20	44.50	52.80	61.00	69.30	77.50	90.00
Windsor	19.50	24.90	35.00	43.35	50.80	59.00	66.80	74.90	87.00
Hamilton	18.30	22.30	28.60	33.90	38.70	43.60	48.70	53.50	61.10

MINIMUM WEIGHTS (lb.)
(Rates expressed in dollars per hundredweight)

	500	1,000	2,000	5,000	10,000	20,000	30,000	40,000
Montreal	23.21	18.65	16.32	10.52	7.38	3.82	3.30	2.55
Ottawa	21.04	16.05	13.81	8.82	5.65	2.92	2.53	1.95
Windsor	20.60	15.25	12.60	7.95	5.15	2.60	2.35	1.80
Hamilton	14.78	11.13	7.93	3.66	2.43	1.25	1.11	0.85

FREIGHT RATING

Most freight rates are expressed in dollars or cents per hundredweight ($/cwt.). Table 8.6 shows rates for ranges of weights which change at specific weight levels.

The following examples use the values in Table 8.6 to rate the shipments:

- A truck-load shipment weighing 40,000 pounds from Toronto to Montreal

  40,000/100 = 400 cwt
  unit rate = $2.55/cwt
  cost = 400 × 2.55 = $1,020

- A 320-pound shipment from Toronto to Montreal

  using the 301–350-lb. rate,
  cost = $76.50

- A 38,500-pound shipment from Toronto to Montreal

  using the 30,000 lb. rate,
  cost = 38,500/100 × 3.30 = $1,270.50
  This is more than the 40,000-lb. shipment. Accordingly, it is in the shipper's interest to declare the rate as 40,000 lb. and ship the load for $1,020.

- A 20-pound package from Toronto to Montreal

  using the minimum rate,
  cost = $21.40
  this equates to a unit cost of $107.00/cwt.

The rates in Table 8.6 represent published rates. For a large-volume shipper, following negotiations, the actual charges for a 40,000-lb. load from Toronto to Montreal would typically be between $700 and $800.

LOCAL DELIVERY

Local cartage rates are more flexible than line-haul rates. Shippers often have a choice of paying by weight ($/cwt.), by time ($/hour, $/day, $/month) or by the piece ($/carton). Table 8.7 shows typical cartage rates.

CONSOLIDATION RATES

Many common carriers' rate structures cater for consolidated shipments:
MULTIPLE DELIVERY RATES Multiple delivery rates reduce the costs

TABLE 8.7
LOCAL CARTAGE RATES

Services Available:	Long- and short-term contracts
	Hourly services
	General cartage
	Rail facilities
	Warehousing and distribution
	Fully insured

Area Serviced:	A. Metro Toronto, Bramalea, Mississauga, Markham and Vaughan Townships
	B. Ajax and Pickering

Weight in Pounds	*Per Shipment Charges*	
	A.	B.
1 to 100	$10.00	$14.00
101 to 200	11.00	15.00
201 to 300	12.00	16.00
301 to 400	13.00	17.00
401 to 500	14.00	18.00
	Rates per 100 lb.	
500 to 1,000	2.70	3.60
1,001 to 2,000	2.20	3.25
2,001 to 5,000	2.00	3.05
5,001 to 10,000	1.50	2.55
10,001 to 20,000	1.20	1.35
20,001 to 30,000	.65	.65
30,001 to 40,000	.50	.50
40,001 and up	.45	.45

Vehicle	*Cost per Vehicle and Driver*
Single-axle tractor	$30.00 per hour
Tandem-axle tractor	32.00
Tandem-axle tractor and trailer	35.00
Straight truck — 22 ft.	25.00

Minimum Charge: 3 Hours (tractor and trailer — 6 hours)

of delivering several shipments to different destination points within a delivery region. The combined weight of the individual shipments is used to derive the line-haul rate between origin and destination. The largest shipment is then delivered to its destination point at no extra cost. The remaining shipments are delivered to their respective destination points at local delivery rates. Usually a minimum ($8 to $12) and a maximum

($40 to $50) local delivery charge is applied to each individual shipment.

To illustrate multiple delivery rates, assume a Toronto frozen food manufacturer dispatched four shipments to customers in Montreal. Each shipment would be rated separately. The cost according to the rate tables in Table 8.6 would be:

Shipment Size	Rate/cwt	Shipping Cost
23,000 lb.	$3.82	$ 879
10,000 lb.	7.38	738
5,000 lb.	10.52	526
2,000 lb.	16.32	326
Total Freight Cost		$2,469

Now assume the same shipments were delivered at multiple delivery rates. If local delivery rates were $0.80/cwt., with a maximum delivery charge of $50.00, the transport cost would be:

Consolidated Shipment: 40,000 lb. @ $2.55/cwt. = $1,020
Local Delivery Charge: 23,000 lb. @ no charge
                        10,000 lb. @ maximum   =   50
                         5,000 lb. @ $0.80/cwt. =   40
                         2,000 lb. @ $0.80/cwt. =   16
                        Total Freight Cost $1,126

In this example, multiple delivery rates reduce transportation costs by 54%.

MULTIPLE PICK-UP RATES   Multiple pick-ups are the opposite of the above. The carrier collects shipments from several locations within a city, consolidates them and delivers them to a single location. These arrangements usually concern:

• shippers with several plants or warehouses within a city
• receivers with several suppliers within a city

The combined shipment weight is used to compute the line-haul rate. The first pick-up is free; others cost $30 to $50 each. The exact charge depends on the time taken by the carrier to pick up the goods. Thus, the fee would be much lower to pick up palletized shipments in a single neighbourhood than hand-loaded shipments from extreme ends of the city.

STOP-OFF RATES
Stop-off rates apply where a carrier delivers goods to destination points

along a common route. In a stop-off arrangement, the carrier con-solidates the shipments and uses the combined weight to compute line-haul charges. The rate, however, is assessed to the furthest point. Addi-tionally, for each shipment dropped off en route, there is a stop-off charge of $40 to $60.

As an example, consider the following:

Assume a Toronto shipper has a truckload shipment, half destined for Saskatoon and half destined for Edmonton.

Using Standard Rates:

Toronto to Saskatoon: 20,000 lb. @ $9.25/cwt.	=	$1,850
Toronto to Edmonton: 20,000 lb. @ $10.25/cwt.	=	$2,050
Total Freight Cost	=	$3,900

Using Stop-off Rates:

Toronto to Edmonton: 40,000 lb. @ $8.25/cwt.	=	$3,300
Stop-off charge at Saskatoon	=	55
Total Freight Cost	=	$3,355

In this example, stop-off rates saved 14% on the cost of transpor-tation.

TRAFFIC MANAGEMENT

Traffic management is a specialized function involving the purchase of transportation services. A typical traffic department would be responsible for the performance and annual costs of all outside carriers, including common carriers, local cartage, pool car operators, international freight forwarders and the railways.

The department objective is to provide the required transportation service at lowest cost. To accomplish this, traffic personnel should be familiar with all aspects of transportation, including transportation modes, traffic routes, regulations, tariffs, rates, bills of lading, insurance claims and freight bill auditing. As traffic is but one element of an integrated logistics system, traffic personnel should also have a good understanding of all other logistics activities.

The following checklist reviews the role of the traffic department:

DO TRAFFIC PERSONNEL HAVE THE NECESSARY TRAINING OR EXPERIENCE?

In Canada, the Canadian Institute of Traffic and Transportation (CITT) offers a comprehensive syllabus for those interested in transportation as a professional career. The course covers transportation, physical distribution, accounting, commercial law, business administration, marketing and several other management development subjects. Many organizations enrol their traffic employees in the five-year correspondence course to supplement on-the-job training.

In addition, many colleges and universities in Canada, the United States and the United Kingdom offer day and night courses in transportation and distribution.

ARE FREIGHT CLASSIFICATIONS CORRECT?

Class rates were described earlier in this chapter. A product, however, can fit into a number of different class ratings, depending on description, shipment size and packaging. Thus, if an item is incorrectly described on the bill of lading, it may be subject to higher transportation costs.

The traffic department should examine the accuracy of freight classifications and descriptions for both inbound and outbound shipments. They should also be involved in packaging decisions which may influence a product's rating.

IS THE RIGHT CARRIER USED AT THE RIGHT COST?

The chief responsibility of the traffic manager is to obtain the lowest possible rates, consistent with lead-time requirements. This requires:

- up-to-date knowledge of tariffs and traffic developments
- good carrier relations
- negotiating skills
- records to measure current rates and deviations from budget
- programs to periodically review and negotiate all rates and services

To minimize costs on all routes, the traffic manager needs to specify the most suitable mode and negotiate the best rates.

- For long-distance shipments, railcar, pool car, piggyback or common carriers may be used. Commodity or FAK rates may be negotiated for recurring large shipment sizes.
- When shipments can be consolidated, multiple delivery, multiple pick-up or stop-off arrangements should be established.
- Small packages should be shipped by the most appropriate mode. Courier, rail express, bus express or mail may eliminate the high cost associated with frequent minimum billings.
- For local deliveries, reliable cartgage companies should be appointed. The best rate structure (by weight, piece or hour) will depend on the characteristics of the shipment.

IS CARRIER PERFORMANCE ASSESSED?

Carriers should not be selected based on costs alone. Service is equally important. The following questions should be addressed when assessing carrier service:

• Does the carrier arrive at the shipping dock on time?
• Is the carrier responsive to special requests?
• Does the carrier operate reliable equipment?
• Are claims minimal and quickly settled?
• Does the carrier arrive at the destination points on time?

When a carrier's performance falls below par, the traffic manager should discuss the problem with the carrier's personnel. This usually results in immediate improvement in service. However, if service continues to be erratic, a more reliable carrier should be appointed. After all, the customer judges the supplier, and not the carrier, on lead-time performance.

HAVE SPECIAL RATES BEEN NEGOTIATED WITH CARRIERS?

Until reregulation, freight rates in Canada were controlled and had to be published. In reality, special under-the-table deals were generally established between shippers and carriers, tailored to benefit both companies. As a rule of thumb, if you were shipping products at published rates, you were paying too much. The ability to negotiate effectively is a key success factor for all traffic departments.

ARE RATES PERIODICALLY SOLICITED FROM COMPETING CARRIERS?

There is a tendency among some traffic managers to stick with the carriers they know and with whom they have developed good lines of communication.

However, traffic managers should still solicit rates and services from competing carriers periodically — at least once per year for each major traffic lane. If there is a significant difference between the quoted and current rates, this can often be used as leverage to negotiate lower rates with the current carrier. Alternatively, the traffic manager may wish to introduce the competing carrier as a second carrier.

The use of two carriers is usually a highly effective means of keeping both carriers honest and responsive to service reliability requirements. The new carrier is anxious to demonstrate the ability to provide good service at a highly competitive price, with the hope that this will eventually lead to a greater share of the customer's business. The original carrier must now work equally hard to maintain its share of the action. If service or rates change, the traffic manager can reward or penalize either carrier by adjusting its share of the business.

ARE STEPS TAKEN TO MINIMIZE FREIGHT DAMAGE?

When goods are damaged in transit, everyone loses, but the shipper is the biggest loser. At best, if and when the claim is settled, the shipper recoups the replacement value of the damaged or missing goods. But there is no compensation for the inconvenience and loss of customer goodwill.

As a rough guideline, most industries experience a loss during transit of 1% of the shipping charges. This will vary, of course, depending on the type of products handled. However, if the loss for a fairly durable product far exceeds the 1% figure, something is wrong.

Many companies have established claim prevention programs. The reasons for damage are recorded and analysed. This data indicates recurring sources of damage, which can then be rectified. Typical problem areas are:

- Incompetent carriers. Records may indicate that a high percentage of claims are filed with a particular carrier. Poor equipment or careless handling may be responsible.
- Poor packaging. Inadequate packaging specifications, or the constant reuse of cartons designed for a single trip, result in crushed, broken or lost contents.
- Poor shipping or receiving. Damage may be traced to a particular warehouse or customer. Careless handling or inadequate equipment may be to blame.

To prevent damage, the shipper should, before loading, quickly examine the interior of the carrier's vehicle for potential problems:

- Has the inside of the van or trailer been swept out?
- Are there any nails or splinters sticking out of the floor or walls?
- Are there any damp patches indicating roof leaks?
- Are there any strange odours from previous shipments, which may contaminate the product?

ARE CLAIM PROCEDURES ESTABLISHED?

Damaged and lost goods on public carriage are significant problems. Each year claims cost public carriers more than $50 million in Canada. The traffic department should establish claim procedures to ensure prompt identification, filing and collection of claims.

Processing claims is a time-consuming and costly procedure for both traffic and carrier personnel. The receiver must identify damaged or lost goods as soon as possible after delivery. The claim must be in writing, setting out particulars of the origin, destination, date of shipment and estimated amount claimed for damage or loss. The carrier may then elect to examine the damaged goods. Finally, if settlement is not forthcoming, regular follow-ups with the carrier are necessary to discuss the status of the claim.

Some claims are refused. The carrier may feel there is insufficient proof that damage occurred while the goods were in its care. The carrier's contract leaves a lot of room for contention: as an example, Air Canada's "condition of contract" includes the clause "carrier is not liable for any damage or loss, unless such damage is proved to have been caused by the negligence or willful fault of the carrier, and there has been no contributory negligence of the shipper or consignee."

The best chance of obtaining claim settlement occurs when damaged or lost goods are identified by the receiver on arrival. Cartons that are bulging or damp or rattle inexplicably should be opened to examine the contents. Cartons that are split or broken open should be checked for the possibility of pilferage. Any indication of damage should be written in detail on the carrier's pro bill.

To avoid limiting the carrier's liability, shippers of high-value items should record the real value of the goods on the face of the bill of lading. Otherwise, claims are restricted to the amount written on the back of the bill of lading. Typical bills of lading read as follows:

- Common Carrier. "The amount of any loss or damage for which the carrier is liable should not exceed $1.50 per pound unless a higher value is declared on the face of the bill of lading by the consignor."
- Air Forwarder. "If the shipper does not declare the value of the shipment, liability is limited to $50, or if less, to the actual value of the shipment."

ARE FREIGHT BILLS AUDITED?

A company with annual sales of $50 million is likely to make over 1,000 separate shipments per month, using up to 100 different carriers. The freight bills covering these shipments can contain any number of errors, such as incorrect product description, incorrect calculations, incorrect classifications, etc. The time, effort and cost of checking each bill in detail before payment (pre-audit) is prohibitive for many companies. In fact, the savings do not always justify the cost of the audit. Some companies check only the larger bills on a sample basis. This cuts down on the clerical work and catches major errors.

Alternatively, companies can check the bill after payment (post-audit) and file claims with the carrier for any overcharges. Many companies use auditing services to check or double-check their bills. These freight auditing companies are usually paid a percentage of any cost recovered.

More progressive companies are now using computers to audit their bills. The program checks the invoice with the bill of lading, using updated freight rates and terms. Most companies recoup between 1% and 2% of their overall freight bill through a post-audit.

HAVE CONSOLIDATION PROGRAMS BEEN ESTABLISHED?

Freight consolidation is the most effective method of reducing transportation costs. When goods are consolidated, the larger shipment sizes travel at lower freight costs per hundredweight. When separate shipments are consolidated, multiple delivery rates or stop-off rates can be arranged with carriers.

Not all consolidation programs are beneficial. Some traffic departments have been guilty of surreptitiously holding back orders beyond the planned lead times. Although this strategy reduces transportation costs, it adversely affects customer service levels.

In more progressive companies, consolidation programs to customers are established jointly by the distribution and marketing departments. Lead times take into account both competitive service levels and distribution costs. Typical consolidation opportunities stem from:

- Establishing scheduled delivery days to customers in major cities or marketing areas. Instead of shipping daily to each city, one, two and maybe three specific delivery days are designated. As most customers order only once a week, this program does not affect their delivery frequency, but merely co-ordinates their ordering and delivery patterns.
- Selling truck-load shipments to major customers. In exchange, the customer may expect some form of volume discount.
- Arranging shipment to a customer's distribution centre instead of drop-shipping to the individual outlets. Again, the customer may expect a discount to cover the extra handling and delivery cost.
- Evaluating the trade-off between transportation and branch warehouse inventory. Less frequent deliveries reduce transportation costs but increase field inventory levels. Lowest overall costs occur when the replenishment period minimizes the sum of transportation and inventory carrying costs.
- Reducing order-processing times in other activities. Time saved in order transmission (send electronically or by courier instead of mail), order processing (computerize order entry and sequence picking slips, improve warehouse layout and handling methods) allows more time to consolidate orders and still remain within planned order lead times.
- Pooling freight with other companies. Certain industries have formed shippers' associations to pool their freight and reduce overall costs. Also some public warehouses pool their clients' orders, thereby creating freight savings.

DO YOU HAVE ACCESS TO A COMPUTERIZED TRANSPORTATION INFORMATION SYSTEM (CTIS)?

Unfortunately, the traffic department has invariably been the last area to receive any attention from the systems department. Even today, most traffic managers work in the dark ages, obtaining rate information from a tariff library, writing bills of lading by hand and tediously matching each freight invoice with the bill of lading. Management information reports, if available at all, are compiled manually on a note pad.

This situation is changing rapidly. In recent years great strides have been made in the availability of computerized transportation information systems (CTISs). A CTIS is defined as an automated means of providing rapid access to transportation rates, routings and related information from a single, easily updated data base.

In Canada, only about 15% of large shippers, and virtually no smaller shippers, have developed their own in-house CTISs. The trend, however, is for shippers to use external CTIS suppliers, who have extensive data bases. With a wide base of CTIS users, these suppliers can afford to continuously update tariffs and develop improved information systems.

In the United States, the three major suppliers of CTISs are Distribution Sciences Inc., Numerax and Rand-McNally-TDM Inc. In Canada, CTIS services are provided by Distribution Sciences Canada Ltd. (a joint venture between James T. Girvan & Associates, an organization specializing in freight bill auditing and Distribution Sciences Inc.) and the Goods Distribution Systems Office (GDSO) of the Ontario Ministry of Transportation and Communications.

The services provided by these CTIS suppliers include rate information, freight bill auditing, information on alternative routes and carriers, assembling consolidations and generating freight bill payments. In addition, these firms add customer-specific information to their extensive data bases, including commodity and competitive rates, and they generate custom-made management information reports.

In 1983, the Coopers & Lybrand Consulting Group conducted a major study for the GDSO to determine the market potential. Figure 8.2 indicates the type of information shippers need from a CTIS. This information was obtained from a detailed survey of 150 shippers across Canada.

The GDSO is now examining the viability of a CTIS for the marine mode. This will provide information on vessel schedules, line directories, pricing and space needs.

As a rough guideline, the annual cost for regular usage of a CTIS service is about 0.5% of freight costs, with some additional costs for management information systems. The potential savings for most com-

FIGURE 8.2

HOW USEFUL WOULD EACH OF THE FOLLOWING APPLICATIONS OF A TRANSPORTATION INFORMATION SYSTEM BE TO YOUR COMPANY?

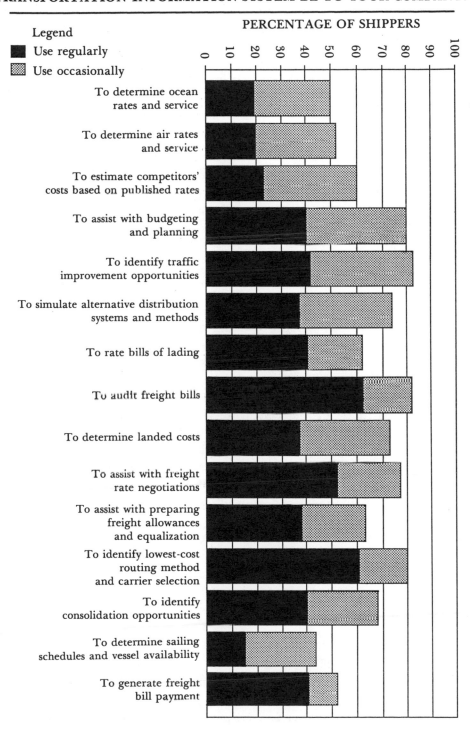

panies from using the data base would be in the region of 1% to 2% of freight costs. In addition, savings of between 5% and 15% of freight costs may be possible through the use of improved management information systems.

The major benefits to shippers include:

• lower freight charges
• reduced overpayments
• reduced landed costs on inbound goods
• savings in freight tariff library subscription
• improved management decisions and control

A further benefit is the improved productivity of traffic personnel. Less time is spent maintaining a tariff library and auditing freight bills. The time saved can be used to identify opportunities to further reduce freight costs.

FLEET MANAGEMENT

Many companies operate their own trucks. These private fleets are generally used to deliver local customer orders, where control of service and company image is a key factor. Over the last few years, however, more and more companies are using this same fleet to backhaul inbound shipments from suppliers. This generally leads to improved control over inbound shipments, as well as lower costs for inbound transportation.

Canada is following the United States in deregulating the trucking industry. It is expected that the carriers will become more competitive. Accordingly, some companies may abandon their private fleets and rely entirely on common carriers. Other companies may use their private fleet to operate as common carriers, shipping third-party goods for an agreed rate. This will help to reduce deadhead miles, fill unutilized capacity and generate revenue.

Managing a private fleet operation requires a wide range of skills: analytical, managerial, technical and financial. The major responsibilities are:

• routing and scheduling trucks
• supervising drivers
• specifying trucks
• controlling truck operating costs
• acquiring trucks through purchase or lease

For a small fleet of five to ten trucks, one person may be responsible for all these functions. For larger fleets, these responsibilities may be split between dispatchers, garage supervisors and purchasing personnel. The major private fleet responsibilities are reviewed below.

ROUTING AND SCHEDULING

Routing and scheduling concerns the planning and performance of the daily delivery operation of each truck and driver. No two routes are alike; no two days are alike. The dispatcher, therefore, requires an analytical mind and knowledge of the customers and delivery area in order to plan the ever-changing delivery operation. On a daily basis the dispatcher is responsible for:

* assigning shipments to each truck
* co-ordinating load sizes with truck capacities (weight and cube)
* establishing the routes and sequence of deliveries
* planning arrival and departure times for each delivery
* levelling the work-load between drivers
* taking appropriate action to maintain deliveries during driver holidays, illness, truck breakdowns and maintenance
* measuring and controlling driver performance

Whereas public carriers usually employ skilled dispatchers to perform these functions, many smaller private fleets rely on the discretion of shippers or drivers. This often results in inefficiencies due to:

* lack of training
* insufficient time available
* absence of fleet performance objectives or measurements

The following sections discuss methods of measuring fleet performance and identifying opportunities for improvement.

MEASURING FLEET PERFORMANCE

No route can be effectively planned or controlled without some idea of how delivery performance stacks up against expected standards. Drivers spend most of their working (or paid) day with no direct supervision. Unless reasonable controls are in place, inefficiencies tend to creep in.

There are two main parameters to measure:

FLEET UTILIZATION
Fleet utilization is the fraction of time when trucks are effectively moving goods, i.e., when the wheels are moving. As utilization of equipment and drivers increases, the transport costs per mile or per unit-load decrease. This comes about because fixed costs (depreciation, insurance, licence and drivers' wages) are spread over more miles and hours of operation. By reducing the time taken in stationary activities (loading, unloading, waiting, etc.), utilization of trucks and drivers improves.

LOAD FACTOR
The load factor is the fraction of the available truck capacity (volume and

weight) that is filled with goods. As fleet utilization improves, the trucks have more time to make more deliveries. This in turn leads to a higher load factor. If routes can be planned to carry backhauls on the return trip, or make second deliveries, the load factor can be essentially doubled. Naturally, the more goods carried per truck, the lower the transportation cost per unit-load.

The key to efficient routing and scheduling is high fleet utilization and a high load factor of the trucks. To control these parameters, standards can be developed and performances measured for all fleet activities. These standards include:

- average time taken for documentation and pre-delivery inspection (minutes)
- average time required for truck loading and unloading (pieces/hour, pallets/hour)
- waiting times prior to unloading (minutes)
- travelling in town (mph)
- travelling out of town (mph)
- load factor (% of truck capacity filled, lb. per load, pieces per load or cube of load)
- distance travelled (miles)
- number of deliveries

These standards are usually established by analysing driver route sheets or tachographs. It is also advisable to occasionally accompany the drivers on their routes. In this way, the transportation manager can gain first-hand experience of the problems facing the drivers, such as delays at customers' premises, inadequate receiving facilities, poor access, no-stopping regulations, etc. The transportation manager can, in some cases, take action to overcome the problems, but in other cases must adjust the standards to account for exceptional circumstances.

Once established, the standards are still only guidelines for measuring performance. On any day, conditions such as traffic congestion, truck breakdowns or a receiver gone AWOL can soon disrupt a route's efficiency. Nevertheless, consistent below-average performance can be easily identified and action taken to rectify the situation.

The data for analysing performance can be extracted from driver route sheets, tachographs or on-board recorders. These are reviewed below.

DRIVER'S ROUTE SHEETS Route sheets are filled in by the drivers, detailing relevant data about each trip. Figure 8.3 shows a typical route sheet. This identifies the truck and driver, shipment details, mileage and times involved in driving, waiting, loading and unloading. It also provides space for the driver to record any mechanical or delivery problems.

FIGURE 8.3
DAILY DRIVER LOG REPORT

Driver: _____

Plant: _____

Date: _____
Truck #: _____
Trailer #: _____

Hubodometer Finish: _____ KM
Hubodometer Start: _____ KM
Daily Total KM: _____ KM

Time Finish: _____
Lunch: _____
Time Start: _____
Total Hours: _____

Stop #	D	Destination	Bol #	Customer	Product	Units Delivered	Time Arr.	Time Dep.	Hub Reading	Comments
1										
2										
3										
4										
5										
6										
7										
8										
9										
10										

Fuel: _____
Oil: _____
Misc: _____

Delay Report

Mechanical Report

_____
Signature

Drivers' route sheets are cheaper than tachographs and easier to analyse. They are, of course, less accurate, relying partly on drivers' integrity. But, coupled with expected work standards and with follow-ups on questionable data, they prove adequate to control many fleet operations.

TACHOGRAPHS Tachographs are measuring instruments that fit into the truck cab. They accurately record route details, including speeds, miles travelled and stationary periods. Figure 8.4 shows a typical tachograph output. The disadvantages of tachographs include equipment expense, drivers' dislike of the "spy in the cab" and the time taken to extract and analyse data from the graphical charts.

ON-BOARD RECORDERS On-board recorders couple the accuracy of the tachograph with the more readily available information of the driver route sheets. They provide information on route activities, speeds and revs. In addition, they can compile the drivers' payroll and provide custom management reports.

FIGURE 8.4
A TACHOGRAPH OUTPUT

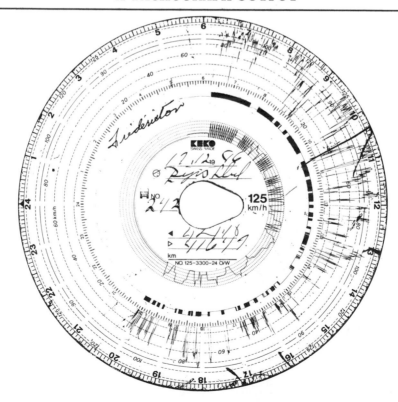

On-board recorders record information punched in by the driver to identify a change of activity, e.g. driving, coffee break, waiting, unloading, fuelling, trailer switch, etc. If the driver fails to punch in the information, the recorder will identify time unassigned. The information is stored on a cassette. Back at the terminal, the cassettes are fed into a personal computer which transcribes the relevant route information into hard copy, including:

- driver and truck information
- log-in time
- time taken to check truck
- driving time
- driving speed
- coffee and lunch break
- delivery and pick-up location
- unload and load times
- trailer switch times
- log-out time
- total hours
- fuel usage
- maximum speed
- truck revs
- fuel consumption

This information can then be summarized to provide customized management reports on truck and fleet utilization, load factors and driver performance.

There are several suppliers of on-board recorders, including Rockwell's Tripmaster and Cummins Engineering's Cadec system. These are being used by many companies with considerable success. The cost per unit ranges from about $2,000 to $4,000, including set-up. Most companies achieve a pay-back within a year. Publix Super Markets, for example, used the information from Rockwell's Tripmaster to reduce their fleet cost per mile by 36.6%.

Simply tracking performance often leads to immediate improvements. One company discovered this after a branch manager introduced driver route sheets. For years the company had hired two trucks on an hourly basis to deliver customer orders. Every week the carrier invoiced the company for 80 hours' usage at $30 per hour.

Then, at the request of the head office transport department, the branch manager arranged for the drivers to fill in route sheets. Due to staff shortages, vacations and other priorities, the manager never got around to looking at the completed sheets. Nevertheless, the invoices for the next five weeks were for 68, 63, 65, 58 and 62 hours' usage, representing an average 20% cost reduction.

PLANNING DELIVERY ROUTES

Delivery routes are generally planned and scheduled by experienced dispatchers. These professionals have often spent many years on the road and somehow remember the details of every stop — location, access, unloading constraints, delivery time requirements, etc.

The dispatcher's job is so highly complex that the chances of always finding optimum routing are practically impossible. For example, if there are 16 stops on a single route, there are more than 10 trillion ways of routing the truck. Many of them, of course, are not practical. But, for a fleet of several trucks, making a total of several hundred deliveries, the number of practical options is enormous.

More and more companies are now using computerized truck routing systems to assist the dispatchers to plan truck routes, to simulate alternative routing strategies and to control fleet performance. There are several systems available, such as Micro Analytics' TRUCKSTOPS, designed for an IBM-XT or AT, and STSC's TRUCKS, which operates on a mainframe. Prices range from about $2,000 to $80,000 for the PC-driven routing systems and $20,000 to $500,000 for mainframe systems.

The input for these systems includes the customer locations, delivery time requirements, unloading rates, shipment quantities, truck capacities and speed zones. Table 8.8 illustrates the data input requirements and outputs available from a typical routing model. The output sequences the stops for each truck and provides the driver with a detailed route schedule. The planned routes meet time window constraints and minimize overall distance travelled. This leads to more reliable service to customers, lower truck operating costs, less driver overtime and possibly a reduction in fleet size.

These models are used to simulate the effects of alternative trucking strategies, including:

- truck capacities
- unloading methods
- driver hours
- delivery time windows
- work-load balancing

These simulations enable the dispatcher to fine-tune the routing process. Typical savings from the use of computerized routing packages range from 5% to 10% of fleet operating costs.

The TRUCKSTOPS micro-software package is being used successfully by many companies. The success stories include:

TABLE 8.8

TRUCKSTOPS FLEET ROUTING SYSTEM COURIER ROUTE

TRUCK-ROUTE SEQUENCING/SIMULATION PROGRAM INPUT DATA

Stop Data Input File	D:STTHE1 • SDF
Parameter File	D:ST THERES • PAR
Truck Designator	VAN
Capacity	50
Departure Time	500
Unloading rate	60 units/hr
Orig. Coordinates (STE THERE)	1061, 451
Dest. Coordinates (STE THERE)	1061, 451
Normal Workday	6 Hrs.
Total Load	25

Zone	Type	Speed	Range
L.R.	CROW	50	> 35
M.R.	CROW	40	> 4
S.R. 1	CROW	25	< 4
S.R. 2	CROW	30	< 4
S.R. 3	CROW	25	< 4
S.R. 4	CROW	30	< 4

*** TRUCKSTOPS TRUCK-ROUTE Sequencing/Simulation Program Output ***

*** Vehicle: VAN, Start: 500, Finish: 1100, Total Time: 360 ***

(continued)

TABLE 8.8 continued

SEQ.	NAME	LOCATION	LOAD	CONSTRAINT	UNLD	ARR	DEP	DIST
		STE THERE					500	0.0
1	J6Z	STE THER-DE	10.0	500-700	15	500	515	11.4
2	1L0	ST-JANVIER P	1.0	500-1000	3	532	535	9.7
3	1N0	ST-LOUIS-TER	1.0	500-1000	3	550	553	6.3
4	1HO	STE-ANN-PLAI	1.0	500-1000	3	603	606	3.6
5	1B0	LA PLAINE PQ	1.0	500-1000	3	615	618	11.4
6	J7K	MASCOUCHE PQ	1.0	500-700	3	635	638	5.5
7	J6W	TERREBONNE P	1.0	500-700	3	646	649	17.2
8	J7P	ST-EUSTACHE	1.0	500-700	13	715	728	7.1
9	1J0	ST-AUGUST-DE	1.0	500-1000	3	739	742	3.4
10	1R0	STE-MONIQUE-	1.0	500-1000	3	750	753	1.2
11	1S0	ST-SCHOLASTI	1.0	500-1000	3	756	759	7.1
12	1K0	ST-BENOIT PQ	1.0	500-1000	3	810	813	8.1
13	1M0	ST-JOSEPH DU	1.0	500-1000	3	825	828	3.4
14	1G0	POINTE-CALUM	1.0	500-1000	3	836	839	8.3
15	1E0	OKA PQ	1.0	500-1000	13	851	904	10.9
16	1P0	STE-MARTH-S-	1.0	500-1000	3	920	923	10.8
		STE THERE				939		

Load: 25 (16 Stops) Cap.: Total: 50 % Used: 50

Distances: Total: 125.56 Stem: 10.76 Bet. Stops: 114.8

Times(m): Total: 279 Travel: 199 Unload: 80

Costs: Total: 84.17 Mileage: 37.67 Hours: 46.5 O.T.: 0

- A major food wholesaler in the midwest increased the productivity of its route sales force by 20%. More deliveries and sales calls were scheduled per sales representative, and the company was able to expand into new sales areas without increasing the size of its sales force.
- A dairy company in New Brunswick cut its four- to five-day delivery week to three days, cut its fleet by 50% and reduced transportation costs by 18%-22%.
- A large grocery chain reduced daily dispatching time from four hours to less than one hour. Fleet size and distribution costs were reduced by 5%-10% without disrupting customer service.

BALANCING DRIVER WORK-LOADS

In some companies, trucks are scheduled on rigid routes or territories. Yet shipment sizes and the number of deliveries may vary daily. Accordingly, some drivers run into overtime while others have spare time on their hands.

A driver who arrives back at the warehouse after eight hours has not necessarily been occupied for all that time. Drivers are human, and a five-hour work-load can easily spread out into eight hours.

To determine route work-loads, there is no substitute for a detailed examination of the time taken in each activity (driving, waiting, unloading). Work-loads can be balanced by applying established standards to each activity.

SPREADING DELIVERIES EVENLY THROUGHOUT THE DAY

Many customers prefer morning deliveries. This has resulted in some fleets being heavily committed in the morning and underutilized in the afternoon. The best way of solving this problem is to negotiate different delivery times with customers. By spreading deliveries more evenly throughout the day, one company recently reduced its fleet size from eleven to seven trucks.

TRANSFERRING UNECONOMICAL DELIVERIES TO PUBLIC CARRIERS

Many companies believe that a private fleet eliminates the need for public carriers. Accordingly, their trucks deliver small packages to customers some 10 or 20 miles off-route. In some cases, the gross margin on these shipments does not even meet the fuel cost of the truck. By handing over the uneconomical deliveries to public carriers (local cartage, couriers, etc.), the fleet can concentrate on more productive deliveries. This, in turn, may lead to reduced overtime and even the elimination of a private fleet truck.

AVOIDING DELAYS AT THE WAREHOUSE PRIOR TO DISPATCH

Twenty to thirty minutes is often sufficient time for the driver to receive delivery instructions and documentation, check the load and inspect the vehicle. Delays occur when shipments are not ready for loading, docks are congested, etc.

Some companies use drivers to load trucks. If the trucks are loaded by hand, the time taken cuts into available delivery time and hence utilization. Additionally, this work could be performed at lower cost using warehouse workers rather than the higher-paid drivers.

Guidelines can be established according to the particular duties of the driver prior to departure. The reasons for pre-delivery delays should be examined and resolved.

MINIMIZING WAITING TIMES AT CUSTOMER PREMISES

Delays at customer premises are becoming occupational hazards. These are particularly prevalent at food stores and distribution centres. Reasons for delay include:

- waiting for other trucks to unload
- receivers unavailable (many receivers will not accept shipments during their lunch hours)
- congested receiving area

Some companies accept the problem and allow up to four hours' waiting time when delivering to certain customers. Other companies attempt to deal with the problem by monitoring all delays from the drivers' route sheets. When recurring delays occur, they discuss the issue with the customer. Often this can lead to pre-arranged delivery times in off-peak periods.

One fleet manager, while visiting the receiver at a customer's warehouse, noticed that one of his drivers was letting other trucks push in front of him. The fleet manager asked the receiver to investigate. The driver told the receiver, "Don't worry about it — I'm paid by the hour." That was one of the last hours he was paid.

Some waiting time is often inevitable. Can this time be used productively? For example, can the driver move the shipment closer to the truck doors in preparation for unloading?

REDUCING UNLOADING TIME

A large proportion of delivery time can be spent unloading trucks at customers' premises. It is, therefore, important that the most suitable handling methods are used. Unitized loading methods such as pallets and wheeled cages can greatly minimize this time. Unloading aids such as roller conveyors, hand pallet trucks and tailgate lifts also help to speed up the unloading operation. To effectively control the unloading operation, handling-time standards should be established and measured. Standards usually take the form of the number of pieces (individual cartons) or pallets unloaded per hour. This information can be taken from the drivers' route sheets.

SPOTTING TRAILERS

Perhaps the most effective method of minimizing both waiting and unloading times is to eliminate them altogether. Many companies "spot a trailer" (leave a trailer) at customer or branch warehouse premises. Whenever they make a delivery with a loaded trailer, they switch trailers (unhitch the loaded trailer and hitch up to the empty trailer). The receiver then unloads the full trailer when it is convenient, and the tractor and driver are not held up. This tactic is effective when several truckload shipments are delivered to a location each week.

The cost of spotting a trailer is the daily capital depreciation. For most trailers this is unlikely to exceed $20 to $25 per day. Against this cost, the company must assess the value of the time saved by the tractor and driver (about $30 to $40 per hour) for a city delivery.

INCREASING THE HOURS OF TRUCK USAGE

Many companies operate their trucks for less than 40 hours per week. In contrast, some companies double-shift their trucks to achieve more than 80 hours per week usage. In the oil industry, three drivers are assigned to each truck. The drivers work four 10-hour shifts. Each truck operates six days per week to give a total utilization of 120 hours/week. This greatly improves utilization because the fixed truck costs are spread over many more hours.

In some industries, it may not be possible to run all trucks on two shifts. Only a few customers are willing to receive shipments beyond the normal working day. However, if several such customers can be arranged into practical routes, one or two trucks may be doubled-shifted. Additionally, stock transfers to branch warehouses may be possible on a night shift. Trailers can be spotted at the warehouse and switched to avoid the need for night employees.

PAYING MILEAGE OR TRIP RATES TO LONG-DISTANCE DRIVERS

On line-haul trips, where the round-trip journey may take 15 to 16 hours (for example, Toronto to Montreal and return), a "job and finish rate," "trip rate" or "mileage rate" arrangement often benefits both company and driver. In this arrangement, the company pays the driver a set rate for the trip, for example 30¢ per mile or $204 for Toronto to Montreal round trip. The driver may complete the journey in as little as 14 hours but still receive the 30¢ per mile or $204 trip rate.

This arrangement provides an incentive for the driver to return the truck as soon as possible, making it available sooner for loading or for a second driver to use. Care must be taken, however, to ensure that the driver does not exceed speed limits. Otherwise, the extra fuel usage may outweigh the savings in truck and driver time. Tachographs can be used to control the driver's speed.

Arrangements should be made for the driver to get a rest or sleep period on the longer routes. Drivers should be paid for motel accommodation (about $40 or $50) or provided with sleeper cabs.

Payment is easier to compute and to control using trip rates than it is with hourly rates. With hourly rates, drivers are penalized financially for returning the truck early and rewarded for spending excessive time in roadside cafes. With trip rates the driver receives the same pay no matter how many hours the trip takes. Some companies, however, make concessions when delays result from causes beyond the driver's control, such as breakdowns or excessive waiting times at customers' premises.

COLLECTING BACKHAULS

Many private fleets deliver goods in one direction only. Major savings can be achieved by collecting inbound raw materials or merchandise on the return trip. Instead of a company purchasing these products FOB (free on board, or freight on board) the receiving warehouse, arrangements are made to purchase the goods FOB the supplier location — i.e., the ownership of the goods changes hands prior to transportation. In return, the company arranges a freight allowance with the supplier, thereby generating revenue for the private fleet. Steinberg's fleet in Montreal, for example, generates well over $1 million on its backhaul program.

An effective backhaul program is based on a win–win situation for the supplier and the customer. The freight allowance is generally slightly less than the supplier normally pays the carrier, hence the supplier achieves a freight savings. The allowance should, however, cover all out-of-pocket expenses for the customer (including off-route mileage, waiting and loading time for expenses for the truck and driver and any additional expenses in unloading, scheduling and administration) plus a profit.

Not all suppliers are willing to allow customers to pick up their orders. Some suppliers build the cost of transportation into the purchase price of the goods. Often they do not keep accurate transport figures. They are uable to deduct the transportation value. In some cases, the supplier would actually reduce the efficiency of its own transportation system if some, but not all, customers picked up their goods. Instead of combining all customer orders into truck-load quantities, the supplier may have to ship goods to its other customers in LTL quantities. This would increase the supplier's overall transportation costs.

EVALUATING THE OPTIMUM FLEET SIZE

Many companies would prosper by eliminating, or at least reducing, the size of their private fleet. The uneconomical routes should be handed over to public carriers. The converse also applies. Many companies use common carriers on routes which are more suitable for private fleet operations. In both cases, lack of a detailed transportation analysis results in lost opportunities and lower profit.

In evaluating fleet size, three major aspects are considered:

- Will improved routing and scheduling techniques result in fewer trucks and drivers?
- Can a larger fleet size accommodate some shipments currently moved by public carrier? Do the resultant savings justify the cost of the extra trucks?
- Will savings result from having a smaller fleet size and hiring additional units or using common carriers during peak periods?

To determine fleet size, a detailed analysis of all point-to-point shipments must be made for both public carriers and the private fleet. Truck routing models, discussed earlier, are ideal to simulate "what if . . ." questions. For example, what if the fleet were to be reduced by one tractor? The deliveries can then be simulated using the remaining vehicles. Certain less economical routes may be assigned to public carriers. The cost can then be evaluated and compared to the current cost. If this indicates a cost saving, what if the fleet were to be reduced by two or more tractors?

DRIVER SUPERVISION

The private fleet operator must recruit, train, motivate, supervise and pay the drivers. The operator's objectives are to hire and maintain good drivers, pay a fair day's wage for a fair day's work and ensure good labour relations.

There are good, bad and militant drivers. Good long-distance drivers can command annual wages of well over $40,000, and earn every penny of it. Bad drivers can write off $100,000 tractor-trailers plus contents. Militant drivers can close down a company's entire operations.

For many companies, contract clauses negotiated by the unions increase the costs and restrict the flexibility of private fleet operations. These clauses include:

- driver wages and benefits higher than those paid by carriers
- overtime after seven and a half or eight hours
- double time on Saturdays and Sundays
- limitations to shift starting times
- restrictions to loading and unloading tasks
- restrictions in contracting out uneconomical deliveries to carriers
- restrictions in contracting out peak loads to carriers
- restrictions in hiring temporary drivers to meet peak loads or vacation schedules
- restrictions in lay-offs, even if workload is reduced

If these clauses result in lower customer service or excessively high costs, management should evaluate the benefits of renegotiating them. Are the benefits sufficient to give ground in other areas, such as benefits, or even sufficient to risk a strike?

If a common ground between management and the unions cannot be reached, recent reregulation has provided the incentive for some companies to abandon their fleets. The opportunity is now available to contract out their entire trucking operation to common carriers, as indeed was the experience in the United States following deregulation.

More and more private fleet operators are moving away from employing their own drivers. Instead, they are leasing the drivers or using brokers or owner-operators. This allows them the flexibility to improve routing and scheduling procedures and to achieve higher fleet utilization. These alternatives to company-employed drivers are reviewed below.

DRIVER LEASING

Over the last few years, there has been a growth in driver leasing. Organizations such as Driver Leasing and United Driver Services are in the business of recruiting and employing competent drivers. These organizations, in turn, lease their drivers to companies on a long-term basis to operate owned or leased trucks.

The day-to-day control of the drivers usually rests with the private fleet operator. But all the administrative duties, including payroll, union contract negotiations and grievance settlements lie with the leasing company. Thus the private fleet can operate without a lot of complex personnel responsibilities.

Driver leasing companies are usually more experienced than private fleet operators at recruiting drivers. They check previous employment records, arrange DOT physical examinations and test the drivers. In addition, they provide safety programs and labour productivity reports.

Avoiding industrial relations problems is often cited as the main reason for leasing drivers. The private fleet operation is not the driver's employer. As such, drivers cannot picket that company's premises in the case of strike action. But, as the leasing companies are often more experienced working with unions, such industrial disputes are few and far between.

BROKERS AND OWNER-OPERATORS

There has been a major trend in the trucking industry for both carriers and private fleet operators to use brokers and owner-operators. A broker will typically own several tractors and employ several drivers. An owner-operator owns his or her own tractor.

The trucks and drivers are contracted to a company, usually on a long-term basis, and an agreed rate — for example $1.00 to $1.15/mile, with a minimum annual usage of 100,000 miles. The broker or owner-operator is responsible for providing a reliable driver and maintaining the tractor in good working condition. The company has all the benefits of routing and scheduling a private fleet, without many of the responsibilities for control and administration.

As independent businesspeople, brokers and owner-operators are usually willing to work long hours and haul long-distance routes which may keep them away from their home base for several days. At the end of three or four years, they have generally paid for their tractors and made a relatively high income. In addition, tax write-offs (truck, depreciation, operating expenses, travelling expenses, office in the house, spouse's income to maintain the paperwork, etc.) help to maintain a high standard of living.

The downside to brokers and owner-operators can be driver burnout. Some of these operators are too keen to work every hour available and tend to drive too long. In some cases, drivers have been guilty of popping pills to stay awake. This is dangerous both to their own health and to safety on the road.

Some companies have successfully converted company drivers into owner-operators. These companies assist the drivers by:

- arranging the necessary financing for the tractor
- providing financial training to ensure that the drivers hold back part of the revenue for the inevitable major repair
- establishing fair mileage rates to ensure that the owner-operator can cover expenses and make a decent living

With a good owner–operator program, both company and drivers benefit.

TRUCK SPECIFICATIONS

To operate a fleet efficiently, it is imperative to use the right truck for the job. Poor truck selection inevitably leads to unnecessarily high costs for the life of the trucks. If they are overspecified, the fixed costs will be too high. If they are underspecified, the variable costs will be too high.

Before selecting a truck, background data are needed on all aspects of the truck's expected application, including:

• types of product carried
• average and maximum loads
• load-handling methods
• annual distances travelled
• type of routes (expressways, secondary highways, urban, etc.)
• potential access problems or height restrictions encountered on the route

Using the above data, the following decisions can be made:

SIZE OF BODY

Vehicle choices range from small pick-up trucks to tractors with double trailers. The overall cube capacities of typical truck bodies are:

14-foot body	700 cubic feet
24-foot body	1,250 cubic feet
45-foot trailer	3,000 cubic feet
2 × 26-foot double trailers	3,500 cubic feet
2 × 48-foot double trailers (Quebec)	6,500 cubic feet

Because of the non-modular nature of most products, these capacities are rarely reached. Eighty per cent of capacity is usually considered to be good utilization.

GAS OR DIESEL

Over the last ten years, there has been a major switch from gas to diesel trucks. Unless the truck is driving very few miles, a diesel truck should be selected. This may cost double the price of a gas truck, but the savings in both fuel and maintenance and the extended economical life of the engine (500,000 vs. 100,000 miles) outweigh the additional capital cost.

MECHANICAL SPECIFICATIONS

Mechanical specifications depend on provincial regulations, load weights, annual mileage and type of terrain travelled. Provincial and state regulations stipulate the maximum weight allowed per axle. Different provinces and states have different weight limitations. Therefore the number of axles required depends on the weight of the load carried and the provinces and states visited. For low-density products, a single-axle tractor with single- or tandem-axle trailer may suffice. As density increases, tandem-axle tractors with tandem- or tri-axle trailers become necessary.

There are an almost unlimited number of combinations of engines, transmissions, differentials, axle ratios, tire sizes, etc. It is beyond the scope of this book to discuss the merits of alternative combinations. However, when fleet operators monitor fleet maintenance and repair records, they can often identify parts and components which have been troublesome. These should be specified differently for replacement vehicles. They can also identify parts and components which have had long life and should be specified again.

The fleet operator should talk to the people who operate and work with the trucks — drivers, shippers and mechanics. These people can often point out problems with current trucks. From previous experience or discussions with drivers from other companies, they also have insight into the qualities of other makes of truck.

OTHER DESIGN FEATURES

Other features to consider when selecting vehicles include:

1. Protective services for products affected by temperature or humidity variation.
   - Refrigerated units (reefers) maintain low temperatures for perishable products.
   - Heaters prevent other products freezing in the winter.
2. Sleeper cabs to allow the driver to rest on long-distance trips.
3. Double decks to provide extra cube utilization for products which are too fragile or shapeless to load more than three or four feet high.
4. Tailgate lifts to speed up loading and unloading at facilities without docks.
5. Cab-mounted wind deflectors, gap sealers, and trailer-mounted "vortex stabilizers" to reduce air resistance by about 20% and achieve fuel savings of about 5.5%.
6. Side doors to provide easy access to the load on multiple delivery routes.
7. Upgraded seating, radio, west-coast mirrors, etc., to improve driving conditions on long tedious journeys.
8. Aluminum frames and wheels to reduce the truck weight.
9. Radial tires to reduce fuel consumption and to minimize the incidence of flat tires. Fuel savings as high as 9% can be expected.
10. Tire pressure control devices, such as the Ettco Automatic Pressure Control, to prolong tire life, reduce fuel consumption and improve safety. This device continually balances the pressure between dual wheels and displays the pressure for easy visual checking.
11. Temperature-modulated fan to minimize the use of the cooling fan, which uses about 5% of rated engine power. Typical fuel savings of 3% to 4.5% can be expected.

12. Retractable fifth wheel position to cater for several trailer sizes.
13. Tag axles or retractable wheels to meet axle-loading regulations for heavy loads, but to save tire wear while dead-heading (driving empty) or carrying lower-weight shipments.
14. Reinforced floors and fully opening doors to allow trucks to be loaded by fork trucks.
15. Smooth interiors to prevent palletized loads from catching on side-wall supports.
16. Strapping and other supports to minimize shifting of products in transit.
17. Adequate lighting for ease of loading, unloading, and product identification.
18. Sign painting to advertise the company's name and products. (It is always a good tactic to get the marketing department to pay for the sign painting.)
19. Placard mount for dangerous goods.
20. Cranes to off-load heavy products or palletized materials at locations which have no handling equipment. (These are widely used by suppliers of construction materials. Palletized loads of bricks or heavy material can be unloaded at the job site in a matter of minutes.)

CONTROL OF TRUCK OPERATING COSTS

Truck operating costs are significant. For example, the cost of running a tractor 100,000 miles per year can be in the region of $30,000 for fuel and $12,000 for maintenance and repairs. Yet many companies fail to seek ways of minimizing these costs. Often their records are inadequate to indicate problem areas or to identify opportunities for improvement.

The most effective method of controlling these operating costs is to keep history records for each individual truck. These records should detail all maintenance and repair work carried out, as well as fuel consumption. History records can be maintained manually on a card system. However, most large fleets have now introduced computerized maintenance reporting systems available on PC mainframe computers.

Data from the history cards should be transferred to management information systems. Tracking the various cost elements of a per-mile basis will spotlight below-average performance by any truck. An examination of the history cards may then indicate whether the problems result from sloppy or inadequate maintenance, poor driving practices or the age of the truck.

FUEL

Most tractors get between four and eight miles per gallon. This depends on truck type, shipment weight and routes travelled. With fuel prices of about $1.80 per gallon in Canada, an improvement of even one mile per gallon can be a significant saving.

Records of the fuel consumption of each truck should be reviewed regularly. Some trucks are gas guzzlers by nature, but a sudden drop in performance may indicate the need for servicing or repairs.

Different driving practices, such as overrevving, speeding, idling, etc., can cause excessive fuel consumption. Driving practices can be analysed from tachometer charts. These record engine RPM, shifting patterns, and speeds travelled. Alternatively, some companies let a driving instructor sit in the cab with their drivers. The instructor can soon identify poor driving habits. Proper re-training can help to improve driving practices and thereby reduce fuel consumption.

Fuel cost per gallon should also be examined. In the absence of company pumps, special price arrangements can often be made with local garages. Failing this, drivers should be instructed to visit discount fuel stations. Variations in fuel prices from garage to garage can add several cents to a gallon of fuel. One company, shipping into the U.S., found a ten-cents-per-gallon variation. The drivers were filling the tanks at stations offering quadruple Green Shield stamps.

Fuel economy can be improved with the help of cab-mounted air deflectors. For a cost of about $800, fuel consumption can be reduced on the highway by about 6%. On an annual usage of 100,000 miles this would result in a yearly saving of $1,800 per truck.

MAINTENANCE AND REPAIRS
A good preventive maintenance program helps to reduce repair costs. Figure 8.5 shows a typical preventive maintenance work-sheet. This not only ensures the truck is maintained in top condition, but also identifies areas where repairs are needed. This in turn reduces the number of times the truck breaks down en route.

REPLACEMENT DECISIONS

While some trucks should have been scrapped years ago in the interest of company profit, others are replaced prematurely, thereby increasing costs. Like most machinery, trucks become less productive with use and age:

• Engines burn more fuel and oil.
• Parts become worn and need replacement.
• Breakdowns are more frequent.
• Time spent in the workshop increases.

At some point, fixed costs (depreciation) plus operating costs (fuel, maintenance and repairs) of old trucks are more expensive than the higher fixed costs but lower operating costs of new trucks. This is the time to replace.

FIGURE 8.5
IMPERIAL OIL LIMITED

(ESSO) TRUCK AND BUS PREVENTIVE MAINTENANCE WORK SHEET

DATE _____ 19____ EQUIPMENT # _____ PRESENT MILEAGE _____

ACCOUNT_____ MAKE _____ STARTING MILEAGE _____

ADDRESS _____ YEAR AND MODEL _____

√ – CHECK IF O.K.   X – ADJUSTMENT MADE   O – REPAIRS NEEDED

☐ GROUP A SERVICE_____MILES
(CHECK EACH ITEM, EVEN THOUGH SUCH AS ITEMS **4 & 8** ARE INSPECTED AT MUCH SHORTER INTERVALS)

☐ 1. COMPLETE CHASSIS LUBRICATION.
☐ 2. CHECK REAR AXLE LUBRICANT LEVEL; ADD LUBRICANT IF NECESSARY. EXAMINE FOR OIL LEAKS.
☐ 3. CHECK TRANSMISSION LUBRICANT LEVEL; ADD LUBRICANT IF NECESSARY. EXAMINE FOR OIL LEAKS.
☐ 4. CHECK CRANKCASE LEVEL, AND EXAMINE FOR OIL LEAKS.
☐ 5. INSPECT PCV VALVE.
☐ 6. INSPECT FUEL SYSTEM FOR LEAKS.
☐ 7. CHECK MANIFOLD HEAT VALVE.
☐ 8. CHECK BATTERY VOLTAGE. CLEAN CORRODED TERMINALS. HYDROMETER READING: 1____ 2____ 3____ 4____ 5____ 6____. ADD WATER IF NECESSARY.
☐ 9. CHECK COOLING SYSTEM FOR LEAKS. INSPECT WATER PUMP AND TIGHTEN HOSE CLAMPS, IF NECESSARY.
☐ 10. FILL RADIATOR WITH OR CHECK ANTI-FREEZE AS NECESSARY. (ANTI-FREEZE: SAFE TO ____DEG. F.)
☐ 11. EXAMINE FAN. CHECK BELT FOR ADJUSTMENT.
☐ 12. RECORD CHARGING RATE. ____AMPS.
☐ 13. RECORD OIL PRESSURE. ____LBS.
☐ 14. CHECK CLUTCH PEDAL CLEARANCE.
☐ 15. CHECK GAS GAUGE, AIR GAUGE, HORN, HEAT INDICATOR, WINDSHIELD WIPER.
☐ 16. CHECK PLAY IN STEERING WHEEL AND STEERING CONNECTIONS.
☐ 17. CHECK POWER STEERING RESERVOIR LEVEL.
☐ 18. INSPECT RADIUS RODS.
☐ 19. INSPECT SPRINGS AND SHACKLES.
☐ 20. INSPECT BRAKES, CHECK CONNECTIONS AND FLUID LEVEL.
☐ 21. DRAIN AIR TANKS.
☐ 22. TIGHTEN ALL WHEEL NUTS AND/OR RIM BOLT NUTS.
☐ 23. TEST AND ADJUST LIGHTS.
☐ 24. INSPECT BODY HARDWARE AND DOORS.
☐ 25. INFLATE AND INSPECT TIRES.
☐ 26. INSPECT SAFETY EQUIPMENT (FLARES, FLAGS, TOOLS).

☐ GROUP B SERVICE_____MILES
☐ 27. CLEAN FUEL PUMP, STRAINER, CARBURETOR BOWL. ADJUST FLOAT LEVEL, AND SERVICE AIR CLEANER.
☐ 28. TIGHTEN CYLINDER HEAD, MANIFOLD, GOVERNOR, AND CARBURETOR FLANGE BOLTS.
☐ 29. CLEAN AND ADJUST SPARK PLUGS.
☐ 30. CLEAN AND ADJUST DISTRIBUTOR POINTS, AND CHECK IGNITION WIRING.
☐ 31. CHECK IGNITION TIMING (NEON LIGHT).
☐ 32. ADJUST CARBURETOR. (USE EXHAUST GAS ANALYZER AND/OR VACUUM GAUGE WHEN POSSIBLE).
☐ 33. CHECK GOVERNOR AND SET.
☐ 34. CHECK WHEEL BEARINGS AND STEERING KNUCKLES.
☐ 35. TIGHTEN SPRING U BOLTS AND ALIGNMENT CLIPS.
☐ 36. TIGHTEN REAR AXLE SHAFT NUTS OR FLANGE BOLTS.
☐ 37. CHECK PROPELLER SHAFT AND UNIVERSAL JOINTS.
☐ 38. CHECK BODY OR CAB HOLD-DOWN BOLTS.
☐ 39. CLEAN AIR COMPRESSOR FILTER AND CHECK DELIVERY.

☐ GROUP C SERVICE_____MILES
☐ 40. CLEAN CRANKCASE VENTILATOR/PCV VALVE.
☐ 41. ADJUST VALVE CLEARANCE.
☐ 42. CHECK CYLINDER COMPRESSION WITH GAUGE.
☐ 43. CHECK FUEL PUMP PRESSURE, AND TIGHTEN DIAPHRAGM SCREWS.
☐ 44. TIGHTEN STARTER SWITCH, COIL, AMMETER, AND DISTRIBUTOR CONNECTIONS, AND TEST COIL.
☐ 45. CLEAN AND EXAMINE STARTING MOTOR, GENERATOR, ALTERNATOR, AND VOLTAGE CONTROL UNIT.
☐ 46. TIGHTEN MOTOR MOUNTING BOLTS.
☐ 47. CHECK CASTER, CAMBER, TOE-IN.
☐ 48. CHECK WATER TEMPERATURE (USE THERMOMETER), AND REPLACE THERMOSTAT IF NECESSARY.

☐ OTHER SERVICES   MILES
☐ 49. CLEAN AND REPACK WHEEL BEARINGS. . . . . ._____
☐ 50. LUBRICATE SPEEDOMETER CABLE. . . . . . . ._____
☐ 51. REPLACE SPARK PLUGS . . . . ._____
☐ 52. REPLACE DISTRIBUTOR POINTS AND CONDENSER . . . . ._____
☐ 53. INSPECT DISTRIBUTOR ASSEMBLY FOR WEAK SPRINGS AND WEAR . . . . ._____
☐ 54. REPLACE OR RECONDITION MAGNETO AND IMPULSE STARTER . . . . ._____
☐ 55. REPLACE OR RECONDITION FUEL PUMP . . ._____
☐ 56. REPLACE OR RECONDITION CARBURETOR . . ._____
☐ 57. REPLACE HIGH TENSION WIRES, DISTRIBUTOR CAP, AND ROTOR . . . . ._____
☐ 58. REMOVE OIL PAN, CLEAN OIL PAN, PUMP SCREEN AND CRANKCASE, INSPECT OIL PUMP ASSEMBLY AND LINES. . . . . ._____
☐ 59. INSPECT COMPRESSOR LUBRICATION SYSTEM . ._____
☐ 60. CLEAN AND INSPECT TRANSMISSION AND DIFFERENTIAL CASES. . . . . ._____
☐ 61. FLUSH COOLING SYSTEM . . . . ._____
☐ 62. PCV SYSTEM – CLEAN HOSES AND FITTINGS – REPLACE VALVE . . . . ._____

☐ SPECIAL REQUIREMENTS
☐ 62. CHANGE CRANKCASE OIL_____MILES
☐ 63. CLEAN OR REPLACE FILTER ELEMENT_____MILES
☐ 64. CHANGE AIR COMPRESSOR OIL, IF SEPARATE SYSTEM _____MILES
☐ 65. AUTOMATIC TRANSMISSION: CHANGE FLUID AND ADJUST BANDS _____MILES
☐ 66. _____

☐ EMISSION CONTROL SERVICES
_____
_____

☐ OMIT ITEMS
_____
_____

GROUP A SERVICE IS USUALLY DONE AT 1000 TO 1500 MILES.
GROUP B SERVICE IS USUALLY DONE AT 2000 TO 3000 MILES.
GROUP C SERVICE IS USUALLY DONE AT 4000 TO 6000 MILES.
OTHER SERVICES ARE PERFORMED AT VARIOUS INTERVALS. GENERALLY IN THE RANGE OF 10,000-20,000 MILES, DEPENDING ON CONDITIONS.

AFTER ABOVE WORK IS COMPLETED, ROAD TEST, AND
NOTE GENERAL CONDITION_____
_____
_____
_____
_____

TIME SPENT ON ABOVE WORK _____
MECHANIC

NOTE – ITEMS MARKED "O" SHOULD BE LISTED ON OTHER SIDE.

When trucks have been written off company books, the apparent zero depreciation cost can be misleading. Usually this practice is merely an accounting write-off for tax purposes rather than the true value. Yet many companies incorrectly assume that these trucks operate at lowest cost, because no fixed costs are assigned to the truck. The way many companies operate budgets, this appears true. The transport department is only charged the variable cost. Yet, in reality, the true value is the resale or trade-in value. The true depreciation factor is the expected loss of value of the truck in the forthcoming year plus the expected return on capital tied up in the truck. When the true value is taken into account, the company is usually better off replacing these trucks when variable costs are high.

Some companies replace trucks after fixed periods of service. This is also a drain on company profits. The operating costs of the better trucks may be quite low. Also, major mechanical components may have been recently replaced to give the truck a new lease on life. In these cases, the depreciation factor plus operating costs may still be far lower than those of replacement trucks.

The most profitable time to replace trucks can only be determined from true values and accurate records of the operating costs of each individual truck. Tracking these elements on a per-mile basis will spotlight high-cost trucks. An examination of past repairs and performance will indicate whether these trucks should be replaced. Until replacement time, high-cost trucks should be placed on low-mileage routes to minimize operating costs.

PURCHASE OR LEASE

The three principal methods of acquiring trucks are:

- purchase
- financial lease
- maintenance lease

Under the purchase and financial lease options, the fleet operator arranges and pays for all maintenance and repairs to the trucks. The choice between these two acquisition methods is strictly a financial consideration, i.e., which method best suits the individual company's financial policies and working capital situation.

In contrast, under a maintenance lease, the lessor looks after the control and costs of maintenance and repairs. This relieves the fleet operator from much of the responsibilities, time and expertise required to operate the fleet. Because of these benefits, many fleet operators are acquiring trucks by this method. The following sections discuss the major issues concerning each option.

OWNERSHIP Companies can purchase their trucks from dealers. There are possible investment tax credits and depreciation allowances associated with ownership. A major issue to consider is the management time and administration work involved in operating and maintaining the fleet. Namely:

• setting up and controlling preventive maintenance programs
• establishing, recording and analysing truck history records
• obtaining a reliable garage to do servicing/repair work
• arranging for towing and repair work when the truck breaks down en route
• acquiring additional trucks during breakdown or major repair work
• arranging to have the trucks washed on a regular basis
• recording and submitting fuel tax records
• obtaining licences and insurance

FINANCIAL LEASE The financial lease is an agreement in which the lessee makes a series of periodic lease payments. These payments normally total the full price of the asset, together with the lessor's profit. Under a financial lease, the lessee pays all costs connected with the equipment, such as fuel, maintenance, repairs, licences, insurance, etc., in a similar manner to ownership. Management and administration time is also the same as that of ownership.

Financial leasing is extremely flexible. Rental schedules can be tailored to individual requirements. Leases can be structured for monthly, quarterly, semi-annual or annual payments, as well as irregular or skip payments. At the end of the lease, the lessee may:

• return the equipment to the lessor
• purchase the equipment
• renew the lease at much lower rates
• arrange with the lessor to trade in the equipment and negotiate a new lease for its replacement

The advantages of financial lease over outright purchase include:

• No capital outlay is necessary.
• Present fleet investment can be converted to cash.
• Trucks can be purchased by the financial leasing company at wholesale prices.
• The entire cost of the lease is treated as an expense. As such it is tax deductible. (Before signing a leasing agreement, it is advisable to check that it meets the guidelines set out by Revenue Canada Taxation. Some agreements can be construed as a disguised purchase.)
• Continued inflation makes it attractive to defer as many payments as possible. These can be made with tomorrow's inflated dollar.

MAINTENANCE LEASE The maintenance lease has all the benefits of the financial lease, with the following additions:

- The lessor is responsible for licensing the trucks in the home province.
- The lessor is responsible for all maintenance and repairs.
- Replacement trucks are provided during breakdown and extended servicing downtime.
- Weekly truck washing and inspections are often included in the lease cost.
- On a "wet lease," fuel is supplied at reduced costs.
- Much of the administrative work associated with fleet operation is done by the leasing company, including servicing schedules, repair records, fuel control and, for a wet lease, fuel tax records.
- Convenient servicing arrangements can usually be made. The major leasing companies often operate two or even three shifts at their service centres. This allows trucks to be serviced or repaired at times which do not disrupt the normal delivery operation.
- Leasing companies can provide good service at low costs. They are able to purchase parts and supplies at about 20% below the price paid by private companies. They also attract and hold superior maintenance personnel.
- Additional trucks can often be leased for short periods at favourable rates. This is useful for companies that experience variable work-loads.
- Maintenance leases provide for accurate fleet budgeting.

When comparing alternative maintenance leasing companies, the following points should be considered:

- Leases can be quoted in several different ways. In particular, each lease contains a provision for escalation charges. These usually increase the lease and operating costs proportional to increases in the consumer price index. But different base indices may be used. To compare apples with apples, it is advisable to evaluate the overall cost of the trucks over the life of the contract.
- Is the servicing centre of the leasing company conveniently located to the truck's home base? This is particularly relevant on a wet lease arrangement. If the trucks must travel several miles off-route every time they need refuelling, the advantages of lower fuel cost are lost.
- Does the leasing company have adequate fuelling, servicing and repair facilities in the territory travelled by the fleet? If not, has it made arrangements with reliable garages to handle fuelling and repairs quickly?

TRANSPORTATION DIAGNOSTIC

A detailed review of most transportation operations will result in at least a 10% cost reduction. This is based on the experience of the authors, who have conducted more than a hundred transportation diagnostics in a variety of industries, including food, retail, automotive, oil, hard goods, electrical, mining and fertilizer. In most cases, these savings do not imply that the transportation managers are doing a bad job, but rather that they (1) had insufficient information to make effective and timely decisions and (2) lacked support from other departments within their companies to effect the necessary changes.

Two examples of these points follow.

EXAMPLE 1

The logistics function of a food manufacturer in the province of Quebec was split between the plant manager and the distribution manager. The plant manager was responsible for all inbound raw materials and supplies, the distribution manager for all outbound customer deliveries. The plant manager had a single tractor-trailer, which made two trips per day to Montreal, some 50 miles from the plant, to collect glass jars. The plant was operated on just-in-time principles, and hence the plant manager needed to ensure the reliability of the inbound flow of glass jars. To achieve this, the plant manager allowed no one else to use the plant's tractor-trailer.

Meanwhile, the distribution manager dispatched three tractor-trailers every day to Montreal to make customer deliveries. At peak periods, when a fourth truck was needed, outside carriers had to be used, even if the plant truck was lying idle. Figure 8.6 illustrates the traffic flows.

FIGURE 8.6
FOOD COMPANY IN QUEBEC

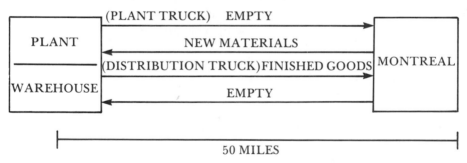

The distribution manager was confident that it would make sense to combine the fleets, delivering customer orders on the outbound trip and collecting glass jars as a backhaul. The only thing standing in the way was fear: like others in the organization, the distribution manager had strong misgivings about crossing the crusty old plant manager.

However, having paid outside consultants vast quantities of money to review the distribution operation, the president of the company was obliged to heed one of the early and obvious recommendations: give the distribution manager the responsibility of hauling the inbound supply of glass jars on a backhaul. The recommendation was implemented. To this day, several years later, the plant has always received the glass jars on time. Again, fear is a great motivator. The company saves about $60,000 per year.

EXAMPLE 2

A retail chain in Toronto ran a fleet of trucks to deliver store orders across Ontario from the central warehouse in Toronto. The stores received one to two LTL shipments per week on specified days. The schedule had been established a few years earlier in a worthwhile attempt to level the demand on the warehouse. The company lacked the necessary information to determine whether the current schedule was the most cost-efficient.

The company commissioned a study to conduct a detailed transportation diagnostic. The project team started from a "green fields" approach. They assumed that any store could receive a delivery on any day. Using a truck routing model, they found that all deliveries could be achieved with fewer trucks if the store groupings were changed. For example, the store in Windsor received a delivery every Monday and Thursday, the store in Sarnia every Tuesday and Friday. If both store orders were on the same truck, the overall delivery distance, and hence costs, would be reduced significantly. This required changing the ordering and delivery days of each store.

The project team conducted further simulations to determine the lowest-cost trade-off between warehouse load levelling and truck utilization. The optimum solution called for a slight increase in warehouse handling costs, but major savings in transportation. These changes led to net annual distribution savings of $170,000.

DEVELOPING A TRANSPORTATION PROFILE

The more progressive companies, which have good systems and transportation information systems, have the necessary data to review their operations periodically. The vast majority of companies, however, have lots of manual data, but no information. Introducing a transportation information system is usually relegated to future considerations by overburdened systems people. Yet there is now hope. The advent of the personal computer (PC) allows all companies to conduct a transportation diagnostic.

The following work-steps indicate the data requirements and the typical improvement opportunities available to most companies. This diagnostic can be accomplished in-house, if a company has the necessary skilled personnel who have time available to conduct the study. Alternatively, a company can hire skilled transportation consultants to work with them. An experienced transportation consultant can conduct a typical transportation diagnostic in about 10 to 15 work-days, at a cost of $10,000 to $15,000.

The base data for a transportation diagnostic is a detailed list and summary of all point-to-point movements within a representative time-frame. The work-steps are as follows:

1. *Select a representative business period.* This may range from one to three months, depending on sales fluctuations. Details of each shipment made during this period are listed by:
   - origin
   - destination
   - type of shipment (stock transfer, customer delivery, pick-up)
   - date
   - mode (common carrier, pool car, express, etc.)
   - pieces or cartons
   - weight
   - cube (if available)
   - freight charge

   Depending on the type of freight, some companies may also wish to identify commodity, density factor, consolidated shipment, individual customers, specific carriers, demurrage charges, etc.

2. *Obtain detailed information on all shipments within the selected time-frame.* Source documents are usually pro formas or bills of lading. Table 8.9 shows the detail of a typical logistics profile sorted by origin. The data could alternatively be sorted by carrier, date or destination point. Table 8.10 summarizes the shipments to show average weights, costs, rates, etc.

3. *Identify potential improvement opportunities.* The logistics profile provides the data to review the efficiency of the operation and to assess potential cost savings. Typical questions to be addressed include:
   - Can the incidence of minimum billings be reduced?
   - Is the best type of transport used for small packages?
   - Why were expensive modes of transport used?
   - Is there a difference between rates provided by carriers on similar routes?
   - Is there a large variance between local cartage rates in different towns?
   - What are the effects of shipping fewer but larger loads to branch warehouses?
   - Are goods cross-hauled between warehouses? What are the reasons and the costs?
   - Can shipment sizes be increased by establishing "scheduled delivery day" programs?
   - Where and why do demurrage charges occur?
   - Are there opportunities to consolidate shipments using stop-off methods?
   - Are all opportunities for load consolidation being used advantageously?
   - Can some routes be better serviced by private fleet trucks? Potential opportunities include regular two-way hauls or high local delivery costs.

The following case example illustrates how a transportation profile was used to reduce freight costs.

CASE EXAMPLE

A packaged food manufacturer with plants in Toronto and Montreal supplies several hundred products to thousands of customers across Canada. It operates distribution centres in Toronto and Montreal and utilizes public warehouses in Halifax, Winnipeg, Calgary and Vancouver. At the time of the review, the private fleet consisted of five trucks in Toronto. These were used to pick up raw materials from local suppliers and to make local customer deliveries. All other deliveries were made by public carriers.

STUDY PROGRAM

A transportation profile was developed and reviewed to identify potential cost-saving opportunities.

SUMMARY OF RESULTS

Annual transportation costs were in the region of $1.2 million. The detailed transportation review identified opportunities to reduce this freight cost by more than 15%. Annual savings stemmed from:

REDUCING LOCAL CARTAGE COSTS

Table 8.11 shows average local cartage shipment sizes and rates across Canada. A comparison of rates in each city showed relatively high rates in Vancouver, Calgary and Toronto (private fleet). An examination of individual shipments and bills of lading in Vancouver and Calgary indicated:

- Vancouver rates were not out of line. Higher wages and different delivery rates for the four zones of Greater Vancouver accounted for the relatively high cost.
- Certain carriers were charging higher-than-average rates in Calgary. A change of local carriers resulted in better rates and lower costs.

ELIMINATING A TRUCK AND DRIVER FROM THE TORONTO FLEET

The Toronto private fleet consisted of four straight trucks, one tractor and two trailers. Table 8.11 indicates that private fleet costs were high ($0.95/cwt.).

A detailed examination of drivers' route sheets indicated several areas for improving the operations of the four trucks.

- Drivers were delayed up to an hour at the warehouse prior to deliveries. Preloading the trucks would save up to 45 minutes per vehicle.
- Frequent delays occurred at certain customers' premises. Discussions with the customers' receivers resulted in prearranged delivery times at off-peak periods.

TABLE 8.9
FREIGHT ANALYSIS DETAIL

ORIGIN – MONTREAL

DESTINATION		DATE	MODE	CONS.	PIECES	WEIGHT	FREIGHT CHARGES	FREIGHT COST/ CWT.
Vancouver	Branch warehouse	07-27	Pool car		1,330	29,640	1,599.00	5.39
		08-25	Pool car		661	12,557	822.48	6.55
		08-31	Pool car		52	1,228	84.12	6.85
Vancouver	Major customer	08-25	Pool car		910	34,580	1,843.11	5.33
Vancouver	Food service	06-11	Pool car		225	11,435	748.99	6.55
		08-23	Pool car		165	8,340	571.29	6.85
Other B.C.	Other customer	06-09	Common carrier		2,428	47,666	2,275.00	4.77
Edmonton	Branch warehouse	06-20	Common carrier		504	10,584	356.68	3.37
		07-12	Pool car		1,355	28,135	1,497.00	5.32
		08-05	Pool car		250	13,320	1,044.28	7.84
		08-10	Pool car		365	10,204	582.65	5.71
		08-24	Pool car		724	15,302	873.74	5.71
Edmonton	Other customer	06-23	Pool car		1,415	24,780	1,434.76	5.79
		08-24	Pool car		225	7,150	437.58	6.12
		08-24	Pool car		195	6,730	411.88	6.12
Calgary	Other customer	06-22	Pool car		50	2,650	162.18	6.12
		08-25	Pool car		470	15,990	913.03	5.71

Location	Customer type	Date	Mode				
Other Alberta	Other customer	06-23	Pool car	99	5,050	431.78	8.55
		07-12	Pool car	155	7,605	616.77	8.11
Winnipeg	Branch warehouse	06-13	Railcar	29	44,992	1,562.72	3.47
		07-27	Common carrier	900	17,500	726.00	4.15
		07-28	Pool car	855	19,260	782.00	4.06
		08-22	Pool car	680	12,175	628.23	5.16
Sault Ste. Marie	Other customer	06-02	Common carrier	69	1,885	167.20	8.87
		08-02	Common carrier	35	7,610	446.54	5.87
Sudbury	Major customer	06-17	Common carrier	72	2,429	173.19	7.13
Sudbury	Other customer	06-02	Common carrier	150	2,170	154.72	7.13
		06-08	Common carrier	45	715	59.20	8.28
		06-17	Common carrier	50	2,020	144.03	7.13
		06-21	Common carrier	90	3,510	250.26	7.13
		07-22	Common carrier	51	737	61.02	8.28
		08-12	Common carrier	50	1,795	134.45	7.49
		08-22	Common carrier	50	2,035	145.10	7.13

TABLE 8.10

FREIGHT ANALYSIS SUMMARY

ORIGIN — MONTREAL

DESTINATION		MODE	NO. OF SHPMTS	NO. OF PIECES	TOTAL WEIGHT	TOTAL CHARGES	$ PER PIECE	$ PER CWT.	$ PER SHPMT	WT. PER SHPMT	PCS. SHPT
Vancouver	Branch warehouse	Pool car	3	2,043	43,425	2,506	1.23	5.77	855.20	14,475	681
		Total dest.	3	2,043	43,425	2,506	1.23	5.77	835.20	14,475	681
Vancouver	Major customer	Pool car	1	910	34,580	1,843	2.03	5.33	1,843.11	34,580	910
		Total dest.	1	910	34,580	1,843	2.03	5.33	1,843.11	34,580	910
Vancouver	Food service	Pool car	2	390	19,775	1,320	3.39	6.68	660.14	9,888	195
		Total dest.	2	390	19,775	1,320	3.39	6.68	660.14	9,888	195
		Total customer	3	1,300	54,355	3,163	2.43	5.82	1,054.46	18,118	433
Other B.C.	Other customer	Common carrier	1	2,428	47,666	2,275	.94	4.77	2,275.00	47,666	2,428
		Total dest.	1	2,428	47,666	2,275	.94	4.77	2,275.00	47,666	2,428
		Total customer	1	2,428	47,666	2,275	.94	4.77	2,275.00	47,666	2,428
Edmonton	Branch warehouse	Common carrier	1	504	10,584	357	.71	3.37	356.68	10,584	504
		Pool car	4	2,694	66,961	3,998	1.48	5.97	1,000	16,740	674
		Total dest.	5	3,297	82,595	4,448	1.35	5.39	741.38	13,760	550
Edmonton	Other customer	Pool car	3	1,835	38,660	2,284	1.24	5.91	761.41	12,887	612
		Total dest.	3	1,835	38,660	2,284	1.24	5.91	761.41	12,887	612
		Total customer	3	1,835	38,660	2,284	1.24	5.91	761.41	12,887	612

Calgary	Other customer	Pool car	2	520	18,640	1,075	2.07	5.77	537.61	9,320	260
		Total dest.	2	520	18,640	1,075	2.07	5.77	537.61	9,320	260
		Total customer	2	520	18,640	1,075	2.07	5.77	537.61	9,320	260
Other Alberta	Other customer	Pool car	2	254	12,655	1,048	4.12	8.28	524.00	6,328	127
		Total dest.	2	254	12,655	1,048	4.12	8.28	524.00	6,328	127
		Total customer	3	504	25,975	1,067	2.12	4.11	355.73	8,658	168
Winnipeg	Branch warehouse	Common carrier	1	900	17,500	726	.81	4.15	726.00	17,500	900
		Railcar	1	29	44,992	1,563	53.89	3.47	1,562.72	44,992	29
		Pool car	2	1,535	31,435	1,410	.92	4.49	705.12	15,718	768
		Total dest.	4	2,464	93,927	3,699	1.50	3.94	924.74	23,482	616

TABLE 8.11
SUMMARY OF LOCAL CARTAGE SHIPMENTS:
SIZES AND RATES

CITY	MODE	AVERAGE SHIPMENT (LB.)	COST/CWT. ($)
Halifax	Carrier	2,413	0.52
Saint John	Carrier	3,258	0.57
Montreal	Private fleet	8,394	0.94
Montreal	Carrier	38,416	0.43
Toronto	Carrier	11,490	0.69
Winnipeg	Carrier	4,291	0.45
Calgary	Carrier	3,890	0.43
Vancouver	Carrier	2,038	0.68

Potential opportunities for improvement:
• Vancouver
• Toronto
• Montreal (private fleet)

• Some drivers ran into overtime, while others had spare time on their hands. Changes to the delivery routes spread the work-load out more uniformly.

These improvements led to the elimination of a truck and driver from the fleet.

REPLACING COMMON CARRIERS BY A PRIVATE FLEET TRACTOR-TRAILER IN THE TORONTO–MONTREAL CORRIDOR

The logistics profile showed regular two-way movement of goods in the Toronto–Montreal corridor. The data were sorted to simulate the effects of a private trucking operation. Table 8.12 shows that three trailer-loads of goods could be hauled weekly in each direction. There would still be excess shipments in one direction. These would continue to be shipped by common carriers.

IMPLEMENTING A SCHEDULED DELIVERY PROGRAM IN SOUTHWESTERN ONTARIO

Analysis of the logistics profile showed the following daily shipment pattern to customers in southwestern Ontario:

• Daily deliveries were made to each town.
• Customers received one or, at most, two deliveries per week.
• Shipment sizes ranged from LTL to 30,000 lb.

TABLE 8.12

ACTUAL SHIPMENTS FROM MONTREAL TO TORONTO

DATE	DESTINATION BRANCH (B) OR CUSTOMER (C)	WEIGHT (LB.)	ACTUAL CARRIER COST	PRIVATE TRANSPORT SIMULATION TRIP NO.			COMMON CARRIER
				1	2	3	
8/7	C	15,840	396	*			
9/7	B	39,697	568	*		*	
9/7	B	41,960	596		*		
10/7	C	13,615	291			*	
10/7	C	6,450	139			*	
Total		117,562	1,990				
14/7	B	41,454	589	*			
14/7	B	43,924	624		*		
14/7	C	26,460	501			*	
14/7	C	28,800	501				*
Total		140,638	2,215				
22/7	C	25,200	501	*			
22/7	C	25,344	501				*
22/7	B	45,363	644				*
23/7	B	44,559	633		*		
24/7	B	48,972	735			*	
Total		189,438	3,014				

This suggested that a consolidation program could be established. Scheduled deliveries could be made to each city on a two-day per week basis. This would not cut back the frequency of service to customers, but would require them to place their orders on set days. After some consultation, the marketing department endorsed the scheduled delivery program.

The logistics profile was summarized to simulate shipment weights based on two deliveries per week. This showed that consolidated shipment sizes would range from 20,000 lb. to 45,000 lb. to major cities — Hamilton, Kitchener, London and Windsor.

Using data from the logistics profile, the traffic manager negotiated a multiple delivery program with several carriers, obtaining improved rates and terms. These include:

- competitive multiple delivery rate
- special rates for 45,000-lb. weight brackets
- multiple delivery rates to include larger delivery areas (e.g., Burlington and Oakville were combined with Hamilton)

The consolidation program was simulated over a 12-week period. The line-haul plus local delivery costs were compared to the actual costs over the same period. The simulation indicated potential annual transportation savings of more than $55,000. A reserve of $10,000 was subtracted from the potential savings. This allowed for LTL deliveries of emergency shipments to be made outside the consolidation program. This strategy overcame the marketing department's fear of possible reduction in customer service.

CHAPTER 9

Purchasing

INTRODUCTION

The distribution department is responsible for the timely delivery of the required goods and services at the correct location and at the least cost. Purchasing is an integral component of this department; purchasing staff are responsible for all arrangements between the company and its suppliers.

Supply contracts can influence inventory, transportation and operations strategies. The purchasing group will be involved in sourcing, qualifying suppliers, preparing tender and contract documents, evaluating submissions, negotiating agreements, expediting shipments and monitoring supplier performance.

This chapter discusses the policies and procedures which set the direction and responsibilities of the purchasing department and allow it to carry on its work systematically, considers different types of purchasing systems and agreements and presents techniques which can be used to evaluate the effectiveness of the department.

GOALS AND OBJECTIVES

The *purchasing department* has a number of key goals which enable it to contribute significantly to the overall profitability of the company:

- minimize the total cost of purchases
- ensure reliable timely supply
- minimize purchasing overhead

The specific objectives of *purchasing management* are to:

- ensure that the necessary organization and well-trained staff are in place
- ensure that the policies and procedures are maintained
- implement and maintain information systems and communication channels with other departments and suppliers

The specific responsibilities of the *purchasing agent* are to:

- identify suppliers and thus ensure competitive pricing
- identify means of reducing overall costs through negotiation, substitution, purchasing systems or order consolidation
- communicate opportunities for savings to the client groups
- qualify suppliers on the basis of product quality and delivery performance
- prepare clear and concise bid documents
- evaluate tenders and bids
- negotiate the best terms for each purchase
- monitor supplier service performance
- improve purchasing methods and, thus, productivity

SUPPLY MANAGEMENT

Sourcing of goods and services in most corporations draws on an established network of suppliers. But new manufacturing directions, new purchasing approaches or an unsettled economic environment can upset supply-and-demand patterns. The network cannot always adapt. The purchasing department must take an active role in protecting sources of supply, particularly for raw materials.

There are three main factors affecting sources of supply:

- Loss of supply. A surge in demand from competitors, or reduced production caused by political unrest, resource depletion, strikes or vendor financial failure can have devastating effects.
- Opportunity for improved pricing. To gain an edge in their market, companies are looking farther afield for sources, arranging long-term contracts in return for guaranteed pricing and starting up joint ventures with suppliers.
- Opportunity from new technology. The application of new methods and new equipment to the operation of a plant will result in a significant change in the pattern and nature of the demand for goods and services. Some vendors will not be positioned to react to new demands for enhanced communications and superior service.

In the light of "just-in-time" approaches, the supply management role is replacing the purchasing strategies of the recent past. The purchasing department must become proactive and forward-looking. Planning, sourcing and evaluating alternatives must be emphasized over the tendering and purchase order preparation tasks.

The importance of the supply management role cannot be over-emphasized in light of the following two factors:

- The strategic importance of purchasing. Raw materials costs represent a large component of finished goods costs. As the complexity of the operation grows, the number and locations of potential suppliers are significantly increased.
- The complexity of the supply market. The selection of suppliers may depend on world conditions, exchange rate forecasts and political conditions, as well as product unit price and quality.

A successful supply strategy must consider:

- Opportunities to consolidate the requirements of several plants, departments, divisions, subsidiaries or joint venture partners.
- Ways and means of avoiding bottlenecks and disruptions of supply, by assuring the viability of suppliers or developing alternative sources of supply.
- The acceptable level of risk associated with each contract. Increased risk will generally result in lower pricing and more flexibility. However, the use of multiple sourcing, long-term contracts and shared investment through joint ventures are all ways to hedge.
- A "make or buy" policy? Security of supply is assured through vertical integration of supply, manufacturing and distribution. However, where excess capacity exists in an industry, contracting for services is often cheaper.
- Supplier co-operative programs. Involving suppliers early in the development process can gain their commitment and result in cost savings.
- Competitor co operative programs. Items of small demand cannot be produced efficiently, but if the needs of several organizations are considered, a reasonable production run can be assured.

This proactive approach is vital for firms in all industries. The risks must be assessed and a rational approach to finding ways to minimize exposure developed in order to secure the future of the organization.

TYPES OF PURCHASE ORDERS

There are a number of strategic approaches to purchasing, depending on the characteristics of the goods and services. The purchasing agent must fully understand the advantages and disadvantages of each. The following section outlines the strengths and weaknesses for both purchaser and supplier.

There are six types of purchase strategies. Each has a different balance of risk for the buyer vs. the vendor. In general, the more precise the quantities and delivery dates, the less business risk for the supplier. The purchaser can expect favourable terms in the purchase agreement. When the specifications are non-standard or loose, quantities are unknown, reorder possibilities are slight or any other condition is unfavourable, the supplier will expect terms which put more of the risk on the purchaser.

FIRM FIXED-PRICE AGREEMENT

The most common type of purchase order is the firm fixed-price agreement. The goods or services are supplied for a fixed cost, with no provision for change. The onus is clearly on the supplier, with minimum risk to the buyer. This agreement is used when the requirements are clear, sourcing is straightforward, and the price can be agreed on in advance.

Purchases from suppliers' catalogues for immediate delivery are made using this type of contract.

REPRICING AGREEMENT

If there is a possibility of changes in the customer's requirements, in terms of location or quantity, or if the contract is for a long term so that the raw materials or labour input costs cannot be accurately predicted, repricing clauses may be negotiated. The items which can be adjusted are all embodied in the contract. The agreement contains review milestones, based on time, quantity or percentage complete.

The repricing agreement allows the risk to be shared between the buyer and the seller. The supplier takes all the risk to the first milestone, as above, but the buyer shares in the risk for the variable inputs after that time. For example, a purchaser may have placed an order for 500 units of a specially manufactured item, but finds that only 300 are needed. The supplier is entitled to increase the unit price to offset the fixed costs, which would otherwise have been spread over the full order.

INCENTIVE AGREEMENTS

The agreements for construction projects, development of manufactured products, or fabrication of parts may include specific incentive provisions. For long contracts, there may be a monetary bonus for the supplier to complete the project ahead of schedule, provide products or services with exceptional performance, or develop cost savings in the project. Similarly, there may be penalty clauses for poor performance.

Normally there is a target cost, agreed schedule of completion, and measurable performance criteria. The incentive clauses are used to compensate the supplier for providing the buyer with a superior product or for making it available early. Similarly, penalties compensate the purchaser for lost revenue from underperformance or unavailability. Road construction projects are typically carried out under such agreements. Early completion means reduced congestion and, thus, time saved by motorists. The road contractor is encouraged by the bonus to complete the project early.

Care must be taken in establishing bonuses and penalties to ensure that the incentives are worthwhile. If the rewards are insignificant, the incentive will be ignored. If the rewards are too great, quality may suffer. Structuring the incentive may require special accounting procedures, particularly when a target profit margin is used as measurement criterion.

ESCALATION AGREEMENT

An escalation agreement protects the supplier against a predefined set of factors. These types of contracts are used when the prices of the raw materials are subject to unstable market conditions or when the agreement will extend over a long period of time. Prices are raised on the basis of predetermined formulae, usually on the basis of labour contract results or commodity price fluctuations. In times of high inflation, this type of agreement is common except for the shortest-term supply periods.

As with the repricing agreement, the buyer is sharing the risk with the supplier. In contrast, the changes are based on market change trigger points, not milestones in the agreement. Errors in estimating quantities of labour or materials, however, remain the responsibility of the supplier. Of course, escalation of prices covers only the undelivered portion of the order, or services which were incomplete before their costs rose.

COST-PLUS AGREEMENT

A cost-plus contract stipulates that the buyer will pay the seller the seller's actual costs to produce the goods or provide the service, plus some amount of agreed-on profit. Because it places the balance of risk with the buyer, this type of contract should be used only when the timing or project definition precludes accurate costing. The contract must have a clear definition of the requirements, a well-defined scope of allowable costs, a formula for accounting for costs and profit, and provision for adequate inspection and cost auditing by the buyer. Also, to lessen the risk, there is normally an upset cost established. Defence contracts are frequently written in this form.

A variation of the cost-plus profit contract is the cost-plus profit-plus incentive, which includes bonus clauses for performance. This type of agreement is used to motivate suppliers to keep costs below a targeted amount.

TIME AND MATERIALS CONTRACT

A form of the cost-plus agreement is the time and materials contract. Under this type of contract, the buyer normally pays the seller a stated rate per hour or day, plus qualifying expenses for its services. The rates include base salaries or wages, benefits, corporate overhead, general and administrative expenses, and an allowance for profit. Materials and project-related costs are billed at cost, often subject to an administrative surcharge.

This type of contract requires a trust relationship between the supplier and the customer. The seller is usually engaged before the full nature of the requirement is known, and is often required to establish the needs as part of the assignment. Maintenance work and consulting contracts are two examples. To minimize risk, the client must rely on close monitoring and the reputation of the supplier.

PURCHASE ORDER SYSTEMS

Purchasing must have a way of relaying its buying needs to its suppliers' order desks. A key responsibility of management is to develop and maintain a system for the orderly conduct of the business of placing orders with suppliers. Chapter 3 introduced the order desk and its relationship to customers and customer service and introduced the use of electronic data interchange (EDI). This section describes this and five other systems for controlling order status.

TELEPHONE ORDERING

The simplest purchase order system is one in which orders are placed to suppliers by telephone, the requests being recorded manually in logs. Supplies are often ordered this way in industry for maintenance, repairs and stationery. The items being ordered and the suppliers are both usually well known to the buyer, and a relationship of trust has been built up between the parties. The advantages are a quick response capability and minimal administrative cost.

The main drawback is occasional errors in communication between the buyer and seller, with associated problems in controlling pricing and invoicing. With no written contract, disputes may arise. Often, a simple requisitioning system is used to confirm the order and allow for a formal receipt of goods, with proper accounting.

STANDARD PRINTED ORDER

The standard printed purchase order contains all of the elements necessary to complete the transaction. In addition, it will usually include the standard terms and conditions under which the purchase is made, as well as all information necessary to effectively monitor and control the procurement process.

The following data are found on a typical purchase order:

- buyer identification, including name, address, originating requestor and department, purchasing agent, etc.
- shipping instructions and FOB point
- unique order number
- terms of payment
- vendor identification, including contact person
- approval signatures and codes
- description of items, goods or services ordered
- quantity of each item
- unit prices and extensions
- shipping costs and taxes
- control numbers — requisition, cost centre, work order, project, etc.

The purchase order form may have as many as eight carbon copies for simultaneous distribution to all interested parties, as follows:

- The original and first two copies are sent to the vendor, who sends back the acknowledgement copy to be matched with the open order file. Later the vendor will submit a copy with the invoice.
- The third copy goes to the open order file.
- The fourth copy alerts accounts payable of the commitment.
- The fifth copy opens an expediting file and may be used to monitor supplier performance.
- The sixth and seventh copies go to receiving: one copy to release the expediting and open order files after goods are received, and the other to verify receipt to accounting so that the invoice can be paid.
- The eighth copy is sent to the originating requestor.

Processing so many pieces of paper through so many hands is costly. It is estimated that the cost to issue and process a purchase order is over $50 for most large organizations. With a large number of small orders to a single supplier or a periodic reorder of specific goods or services, there are opportunities to streamline purchasing and thus reduce cost.

STANDARD ORDER CONSOLIDATION

The time it takes to process a small order is the same as for a large order. Therefore, to reduce costs and allow the appropriate amount of time to be spent on the larger orders, small orders should be consolidated systematically. A number of requests for similar or identical items can be held for bimonthly processing, or for a minimum order size, as long as service is not affected.

The occurrence of many small orders is usually symptomatic of other problems, such as inappropriate reorder quantities, lack of standardization of equipment and materials or inadequate maintenance and operational planning. The logistics approach should be used to analyse any such problem.

BLANKET ORDERING (STANDING ORDERS)

Blanket orders can save significant time and effort and often result in reduced unit prices. If a number of orders are being placed for the same item over time, a series of identical POs will be issued. This repetition can be eliminated by establishing a special agreement with a vendor to release the product from a master purchase order. The supplier agrees to provide the goods or services at a negotiated price for the duration of the agreement, as measured by time or quantity. Authority to draw from the PO can be delegated to the users so that purchasing need not be involved in each release.

In addition to this efficiency, there are other advantages:

- Volume purchases will likely mean lower prices.
- Paper flow is reduced for both buyer and vendor.
- Prices are firm and known, enhancing planning.
- Suppliers will be more reliable if they are given better information.
- Inventory can be reduced.
- Client department convenience is improved.

SYSTEMS PURCHASING

Systems purchasing is a specific form of the blanket order, typically used as a substitute for carrying inventory of low-value, repetitive items. Many companies use systems contracting for their stationery supplies. They carry only a week's stock of pens, paper, etc., and reorder these items as required. Purchasing negotiates a contract for a broad category of items, specifying quality, quantity, service and special terms and conditions, covering from one to three years. One requisition is used to cover a catalogue of items from which approved employees may order directly.

A simplified four-part form replaces the PO. The supplier receives the top three parts, retains one for his or her own records and returns two copies with the shipment so that receipt of the items can be properly recorded and the accounts payable department notified. The originator keeps the last copy.

If a buyer is dealing with only one supplier, the individual unit prices of each item may not be the lowest possible. However, the benefits to the buyer are substantial:

- a high order fill ratio
- delivery schedules planned in advance, resulting in a reliable lead time
- a decrease in inventory carrying costs

- a greatly simplified purchasing process
- reduced administration expense
- more attention paid to the larger contracts with an appropriate improvement in results

Systems contracting also benefits the supplier. He or she is able to provide good service profitably, at a reasonable cost to the purchaser, because of:

- guaranteed business during the contract
- regular cash flow
- predictable profit margins
- increased volume
- better inventory control
- fewer deliveries
- lower sales cost
- less paperwork

ELECTRONIC DATA INTERCHANGE (EDI)

EDI is the most significant change to purchasing technique in many years. It has diverted the efforts of the purchasing agent from paper pushing and paper chasing to sourcing and price negotiation. The elimination of several steps in processing purchase orders has made the function more streamlined, more timely, less costly and, therefore, more responsive to client needs.

The auto industry was the first to recognize these benefits in a big way. By requiring parts component suppliers to link electronically, it was able to institute just-in-time manufacturing techniques which resulted in significant productivity gains.

Order preparation time is reduced. Order accuracy is enhanced. Order tracing and tracking are made easier. Supplier performance monitoring is simplified. Systems contracting is eased.

PRICE EVALUATION AND NEGOTIATION

Price is a key parameter in the selection of a supplier. However, the purchaser must consider more than the tendered unit price when making a choice. The price must be considered as the total value of the right goods at the point of use. Price evaluation requires a valid comparison of the value of competing materials or services in terms of quality, quantity and service.

The delivered price includes more than the unit price paid to the vendor. Freight, packaging, insurance and handling charges, credit terms, taxes, duties and escalation clauses will all affect the future price of goods.

High price may mean high quality. The user departments are responsible for determining the minimum operational and legal requirements, but additional quality features may be appropriate if the life of the product is extended or its operating characteristics are enhanced. On the other hand, overrestrictive specifications for quality reduce sourcing options and may unnecessarily inflate costs.

Unit prices generally decline as the order size increases. However, buying in quantity may not necessarily be advantageous. In deciding on the quantity to order, the evaluation must consider the cost of the capital committed to inventory, storage capability and cost, additional handling requirements and the risk of obsolescence or spoilage. The use of blanket orders may avoid additional costs while gaining the advantage of lower price.

Paying for proven service may be economical, if future added costs can be forgone. Service includes security of supply, on-time delivery, after-sale repair and replacement, training in product use, and parts availability. Consideration should be given to standardizing the product in the operation. For example, the investment required to maintain spare parts for four different makes of fork-lift may be double that for four of one make. Non-standardized equipment also increases training needs.

The analysis of price should consider all of the costs which will be incurred in the purchase and lifetime operation of the goods, or service contract. This is called *life cycle costing*. It involves the estimate of maintenance costs and timing, replacement cost and timing, the cost of downtime and the salvage value at disposal. All costs are converted to current dollars for comparison purposes.

Certain factors affect the decision on the timing of the purchase. Price is determined in the market-place on the basis of supply and demand. Inflated prices will be paid in a sellers' market when demand is high. Large discounts can be expected in the off-season during a buyers' market. A dip in the economy, an increase in capacity to produce a product or service, or the entry of a new competitor may signal a buying opportunity.

Corporate policy may also affect the decision. Many governments, for example, have a policy of sourcing within their own jurisdiction if possible, even to the point of incurring additional cost. Private companies may wish to use affiliates or subsidiaries as suppliers whenever possible.

A dominant purchaser of a specific product or service must also be concerned about maintaining a long-term competitive supplier capability. Consideration should be given to splitting large orders when a competitive supplier may not survive as a result of losing a contract. The presence of the second supplier will also ensure good service from the majority supplier during the contract.

There are many opportunities to negotiate with suppliers on any part of the contract:

- price and escalations
- terms of payment and credit
- specifications for goods or services
- quantity guarantees and discounts
- after-sale service
- delivery and packaging
- incentives and penalties

Effective negotiating requires a special set of skills that are learned over time, but all buyers can become better negotiators if they follow some basic precepts:

- *Set clear objectives.* The objective is not to strip the supplier of profit, but to eliminate unjustified or unnecessary costs. If there is no potential for profit, the level of service and quality of goods or security of supply could suffer. Ideally, both parties should come away from the table feeling satisfied.
- *Plan the bargaining strategy.* Establish an opening position and, above all else, know what you want in terms of specifications and user performance requirements. Determine who will be the spokesperson and plan a tentative timetable. Decide what technical resources and supporting documentation are required at the negotiations.
- *Have a positive attitude.* Enter the negotiations confident of success. Take a friendly but firm position. Try to understand the position of the supplier and adjust to new information.
- *Define a fall-back position.* Establish the issues on which you can be flexible and define the farthest you will move from the initial position. Review the possible trade-offs and protect the most important concerns.
- *Negotiate from a position of strength.* Know your supplier. Have all the facts at your fingertips. Have the necessary technical back-up staff available.
- *Have second thoughts.* Before making a firm commitment, take the time to prepare the documents and review your position.

In most foreign countries, negotiation is expected and good negotiating skills are admired. In North America, we are still learning the techniques, but those who can bargain effectively will reap significant benefits.

EFFECTIVENESS OF THE PURCHASING FUNCTION

The process of measuring the effectivensss of the purchasing department is no different than for any other entity within the organization. Determine the department objectives, develop work plans with quantifiable standards and measure performance against these plans. Analyse variance from the plans and make the appropriate adjustments.

Specifically, for the purchasing department, the following factors should be tracked:

- annual and monthly budgets against actual expenditures
- backlog of orders pending
- price reductions measured for individuals and the group as a whole
- identification of new or better sources of supply
- identification of substitution or standardization opportunities
- productivity improvement of the purchasing function
- service given in terms of elapsed time for purchasing activities
- specific projects aimed at work simplification or system improvement (should be tracked independently)

Purchasing is a profession and must be carried out in a professional manner. The purchaser must have the integrity and professional competence to carry out the objectives of the department and provide a high level of service to all user departments.

SUMMARY

An effective purchasing function is vital to the economic well-being of every company. Working as an integral part of the logistics team, the buyer can esnure reliable, on-time supply of goods and services. The appropriate use of purchasing strategies requires a professional approach to ensure best value for money. Systems purchasing, blanket ordering and life-cycle cost-evaluation techniques will help to achieve this goal. But perhaps the most significant change of recent years is the introduction of EDI, which will drastically reduce paper burden while increasing service levels.

CHAPTER 10

Distribution Resource Planning (DRP)

INTRODUCTION

Most distribution companies use basic reorder point logic to control inventory levels. However, an exciting new technique called distribution resource planning (DRP) is slowly revolutionizing the way in which distribution inventories are controlled. A common theme through all the chapters of this book is that logistics activities must be integrated for all economies to be achieved. DRP is an inventory management technique that recognizes the related activities of customer service, inventory control, warehousing and transportation.

HISTORY OF INVENTORY MANAGEMENT

Prior to the 1940s, companies involved in the distribution of goods tended to focus most of their attention on inventory control, not on inventory management. The primary issue was how to control inventory which had already been produced or acquired. Security measures, physical inventory counts and accounting measurement were emphasized. Little attention was paid to determining how much inventory should be there in the first place.

Operations research, the use of mathematical techniques to solve business problems, came into its own during the latter stages of World War II. One of the areas of particular interest to operations researchers was the calculation of optimum inventory management policies. Many of the so-called scientific inventory management techniques still in use today were developed during this period.

The new scientific rules of inventory management were not widely used until the 1960s. Although the formulae made sense from an academic point of view, the manual calculation of safety stocks and economic order quantities (EOQs) for any but a small number of items was too time-consuming to be practical. The new techniques started to see more applications in the 1960s as large companies began to computerize their inventory systems.

In the 1970s, inventory practitioners began to realize that the scientific techniques did not deliver all they had promised. Specifically, reorder point concepts using statistical safety stocks and EOQs didn't take account of the realities of manufacturing and distribution activities. The shortcomings became more and more apparent as the decreasing costs of computerization allowed more companies to try out the techniques.

The chief problem in using reorder point methods to control manufacturing inventories is that interdependencies between the demand for end-items and the raw materials and components used to build them are not recognized. A technique called manufacturing resource planning (MRP) evolved to address the management of items whose demand is created by the demand for other items. Many organizations have implemented MRP systems to manage inventories in their manufacturing plants. Countless others are analysing MRP to determine whether it makes sense for them.

With all the attention MRP received in technical journals and the constant barrage of advertisements for MRP software in logistics magazines, it wasn't long before distribution managers began to question the value of reorder point techniques for managing the distribution of items to branch warehouses and customers. Reorder point techniques didn't seem to recognize the interdependencies of demand between different levels of distribution. It seemed fairly easy to manage inventories at a central warehouse using reorder points, as long as the central warehouse didn't have to supply any other warehouses. It was the other warehouses, ordering in "economic" lot-sizes, that seemed to cause most of the problems. Once again, the main issue is that reorder point methods don't take account of the fact that demand at one level is affected by inventory decisions made at other levels. A new technique called DRP evolved to address the issue of dependent demand.

This technique was developed by Don Firth in the late 1960s at the Smith's Food Group in the United Kingdom, then a division of General Mills. DRP was used to control inventories at 9 plants and 30 warehouses. Its introduction and use raised customer service levels to almost 100% while reducing inventories by 40%. DRP achieved popularity in the late 1970s following the work of André Martin at Abbott Laboratories in Canada.

WHAT'S WRONG WITH REORDER POINTS?

To fully appreciate the benefits of DRP, one must begin by looking at the limitations of reorder point concepts in a distribution environment.

Reorder point methods are based on the concept that additional inventory needs to be ordered once a reorder point is reached. The reorder point is calculated as the demand which is expected to occur over the lead time necessary to order and receive additional items, plus some quantity of safety stock to cover fluctuations in demand and supply. While reorder points are easy to understand, it is important to recognize the assumptions that must be made in order to calculate them.

First of all, most companies calculate reorder points based on average demand. Any conditions which cause fluctuations in demand will violate the basis on which the reorder points were calculated. A few moments' thought will convince you that demand for many of the items your company sells is not "average." Let's take a look at some of the most common reasons.

- Demand patterns may be changing, either increasing or decreasing.
- Items may have a seasonal or cyclical demand pattern.
- Items may be promoted at different times of the year.
- The nature of the items themselves may cause irregular demand patterns. Spare parts items, for example, may not be needed regularly, but only just in advance of a planned repair or rebuild program.
- Demand for items at the main warehouse in a multi-warehouse situation always fluctuates because of the ordering patterns of the warehouses it supplies.

Most companies that use reorder points to control their inventories calculate order quantities using the basic economic order quantity (EOQ) formula. While the formula has some value as a guideline for determining reasonable order quantities, it does not recognize the fact that many suppliers offer quantity discounts for large-volume purchases. In order to determine if it's worthwhile to take advantage of volume discounts, you also need some idea of the likely timing of future orders. Reorder point inventory systems identify orders which need to be placed now. They don't give any indication of when you can expect to have to order the item again. If you had this information, you could trade off the volume discount against the cost of buying the inventory sooner.

Reorder points are often used to control the replenishment of regional and branch warehouses. Orders are placed as soon as inventories reach reorder points at these warehouses. While this makes sense from an inventory point of view, it ignores the fact that replenishment decisions affect transportation costs.

Suppose, for example, that a regional warehouse is replenished on a weekly cycle from a national distribution centre. Assume that 70 items need to be ordered because inventory levels are below their reorder points. Also assume that the quantities ordered equal half a truck-load. Transportation costs, however, will be minimized if shipments are made in full truck-load quantities. Most companies would find it economical to send additional inventory to the regional warehouse and achieve increased vehicle utilization (or lower freight rates, if common carriers are used). Increased inventory carrying costs will be more than offset by reduced transportation costs.

Reorder point systems, however, can't identify the additional items which should be ordered. As a result, most companies use general rules such as "always fill the truck with our biggest sellers." An effective inventory management system would identify the items which are most likely to be ordered, or needed next.

Note, too, that reorder points don't help you decide which orders can be delayed if you find that a week's orders are slightly more than a truck-load quantity. An effective system would provide the information needed to determine which orders can be delayed without adversely affecting customer service levels. In summary, then, reorder point systems don't take account of transportation issues. Inventory decisions are made without recognizing the impact of these decisions on transportation costs.

Another problem with reorder points is the assumption that additional inventory can always be obtained. Orders for replenishment are placed as soon as warehouse inventories reach reorder points. But what happens if there isn't enough inventory at the supplying warehouse to meet the demands of the warehouses it supplies? How should available inventory be allocated? Reorder point systems can't address this fundamental distribution issue.

Perhaps the biggest problem with reorder points is the implicit assumption that the management of individual items means that total inventories are being managed effectively. Reorder point systems generate orders for individual items based on inventory levels, without taking into account how the recommended orders will affect cash flow, warehouse space requirements or transportation costs.

DISTRIBUTION RESOURCE PLANNING (DRP)

DRP is an inventory management technique which has evolved to address the limitations of reorder point methods. Ordering decisions are based on forecasts of future requirements rather than on average historical demand. Inventory levels are projected into the future, based on forecast

FIGURE 10.1
DISTRIBUTION NETWORK

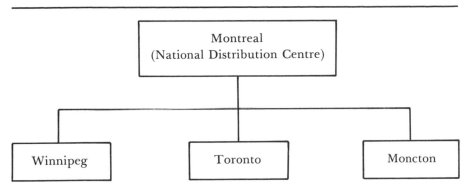

demand. Receipts of additional inventory are scheduled to arrive just before they are required. Lead times are used to determine when these orders have to be placed.

A simple example will help to clarify how DRP works. Assume that the distribution network for a particular item is as shown in Figure 10.1. Customers in western Canada are supplied from the Winnipeg warehouse. Customers in central Canada are supplied from Toronto, and those in eastern Canada from Moncton. The three regional warehouses are all resupplied from the national distribution centre in Montreal, which in turn is resupplied from outside vendors.

The forecast of demand for a particular item at the Winnipeg warehouse is 90 units per week. Experience has shown that safety stock of 50 units is sufficient to cover forecast error. It takes three weeks to order and receive additional items. The item is ordered in quantities of 150 units.

A DRP schedule for the item at the Winnipeg warehouse is shown in Table 10.1. The DRP schedule was completed by calculating the inventory balance expected at the end of each of the eight weeks. A receipt was planned for the beginning of any week in which the projected inventory balance at the end of the week was below the safety stock level of 50 units.

Starting with 200 units on hand, the projected balance at the end of Week 1 is 110 units. This is above the safety stock level of 50 units, so a receipt of additional inventory in Week 1 is not required. The projected balance at the end of Week 2 is 20 units, which is below the safety stock level. A receipt is required in Week 2. With a lead time of three weeks, the order should have been placed two weeks ago. Since the item is ordered in quantities of 150 units, a planned receipt and a planned order of 150 units are marked on the schedule. If 150 units are received at the

TABLE 10.1

Safety Stock	-50 Units
Order Quantity	-150 Units
Lead Time	-3 Weeks

*** Winnipeg ***

	PAST DUE	1	2	3	4	5	6	7	8
Forecast		90	90	90	90	90	90	90	90
On Hand	200	110	170	80	140	50	110	170	80
Planned Receipts			150		150		150	150	
Planned Orders	150	150		150	150		150	150	

TABLE 10.2

Safety Stock	-50 Units
Order Quantity	-150 Units
Lead Time	-1 Week

*** Toronto ***

	PAST DUE	1	2	3	4	5	6	7	8
Forecast		100	100	100	100	100	100	100	100
On Hand	200	100	150	50	100	150	50	100	150
Planned Receipts			150		150	150		150	150
Planned Orders		150		150	150		150	150	150

beginning of Week 2, the projected inventory balance at the end of Week 2 will be 170 units.

The rest of the schedule has been prepared following exactly the same logic. Note that orders should be placed in Weeks 1, 3, and 4.

A DRP schedule for the same item at the Toronto warehouse is shown in Table 10.2. Orders need to be received in Weeks 2, 4, 5, 7 and 8. With a lead time of one week, orders need to be placed in Weeks 1, 3, 4, 6 and 7.

A DRP schedule for the Moncton warehouse is shown in Table 10.3. Additional stock is required in Weeks 2, 5 and 8. With a lead time of two weeks, orders need to be placed in Weeks 3 and 6. An order for 150 units should have been placed last week for receipt in Week 2.

The three DRP schedules show the timing of the orders which need to be placed to keep the projected inventory balances at each location above safety stock levels. The schedule in Table 10.4 shows the total effect of these orders on the national distribution centre. This summary of the planned shipments shows that the demand at the national distribution centre is a function of the timing and size of replenishment orders from the other warehouses. The variable demand shown in this simple example occurred even though all regional warehouses have constant demand and order the same quantity. Fluctuations in the rate of demand at the national distribution centre will vary even more if demand at the other warehouses varies or if they order in different lot sizes.

Since reorder points are usually calculated under the assumption that the rate of demand is constant, a large amount of safety stock would have to be carried at the national distribution centre to provide an acceptable level of service.

The planned shipments to the regional warehouses represent the demand expected at the national distribution centre. This projection of demand can be used to determine when additional stock is required at the national distribution centre. A DRP schedule for the national distribution centre in Montreal is shown in Table 10.5. The DRP schedule shows that additional stock is required in Weeks 3 and 6. With a lead time of one week, orders need to be placed in Weeks 2 and 5.

This example shows how simple DRP really is. Requirements for additional stock are determined at the lowest levels in the distribution network, based on forecasted demand. Requirements at the regional warehouses are then used to determine the dependent demand on the warehouses which supply them. Decisions to replenish the higher-level warehouses are made, taking account of what future demand is expected to be, without assuming that demand will be the same in each period.

TABLE 10.3

			*** Moncton ***						

Safety Stock -25 Units
Order Quantity -150 Units
Lead Time -2 Weeks

	PAST DUE	1	2	3	4	5	6	7	8
Forecast		50	50	50	50	50	50	50	50
On Hand	100	50	150	100	50	150	100	50	150
Planned Receipts			150			150			150
Planned Orders	150			150			150		

TABLE 10.4
PLANNED SHIPMENTS TO REGIONAL WAREHOUSES

	PAST DUE	1	2	3	4	5	6	7	8
Winnipeg	150	150	0	150	150	0	0	0	0
Toronto	0	150	0	150	150	0	150	150	0
Moncton	150	0	0	150	0	0	150	0	0
TOTAL	300	300	0	450	300	0	300	150	0

TABLE 10.5

Safety Stock   100 Units
Order Quantity   600 Units   *** National Distribution Centre ***
Lead Time   1 Week

	PAST DUE	1	2	3	4	5	6	7	8
Dependent Demand	300	300	0	450	300	0	300	150	0
On Hand	550	250	250	400	100	100	400	250	250
Planned Receipts				600		500	600		
Planned Orders			600			500			

Although we've used a simple example to introduce the DRP concept, rest assured that DRP can be used effectively in complex distribution networks where warehouses supply some customers directly as well as other warehouses.

WHAT ABOUT REORDER POINTS?

The use of reorder point logic to control the replenishment of the warehouses in the preceding example would have resulted in substantially higher inventory levels. Demand at Winnipeg, Toronto and Moncton is 90, 100 and 50 units per month, respectively. Since these warehouses are resupplied from the national distribution centre, average demand at the national distribution centre will be 240 units per month. For the sake of simplicity, we assume that the national distribution centre doesn't supply any customers directly. With a lead time of one week, the reorder point should be 240 units, plus some extra quantity of safety stock. A moment's thought, however, should convince you that the "average" demand may be very misleading.

The summary of planned shipments to the regional warehouses shown in Table 10.4 shows that demand can be as low as 0 units if none of the warehouses places orders, and as high as 450 if all order in the same week. If replenishment of the national distribution centre is controlled using reorder point logic, the reorder point must be at least as high as the maximum demand which can be expected to occur over the lead time. In this example, a reorder point of 450 units is required. The use of any value less than 450 units will result in stock-outs in any week when all warehouses place an order.

Assuming we use a reorder point of 450 units, the inventory levels we expect at the national distribution centre are as shown in Table 10.6. Comparing the inventory levels at the national distribution centre using DRP and reorder points, we see that:

• DRP results in an average inventory of 250 units.
• Reorder points give an average inventory of 625 units.

The use of DRP logic, in this case, provides the same level of service (100%) as reorder points, but with 60% less inventory!

The reason for the sizeable difference is that DRP takes account of the fact that demand at the national distribution centre is a function of the ordering patterns of the warehouses it supplies. Reorder point logic, on the other hand, results in orders being placed whenever the balance on hand falls to 450 units. By taking account of the ordering patterns of the warehouses, the orders placed in Weeks 1 and 4, using reorder point

TABLE 10.6

Reorder Point   450 Units
Order Quantity   600 Units   *** National Distribution Centre ***
Lead Time   1 Week

	PAST DUE	1	2	3	4	5	6	7	8
Dependent Demand	300	300	0	450	300	0	300	150	0
On Hand	550	250	850	400	700	700	400	850	850
Planned Receipts			600		600			600	
Planned Orders		600		600			600		

logic, can be safely delayed until Weeks 2 and 5 because the expected demand in Weeks 2 and 5 is 0. Delaying the placement of these orders results in a substantial reduction in inventories.

INVENTORY ALLOCATION

One of the real-life problems in inventory management is determining how to best allocate inventory to warehouses when demand exceeds supply. Using our previous example, we'll demonstrate that DRP provides a planner with considerably more information for making allocation decisions.

The reorder point schedule for the national distribution centre (see Table 10.6) shows that an order will be placed in Week 1, when the inventory level drops to the reorder point. With a lead time of one week, additional stock should arrive in Week 2. What should a planner do if the order is delayed and is not received until the end of Week 3?

The expected inventory balance at the end of Week 1 is 250 units. If the shipment is not received in Week 2, the expected ending balance for the week is also 250 units, since none of the regional warehouses places orders for replenishment. In Week 3, however, each warehouse places an order for 150 units, for a total demand of 450 units. Since there are only 250 units on hand, an inventory planner would have to determine how the 250 units should be allocated.

Since the orders at each warehouse have been generated independently of the other warehouses, a planner at the national distribution centre has no insight as to what the requirements at each one actually are. Most companies, faced with this problem, attempt to allocate the inventory on some sort of "fair-share" basis. Most fair-share algorithms base the allocation on the percentage of total demand represented by each warehouse.

In this example, each warehouse orders 150 units at a time, so fair-share allocation would distribute the 250 units as follows:

• 83 units to Winnipeg
• 83 units to Toronto
• 83 units to Moncton

This allocation, however, while conveniently easy to calculate, totally ignores what the requirements at each location are.

DRP gives an inventory planner considerably more information for making an intelligent allocation decision. The DRP schedule for the national distribution centre (see Table 10.5) shows that 600 units need to be ordered in Week 2, to arrive at the beginning of Week 3. If we assume again that receipt of the order is delayed until the end of Week 3, an inventory planner will have to determine how to allocate the 250 available units.

The first thing a planner using DRP would do is determine where the demand is coming from. The schedule of planned shipments to the regional warehouses (see Table 10.4) shows that orders have been placed by the Winnipeg, Toronto and Moncton warehouses.

The next step is to determine what the requirements at each of these locations actually are by looking at the corresponding DRP schedules.

- The DRP schedule for Winnipeg (see Table 10.1) shows that the order in Week 3 is scheduled to be received in Week 6. Forty additional units are required in Week 6 to meet the forecasted demand. Another 50 units are required to cover safety stock requirements. Sixty additional units are needed, because the branch is replenished in quantities of 150.
- The DRP schedule for Toronto (see Table 10.2) shows that the order in Week 3 is scheduled to be received in Week 4. Analysis of the requirement, however, shows that only 50 more units are required to meet the forecasted demand for Week 4. Another 50 units are required to maintain the desired level of safety stock. Fifty more units are ordered because the normal order size is 150 units.
- The DRP schedule for Moncton (see Table 10.3) shows that receipt of the order placed in Week 3 is expected in Week 5. No additional stock, however, is necessary to meet the forecasted demand for Week 6. Fifty units are required to cover safety stock requirements, and another 100 have been ordered because the normal order quantity is 150 units.

These requirements are summarized in Table 10.7. Only 90 units need to be shipped from the national distribution centre to fully satisfy the demand which has been forecasted at each of the other warehouses. An additional 150 units (240 units in total) need to be shipped to the regional warehouses to maintain desired safety stock levels. An additional 210 units (450 units in total) are required because these warehouses are replenished in lot sizes of 150 units.

Using DRP, a planner can see that the 250 units available for distribution are sufficient to meet the forecasted demand at each warehouse and

TABLE 10.7
SUMMARY OF REQUIREMENTS IN WEEK 3

	FORECAST	SAFETY STOCK	REPLENISHMENT SIZE
Winnipeg	40	50	60
Toronto	50	50	50
Moncton	0	50	100
	90	150	210

to maintain the desired levels of safety stock. The best way to allocate the 250 units, therefore, is:

- 90 units for Winnipeg
- 100 units for Toronto
- 50 units for Moncton

The ten units left over can be kept at the national distribution centre or sent to one of the three other warehouses.

A planner using reorder points and fair-share logic would have distributed 83 units to each branch. Inventory levels at Winnipeg and Toronto would then be below safety stock levels, while inventories at Moncton would be 33 units higher than necessary.

The problem with reorder points and fair-share allocation is that the fair shares are usually based on the quantities ordered by each branch. These order quantities, as shown in our example, are composed of requirements for forecast demand, safety stock and replenishment quantities. Planners need to know the true requirements for forecast demand and safety stock to make intelligent allocation decisions. DRP, unlike reorder points, gives planners this information.

Use of DRP in this simple example resulted in inventory reductions of 60% and, at the same time, gave planners better information to enable them to plan for and achieve even higher levels of customer service.

TRANSPORTATION PLANNING

Earlier in this chapter, we suggested that one of the limitations of reorder point techniques is a lack of integration between inventory management and transportation planning. Orders for replenishment are launched as soon as reorder points are reached, without regard for the effects that the timing of these orders will have on transportation costs. Reorder points can't give any indication of the timing of future orders.

DRP can be used as a tool for co-ordinating the activities of the inventory planning and transportation functions of your business. DRP schedules show the items which need to be shipped between warehouses, the quantities required and the timing of the shipment. Essentially, then, DRP simulates what is expected to happen over the next several planning periods.

This simulation of future activity can become very useful for planning transportation if additional data (such as weight, cube and quantity per pallet) is specified for each item. Schedules of future shipments can be produced which show:

- the planned shipments to other warehouses

- planned shipment quantities
- the number of pallets to be shipped
- shipment weight
- shipment volume

An example of a transportation planning report is shown in Table 10.8.
The information shown on the transportation planning report is invaluable for managing the operations of your transportation department, since it can be used to increase vehicle utilization. The sample report shows that the shipments planned for Week 5 are less than a full truck-load. Up to three more pallets of product, with a volume up to 505

TABLE 10.8
DRP TRANSPORTATION PLANNING REPORT

Source: National Distribution Centre   Destination: Toronto Warehouse.

WEEK	ITEM	QUANTITY	WEIGHT	CUBE	PALLETS
5	11035	2,000	15,000	100	2
5	21234	7,000	7,000	250	2
5	32215	3,200	3,200	275	3
5	32218	2,500	12,000	180	3
5	39216	6,700	1,750	270	3
5	52118	9,200	500	450	1
5	57764	50	1,000	400	1
5	72915	12	2,500	30	1
5	88789	8	75	40	1
5	91022	982	100	120	1
5	98983	7	250	80	1
			43,375	2,195	19
6	12038	300	3,000	200	1
6	18703	100	4,500	150	2
6	19703	50	200	300	2
6	23206	2	570	150	1
6	41610	5,100	4,310	150	1
6	55573	275	2,700	200	1
6	83020	100	1,500	250	2
6	88763	250	700	250	2
6	94872	505	25	300	3
			17,505	1,950	15

Truck Capacity: 45,000 pounds
2,700 cubic feet
22 pallets

cubic feet and a weight not exceeding 1,625 pounds, can be shipped on the same truck. Item number 83020, which is to be shipped in Week 6, can be shipped a week early (provided that there is sufficient inventory at the national distribution centre) to increase the utilization of the truck. The cost savings associated with a higher level of vehicle utilization will almost certainly outweigh the costs associated with shipping selected items a week early.

This type of report can also be used if the shipments planned for a particular week exceed the available shipping capacity. If, for example, the total weight of shipments planned for Week 5 totalled 47,000 pounds, the Transportation Planning Report could be used, in conjunction with DRP inventory planning reports, to identify shipments which can be delayed without affecting customer service.

Reports of planned future shipments generated using DRP logic can also be used as a basis for negotiating freight rates with common carriers or for rationalizing the use of company-owned vehicles. DRP identifies the quantity, size and timing of transportation requirements. Some companies which have implemented DRP have also found that schedules of future shipments can be used as a basis for identifying backhaul opportunities. Knowledge of when company trucks will be resupplying warehouses allows transportation planners to arrange pick-ups from vendors in the same area. Intelligent use of DRP transportation data can reduce both outbound and inbound transportation costs.

FINANCIAL PLANNING

DRP is also an effective tool for financial planning. It can be used to determine realistic estimates of inventory investment which can, in turn, be used to evaluate the effects on cash flow. Estimates of future inventory investment are traditionally based on:

- past experience
- inflation factors
- judgmental factors, to reflect changing business or market conditions

DRP can also be used to simulate the levels of inventory investment which are required to meet expected demand and satisfy customer service objectives. DRP projections of aggregate inventory balances can be converted to dollars, using the unit cost for each item. These projections are useful for determining the timing of cash outlays for purchasing additional inventory.

Volume discount schedules can also be incorporated into DRP so that purchasing decisions are evaluated, taking account of discount opportunities. Since DRP projects the timing of future orders, it's possible to determine the extent to which future orders have to be advanced in order to obtain the volumes necessary for different price breaks. The inventory carrying costs associated with ordering inventory sooner than it is actually needed can be compared to the savings that can be obtained through lower unit purchase costs. Analysis of volume discount opportunities is much more difficult if reorder points are used instead of DRP, because the timing of future orders is not known.

NETWORK ANALYSIS

DRP is an effective tool for analysing alternative distribution network strategies. It can be used to address major issues such as:

- warehouse rationalization
- changes to warehouse stocking policies
- use of alternative modes of transport
- changes in product mix

DRP determines future requirements, based on the current distribution network and company policies. Many commercially available DRP software packages allow users to create a copy of the DRP data base at any time. DRP logic can then be used to simulate the effects of any changes made to the existing network or policies.

Suppose, for example, that a company wishes to evaluate the effects of supplying one area of the country directly from a main warehouse, instead of from a branch warehouse located near the customers. This change in the distribution network will likely result in lower inventory levels and costs and lower warehousing costs, but transportation costs will be higher. DRP can be used to simulate the inventory and transportation costs for the current and proposed networks to determine the specific trade-offs involved.

DRP INTERFACE WITH MANUFACTURING

DRP is a technique for controlling distribution inventories. Many distributors, though, do some or all of their own manufacturing. Obviously DRP has to be integrated in some fashion with the system used to control manufacturing inventories.

Some organizations which do not yet see the value of integrating manufacturing and distribution activities under the umbrella of logistics view distribution only as the activity of distributing inventories which are available as the result of production. In other words, the manufacturing department determines what to produce (usually to minimize manufacturing costs) and then relies on the distribution function to find the best way to distribute these products to customers. The value of DRP to this type of organization lies in the improved ability DRP offers for determining the best allocation and distribution of products. DRP can be used to maximize customer service and minimize transportation costs. It will have little or no effect on inventory levels, if these are determined by the manufacturing group.

Organizations which recognize the importance of integrating manufacturing and distribution activities can achieve even greater benefits from using DRP. DRP requirements at the top level in the distribution network are used to drive the manufacturing system. Companies which use MRP to control manufacturing activities can use DRP to develop the manufacturing master schedule which defines what will be manufactured and when it will be completed. The expected dates when manufactured items will be available for distribution must be communicated back to DRP, so that future requirements can be calculated, taking account of the planned receipt of items already scheduled in the manufacturing process.

DRP INTERFACE WITH PURCHASING

The planned orders at the top level in the distribution network indicate when additional stock from outside the distribution network is required. For items purchased from outside suppliers, these planned orders represent purchase orders which need to be released. Since DRP also identifies the timing of future orders, these requirements can be used to:

• place purchase orders with suppliers
• evaluate volume discount opportunities
• negotiate blanket orders or contract purchasing arrangements

The expected receipt date for each purchase order needs to be communicated back to DRP, so that future requirements can be determined taking account of what has already been ordered.

FORECASTING DEMAND

The type of forecast data required for DRP is significantly different from that commonly used by organizations using reorder point logic. One of the biggest differences is that DRP requires forecasts of demand at the lowest echelons in the distribution network (i.e., the facilities which actually serve customers). Forecasts of demand at higher levels are not necessary (unless these locations also supply some customers directly) since they can be calculated based on the dependent demand of the warehouses they supply. In the example given earlier in this chapter, forecasts of customer demand were used for the warehouses at Winnipeg, Toronto and Moncton. The projection of demand at the national distribution centre was calculated by adding up the orders from the three regional warehouses.

Many organizations, however, tend to develop forecasts for only the total demand of their products. This is probably a carry-over from when distribution was viewed as a secondary activity. Forecasts of total demand would be used to control reordering from outside suppliers or from the plants. Once the stock was in the distribution network, it was up to the inventory planners or warehouse managers to allocate it as best they could. The fact that DRP requires forecasts at every location where customers are served directly may require a significant change in the procedures and policies used by an organization in developing its forecasts.

The other significant difference between forecasting for DRP versus reorder points is that DRP requires forecasts for each individual planning period, whereas using reorder points requires only a forecast of the demand over the lead time.

Referring to our earlier example, the Winnipeg warehouse has a lead time of three weeks. Using reorder points, all that is necessary is a forecast of the demand over the three-week period. In fact, most companies would set the reorder point based on some average of demand over lead time and leave it unchanged for a substantial period of time.

DRP, on the other hand, requires a forecast for each of the weekly planning periods in order to calculate when planned orders need to be released. While the difference may not appear significant if demand is constant over time, it certainly is when requirements do change over time as the result of trends or sales promotions.

The need to generate time-phased forecasts determines the type of forecasting techniques appropriate for DRP. Specifically, whatever technique is used must generate forecasts for specific future periods of time. Trends and seasonality must be taken account of. Simple forecasting methods like moving averages and basic exponential smoothing cannot be used because they don't generate time-phased forecasts and don't take account of trends and seasonality. More sophisticated techniques such as least-squares curve fitting of multi-term models are most often used, combined with local marketing information such as the timing of upcoming promotions.

Regardless of the specific technique used to generate the forecasts, the most important issues remain the same as those for reorder points:

- Forecast methods must be understood by those who use them.
- Forecast accuracy must be tracked and evaluated.

• Forecast methods should allow the input of judgemental data to account for factors outside the statistical model. The resulting effects of these "adjustments" should also be monitored and evaluated.

It cannot be over-emphasized that the success of any inventory management system is inexorably tied to the forecasts used to drive the system. More accurate forecasts will always make it easier to manage inventories. DRP, though, will always be more effective than reorder point techniques, even if forecast accuracy is low. The dynamic nature of DRP ensures that forecast errors are taken account of and used to update inventory decisions.

DRP SAFETY STOCK

According to reorder point logic, the more safety stock you can justify or afford to carry, the better the service level will be. If you increase the safety stock you carry for a particular item, the reorder point will increase by the same quantity. A higher reorder point will be reached earlier than a low one, so additional stock will be ordered sooner. With more stock in the system, it seems obvious that customer service should improve.

The use of safety stock for DRP is somewhat different. Safety stock may actually obscure what is really needed and when it is needed. Safety stock makes the allocation of available inventory more difficult. Orders from field warehouses will be composed of requirements to meet forecasted demand as well as requirements to maintain desired levels of safety stock. In the allocation example presented earlier in this chapter, we showed that only 50 units of the 150 ordered by the Toronto warehouse were needed to satisfy expected demand (see Table 10.7). The other 100 units represented requirements for safety stock and for satisfying the replenishment lot sizing rule. The order for the Moncton warehouse was caused solely by the safety stock quantity. If no safety stock was specified, an order would not have been planned. We had to determine the specific requirements for forecast demand, safety stock and lot-size before we could make an intelligent allocation decision.

Evaluating the effects of safety stock on inventory decisions, we reach two conclusions:

• A larger quantity of safety stock at any location will increase the service level at that location.
• Placing orders based on safety stock requirements will make inventory allocation decisions more difficult when demand exceeds the inventory available.

Many commercially available DRP software packages are designed to handle safety stock, yet give planners the data they need to make intelligent allocation decisions. This has been accomplished by:

- Defining alternative uses of safety stock:
  - Use safety stock only as a reference. That is, orders are not released based on safety stock requirements, but planners are informed of items which are below safety stock levels.
  - Safety stock is deducted from the current on-hand balance before projections of future balances and orders are made.
  - Orders are planned for release to arrive when the projected on-hand inventory balance falls below the safety stock level.
- Showing the lower-level requirements which cause the orders on higher levels in the network, detailing the requirements which are a function of:
  - demand
  - safety stock
  - lot-sizing rules

These features allow companies to carry safety stock to plan for a high level of service, while at the same time ensuring that planners have the data necessary to make the right decision in times of constrained supply.

Under DRP logic, demand at the levels which supply customers is assumed to be independent and forecastable. Some quantity of safety stock is probably appropriate for each item. The exact quantity depends on the forecast accuracy and the desired level of customer service. Fluctuations in lead time are usually very small since these warehouses are resupplied from feeder warehouses as opposed to manufacturing plants or outside vendors.

Demand at higher levels is dependent on the demand and ordering logic of the warehouses being supplied. Demand at the top levels in the network (i.e., the ones which are supplied from outside the distribution network) is, in turn, dependent on all the warehouses directly and indirectly resupplied. Demand in future periods is known. What is uncertain is the ability of suppliers to deliver within the agreed-on lead times.

Under DRP logic, protection is needed against forecast errors at the levels where customers are actually served. Protection is also needed against fluctuations in supply at the levels where items are sourced outside the distribution network.

The calculation of safety stock levels at the bottom echelons is often based on the historical degree of forecast accuracy and the desired service level. Some companies use a less scientific approach and either specify a fixed quantity of safety stock or express their needs in terms of a number of weeks of forecasted demand.

Safety stock levels can be specified in the same manner for the top echelons. An alternative method called "safety time" may, however, be more appropriate. Safety time is used to advance the release of orders by a specified period of time to cover fluctuations in lead time. We believe that safety time is preferable to safety stock at the top echelons, because:

- The variability is usually related to the timing, not the quantity, of the receipt.
- The use of safety time means that orders are scheduled to be received prior to when they are needed (and this protects against longer than usual lead times); safety stock, on the other hand, is essentially there all the time.

Safety time appears more philosophically sound at the top echelons, is easier to understand and results in lower overall inventory levels.

DRP LEAD TIMES

DRP uses lead times to determine when orders need to be released. Lead times must be specified for each item and for each link in the distribution network. The calculation of these lead times depends on how warehouses are resupplied.

Lead times for items which are supplied from other warehouses in the distribution network are composed of the following elements:

- the time to recognize need to schedule a shipment (i.e., planner review time)
- order processing and picking.time at the supplying warehouse
- transportation time
- time for receipt, inspection and put-away at the receiving warehouse

These elements are fairly predictable at most companies. Order processing, picking and shipment to other warehouses are usually based on regular, predictable cycles.

Lead times for items obtained from outside the distribution network (i.e., manufactured or purchased items) are usually more variable, for a variety of reasons. Order processing and picking time is the function of each of your individual suppliers and their own internal policies on customer service and inventory management. Transportation time may be more variable as well, since usually it's your suppliers who decide on the mode of transport to use. The lead times you should use for these types of items are the normal procurement or manufacturing lead times, taking account of the ordering, manufacturing and distribution cycles of your suppliers. It will probably be appropriate to carry some quantity of safety stock or to use safety time to offer a degree of protection against variability in these lead times.

DRP ORDER QUANTITIES

Order quantities must be specified for each item, at each stocking location. These order quantities can be expressed as a fixed quantity or as a specified number of weeks of future requirements. The selection of appropriate order quantities depends on how warehouses are resupplied.

For warehouses supplied by other warehouses in the company's distribution network, order quantities should be based on:

- the frequency of shipments to the warehouse
- quantities required for efficient materials handling (e.g., carton or pallet)

Order quantities should normally be in multiples of cartons or pallets to maximize materials-handling productivity, and must be large enough to cover demand over the period of time until the next shipment is received. Order quantities which are larger than necessary will draw excessive stocks out to the field warehouses, and may adversely affect customer service at other stocking locations.

If we try to use the basic EOQ formula to calculate order quantities for branch replenishment, we have to estimate the cost of placing an order for replenishment. Although this cost is difficult to estimate, it is probably small. All of the main cost elements are essentially fixed costs. We have to have planners, pickers and receivers on staff, and their work-load doesn't change much if we ship one pallet a week instead of two pallets every other week. Transportation volumes don't change either; we just have a larger mix of items on a particular shipment. A small cost to place an order will result in a small EOQ, which supports the rough guideline we presented earlier: replenishment quantities for field warehouses should be as small as possible, yet large enough to achieve materials-handling economies.

Order quantities for items at the top echelons which are obtained from outside the distribution network should be based on:

- procurement cycles
- normal package quantities
- ordering costs versus holding costs
- volume discount opportunities

We'll review each of these in turn.

First of all, order quantities must be at least as large as the expected demand at the top echelon over the procurement cycle. As an example, if an item is manufactured at a company plant and is produced only once a month, the order quantity must be at least as large as one month's expected demand.

Second, order quantities should obviously be in multiples of standard pack sizes or manufacturing run quantities.

Third, the trade-offs between ordering costs and holding costs should be used as a guideline for setting appropriate order quantities.

Finally, in some situations, volume discount opportunities may make it worthwhile to order items in larger quantities and obtain price discounts which more than offset the increased costs of carrying larger inventories.

DRP PLANNING HORIZON

DRP determines the timing of orders for several periods into the future. One of the issues in implementing DRP is determining the length of planning horizon required.

The planning horizon must be at least as long as the total cumulative lead time, from manufacturing or procurement at the top echelon to the receipt of items at the lowest levels in the network. Consider the following example for an item purchased from an outside supplier.

Lead time to purchase items from supplier to replenish the national distribution centre in Montreal	6 weeks
Lead time to replenish a regional warehouse in Vancouver from the national distribution centre	2 weeks
Lead time to replenish a local warehouse in Prince George from the Vancouver warehouse	1 week

The planning horizon must be at least as long as nine weeks, the total cumulative lead time. If additional inventory is required at Prince George in Week 9, it must be shipped from Vancouver in Week 8. If we project that there will be insufficient stock at Vancouver in Week 8, it must be sent from the national distribution centre in Week 6. If we project that there won't be enough stock at the national distribution centre to make the shipment, additional stock will have to be ordered from the supplier. With a lead time of six weeks, the stock must be ordered in the current week for it to be available in Prince George in Week 9. If the planning horizon was less than nine weeks, we wouldn't be able to react soon enough to ensure that additional stock is available when it is required.

Many companies which use DRP use a planning horizon which is substantially longer than the total cumulative lead time for particular items. Longer planning horizons are useful for estimating longer-term requirements for inventory investment, warehouse space and capital equipment. Estimates of longer-term procurement requirements may also be useful for negotiating blanket orders and systems contracts with suppliers.

DRP ACTION MESSAGES

Commercially available DRP software packages identify special conditions which inventory planners should review. These conditions are reported to planners via action messages which are printed each time the DRP planning process is run. Examples of the conditions which are typically reported to planners are shown below and are ranked in order of decreasing priority.

- Currently out of stock — no outstanding orders
- Currently out of stock — expedite outstanding order
- Projected out of stock within lead time — no order outstanding
- Projected out of stock within lead time — expedite outstanding order
- Below safety stock
- Projected below safety stock within lead time
- Release order now
- De-expedite scheduled due in
- Inventory exceeds XX weeks of supply
- No action necessary

Action messages focus planner attention on the items about which decisions need to be made. Many of the messages have a timing element to them, because DRP is a time-phased inventory planning system.

FIRM PLANNED ORDERS

The timing of planned orders and receipts is updated each time the DRP planning process is run. This recalculation of requirements ensures that supply is kept in tune with demand, taking account of the differences between forecasted and actual demand.

As part of the replanning process, DRP identifies shipments which need to be advanced to ensure stock availability and those which can be safely delayed without affecting customer service. At times, it may be appropriate to lock in the timing of planned shipments so that they won't be rescheduled the next time DRP is run. This is usually handled by designating orders as "firm planned orders." Examples of situations where firm planned orders would be used include:

- firming up transportation schedules to achieve a high level of vehicle utilization
- planning stock buildups necessary because of planned shut-downs for vacations or retooling
- shipping less than normal lot-sizes to warehouses because of limited stock availability

The quantities and timing of firm planned orders are left unchanged when DRP schedules are updated.

DRP SOFTWARE

The availability of computer software packages for DRP is still limited. There are only a few suppliers of DRP packages that run on mainframe computers or minicomputers. Three of these are:

- American Software
- Cullinet — DMS
- MSA

These packages typically come complete with modules for forecasting, inventory management and DRP. Some have additional modules for order processing and warehousing which can be integrated with the DRP modules. The costs of these packages range from about $100,000 to $300,000, depending on the modules purchased.

A small number of DRP packages are available for microcomputers. The practicality of using microcomputer-based packages depends on the number of items, the number of stocking locations, and the manner in which inventory balances at regional and branch warehouses can be communicated back to the computer which does the DRP replanning. The use of microcomputers will become more prevalent as their networking capabilities are improved.

The limited number of commercially available packages and their relatively high cost has led many companies to consider developing their own DRP systems. The high cost and risks associated with custom development have prevented many organizations from implementing DRP. Over the next three to five years, however, we can expect to see a dramatic increase in the number of DRP packages available for distributors.

CANDIDATES FOR DRP

Virtually any organization with inventory can benefit from the use of DRP. The benefits, though, will clearly be more significant for some types of businesses.

In general, the benefits of using DRP will be more significant given:

- high customer service requirements
- a multi-echelon distribution network

Examples of the types of businesses which have successfully implemented DRP include:

- grocery products
- dairy products
- building supplies
- hardware items
- electrical supplies
- plumbing supplies
- maintenance supplies
- oil companies

The way in which DRP is implemented depends on the characteristics of the particular business. In the grocery business, for example, the planning periods are normally expressed in days instead of weeks. Companies using DRP to control maintenance inventories, on the other hand, may use a planning horizon of several years because of items with long lead times. While the ways in which DRP is implemented in various organizations may be quite different, the issues and potential benefits are similar.

BENEFITS OF DRP

In the previous sections of this chapter, we've described the significant benefits which can be achieved by using DRP, including:

• lower inventories
• better allocation of inventory
• higher levels of customer service
• lower transportation costs
• comprehensive evaluation of purchase volume discount opportunities
• network simulation and evaluation capability

Companies which have implemented DRP have characteristically achieved inventory reductions of 10%-30%, improvements in customer service of 5%-10% and reductions in transportation costs of about 5%-15%. Use these rough percentages to determine the potential cost reduction opportunities for your organization, and see if you can afford not to take a closer look at DRP.

Direct Product
Profitability (DPP)

INTRODUCTION

Every so often, a new concept, technique or management tool comes along that has a major influence on how we do business. Direct product profitability (DPP) is being heralded in such terms. The Canadian Grocery Distributors Industry devoted its entire midwinter conference in 1986 to it. The Food Marketing Institute (FMI) has helped to develop a unified DPP model for the entire industry, and *Canadian Grocer* magazine endorses DPP as the best management tool of the 1980s.

WHAT IS DPP?

DPP is a highly sophisticated decision support tool designed to calculate the real costs and profitability of distributing each individual product item for the manufacturer, through all the distribution activities (transportation, handling, storage, order processing, etc.) to the final customer.

DPP is defined as the net profit contribution from the sale of a product, after direct allowances and other discounts are added and all direct costs of distribution are subtracted from the gross margin.

DPP = An item's gross margin + discounts and allowances
   − direct distribution costs

Figure 11.1 illustrates the general DPP formula. This formula is used in Table 11.1 to develop the DPP for a typical grocery product item. This

FIGURE 11.1
DPP FORMULA FOR EACH ITEM (SKU)

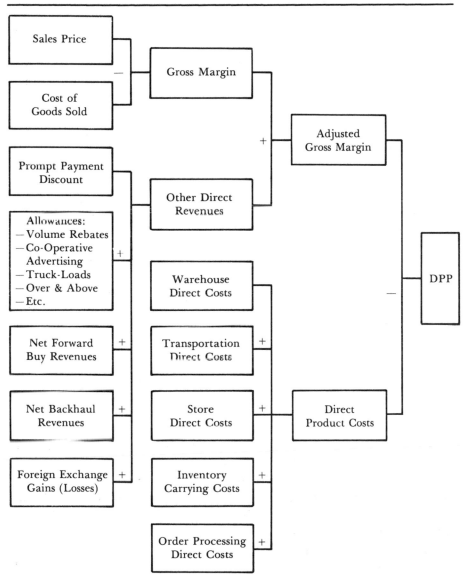

example shows how DPP provides a more accurate guide to an item's profitability than the traditional gross margin assessment. The item appears to have a favourable adjusted gross margin of 24%. However, following a DPP assessment, the profit contribution is found to be only 2%. Armed with this information, management can seek ways of improving the item's profitability by either reducing costs (e.g., better handling methods, lower inventory levels) or improving adjusted gross margins

TABLE 11.1
DPP CALCULATION
(DEVELOPING DPP FOR AN INDIVIDUAL ITEM)

	DOLLARS PER CASE
Retail Price	$20.00
Cost	16.00
Gross Margin	4.00 or 20%
Plus Discounts and Allowances:	
Payment discount	0.30
Merchandising allowance	0.40
Backhaul allowance	0.15
Total allowance	0.85
Adjusted Gross Margin	4.85 or 24%
Minus Direct Distribution Costs:	
Warehouse space	0.10
Warehouse handling	0.45
Warehouse inventory expense	0.20
Transportation to stores	0.15
Retail space costs	0.85
Retail handling	1.40
Retail inventory expense	1.30
Total direct product costs	4.45
DPP =	$ 0.40 or 2%

[e.g., lower purchase price, higher direct revenues, increased retail price (if not governed by competitive pressures)].

Thus, DPP provides management with a tool to highlight which items must be concentrated on in order to improve profitability. In addition, the detailed distribution information available from the DPP model provides valuable information to help identify potential distribution improvement opportunities.

Some retailers are realizing added profit of up to 2% of sales through the use of DPP.

WHO IS USING DPP?

DPP is already being used by many companies. In a 1986 Touche Ross survey of 550 food trade firms, 27% of the responding manufacturers and 17% of the retailers said they used it. These companies include leaders in the industry such as Steinberg, Safeway, Procter and Gamble, General Foods and Heinz.

Department store chains have used DPP models to make merchandise routing decisions, i.e., which products should be shipped to the stores directly from the suppliers and which should be distributed via a distribution centre. These stores include Miracle Mart, Simpsons, The Bay, Woolworth and Beaver Lumber. DPP models are now being developed for the drug industry and have been used by Hy & Zel's (a Toronto drug chain), Bi-Lo in Mauldin, S.C., and Tom Thumb Supermarkets in Dallas.

Over the next few years, other industries are likely to develop their own DPP models.

WHAT ARE THE APPLICATIONS?

DPP is already being used extensively by leading grocery and drug manufacturers, wholesalers, distributors and retailers as a support tool to improve profitability. Typical applications are listed below.

1. *Focus on profitable items.* DPP identifies which items are contributing most to the bottom line. Figure 11.2 shows a merchandising matrix based on a DPP assessment of different products. The DPP information allows man-

FIGURE 11.2
DPP MERCHANDISING MATRIX

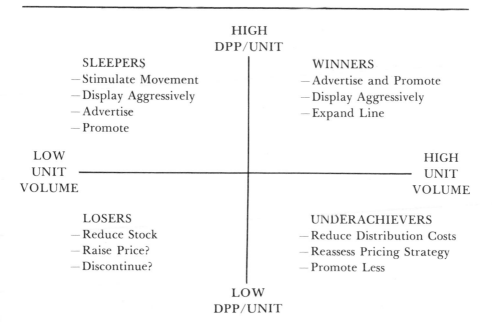

agement to develop strategic plans based on an item's current or potential profitability.

2. *Item elimination.* DPP identifies which items are losing money. DPP can then be used to simulate alternative strategies to either reduce costs or increase margins to turn those products around. If all else fails, these items can be red-circled for possible elimination.

However, items should not be arbitrarily eliminated. Certain items are required to round out a line or to give a good product mix. For the retailer, some products are essential as traffic builders. DPP at least indicates the cost of rounding out a product line or generating traffic.

3. *Item selection.* When adding new products to the line, a DPP assessment will determine which items will genuinely increase profits and which are marginal at best.

4. *Promotions.* Based on DPP information, high-profit items can be identified as best for promotional activities. DPP will also identify which items cannot be reduced in price without making them money-losers.

5. *Pricing.* Products which have a low or negative DPP may require a price increase. On the other hand, it may be worthwhile to reduce prices of products which have a very high DPP in order to increase sales. However, pricing decisions must also take competitors' pricing strategies into account.

6. *Shelf space allocation.* Products which have low DPP are likely to receive less shelf space at retail stores. Items with high DPP might be given more facings.

7. *Private label vs. national brand label.* DPP information allows retailers to review the merits of their private label versus national brands. Which warrants the greater shelf space? Is private label truly profitable, or merely taking sales away from a more profitable national brand — or vice versa?

8. *Product routing.* DPP models have been used extensively to identify the lowest-cost method of routing products from suppliers to stores, that is, direct-store delivery or distribution through the retailer's distribution centre.

9. *Distribution operations.* DPP models can be used to identify where high costs are incurred in the distribution chain and to simulate "what if" strategies to reduce these costs. These strategies can include:
   - cross-dock vs. storage
   - alternative handling and storage methods
   - minimum order quantities
   - alternative picking methods
   - different pallet patterns
   - private fleet vs. common carrier
   - fleet routing
   - drop trailer
   - backhauls and allowances
   - increased inventory turnover

10. *Distribution channel selection.* DPP may indicate that the cost of dis-

tributing certain items is unprofitable. However, external distributors or rack jobbers may be better equipped to distribute these items at lower cost.

11. *Packaging changes*. DPP models have been used to access the impact of changing packaging sizes and methods. As many of the distribution costs are directly related to product cube, a reduction in packaging size may allow more cases per pallet, hence improved storage and transportation cube utilization.

12. *Supplier selection*. Inbound movement from suppliers to the customer's plant, distribution centre or stores can be a significant cost element. In each case, alternative strategies can be simulated to reduce costs, including consolidation of inbound products, backhauls and even a switch to local suppliers.

13. *Full case vs. broken case*. A DPP assessment may indicate high inventory carrying costs of slow-moving items, particularly at retail store levels. Accordingly, DPP can be used to assess the trade-offs between the increased handling cost of breaking the cases at the distribution centre and shipping to stores in units vs. the cost savings from improved inventory turnover. The converse also applies.

CAN DPP BE USED BY ANYONE?

DPP can be used by all industries. There are no real drawbacks to the DPP concept. Application, however, may be another story. Although DPP provides the relevant information on which to base decisions, the ability of the decision maker to take full advantage of this information will depend on the individual's business acumen and management skills. For example, if a DPP assessment shows that a product is losing money, an obvious solution is to drop the product. However, more creative ways to improve its performance should be reviewed, such as:

- changing the distribution channel — e.g., using a distributor
- improving the distribution network and operations
- changing suppliers
- changing procurement methods
- changing the product's design or packaging
- adjusting prices
- changing marketing strategies

The use of DPP will differentiate between the average and the smart manager.

CAN WE DEVELOP A DPP MODEL?

Obtaining a DPP model is no problem. Models can quickly be developed in-house or obtained from industry associations, such as the National

Mass Retailing Institute and the Food Marketing Institute. The models are a basic spreadsheet application. All that is required is an IMB-PC or clone, a LOTUS 1-2-3 Spreadsheet, expertise in logistics, a major commitment of time and resources.

This latter requirement may become an obstacle for some companies. Yet it is of the utmost importance that the DPP project has the understanding and support of the entire top management team (President, VPs for Finance, Marketing, Operations and Distribution, etc.).

The major effort in developing a DPP model is to obtain the necessary data. Table 11.2 provides an example of the information needed to calculate the distribution costs in the retail industry, from warehouse to stores. Similar detail is required for in-store costs.

These figures show how the distribution function is broken down into each individual activity as an item moves from a retail warehouse to a store check-out counter. Each handling, storage or movement of the case incurs a cost.

In developing a DPP model, the major effort and skills are focused on developing the productivity factors, such as pallets, cases or cubic feet per hour, for each activity (receiving, put-away, replenishment, selecting, etc.). Once these factors have been evaluated, the DPP model simply multiplies the productivity factor by the cost of each activity [wage rates

TABLE 11.2
FMI SEPT. 1985 DPP MODEL WAREHOUSE COSTS

	INDUSTRY FACTORS DATA UNITS	MODEL FACTORS DATA UNITS
Wage Rate:	$22.00 $/hr	
Receive (at whse):		
Supplier Truck (unitized)	44.00 pal/hr	$0.500 $/pal
Backhaul — All (cube)	44.00 pal/hr	$0.500 $/pal
Deadpile only (case)	200.00 cs/hr	$0.110 $/case
Rail — All (cube)	33.00 pal/hr	$0.667 $/pal
Deadpile only (case)	200.00 cs/hr	$0.110/case
Addl. deadpile (weight)	5000 lb/hr	$0.004 $/lb
Move Across Dock, no put-away	22 pal/hr	$1.00 $/pal
Put-away:	12.00 pal/hr	$1.833 $/pal
Replenish:		
Cube-related	15.00 pal/hr	$1.467 $/pal
Case-related	120.00 cs/hr	$0.183 $/case
Weight-related	3000 lb/hr	$0.007 $/lb

TABLE 11.2 continued

	INDUSTRY FACTORS DATA UNITS	MODEL FACTORS DATA UNITS
Select Order by Case:		
Overall selection rate is	120 cases/hr	
Outgoing pallet driving is	10% of case selection activity	
with an average size of	65 cf/pallet	
which holds an avg of	60 cs/pallet	
Case weight accounts for	10% of avg non-cube-related hrs	
Weight of the avg case is	25 lb/case	
Cube-related portion is:		
for the first case	20.00 pal/hr	$0.017 $/cf
for other cases	15.00 pal/hr	$0.023 $/cf
Case-related portion of:	148 cs/hr	$0.149 $/case
Weight-related portion is:	3700 lb/hr	$0.06 $/lb
Load Outgoing Truck:		
Unitized	20.00 pal/hr	$0.017 $/cf
Deadpile case-related	120.00 cs/hr	$0.183 $/case
Deadpile weight-related	3000 lb/hr	$0.007 $/lb
Warehouse Space Costs:	$1.00/cf/yr of avg inventory	
Warehouse Equipment:	$0.010/cf of product moved	

Warehouse Inventory Estimates:
The average days of warehouse inventory is estimated to be
20.00 days of supply plus 10% of store inventory.
The minimum inventory is 10 days of supply, and
the maximum inventory is 30 days of supply.

Interest Rate:	15.0% per yr	0.0411% daily
Process Invoice:		
Rcv thru whse	$2.00/invc	$0.002/case
avg cases on whse invc	1000 cs/invc	
Rcv DSD or drop shipment	$2.00/invc	
avg cases on DSD invc	50 cs/invc	

Transportation from Warehouse to Store:

Deliveries to store/wk		5 del/wk	
Cost per mile driven	$3.500/mile		
Avg cubic feet per load		1050 cf of products per trip	
Avg haul distance per load		100 mi/trip	
Avg cost per cf of product			$0.333/cf

($/hour), trucking rates ($/mile or $/hour), etc.] to obtain the costs for each activity. The model then adds the cost of each activity to derive the direct product cost.

Unfortunately, very few information systems provide the level of detail needed to develop the productivity factors. Most information systems provide only global measurements, such as total warehousing costs, broken down into salaries, benefits, space and equipment costs.

Warehouse productivity measurements, for example, usually stop at warehouse costs as a percentage of sales or number of cases picked per worker-hour. They do not differentiate between the cost of storing and handling products with different dimensions or handling requirements.

To get meaningful distribution data, most companies must make a significant effort to improve their management information systems. This requires a strong commitment of both time and money.

The lack of data is indeed a set-back for DPP implementation. However, it should not prevent a company from developing a DPP model. Very few of the companies which are now using the DPP concept had adequate data when they first embarked on the project. In fact, because of the high-level focus on DPP, top management is realizing the importance of distribution. This, in turn, is leading to a greater priority for the MIS departments to concentrate on providing information systems for the distribution function.

Nevertheless, it is not advisable to wait for the MIS to provide a good distribution information system. This can take years. Instead, the relevant data can be derived from a detailed diagnostic of the distribution operations. Necessary data can be derived from observations, sampling and collecting live data over a four-to-eight-week time-frame.

HISTORY OF DPP

DPP is not new. Under many other names, DPP techniques have been used by a few progressive companies and distribution consultants for more than twenty years. However, many of the models developed were designed for a specific application and required extensive data and expensive mainframe computer support.

The recent surge of interest stems from

- food industry leaders demonstrating the improved decision-making capabilities resulting from DPP
- fierce competition forcing retailers to reduce costs
- the ability to develop DPP models on the PC which can later be developed on the mainframe

• the increased importance of logistics in the eyes of top management

Some of the early work on DPP models was undertaken by McKinsey & Co. and General Foods. They conducted one of the first DPP studies in the mid-1960s when they used DPP techniques to look at 16 products such as soap, canned tuna and breakfast cereal. This provided the first illustration of how different a DPP assessment was from the traditional gross margins.

In 1967, the National Association of Food Chains (NAFC), a predecessor to today's Food Marketing Institute (FMI) embarked on a more comprehensive project called COSMOS (Computer Optimization and Simulation Modelling for Operating Supermarkets) to illustrate how DPP could be implemented. However, the problems associated with assembling the necessary data and processing it through mainframe computers of the time proved to be too laborious for day-to-day use.

In the 1970s the Stevenson Kellogg Ernst & Whinney consulting group conducted several major distribution projects using DPP principles. These included product-routing projects for major Canadian retailers (store direct vs. cross-dock vs. warehouse) and international projects to assist countries in developing their export markets for fresh produce.

In these export market development studies, a team of marketing professionals examined the seasonal import volumes and prices of a variety of products at all potential foreign markets. At the same time, a team of agricultural and distribution experts developed the costs of farming, post-harvest handling, grading, cleaning, packing, storing, transporting and export marketing to determine the direct product costs of landing each product at each potential export market. Figure 11.3 identifies the major links and activities in the total system.

A computer program was then used to develop the direct product profitability of each product at each potential market. The products with a high DPP were identified. For each of these products the consultants then prepared production, distribution and export marketing strategies to develop the export program.

By 1984, several manufacturers had developed their own in-house DPP models to assist them with their product presentations to retailers. These models were developed with differing levels of sophistication and by people with different levels of skills and experience in distribution. Inevitably, they showed conflicting results.

At the FMI Midwinter Executive Conference, in January 1985, the FMI announced its intent to co-ordinate one unified DPP model. This was completed eight months later with the help of a number of companies, including Procter and Gamble; Cresap McCormick and Paget;

FIGURE 11.3
HORTICULTURE AS A TOTALLY INTEGRATED SYSTEM

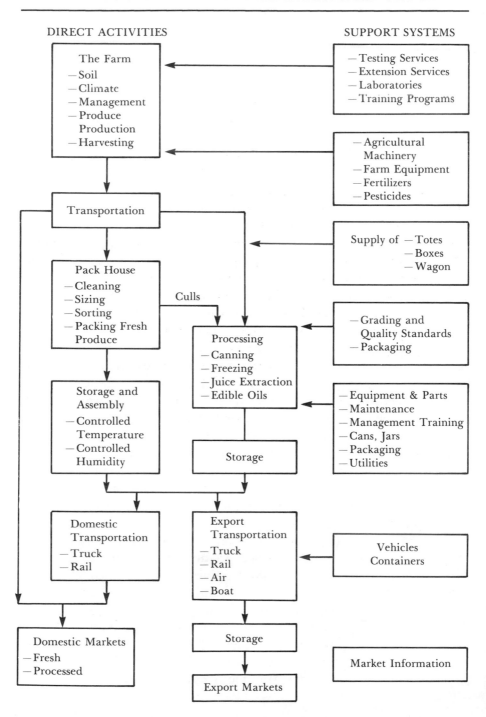

McKinsey; Touche Ross; and Willard Bishop. The end product is a complete DPP methodology for dry grocery products, a set of three technical and user manuals, DPP software designed for use on an IBM personal computer or clone, equipped with LOTUS 1-2-3 and an accompanying education program. This model is available to all members of the industry.

These unified models comprise a set of flow charts, definitions, technical manuals and PC software. The models contain no data. This was a deliberate decision, as DPP is specific to each manufacturer, distributor and retailer. Each company has its own unique productivity levels, labour rates and methods of distributing the product.

The FMI is now offering an ongoing series of educational programs for manufacturers, distributors and retailers. The DPP Council is expanding the original dry grocery model for all products, including perishables.

In 1986, the National Mass Retailing Institute developed a unified DPP model for the department chain store industry. Procter & Gamble was also working on developing a DPP model for the chain drug store industry.

DPP VS. GROSS MARGINS

Today, many management decisions are made on gut feelings and inaccurate information. This is particularly true in the case of gross margins, the traditional yardstick used to assess an item's profitability.

In the retail food industry, for example, gross margins historically equal about 21%. This covers costs and allows an adequate profit. However, when the true costs of distributing specific items can vary from 1% to 40% of an item's retail price, items with a high gross margin may actually contribute less to the bottom line than those with low gross margins. This is particularly true for low-value, bulky items, which

- take up more space in a warehouse — hence a higher % space cost
- take up more space in a truck — hence a higher % transportation cost
- take up more time in picking and handling activities — hence a higher materials-handling cost

As an example, compare the costs of distributing a coffee item and a paper towel item. The cube of the coffee item is approximately 55 cubic inches; that of the paper towel is 440 cubic inches, eight times larger.

The cost of distributing the coffee item, which sells for $3.30, may be as low as 5¢ or 1.5% of sales. The cost of distributing the paper towel, which sells for $1.75, may be as high as 35¢ or 20% of sales. When the paper towel is on promotion as an advertised special, it may sell for $1.29.

It will still cost 35¢ to handle — 27% of sales. The gross margin for both of these items may be 25%. DPP recognizes the different costs of distributing these items, and hence indicates the profitability of each item.

Gross margin decision-making can be way off base, resulting in dropping highly profitable items and promoting money-losers. For example, consider the decison-making process of two products with the following characteristics.

	Product A	*Product B*
Case size	1 cu. ft.	1 cu. ft.
Weight	15 lb.	15 lb.
Cost/case	$5	$50
Weekly sales	1,000 cases	100 cases
Sales value	$5,000	$5,000

If we look at these products from a gross sales point of view, we have two identical products. But if we take the next step and compare gross margins and average distribution costs (usually the only distribution data available)

$$\text{Average distribution costs } (\%) = \frac{\text{Total (warehouse + transport + inventory carrying costs + order processing costs, etc.)} \times 100}{\text{Total Sales}}$$

we obtain the following information for decision making.

	Product A	*Product B*
Sales value	$5,000	$5,000
Gross margin	$1,000 (20%)	$500 (10%)
Average distribution costs (3%)	$150	$150
Expected profitability	$850	$350

Based on a gross margin assessment, Product A is clearly a winner and would deserve considerably more management attention than Product B.

Under the DPP concept, the actual cost of distributing each individual product is taken into account. In the above example, let's assume that the products are distributed in a similar manner. The storage, handling and transportation costs to distribute the two identical cases will be the same — say $1.00/case. In reality, there will likely be some variance in inventory carrying costs, order processing, etc., but if the product has a high turnover, this will be relatively small.

If we now compare the products from a DPP point of view, we have the following information.

	Product A	Product B
Gross margin	$1,000	$500
Weekly sales	1,000 cases	100 cases
Distribution cost/case	$1	$1
Distribution cost	$1,000	$100
DPP	0	$400

Based on a DPP assessment, the relative profitability of the two items is reversed. Again Product A requires management attention. DPP indicates that it is time to determine whether to restructure the pricing of this item, identify lower-cost distribution methods, or even to drop Product A.

RETAIL SHELF SPACE

We have discussed how DPP is used to determine the profitability of individual items from the manufacturer's plant to the final customer. However, for retailers, shelf-space allocation is also a key concern.

For a retailer, every square foot of the store is valuable real estate. For years, retailers have measured their success on sales per square foot. With the advent of DPP models and shelf-space allocation models, retailers can now measure the sales and profitability per square foot of shelf space, and the profitability of individual items relative to the amount of space required to merchandise the product. As an example, consider the allocation of shelf space for two competing products. Table 11.3 calculates the DPP per square foot of shelf space.

TABLE 11.3
CALCULATING DPP PER SQUARE FOOT OF SHELF SPACE

	COST PER CASE	
	ITEM A	ITEM B
Gross margin	$10.00	$8.60
Plus discounts and allowances	1.00	.90
Equals adjusted gross margin	11.00	9.50
Less direct product costs	6.00	4.00
Equals DPP	5.00	5.50
Multiplied by cases per week	5	4
Equals DPP per week	$25.00	$22.00
Divided by shelf space (sq. ft.)	2.0	1.0
Equals DPP per week per square foot of shelf	$12.50	$22.00

While Item A appears to be more profitable based on gross margins, DPP indicates a similar but slightly lower profitability than Item B — $5.00 versus $5.50.

From a retailer's point of view, another major consideration is the profitable use of valuable shelf space. Item A is generating far less profit per square foot of shelf space. Based on this information, a merchandiser may well cut back the shelf space of Item A to one square foot and possibly introduce a new competing item in the space vacated. This will likely hurt the sales of Item A, but generate more sales and profit for the store.

Several commercial software programs are currently available to the retailer. The major systems are Spaceman, Apollo, Sage-AccuSpace and Spacemat. DPP models are now being used by retailers to make crucial merchandising decisions, including

- item selection
- pricing
- promotion
- shelf-space allocation

They are also being used to identify alternative materials-handling methods to reduce costs and improve profit. For example, several suppliers and grocery retailers are introducing prebuilt displays, which can be moved directly to the retailer's selling floor without handling individual items.

To market their products successfully, manufacturers need to understand how a retailer thinks, how the merchandiser's performance is measured, and how a merchandiser measures suppliers. Progressive manufacturers are using DPP as a selling tool to demonstrate to retailers how they can increase their profitability. These companies are in a better position to demonstrate the profitability of each of their items to the retailer. This results in more items accepted, more facings for existing items, better shelf locations and more promotions accepted. Figure 11.4 shows an advertisement by Frito-Lay.

More and more retailers and manufacturers are applying DPP. Others will be forced to adopt DPP in order to remain competitive. In a 1987 survey by Touche Ross, 100% of all manufacturers who were approached plan to implement DPP within the next four years.

IMPLEMENTING THE DPP CONCEPT

The following check-list outlines a step-by-step approach to implementing the DPP concept. The key work-steps are to

FIGURE 11.4

You guessed it. Frito-Lay. Our Direct Store costs of warehousing, transportation, handling

Nobody knows more about making Direct Product Profit pay off for you than Frito-Lay. Our Direct Store Delivery System maximizes your DPP on snack items by eliminating costs of transportation, warehousing and in-store handling. We do everything for you. The only time you touch Frito-Lay snacks is when you ring up the sale. And our fast-selling line multiplies the high DPP with more turns per year than most other items in your store.

Frito-Lay has conducted more in-depth research on Direct Product Profitability than any other vendor—and we've taken DPP that important extra step: Helping you use DPP to add new profits to your bottom line.

Frito-Lay's Total Snack Program makes DPP work even harder.
You know Frito-Lay products deliver high DPP. But so do many other direct store delivered items. What makes Frito-Lay

products so outstanding is the way our Total Snack Program helps you maximize snack profits:

1. By proper space allocation for Frito-Lay's high DPP products.
2. By displaying according to a proven national pattern.
3. By locating secondary and promotional displays in high traffic areas.
4. By supporting Frito-Lay snack sales with ad features and price reductions during promotional periods.

Your Frito-Lay representative will design a Total Snack Program tailored to your stores. We have the knowledge, experience, and creativity to help you produce important increases in overall store profit. Contact your local Frito-Lay representative. Let's get started today.

Delivery System eliminates your inventory and unsaleables.

Frito-Lay is a registered trademark of Frito-Lay Inc.

- gain full understanding of DPP concepts
- obtain top management commitment
- form project team
- review current distribution operation
- acquire/develop DPP software
- obtain necessary data
- validate model
- run DPP model
- implement DPP program

We comment on each of these steps below.

GAIN FULL UNDERSTANDING OF THE DPP CONCEPT

The first step is to fully understand the DPP concept and to assess the potential benefits it can bring to your company. This can be acquired by reading literature and articles on DPP and attending DPP conferences. More in-depth knowledge can be obtained by contacting managers from other companies that have implemented DPP to discuss the actual benefits realized and the recommended ways of implementing a DPP model. Most managers are very pleased to share this information.

OBTAIN TOP MANAGEMENT COMMITMENT

DPP requires a major commitment in time and resources to obtain the necessary data, to conduct DPP evaluations and to simulate alternative marketing and distribution strategies. Accordingly, it is essential that top management in each department (logistics, marketing, sales, finance, procurement, etc.) fully support the project and are willing to divert their staff's time and effort to the DPP model development and subsequent DPP analysis and decision making.

This generally requires a DPP champion within the company to conduct a pre-implementation assessment of the time and costs of developing a DPP model and the potential benefits to be gained by the company from implementing the DPP concept. The DPP concept must then be "sold" to top management through the use of well-prepared presentations to demonstrate its value to the company.

FORM PROJECT TEAM

Many companies do not have staff available in-house with the necessary skills and experiences to develop the DPP concept. Even employees with the necessary set of skills are unlikely to have the time available to devote to the development of a DPP model.

Accordingly, in these cases it is worthwhile to select an outside distribution consultant to assist with the project. As a rough guideline, depending on how poor the available in-house data is, a DPP expert will likely require 30 to 50 days to identify, collate and input data into a DPP model, validate the model and run the model for a cross-section of items. At an average consulting fee of $1,000 per day, this will cost $30,000 to $50,000.

The consultant should work with a project team which includes members of the marketing, distribution and systems departments. It is essential that these internal resource people participate actively in the project and be committed to the results. It is also important to appoint a project manager who will co-ordinate the project and push it on.

REVIEW CURRENT DISTRIBUTION OPERATION

An important step is for the project team to fully understand the current distribution operations. Based on observations, interviews and data reviews, the project team needs to be familiar with all the following activities for each type of product:

- handling methods (pallet vs. loose vs. breakpack)
- storage methods (drive-in, double-deep, conventional racking, etc.)
- transportation methods (fleet, carrier, rail)
- inventory turnover
- marking activities (labels, tags, etc.)

At the end of this familiarization phase, the team should understand every individual storage, handling and transportation activity incurred by each type of product.

As a by-product from this step, following a detailed review of current activities, many project teams identify potential improvement opportunities in the current methods of distributing products.

ACQUIRE/DEVELOP DPP SOFTWARE

A DPP expert can quickly design and develop the necessary software. Alternatively, the basic spreadsheet can be obtained from such associations as the Food Marketing Institute or the National Mass Retailing Institute.

These models can be modified subsequently to suit a company's individual requirements.

OBTAIN NECESSARY DATA

This is the most crucial part of the project and generally the most time-consuming. Chances are the necessary information will not be readily available. Accordingly, every single distribution activity — receiving, put-away, replenishing, selecting, packing, shipping, etc. — must be examined to develop the productivity factors. For example, how long does it take to unload a typical trailer (1) palletized or (2) hand-bombed? This information can be obtained from collecting live data for a sample of trailers. It may take an average of 44 minutes to unload 22 pallets (2 minutes per pallet) and 4 hours to unload 960 loose cases (15 seconds per case). When multiplied by the labour rate, say $20/hour, the receiving cost per pallet or case can be calculated quickly: 67 cents/pallet, and 8 cents/case hand-bombed. If there are 45 cases on a pallet, the cost of receiving a palletized load will be 1.5 cents/case.

In a similar manner, inventory carrying cost will be derived from an item's turnover performance multiplied by the inventory carrying cost (10% to 18% to cover financing, insurance, damage, obsolescence, etc.).

Thus, if the purchase cost of a case is $20, the turnover for that item is 10 turns and the inventory carrying cost is 15%, the inventory cost per case will be $20/10 × 15% or 30 cents.

Storage costs are generally a function of a product's cube, the number of turns and space costs. Transportation can be a function of either a product's cube or weight, depending on its density. For example, consider a typical tandem-axle trailer with a practical cube utilization of 2,500 cubic feet and a maximum legal pay-load capacity of 45,000 lb. If the weight of the pay-load when using the full 2,500 cubic feet is less than 45,000 lb., then cube information is the deciding factor. In this example, an average load density of more than 18 lb./cubic foot will change the function from cube- to weight-related.

This sort of productivity information is required for each activity and for each type of product handled. In addition, information on product cube, handling methods, turnover, etc. is required for each individual item. Figure 11.5 shows a typical item profile sheet.

VALIDATE MODEL

Once the productivity factors have been entered into the DPP model, the model must be validated to check for possible errors. This is achieved by running the model for a few selected items with different values and cube and turnover characteristics. The results must then be carefully scrutinized to identify unusual results which may highlight apparent errors. Having investigated each anomaly and adjusted all the necessary formulae, the model is ready for DPP application.

RUN DPP MODEL

As a first pass, it is usually best to start small and build up applications as confidence grows with experience. Initially, select a few items, such as low-value, high-cube (hence higher-than-average distribution cost) or

FIGURE 11.5
ITEM PROFILE SHEET

Product name [   ]   Brand size [   ] ml.

UPC [   ]

COST OF GOODS

List case cost [   ] $

Adj. to case cost [   ] $

C.U. retail price [   ] $

Discount terms [   ] %

Net days credit [   ]

CASE RELATED INFO

Case pack [   ]

Case cube [   ] m³

Case weight [   ] kg

No. shelf trays/case [   ]

Cases/incoming pallet [   ]

WAREHOUSE RECEIVING

Receive by: Arrive as: Replenish method:

1 Truck   1 Unitized   1 Unitized

2 Backhaul   2 Deadpile   2 By case

3 Rail   [   ] Repalletized   0 NA
                 (# cases on whse pallet)

4 Cross dock

0 NA   0 NA

DIMENSIONS

Shelf depth [   ]

Shelf height [   ]

Package width [   ]

Package depth [   ]

Package height [   ]   (cm)

STORE RECEIVING

Receiving type: Receive as: No. cases in DSD or drop shipment:

1 From whse   1 Unitized

2 Drop shipment   2 Deadpile   [   ] (0=NA)

3 Backrm   0 NA

4 Aisle ⎤ DSD

5 Shelf ⎦

STORE HANDLING

Pricing required?   Stocking method:

0 No   0 Unit

1 Yes   1 Tray

          2 Dump bin

          3 Pegboard

SHELF STACKING

Layover OK?   Max. stack height:

0 No   [   ] (packages)

1 Yes

MANUFACTURER'S SALES

Total Can. annual case vol. [   ] (thousands)
(Manufacturers only)

% sold in grocery stores [   ] %

RETAIL SALES

Total chain avg wk CASE vol. [   ]

% distribution (avg % ACV) [   ] %

% sold off shelf only [   ] %

- - - - - - OR - - - - - -

Weekly UNIT sales per store [   ]

INVENTORY

Store deliveries/week [   ]
(for DSD products)

Avg STORE inventory [   ] (days)

Avg WHSE inventory [   ] (days)

SHELF PACKOUT

Max. units/facing width [   ]

Number of facings [   ]

- - - - - - OR - - - - - -

Total packout [   ]

FMI UNIFIED DPP METHOD DATA FORM

Collected by: _____   Date: _____

low-margin items, whose profitability is already suspect. Analyse the results by examining the individual distribution components, and identify where the high costs are incurred. Can these activities be simplified or eliminated — for example, by shipping direct from the supplier's plant to customers to avoid high handling costs at a distribution centre? The model should then be rerun to identify the effect of any potential changes to the distribution activities.

The DPP model should then be used for other applications, such as those discussed earlier in this chapter. These will undoubtedly result in better decision-making capabilities and lower distribution costs.

IMPLEMENT DPP PROGRAM

Having successfully applied DPP, the results and applications should be presented to top management to ensure their continued support. The next step is to develop DPP reports for use as a management tool to complement or replace gross margin information.

It is also important to train potential users, such as buyers, merchandising managers and distribution personnel, in the various applications of DPP. Finally, DPP should be continually revised and improved to reflect changes in the distribution parameters arising from productivity improvements.

DPP CASE EXAMPLES

DPP is already being used extensively by leading manufacturers, wholesalers, distributors and retailers. Procter and Gamble makes a DPP assessment for every new product launched to ensure that it can be efficiently and profitably distributed. Roy Kendall, president of Procter and Gamble in Canada, has said that P & G is 100% committed to the idea of DPP. The company will support any project that reduces the overall cost of the entire system from plant to consumer, even if the needed changes increase P & G's own costs.

In this section we outline a few DPP applications in industry.

ITEM SELECTION

Hannaford Brothers Co. in Maine used DPP to assess whether the stores should take on a generic potato chip, which it could price substantially lower than the national brand. The national brand was selling for $2.09 per bag; the generic brand could be priced at $1.39. A DPP assessment showed a DPP for the national brand of 53 cents per bag and a DPP for the generic product of only 1 cent per bag. This was largely due to the fact that the national brand was serviced by the supplier's sales representatives, who looked after tasks like stocking shelves, whereas with the generic brand, all handling was done by store personnel. Following the DPP assessment, Hannaford decided not to take on the generic potato chip line.

DISTRIBUTION CHANNELS

A Procter and Gamble warehousing manager identified the 1,000 most costly items to handle — those with low volume, poor cube utilization, etc. — and obtained a bid from a wholesaler to distribute those items. As a result, the operation became more efficient and the company realized a major net savings.

PACKAGING

Procter and Gamble used DPP to assess the benefits of changing from glass to plastic bottles and to redesign the shape of the Crisco Oil bottle. The result was a lighter, more cube-efficient package that generates a saving of 32 cents per case for the average retailer.

Procter and Gamble redesigned the Downy fabric softener bottle to permit eight instead of six to fit into a case, thereby reducing handling costs through the distribution chain. This saved 48 cents per case. Similarly, Tide detergent was reformulated to make it more dense, so that the same cleaning power could be packed into less volume. This saved 26 cents a case in trade handling costs.

PRODUCT ROUTING

Several department store retailers have used DPP models to identify which products should be distributed through the central warehouse, which should be cross-docked at strategic accumulation locations and which should be shipped direct from suppliers to stores. Tables 11.4 and 11.5 summarize the major distribution cost elements for two items, one a low-value, bulky item and the other a high-value-per-cube item.

Table 11.4 shows that direct shipment of the lampshade incurs greater storage and handling costs at the store level. However, in spite of supplier allowances for cross-dock and warehouse routing, the additional costs of warehousing, inventory and transportation are exorbitantly more expensive than store-direct.

Table 11.5 shows the benefit of distributing a high-value, low-cube item through a central warehouse. The major saving in this particular example is the inventory carrying cost at the store. For many stores, a full case quantity of this product could amount to well over one year's stock. By shipping through a central warehouse, the outer case can be opened

TABLE 11.4
PRODUCT ROUTING COST COMPARISON: PRODUCT 1

Product	Lampshade
Characteristics	Big, bulky
Item value	$2/cu. ft.
Annual volume	$13,000
Supplying location	Montreal

	DISTRIBUTION OPTIONS		
COST ELEMENTS	STORE-DIRECT ($)	CROSS-DOCK ($)	WARE-HOUSE ($)
Warehouse space	—	300	1,650
Warehouse handling	—	900	1,400
Warehouse inventory	—	100	500
Store inventory	650	650	450
Store handling	300	150	150
Transportation	400	950	950
Distribution allowance	—	(650)	(1,050)
TOTAL	1,350	2,400	4,050
% Cost Price	10.4	18.5	31.2

and the products shipped in units to each store on an as-required basis.

Following the results of these product routing studies, the retailers identified which items should be stocked in the central warehouse and which items should be distributed store-direct. These studies generally indicate that high-value, low-cube items should be distributed via the warehouse and low-value, bulky items distributed vendor-direct.

PRICING, MERCHANDISING AND DISTRIBUTION

A national Canadian retailer was having difficulty making a profit. In particular, the pricing strategy seemed out of line vis-à-vis competitors. Although the retailer was offering the lowest prices on certain items, it was not able to compete on many other items, where the competition was seemingly selling the goods at below cost.

In an effort to improve productivity and reduce costs, the company commissioned a study to develop a DPP model to identify the optimal product routing method. As a by-product the study also highlighted the apparent pricing anomalies.

TABLE 11.5
PRODUCT ROUTING COST COMPARISON: PRODUCT 2

Product	Mastermind game
Characteristics	High-value, low-cube
Item value	$60/cu. ft.
Annual volume	$70,000
Supplying location	Toronto

	DISTRIBUTION OPTIONS		
COST ELEMENTS	STORE-DIRECT ($)	CROSS-DOCK ($)	WARE-HOUSE ($)
Warehouse space	—	50	300
Warehouse handling	—	700	1,750
Warehouse inventory	—	550	2,350
Store inventory	7,100	3,550	2,350
Store handling	1,500	800	800
Transportation	550	550	550
Distribution allowance	—	(2,100)	(7,100)
TOTAL	9,150	4,100	1,000
% Cost Price	13.1	5.9	1.4

The company had based pricing decisions on purchase cost minus allowances plus distribution costs. Distribution costs were based on the cost of operating the central distribution centre in Toronto and transporting the merchandise to stores in each province. The total warehouse cost amounted to 12% of the purchase price. Transportation costs varied by province, ranging from 2% for all Ontario stores to 11% of purchase price for all stores in British Columbia. Thus, using gross margin thinking, all products, regardless of cube, value, or handling method, were allocated a distribution charge of 14% of purchase price for Ontario stores and 23% for all British Columbia stores.

The DPP project offered some interesting insights into the problems the company was experiencing in its pricing dilemma. Table 11.6 illustrates the difference between the former distribution charges and the actual distribution costs for three products with differing values per cube. Under the former allocation of distribution costs, the true cost of distributing Item A (low value per cube) is understated by 20% for Ontario stores and 41% for B.C. stores.

TABLE 11.6
COSTS AS % OF PURCHASE PRICE

	ONTARIO STORES	B.C. STORES
AVERAGE DISTRIBUTION CHARGES (ALL PRODUCTS)		
Warehouse	12%	12%
Transportation	2%	11%
Total distribution charge	14%	23%
DPP COSTING		
Item A $5/cu. ft.		
Warehouse	29%	29%
Transportation	5%	36%
	34%	64%
Item B $15/cu. ft.		
Warehouse	12%	12%
Transportation	2%	14%
	14%	26%
Item C $50/cu. ft.		
Warehouse	3.5%	3.5%
Transportation	0.5%	4.0%
	4.0%	7.5%

While using these former distribution charges to compute profitability, these items, on paper, appeared profitable. In fact the retailer had used these types of items to undercut the prices of all competitors and, by so doing, had gained an inordinately large share of the market on these items. In reality, the retailer priced the product well below the actual costs. The more of these items were sold, the greater the drain on profits.

Item B represents the average price/cube of products stocked. Here average distribution costs provide a reasonable guideline.

Item C represents the high-value-per-cube item. The former method of computing distribution costs overstates the actual distribution costs by 10% in Ontario and 15.5% in B.C. Accordingly, the retail prices for these items tended to be higher than those of the competitors, and turnover was much lower.

Having analysed the results of the DPP model, the company made some major changes to improve productivity, including:

- Calculating store retail margins by item, based on the more accurate DPP-computed landed cost as opposed to a global-average landed cost.
- Repricing many items at the retail stores to become more competitive on high-value items and to eliminate losses on low-value items. This led to increased sales.
- Adding selected high-value, low-cube items to the warehouse, leading to reduced overall distribution and retail costs.
- Eliminating many low-value, high-cube items from the warehouse and arranging for store-direct shipments. This also reduced overall distribution and retail costs. In addition, the warehouse space saved was measured in acres! The company relocated to a smaller, lower-cost warehouse.
- Making greater use of rack jobbers to serve stores with high-volume, low-value items which incurred excessive handling costs when distributed through the central warehouse.
- Improving buying and inventory-management techniques, resulting in a higher service level and improved inventory turnover.
- Introducing a cross-dock operation, particularly for promotional items. This also reduced distribution and retail costs.
- Identifying opportunities to streamline the transportation and warehousing operation, resulting in savings of more than $2 million.
- Selecting suppliers based on DPP information. Thus more local suppliers were used to minimize transportation costs, particularly for high cube items.
- Using DPP in item-selection decisions and subsequently in developing the most appropriate routing decisions from suppliers to the stores.

Following the DPP study, the retailer enjoyed considerable success, as measured by:

- increased market share
- increased sales volume
- reduced distribution costs
- improved service levels
- improved inventory turnover

And last, but not least, the company became highly profitable.

CHAPTER 12

Planning for More Profitable Logistics

INTRODUCTION

> Predetermination of results is the main characteristic of the modern method. The acceptance of the haphazard is the main characteristic of the old method. . . .
>
> Predetermination of results is based on scientific certainties modified by experience.[1]

Profitable logistics doesn't just happen. It must be planned. This implies:

- a clear statement of the objective of the logistics system
- a number of optional ways of realizing the objective
- estimating the resources for each option
- evaluating each option in terms of the resources consumed and the attainment of the objective

In this chapter we explore how the planning process is executed in a number of different situations. Most of the emphasis is on planning the network. The development of operating rules has been covered in other chapters such as those dealing with inventories and with transportation.

However, because of the interrelationship shown in Figure 12.1, the operating rules cannot be ignored. Nor can the efficiency with which operations are carried out. The relationship between input and output for each element affects its costs and effectiveness relative to other elements. Low efficiency in one element would cast another element in a more favourable light. In turn, the comparison could result in a

---

[1] Harrington Emerson, *Efficiency as a Basis for Operations and Wages*, reprint of 1909 ed. (New York: Arno Press, 1980).

FIGURE 12.1

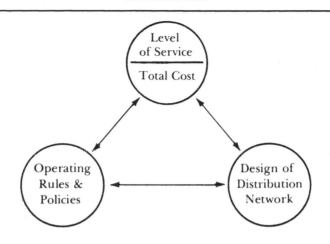

FIGURE 12.2
PLANNING FOR IMPROVEMENT — THE PROCESS

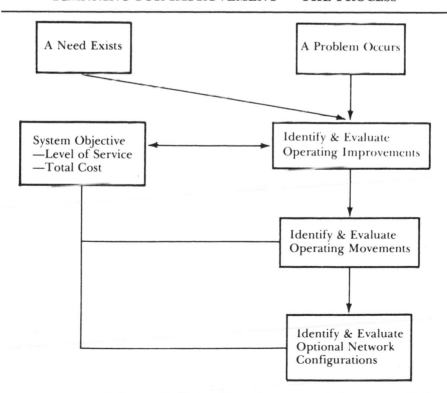

rearrangement of the network to take advantage of the more efficient component.

This interaction between operating efficiency and system effectiveness provides the basis for the planning process which is presented in this chapter (Figure 12.2).

IS THERE A NEED TO EVALUATE THE EXISTING NETWORK?

Seldom do logistics managers face the opportunity of designing a distribution network from scratch. They usually inherit an ongoing system — manufacturing facilities, suppliers, warehouses, transport fleet, order transmission system and so forth. Consequently, it is appropriate that logistics managers and senior management recognize the signals that all may not be well, that the system may need improving and/or fundamental restructuring.

Some of the more important signals are discussed below.

POOR CUSTOMER SERVICE

A logistics system should be designed to serve the market. Its elements should be designed and managed with that end in view. Consequently any indication that service to the market is inadequate or non-competitive may suggest a need to re-evaluate the system. Some of the signals that service is poor are:

• an increasing frequency of complaints from customers
• a survey of competitor's level of service
• increasing frequency of stock-outs, back orders or emergency shipments

CHANGED MARKETING GOALS

Management may decide, for any of a number of reasons, to change its marketing goals. Instead of being defensive, it may decide to become very aggressive in a particular region or distribution channel. Or, with the introduction of a new product line, the company may go for widespread distribution of its product.

Another example is seen in the case of an automotive parts manufacturer. This company had traditionally sold its products through the customary warehouse–distributor–jobber channel. However, sensing a major opportunity in the entry of mass merchandisers into the automotive parts business, the manufacturer elected to support this channel. This new channel, with its different concepts of supply and service, forced the manufacturer into a total re-evaluation of its logistics system.

CHANGED COMPETITIVE POSITION

A few years ago an offshore manufacturer of electrical and electronic hardware and systems decided to enter the Canadian lamp market. Its initial entry strategy was based on low prices and widespread availability of product. Market share increased rapidly to about 10% at the expense of the established firms. This changed competitive position forced at least one of the majors to re-evaluate its logistics network and operating policies.

Other competitive factors that might call for a similar re-evaluation include:

- change in competitor's pricing policy from FOB to delivered pricing, for example, or vice versa
- loss or acquisition of a major customer
- gradual increase, or decrease, in market share which after a number of years has become significant

EXCESSIVE INVENTORIES

What is "excessive"? Of course, there is no easy definition, but some of the indicators that might suggest a re-evaluation of the system include:

- A comparison of turnover with published industry data.
- A historical comparison of inventory-turns with past years' data.
- An analysis of the return generated by the increased investment in inventory. Many companies expect a return of 25% or more from investments in fixed assets. However, without realizing it, they frequently enjoy returns of less than 12% from the investment in inventory.

If analysis reveals, by any criterion, that inventories are excessive, it may indicate the need to re-evaluate the design of the network and/or operating rules and policies.

EXCESSIVE COSTS

Again the question might be asked — "What is excessive cost?" The answer is even more elusive than when asked of inventories. Measurement of inventories is fairly consistent across an industry — industry statistics tend to provide useful bench-marks. Measurement and reporting of logistics costs, however, show no such consistency. Experience of many industries shows a wide divergency of elements included in the costs of logistics:

- Most companies include costs of outbound transportation from plant to distribution centre.
- Many companies omit delivery costs from the final shipping point to the customer.
- Many companies include the variable costs of field warehousing; some omit the fixed costs such as rental, utilities, etc.

- Many companies omit plant warehousing and shipping costs from logistics costs.
- Inventory costs seldom appear as a component of logistics.

Because of this inconsistency, be on guard against using published comparisons unless all elements are explicitly identified.

The definition of "excessive" tends, therefore, to reflect:

- Historical trends, as a per cent of sales revenues.
- "Key" indicators which represent the dominant cost element in the logistics system. These indicators might include:
  - transportation costs — dollars per hundredweight or per cent of sales.
  - warehousing or depot costs — per order, or per hundredweight.
  - delivery costs — per order.
- Periodic comparisons based on an industry-wide cost-collection project.

On an ongoing basis the first measure, historical trends, is the most meaningful. Any significant increase in logistics costs will reduce net income. Consequently, continuous monitoring of logistics costs, as a per cent of net sales revenue, will give timely notice of a potential decrease in revenue. It will signal when costs exceed an acceptable range. This warning will be more timely than merely watching net income. This latter figure is the result of many influences — material costs, labour, overhead, utilities, etc. — so that variance in logistics costs tends to be overshadowed.

PENALTIES

Penalties — for small shipments, back orders, overtime, damage, demurrage, etc. — tend to be the micrometer which monitors the fine variances in logistics performance. Small deviations in the logistics system tend to produce relatively large variances in these indicators.

Consequently, periodic reporting and tracking of trends will give timely warning of a need to redesign the system.

NEW PRODUCT

The routine introduction of new products to replace matured products having similar characteristics, in the same market, for the same customers, is not usually of significance.

However, occasionally a product will be launched which differs fundamentally from the basic line. The difference may be:

- in the market served — food service instead of consumer, mass merchandisers instead of specialty retail stores
- in the physical characteristics of the product — its configuration, density, value, handling characteristics, perishability, life cycle

- in the nature of the demand — predictable or unpredictable, stable or volatile, steady or seasonal

For example, a manufacturer of packaged foods, nationally advertised, introduced a line of institutional food products. The requirements of institutional buyers differed from those of supermarkets and grocery chains (the traditional market). As a result, the company was obliged to re-evaluate its logistics system. A chain of distribution centres across the country became necessary in order to meet the service requirements of the new customers. Inventory policies were revised to handle the increased volatility of demand.

MERGERS OR ACQUISITIONS

Merger or acquisition is an obvious opportunity to explore potential improvements in logistics. The higher volume of goods, especially if sold through the same channels to the same or similar customers, provides a means of achieving economies of scale in transportation and warehousing. But, more relevant in many instances, the higher volume will permit more frequent, economical shipments to customers. In turn, this better customer service may be used as an effective marketing tool.

In short, a merger would normally suggest a total re-evaluation of market objectives, levels of service and total logistics costs.

CHANGE IN AVAILABILITY OF CREDIT

An essential component in managing logistics is the set of trade-offs involving inventory levels:

- inventory cost vs. customer service
- inventory cost vs. transportation
- inventory cost vs. production costs

Consequently, whenever the cost of inventory changes, the optimal balance between inventories and other elements also shifts. For this reason any material change in the cost of capital should lead to a re-evaluation of at least the operating rules and policies in the system. It is less likely that the network will need revision.

ADDITIONAL PRODUCTIVE CAPACITY

Production facilities tend to be a dominant anchor point in every logistics network. Their location and capacity have a lasting impact on the costs and effectiveness of the system.

Because of this lasting effect, every major addition to productive capacity should be based on an evaluation of expected logistics costs over the ensuing ten years or so. For some products, notably primary materials, there may be little flexibility in the choice of location for the manufacturing facility; any economic study would show the best location is close to the source of materials.

For manufactured goods the choice is not so simple. Changing economic growth rates, the emerging importance of western Canada, especially Alberta, and gradual shifts in the power and control within marketing channels all highlight uncertainties implicit in investing in capital facilities.

And of course, the same risk is present, albeit on a smaller scale, whenever small additions are made to existing facilities. Installing a new packaging line, adding to processing equipment, enlarging the shipping department — all imply the present logistics network is the most appropriate and will remain so.

A number of companies overcome the problem by having, and periodically updating, a plan of the "ideal" logistics system ten years in the future. This plan incorporates:

- Projections and estimates of the demand for the company's products in each geographic region. These documents reflect the company's marketing goals, product lines, market share, channels, etc.
- Estimates of costs of materials and of production at various levels of throughput.
- Estimates of costs of transportation and of redistribution.
- Potential "breakthroughs" in logistics practices.
- A number of optional "scenarios" wherever uncertainty exists.

Evaluation of optional locations, using these inputs, aids management to select the "best" overall configuration of the logistics network in the next decade. This configuration is then the master plan for all capital investment decisions. New plant locations are the most obvious result of such an approach. It also applies, however, to lesser investment decisions. By referring them to the master logistics plan, management is assured that all its investments are compatible with the optimal future logistics system.

RENTING WAREHOUSE SPACE

Frequently, the first indicator of an overloaded logistics system is the need to rent outside storage space. Such a decision should call for a reevaluation of the overall flow of goods from plant to consumer. This would assure management that the most effective configuration, or network, was being used.

Typical of the options that should be evaluated when considering the need for additional space are:

- changing production rules to reduce the level of inventory and, in turn, the need for space
- transferring inventory directly from the production line to field warehouses instead of using the plant warehouse as a central warehouse for all items
- revised order processing and stock replenishment procedures in order to achieve higher inventory turns and hence a lower storage requirement

Unfortunately the problem is seldom seen as part of a total system. Outside storage space is frequently acquired close to the plant or to the crowded facility. Goods are then transferred back to the original warehouse where they are assembled with other goods at the loading dock.

The transfer costs and outside storage costs are additional expenses for which little value (from the consumer's viewpoint) is received. Frequently these expenses can be eliminated or greatly reduced by a review of the total system.

NEGOTIATING UNION CONTRACTS

Contract negotiations often provide management with an opportunity to remove some of the cost-causing constraints in the logistics system. This applies especially to private trucking operations where clauses relating to overtime, drivers' schedules, etc., impede management's ability to operate the most effective system.

If management believes such constraints are adversely affecting costs or levels of service, it should calculate what the costs and/or level of service would be without the constraints. This puts a value on their removal. It provides management with the information needed to negotiate effectively. Conversely, the total system cost analysis will enable management to determine, ahead of time, the full impact of union demands.

In some cases, management must fight in order to remove constraints that reduce competitiveness and inhibit growth. As an example, Steinberg, the wholesale and retail food giant, operates a fairly traditional logistics network in the province of Quebec. A central warehouse complex in Montreal supplies the 120 stores across Quebec with grocery, produce, dairy, and frozen products.

In 1987, contract talks between management and the union, representing the warehouse and transport employees, hit an impasse. In order to successfully expand the wholesale operation, management needed changes in the restrictive union contract. Three major issues were placed on the table to obtain the necessary flexibility for growth. The union representatives refused to even negotiate these issues. When the contract expired, the union took the 1100 warehouse and transport employees out on strike.

In previous strikes, stock in the stores rapidly depleted, sales dropped drastically, and management usually succumbed to union demands, probably the reasons that the previous contracts were so restrictive.

Maintaining supplies during a strike in the province of Quebec is difficult. Quebec has a fairly unique "anti-scab" law that restricts companies from operating facilities during strikes. Whereas arrangements can be made for produce and meat to be shipped from wholesalers direct to stores, there are no grocery wholesalers large enough to supply all store demands.

In 1987 Steinberg prepared an innovative strike contingency plan, using advanced just-in-time logistics principles. Arrangements were made with each supplier to ship direct to the stores. In order to avoid the congestion of thousands of LTL shipments, a supplier consolidation program was established. Figure 12-3 illustrates the network. The stores ordered daily, using modern scanning equipment. A computerized system captured the orders, totaled them, and placed a single order to each supplier.

The suppliers picked the cumulative orders and shipped them to designated public warehouses. The public warehouses sorted the products by store and consolidated them into a single shipment for each store. This in turn eliminated the otherwise excessive congestion at store level had each supplier shipped direct to the stores.

The just-in-time logistics strategy resulted in significant benefits for the suppliers, Steinberg, and Steinberg's customers. The suppliers achieved economies over the alternative direct delivery to the stores:

• Receiving one consolidated order for all stores instead of 120 individual orders, hence lower order processing and accounting costs.
• Picking one order instead of 120 individual orders, hence lower warehousing costs.
• Consolidating store deliveries with other suppliers to achieve truckload shipments instead of high cost less than truckload shipments.
• Eliminating congestion at the stores, hence reducing excessive waiting time.

As discussed in Chapter 2, key customer service activities include reliability and flexibility to handle unusual situations. The grocery suppliers performed admirably. They gave the necessary support to maintain a continued supply to the stores. Whereas normal lead times are five to ten days, the suppliers provided a special two-day lead time service as required by the contingency plan.

The public warehouses and carriers provided the suppliers the necessary distribution service to meet the tight lead time requirements of the stores. Each day, up to 65,000 cases were delivered to the public warehouses, sorted, and delivered to the stores. At the end of each day, the

FIGURE 12.3

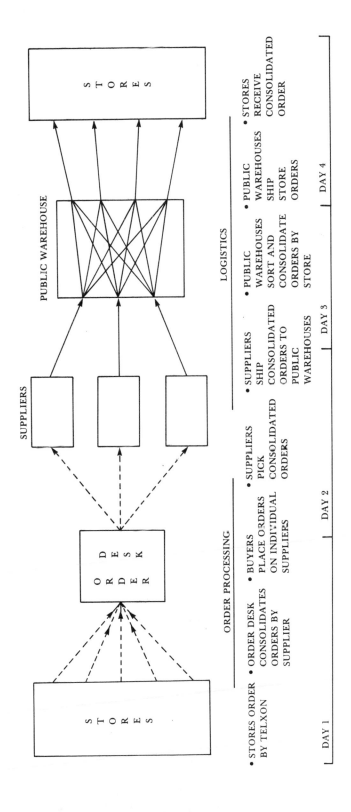

floors of the public warehouses were empty. The service provided by these companies was exceptional. As may be expected in such an operation, every one of Murphy's laws, and more, occurred. Yet due to the professionalism of the staff involved, all problems were resolved, and the store lead times were met.

The just-in-time operation grew more powerful on a daily basis. Suppliers got used to the short lead times, the public warehouse staff became highly experienced in the custom designed cross dock operations, and the carriers became familiar with the routes and access to each store. Store shelves remained full, and most customers never even realized there was a strike. The contingency plan could have been maintained forever. Fortunately, however, after four weeks, Steinberg labour relations team successfully negotiated a new contract, which was ratified. The new contract provides Steinberg with a greater flexibility to expand its wholesaling operation across Quebec.

REVISION IN FREIGHT RATE SCHEDULES

Transportation costs appear in most of the trade-offs in the design of the system and its operating rules:

- inventory costs vs. transportation in the selection of branch stocking rules and the mode of transportation
- transportation costs vs. order frequency in establishing customer service policies
- transportation costs vs. warehousing costs in determining the number and location of stocking points and distribution centres

Consequently, whenever transportation costs change significantly, it is essential to re-evaluate the performance of the entire system.

A survey was conducted of shippers shortly after the energy crisis in 1973. It indicated that some 63% of them had critically evaluated their logistics system to ensure they still provided the most appropriate balance between costs and level of service.

APPARENT UNDERUTILIZATION OF LABOUR, CAPITAL OR EQUIPMENT

An efficient, effective distribution system should represent the best balance between human capital and material resources. To the extent that any are significantly underutilized, the system is out of balance. Some redesign should improve either costs or performance.

Some of the indicators that might suggest such underutilization are:

- highly variable work-load in shipping or in the warehouse. If the capacity exists to handle the peak load, it is much underutilized at other times.

- employees apparently idle for substantial periods of the day.
- materials-handling equipment either idle or moving without loads.
- trucks arriving or departing only partly filled (in terms of weight and/or cube).
- trucks waiting to be loaded or unloaded.
- poor utilization of the total space in the warehouse — little stacking of goods, excessively wide aisles, etc.

Where management suspects that its resources are underutilized, a simple work-sampling study, based on random observations over a period of time, will confirm or negate the hypothesis.

DUPLICATION OF ACTIVITIES

A logistics system exists to serve the customer or consumer profitably. It cannot meet this goal if there is a needless duplication of activities between the plant and the end-user.

Duplication can occur because management does not know what is happening beyond its legal domains. It is suggested that each company flow-chart the movement of goods from the end of the production line to the ultimate consumer. Changes of ownership should be ignored. The emphasis is on cost-incurring activities — transportation, handling, storage, inventories, order processing — along the system.

With such information management will spot those activities that add little to value, only to costs. Optional steps to eliminate or minimize duplication will emerge. In turn, this will suggest some re-evaluation of the entire system.

CURRENT SERVICE LEVEL AND COSTS

As the local wag said in answer to the question, "How would I get to . . .," "I wouldn't start from here if I were you"; so, in planning to improve the logistics system it would be much neater, more satisfying, more ideal, if we didn't have to start with the existing system, if only we could start from scratch to design the new system.

But plants exist. So do warehouses, customers, order-processing facilities and all the trappings of a system that has been moving goods to the customer. It may not be the most efficient or effective system, but it has been doing the job. Consequently the first step in planning for improvement is to determine the cost and performance of the present system.

SERVICE LEVELS

Two aspects of service level are critical to the design and evaluation of the distribution system. They are:

- order cycle time
- order fill rate

The former reflects the time that elapses between an order being generated by the customer and the customer receiving the goods. The latter measures the fraction of an order that is shipped.

Because of their importance in achieving company marketing objectives, these measures are discussed in further detail.

ORDER CYCLE TIME: THE CONCEPT

The most frequently encountered measure of order lead time is the time that elapses between the receipt of an order at the sales office (customer service desk) and the dispatch of the goods by carrier.

This measure is easy to monitor. It is entirely under the control of the shipper; if it becomes excessive the shipper has all the power needed to reduce it.

But, from the customer's view point, this limited definition of order cycle time is largely irrelevant. The customer is concerned with issues such as:

- How big should inventories be?
- When should a stock replenishment order be issued?
- What promises can be made to customers concerning delivery of an item on order?

These questions are not answered by the conventional measure. They can be resolved only by a system which manages, and monitors, all the elements shown in Table 12.1. The system must measure more than the mean time to satisfy a customer's order. It must also monitor the variance in each element and in total.

TABLE 12.1
ELEMENTS OF ORDER CYCLE TIME

ELEMENT	PACKAGED FOOD MANUFACTURER		PHAR-MACEUTICAL MANUFACTURER	
	MEAN	RANGE	MEAN	RANGE
Transmit order:				
customer to supplier	1 day	0–2	5 days	2–10
Process order in office	2.5 days	1–4	1.5 days	1–2.5
Fill order	1.5 days	1–3	1.5 days	1–3
Shipment of goods:				
supplier to customer	2 days	1–4	8 days	5–15
TOTAL	7 days	4–10	16 days	10–25

The two companies depicted in Table 12.1 illustrate the importance of the total order cycle. The grocery manufacturer had systematically analysed each element of the system. Orders were telephoned into the order desk. An INWATS code was available to enable long-distance customers to telephone orders at no additional cost.

At the end of the day orders were batched for processing the following day through inventory allocation, credit and preparation of billing and order picking documents. Occasionally a question arose concerning credit. Normally, however, the order would be processed in one day.

The shipping documents were delivered to the warehouse overnight. Usually they would be picked and assembled the following day. However, it was not unusual at the beginning of the week for the surge in the workload to take two days to clear the shipping department.

Delivery to most customers was overnight. But small orders to remote locations were consolidated and cross-docked, sometimes taking up to four days.

Table 12.1 is a summary for all customers in the region. More detailed analysis by customer category showed less variance within each class. This supplier, the packaged food manufacturer, was able to discuss delivery objectively with customers. A request for better service could be handled rationally — its implications evident for all to see.

Not so the pharmaceutical manufacturer. This company had received numerous complaints about delays in receiving orders. In response, internal procedures had been much improved. On-line inventory updating and production of picking documents had been implemented in the office. A second shift had been added in the shipping department. But still the complaints continued. Subsequent analysis of the total cycle revealed an uncontrolled situation beyond the company's walls:

* Sales representatives were picking up orders and forgetting for several days to mail or phone them to the plant.
* Mail from small urban centres in other provinces was slow and very unreliable.
* Individual orders and shipments were small. They were shipped via a forwarder who waited until a full load was assembled for one destination.
* Further delays were encountered near the destination where orders were cross-docked prior to local delivery.

Analysis of all these elements and evaluation of alternatives led to the opening of a number of distribution centres closer to customers. The company also instituted a more reliable method of ensuring that incoming orders were not delayed.

Obviously the problem and solutions would have gone unnoticed had management not addressed the full order cycle. Evaluation of the current system must always embrace the total time between a customer generating an order and receiving the shipment.

ORDER CYCLE TIME: THE MEASUREMENT

A number of methods are available to measure the various elements shown in the previous section. The more commonly used are:

ORDER TRANSMISSION

• Periodic sampling of postmark and the date received (for orders mailed in).
• Sampling of "date of order" and date received.

ORDER PROCESSING

• Periodic sampling (systematically) of the date the order is received and the date the picking documents arrive in the warehouse.

ORDER FILLING

• Similar to order processing: systematic sampling of orders shipped; a comparison of shipping date with the date the order is received in the warehouse or at the order desk. In the latter event, time spent in order processing must be deducted.

SHIPMENT OF GOODS

• Periodic survey of customers. This has the disadvantage of being influenced by subjective considerations.
• Request proof of delivery periodically from carriers. This may be unreliable because of the lack of concern by receivers for the correct date, but it is usually the best source.

ORDER FILL RATE: THE CONCEPT

This is the item most commonly referred to when people discuss "level of service." However, there is no general agreement on an appropriate measure. Some of the measures in fairly common use include:

• fraction of order cycles without a stock-out
• fraction of time out of stock
• per cent of occasions when an order item is in stock
• per cent of demand filled during specified lead time, in terms of value or pieces
• per cent of orders shipped complete (in specified lead time)
• per cent of line items filled completely

As a general observation it is our conviction that, to be relevant as a measure of system performance, the level of service should be customer-oriented; it should reflect the degree to which the customer is satisfied. Such a measure may or may not be related directly to internal measures such as fraction of cycles without a stock-out, per cent availability of goods and so forth.

Even with a customer-based measure, there is considerable variation in the results according to the basis of the calculation. In a similar example to the one discussed on page 38, Table 12.2 shows this in the case of an order for four line items. The level of service, according to the measure used, would vary from 0% to 99.99%:

TABLE 12.2

ITEM	UNIT VALUE	QUANTITY ORDERED	VALUE	QUANTITY SHIPPED	VALUE
ABC	$2	1,000	$2,000	1,000	$2,000
CDE	$12	100	$1,200	100	$1,200
LMN	$50	10	$ 500	10	$ 500
XYZ	$250	1	$ 250	—	—
TOTAL		1,111	$3,950	1,110	$3,700

- order shipped complete — 0
- fraction of lines filled completely — 75%
- fraction of order filled — 1,110 cases ÷ 1,111 = 99.99%
- fraction of order filled (by value) — $3,700 ÷ $3,950 = 94%

Selection of the most appropriate measure should be based on the customer's needs. Is the customer prepared to accept partial orders? If not, a system which monitors the fraction of orders shipped complete is probably the best. If a customer is prepared to accept partial shipments, provided he or she receives the full quantity of each line item, it will be appropriate to measure the fraction of lines filled completely. Another customer may accept any part of an order within the agreed-on lead time. In this case the fraction of demand that is filled could be used.

It should be noted that the measure selected serves as more than a mere monitoring device. It will serve to measure the performance of the system and, implicitly, the people in the system. Consequently they will take whatever action is necessary in order to improve their performance as measured by the system. In this sense it is a motivating device — its implications must be considered carefully before being implemented.

To illustrate: if the number of orders filled completely is the measure, the staff will cannibalize partly filled orders to ensure that the maximum possible number of orders is completely filled. Some customers, who would otherwise lack only one or two items, would find their orders completely decimated.

ORDER FILL RATE: THE MEASUREMENT

Once the measure is selected, monitoring its value is relatively easy. The normal method is to systematically select a sample of orders. For each order the number of cases shipped, lines filled or other parameter is calculated.

THE NEED TO BE SPECIFIC

The unit for measuring service levels is established on overall company and market requirements. However, the quantitative value must be set and measured for specific products, customers and markets. Typical of the categories for which specific measures should be set are:

PRODUCT CATEGORIES
- growth, mature or declining products
- stock or non-stock items
- high-, medium- or low-margin items
- "essential" or non-essential items
- impulse or shopping products
- "branded" or commodity products

CUSTOMER CATEGORIES
- large, medium or small accounts
- chains or independents
- wholesale, mass merchandisers or retailers

MARKETS
- highly competitive or less competitive
- metropolitan, urban or rural
- close to distribution centre or remote

It may not be necessary to set a different quantitative value for each category. However, in selecting the most appropriate measure, and in measuring current performance, it is essential to consider each category separately.

CURRENT COSTS

Just as the levels of service should be specified by customer class and region, so should the costs of distribution. The objective of this step is to identify, or estimate, all costs between the end of the production line and the customer.

A typical format for structuring the cost analysis is presented in Table 12.3. It should list all elements from production line to consumer.

Calculation of some of the costs may present difficulties, especially if they cannot be readily associated with a specific market or channel — inventory costs for example. In general we would recommend the following approach for determining the various components.

FREIGHT AND TRANSPORTATION
The basic source of transportation costs is the freight bill or bill of lading. It documents the weight and charges of each shipment. A representative sample of bills for each type of customer, in each market, will provide both average and total costs. Care must be exercised to ensure that the sample truly represents the activity in that channel. Seasonal variations, abnormalities due to strikes and other variations must be covered and allowance made in extrapolating for the full year, or period under study.

TABLE 12.3
LOGISTICS COST ANALYSIS

	REGION OR MARKET			
	CUSTOMER CATEGORY/MARKETING CHANNEL			
COST ELEMENT	OEM ACCOUNTS	INSTITU- TIONAL MARKET	MASS MERCHAN- DISER	DISTRIBU- TORS
Freight and Transportation				
• Plant–Warehouse				
• Warehouse–Distribution Centre				
• Outside Supply– Distribution Centre				
• Local Delivery				
Warehousing				
• Plant Warehouse				
• Distribution Centres				
Packaging				
• Pallets				
• Shrink-wrap				
• Cartons				
Inventories				
• Plant Warehouse				
• In-Transit to Distribution Centre				
• Customers' stocks				
Order Processing				
• Telex				
• Editing/Checking				
• Computer				
TOTAL				

Local delivery costs may not be so easily determined. Frequently a cartage company is hired by the hour. If this is the case, the delivery cost for each type of account can be estimated by allocating total costs according to the number of deliveries.

If a private fleet is used for local or out-of-town deliveries, an approximation of the delivery cost may be based on the miles travelled to each type of customer.

WAREHOUSING

Current warehousing costs can be related to each customer category by:

- determining an appropriate measure of warehouse activity
- estimating the volume of activity associated with each type of customer
- pro-rating the total costs on the basis of the level of activity

In most warehouses the appropriate measure of activity is a combination of the number of orders and the number of lines per order. The first step in selecting the measure of activity should be to observe the work of the staff. If necessary, work sampling might be employed. The purpose of the observations is to determine, if possible, whether the time spent filling an order is more or less constant, or whether it varies greatly with the number of line items.

A more sophisticated approach is to employ regression techniques of the form:

Workload $= aX_1 + bX_2 + c$
Where X_1 = number of orders
X_2 = number of line items
a,b,c are constants

Once the appropriate measure of activity is established, the volume of activity can be ascertained by sampling a batch of orders in each customer category. The number of orders and/or line items in the period is tallied and the relative work-load in each category estimated.

The relevant costs of each category are estimated by pro-rating total costs on the basis of the relative work-load. For purposes of long-term comparison it is appropriate to use the total warehousing costs — labour, benefits, supplies, equipment, space and utilities. Admittedly, space and utilities are not variable in the short term. However, in the longer term covered by the planning period, it is reasonable to assume that all these costs are variable. Space could have other uses, equipment could be transferred to another site and so forth.

PACKAGING

These costs are relatively easy to determine. They are almost entirely variable. Usually they can be closely identified with particular product or customer categories.

INVENTORIES

Estimating the inventory costs associated with each class of customer presents some unusual problems unless each class of customer takes a mutually exclusive line of products.

Inventory levels, and hence costs, are a function of many factors including the demand and variability of demand, customer service policy, replenishment lead time and so forth. However, unless the company has an explicit policy stating that levels of service must be different for each class of customer, it is probably appropriate to allocate inventory costs on the basis of the sales volumes to each category.

Obviously the cost of inventory must include all those elements whose magnitude varies with a change in the level of inventories. As discussed in Chapter 6, it should include capital invested, insurance, space, heat, light, obsolescence, deterioration and record-keeping. In some communities it should include the municipal taxes that are levied on goods in storage.

ORDER PROCESSING

These costs, as with warehousing costs, are a function of the number of orders and the numbers of lines per order. Observation of the order processing activities will usually provide a basis for determining the propor-

FIGURE 12.4
RELATIONSHIP OF COST, EFFECTIVENESS AND
EFFICIENCY OF A LOGISTICS SYSTEM

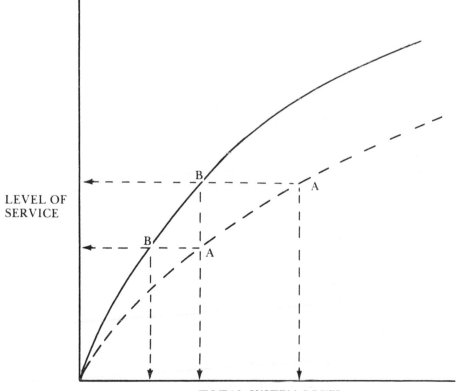

LEVEL OF
SERVICE

TOTAL SYSTEM COSTS

tion of time associated with the order and the proportion with the items being ordered.

Such observations are usually sufficient to estimate how these costs should be assigned to each customer category. It should be pointed out that errors here are not critical. Order processing costs are usually an order of magnitude less than the costs of handling, transportation and inventory.

Completion of these steps — determining the level of service and total costs — enables management to fix the performance of the present system. It provides the basis for exploring possible improvements in the effectiveness of the system — higher levels of service, for example (AA in Figure 12.4), or what is usually more significant, possibly improving the efficiency, thereby realizing a higher level of service for no additional cost, or the same level of service for a lower cost (AB).

POTENTIAL IMPROVEMENTS IN THE EXISTING SYSTEM

Before management considers the costs and benefits of fundamental changes in the system, it is essential to determine the gains to be realized from fine-tuning the existing system. This serves two purposes. It provides an honest basis for evaluating the costs and benefits of major changes in the system. And it usually indicates how significant benefits can be realized for a minimal outlay.

Many of the potential improvements have been discussed in detail in the sections of the book dealing respectively with inventories, transportation, warehousing and so forth. Others will emerge from an analysis of the operations and costs described in the previous section.

Some of the more common improvements are listed in Table 12.4. This might be considered a first-round check-list. It should be applied to every logistics system once the basic data on levels of service, movement and costs have been determined. The principles underlying these improvements are reviewed briefly below. For more detail the reader should refer to the chapter dealing with the specific subject.

TRANSPORTATION

The objective behind most of the suggested improvements is to raise the utilization and/or load factor of the vehicle. Small shipments, whether handled by company fleet or outside carrier, are costly. Anything that can be done to consolidate small shipments, eliminate small orders and increase the size of the load will usually reduce transportation costs.

TABLE 12.4
POSSIBLE IMPROVEMENTS IN PRESENT SYSTEM

TRANSPORTATION
* Reduce small shipments by reducing multiple, emergency or back orders: guaranteed deliveries.
* Arrange for consolidations to regional break-bulk points.
* More economical modes, containers, piggybacks.
* Two-way movement may offer advantages for private or contract carriers.
* Improved negotiated rates

WAREHOUSING
* Work standards for employees.
* Scheduling of employees: staffing charts.
* Best relation between bulk and forward storage.
* Locations of popular items.
* Mechanization: lift trucks, conveyors.
* Delivery truck scheduling.
* Buying "rules" or procedures.

ORDER PROCESSING
* Paperwork simplifications.
* Reduce number of orders processed, especially back orders and emergency orders.
* Data processing.
* Reduce delays in the paper system.

INVENTORY MANAGEMENT
* Transfer inventories to plant.
* Determine optimal replenishment rules.
* Reduce in-transit time.
* Improve sales forecasting.

WAREHOUSING

Here the initial thrust is to obtain higher labour productivity. Better methods, more mechanization, engineered standards, better planning and scheduling of the daily work-load and labour reporting further this objective. A second thrust should be to improve space utilization. Stacking, racking and use of narrow aisles typify this type of improvement.

ORDER PROCESSING

Work content and elapsed time are both important in order processing. Simplifying the order form, eliminating duplication, adopting a one-write system and using data terminals all reduce the work-load.

Elapsed time is critical because, as seen earlier, the customer is concerned with total order cycle time. A day saved in order processing could mean one day less is required to have the order in the customer's hands. Or it could make available one extra day for further order picking and/or consolidating orders. The pay-off from having time available to pick and ship orders usually outweighs severalfold the added cost of improving the order processing system.

INVENTORY MANAGEMENT

The first step in optimizing inventory levels lies in introducing systematic re-ordering rules. Order quantity and order points can both be calculated scientifically to provide the optimal trade-off between customer service and system costs.

Other directions offering significant pay-offs are reduced replenishment cycle time and better forecasting. Safety stocks are heavily influenced by both the length of the replenishment cycle and its variability. Efforts to improve these parameters will yield substantial benefits.

Better sales forecasting offers handsome returns. The major reason for safety stocks is the uncertainty in the forecast, the deviation between forecast and actual sales. A 50% reduction in this deviation would result in a corresponding decrease in safety stocks.

As stated at the beginning of this section, the prime purpose for identifying and evaluating the pay-off from these improvements is to provide a datum for evaluating major system changes. It is not necessary to implement these changes before proceeding to the next step.

FIGURE 12.5
MARKETS/CUSTOMERS

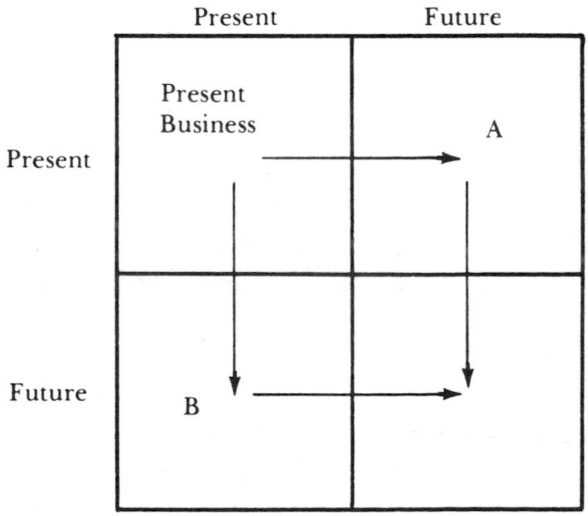

Upon completion of this step, the data in Table 12.4 should be updated to present the details and summary of "Present System — Lowest Cost Operation" for the present level of service. If Point A in Figure 12.5 represented current actual costs, Point B represents this new datum.

DESIGNING THE NETWORK

Once management has estimated the optimal total cost/level of service for the existing system, it is in a position to evaluate optional designs of the network. This section presents an approach which has been tested and found successful in a number of applications. The principles would apply also to the design of a new network. However, as pointed out earlier, the vast majority of studies start from an existing logistics system.

FUTURE DEMAND

Networks should be designed for future, not past, business. Despite the self-evident nature of this statement, too many logistics investment and policy decisions are made without sufficient analysis of future business.

The framework for this analysis is shown in Figure 12.5. The starting point for the projection is today's business: today's product range, market regions or territories and customer categories.

From a logistics viewpoint, considerable aggregation of data is desirable. Products should be grouped into major categories according to their physical characteristics and market served. For example:

- A cigarette manufacturer would group all products into one category.
- A packaged food manufacturer might have three categories:
  glass products
  canned products
  dry groceries (cake mix, cereals, etc.)
- A home-improvement distributor may have to employ a larger number of groupings:
  rough lumber
  panelling and plywood
  home workshop
  tools
  electrical, plumbing hardware
  portable appliances
  home entertainment
  lawn and garden
  furniture, etc.
- A national baker may find that the logical groupings are:
  bread
  buns, rolls
  sweet goods, cakes, etc.

The grouping represents a deliberate compromise. Too much detail calls for unnecessary work and precision. Too little detail may result in significant shifts in the market going unnoticed.

It is not the purpose of this section to discuss details of how forecasts should be prepared. That is a separate topic — many publications cover the subject in great depth. However, it is relevant to touch on some of the most important elements.

FUTURE MARKET FOR PRESENT PRODUCTS

The starting point is usually the per capita total consumption of the product, from all suppliers. This might lead to the following types of analysis:

- total per capita consumption
- analysis of regional per capita variations
- analysis of trend over last five to ten years — decreasing, increasing per capita consumption
- outlook for the future — gradual levelling of regional disparities, relationship of regional disparities to other economic measures such as per capita income, number of housing starts, etc.
- changes in life-style that will explain or affect consumption (for example, the trend to convenience foods and eating out is having a marked effect on manufacturers of traditional foods)
- substitution of new products

Then, within the total market development, the firm must consider its own position:

- trend in market share in each major region
- rationale for gaining or losing market share
- marketing strategy — does the company have plans that will change the trend? — new products, more advertising, more outlets, wider market distribution, additional distribution channels, accounts and so forth
- changing competitive position (Are competitors becoming more or less aggressive in promoting their products? Have any corporate mergers, affiliations or divestitures taken place that will influence the strength or resources of competitors?)

This two-stage process of viewing the market in total, and the firm's share in it, is critical. A view of only the firm's growth may hide significant trends in the market at large. For instance, one major company projected a continuation of its current high absolute growth rate over the ensuing eight years. The resulting figures were indeed attractive. But, subsequent analysis of the total market revealed that the firm would need a 110% share of the total market to realize its projected growth!

PRESENT MARKET FOR FUTURE PRODUCTS

What plans does the company have to introduce *significantly* different products? Significant in this context means satisfying a different need, as opposed to additional items in present product categories.

Does the company plan an acquisition or merger? Are new products being tested in the research department? Is the company actively searching for new items that could be imported or manufactured under licence?

Once the products have been defined, the process outlined in the previous section should be repeated:

- What is the total market — by region?
- What share should the company expect?
- Will distribution be regional or national?
- Will the product be confined to one or two distribution channels, or will it be subject to widespread distribution?

FUTURE MARKETS FOR FUTURE PRODUCTS

This is a more speculative opportunity than the two previous cases. It should not be overlooked, however, if company plans indicate a potentially significant impact on the distribution system.

The results of this activity should be an estimate of the increase and/or shift in the movement of goods to each major region and to each distribution channel.

The definition of "region" frequently presents some difficulty. It is hard to present firm rules. The definition depends very much on the nature of the problem and the product in question. To illustrate:

- If the company wishes to design the most appropriate delivery network for distributing bread and baked goods, the "region" will probably be a municipality or county. The same would apply to beer, where the system is specified to the level of the individual retail outlet.
- If the manufacturer sells to distributors or to mass merchandisers who do their own distribution, a region may be a small province or a sector of a large province such as northwestern Ontario, lower mainland B.C. or the major metropolitan areas.

A key element in this definition is the nature of the customer's operation. Is it the final reseller, or is it an intermediate distributor?

ORDER CYCLE TIME: THE FIRST CONSTRAINT

The first parameter in configuring the network is the required service level. How long is a customer prepared to wait between issuing the order and receiving the goods?

Same-day delivery implies a shipping point, and goods within, at most, 50 miles. This usually calls for stocks to be available in all major communities. Twenty-four-hour delivery will usually permit goods to be shipped by truck, or piggyback, up to 500 miles if they are going to relatively few destinations. If many destinations are involved, the goods may have to be redistributed from the trucker's terminal. This could call for an extra day. Conversely, it might limit next-day delivery to a radius of 300 miles or so.

THE CRITICAL TRADE-OFFS

A second focus of the design is a review of the present total logistics costs in order to identify the largest components. The objective of the redesign is to reduce or eliminate these largest components without incurring corresponding increases in the other elements.

To illustrate, if the largest cost element is:

- line-haul transportation, the redesign should explore the implications of:
  - reducing the frequency and increasing the size of shipments
  - consolidating shipments to adjacent locations
  - reducing the number of destinations to which goods are shipped
- local delivery costs, the manager should examine alternative ways and implications of:
  - eliminating local delivery, drop-shipping directly from the plant or principal shipping point
  - arranging for distribution points to be closer to the market; increasing the number of distribution centres and/or cross-docking facilities
  - consolidating local deliveries into fewer, scheduled runs
  - pooling, or combining shipments, with those of other suppliers serving the same market
  - redesigning local delivery routes
  - installing bulk systems on customers' premises; replenishing on basis of optimal delivery/inventory schedule.
- inventory cost, some of the options to be explored include:
  - eliminating inventories from various points in the system: pulling them back from regional centres to a central warehouse, supplying remote customers directly from the central supply point, cross-docking at a regional terminal
  - adopting a faster mode of transportation, e.g., air freight, in order to reduce the lead time and/or develop a capability to ship directly to customers
  - improving forecasting, order processing and transmission
  - "managing" customers' inventories; developing systematic reordering rules
  - consolidating customers' and suppliers' inventories
  - reducing the number of stages in the system between supplier and customer
- warehousing costs, it would be appropriate to examine the feasibility of:
  - reducing the number of warehouses
  - increasing direct shipments from principal point of supply to customers
  - installing a mechanized and/or computer-controlled warehousing system
  - using public instead of private warehousing facilities, especially if the level of activity is highly variable
  - reducing the number of stages: consolidating warehouses into fewer, larger outlets

The above approach gives a general indication of the direction management should seek in restructuring or redesigning the system. The principal thrust, initially, should always be towards reducing the largest cost component in the system.

LOCATION OF DISTRIBUTION CENTRES

A number of sophisticated mathematical techniques have been developed to find the theoretical optimal location of "n" shipping points to serve a given market. Unfortunately their application in the Canadian context is relatively limited.

A better approach, in general, is one which reflects the realities of the Canadian economy — a relatively small number of "natural" centres able to serve the immediate and possibly adjacent provinces. In this method the manager selects as the first centre either:

• the plant location, if the company is a manufacturing enterprise
• the centre of largest projected demand — usually Toronto or Montreal for consumer products

Following this selection, a number of radii are drawn reflecting the area that could be served within one day, two days, three days, etc. — the time representing the full order cycle from the generation of an order by the customer to the receipt of goods.

This definition of one-day, two-day, three-day zones, etc., reflects the fact that, provided the volume is adequate to produce reasonable transportation rates, the cheapest distribution is direct shipment: source to customer.

The zones are then compared with present or potential customer service requirements. The comparison defines the area that can be served out of the principal shipping point consistent with meeting customers' needs.

If this first step does not embrace the entire country, it is repeated in the second-largest market outside the initial service area. This might be Alberta, for example, in which Calgary or Edmonton is the focus, depending on the relative demand. And the iterations continue until all, or the vast majority, of the market is covered.

TRADE-OFF — TRANSPORTATION OR CROSS-DOCKING

As stated previously, the lowest-cost method of distribution to a market is by direct shipment; from the plant to the customer, provided the volume is sufficient to obtain attractive transportation rates. However, in some cases the weight of goods, or the cubic volume, going to each destination on a particular day is too small. Further, the required service time may not allow significant day-over-day consolidation.

Under such conditions the first option to be examined is that of cross-docking. Consolidated loads would be shipped into logical "demand centres" in the market area. There they would be received, sorted into individual orders and distributed the same day via local delivery or cartage. The goods would not go into storage in these demand centres. They would be literally transferred from the inbound carrier to the delivery vehicle.

Some examples of demand centres and principal distribution points are shown in Table 12.5. The trade-off implicit in this analysis is shown in Figure 12.6.

TABLE 12.5
DISTRIBUTION CENTRES AND
SATELLITE CROSS-DOCKING POINTS

DISTRIBUTION CENTRES	AREA SERVED	SATELLITE CROSS-DOCKING LOCATIONS
Montreal	Ontario, Quebec	Quebec City Toronto Ottawa
Toronto	Ontario	London Sudbury Lakehead Ottawa
Montreal	Quebec, Maritimes	Moncton
Calgary	Alberta, B.C.	Edmonton Vancouver

EVALUATION OF OPTIONAL CONFIGURATIONS

The above process is continued, in principle, until all markets receive adequate service. The network then consists of:

• one or more points of supply
• regional distribution centres, carrying inventories, serving a region
• cross-docking facilities to permit consolidation of loads and thereby obtain more favourable freight rates

The underlying principle, wherever possible, is to maximize direct shipments consistent with providing adequate service and achieving all possible economies of scale.

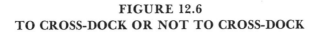

FIGURE 12.6
TO CROSS-DOCK OR NOT TO CROSS-DOCK

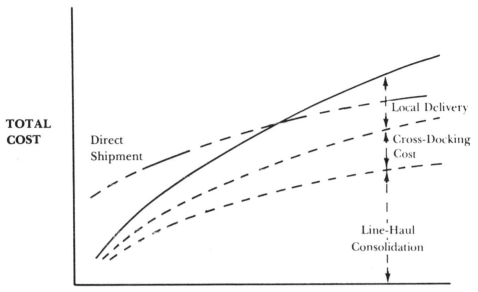

WEIGHT (OR CUBE) OF INDIVIDUAL ORDERS

In an earlier section it was stated that the basis for evaluation should always be total system costs. This criterion demands an explicit analysis of all trade-offs. Further, it provides the means for comparing total costs for varying levels of service.

A typical example of one such total cost analysis is shown in Tables 12.6 and 12.7.

This analysis follows the form presented earlier. It reflects:

- Projections of the quantities of goods moving from the source of supply to regional warehouses and from there to customers by local delivery.
- Analysis of the demand, variability of demand, sales forecast error, safety stocks and total inventories at each point in the system (as described in the section on inventory management).
- A cost of inventory, reflecting the company's expectation of a 20% ROE on invested capital.
- An obsolescence cost which reflects historical experience, subject to the benefit of improved inventory control.
- Warehousing costs which reflect the quantity of goods passing through each warehouse, the optimal methods and equipment and the standard times for each method.
- Transportation costs to the warehouse, based on the annual movement costed at the rate that would be applied to the quantities shipped — truck-load and car-load lots in most cases.

TABLE 12.6

	SYSTEM COSTS ($ 000s)				
NUMBER OF WAREHOUSES	3	6	10	15	20
Service Level — 80%, 24 Hours					
Inventory Costs — 20%	170	185	220	280	360
Probable Obsolescence	85	90	120	190	250
Warehousing Cost	140	180	240	300	370
Transportation to Warehouses	400	360	380	420	480
Local Delivery	300	210	160	125	80
Production or Supply	80	40	35	40	50
Order Processing Costs	20	25	32	55	80
TOTAL SYSTEM COST	1,195	1,090	1,187	1,410	1,670
Forecast Sales Revenue	8,500	8,900	9,100	9,250	9,400
Forecast Manufacturing Profit Contribution (40%)	3,400	3,560	3,640	3,700	3,760
TOTAL SYSTEM CONTRIBUTION	2,205	2,470	2,453	2,290	2,090

TABLE 12.7

	SYSTEM COSTS ($ 000s)				
NUMBER OF WAREHOUSES	3	6	10	15	20
Service Level — 93%, 24 Hours					
Inventory Costs — 20%	240	300	395	540	720
Probable Obsolescence	130	160	210	320	450
Warehousing Cost	155	203	270	350	430
Transportation to Warehouses	415	370	395	435	500
Local Delivery	310	220	165	134	90
Production or Supply	80	40	35	40	50
Order Processing Costs	25	32	40	63	91
TOTAL SYSTEM COST	1,355	1,325	1,510	1,882	2,331
Forecast Sales Revenue	9,800	10,200	10,450	10,630	10,800
Forecast Manufacturing Profit Contribution (40%)	3,920	4,080	4,180	4,250	4,320
TOTAL SYSTEM CONTRIBUTION	2,560	2,755	2,670	2,368	1,989

FIGURE 12.7
RELATIONSHIP OF LOCAL DELIVERY COST TO AREA SERVED

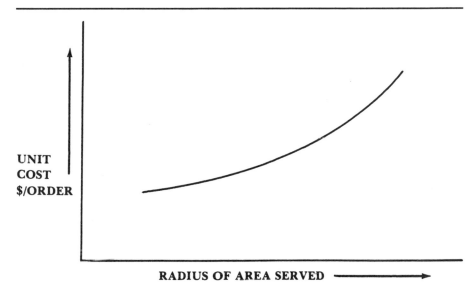

UNIT
COST
$/ORDER

RADIUS OF AREA SERVED ───────▶

- Local delivery based on a formula reflecting the cost per shipment and the area served. The relationship is shown conceptually in Figure 12.7 for a typical market.

The increasing cost as the area increases reflects the higher charges for deliveries outside the immediate urban area. That the curve does not increase more steeply is the result of the majority of shipments going to destinations within the urban area. Increasing the delivery area increases the unit costs of some deliveries, but the number of deliveries is relatively small. Obviously, if the number of shipments increased rapidly the curve would show a much steeper ascent.

Production or supply reflects the possibility of buying goods from outside sources for distant warehouses. This is sometimes preferable to shipping long distances from the plant, especially if the demand for each item is relatively low and unpredictable.

In this example the company wished to evaluate the profit contribution of varying numbers of warehouses:

- three — one in each of Montreal, Toronto and Vancouver
- six — one additional in each of Edmonton, Winnipeg and Moncton
- ten — including Halifax, Quebec City, London and Calgary

From that point, it wished to locate them in all major centres.

Each warehouse was assigned a market territory. All customers in the territory were supplied via the respective warehouse, although large orders would be drop-shipped.

FIGURE 12.8
ADDED CONTRIBUTION FROM MORE EFFECTIVE LOGISTICS

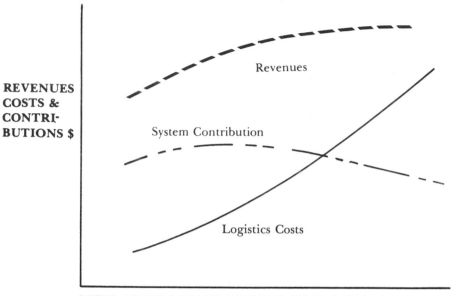

**REVENUES
COSTS &
CONTRI-
BUTIONS $**

Revenues

System Contribution

Logistics Costs

LEVEL OF SERVICE (PROXIMITY OF WAREHOUSE) ———

The first evaluation in the study was an estimate of total system costs. As seen, the six-warehouse configuration is the most attractive. However, another dimension existed in the evaluation. The marketing manager felt strongly that the presence of a warehouse in a community provides a competitive advantage. This advantage results in higher sales volume. In turn, greater profits should be realized. This is illustrated in Figure 12.8.

In order to estimate the overall impact of added warehousing, the marketing staff estimated the probable effect on sales volume. This was converted to additional manufacturing profit contribution. Then, subtraction of logistics system costs provided the "System Contribution." Again, the six-warehouse configuration is most profitable, but only by a small margin of the ten warehouses.

The evaluation was repeated for a high level of order fill. Instead of 80%, management wanted to know how the optimal configuration would change if 93% of orders were filled in 24 hours. As would be expected, inventory costs increased. This penalized the multi-warehouse system more than others. It shifted the preference more in favour of the six-warehouse configuration.

TECHNIQUES TO AID DESIGN

The majority of network design problems in Canada can be approached as described above. The initial step is the selection of the more obvious population centres as focal points for serving a region.

However, this empirical approach can occasionally be complemented through the use of more formal methodology. Some of the better examples are summarized in the following sections.

LINEAR PROGRAMMING: THE TRANSPORTATION PROBLEM

The transportation problem can be stated generally as follows. The system consists of:

- a finite number of shipping points (e.g., factories), each having a specified capacity.
- a finite number of destinations (e.g., warehouses, customers or markets), each with specific requirements.

How should the available capacity be assigned to each market so that the total logistics cost is minimized? A specific example of this type of problem is illustrated below. A manufacturer has three plants which are located in Montreal, Toronto and Quebec City. Their capacities are:

Montreal	200 cwt. per week
Toronto	100 cwt. per week
Quebec City	150 cwt. per week

These plants ship their goods to five principal distribution centres, for which the forecast demand is:

Distribution Centre No. 1	80 cwt.
Distribution Centre No. 2	90 cwt.
Distribution Centre No. 3	100 cwt.
Distribution Centre No. 4	70 cwt.
Distribution Centre No. 5	60 cwt.

Transportation costs from each plant to each distribution centre are shown in Table 12.8.

A well-documented technique which systematically evaluates the cost of supplying each warehouse from each plant will produce the optimal allocation shown in Table 12.9. This method has several applications. It will establish the lowest-cost logistics pattern for a given plant–warehouse configuration. This is the most common use. But, it can be used also as a

TABLE 12.8

FROM PLANT	TO DISTRIBUTION CENTRE				
	NO. 1	NO. 2	NO. 3	NO. 4	NO. 5
Montreal	$5/cwt.	$1/cwt.	$6/cwt.	$3/cwt.	$1/cwt.
Toronto	$2/cwt.	$3/cwt.	$4/cwt.	$5/cwt.	$4/cwt.
Quebec City	$4/cwt.	$2/cwt.	$3/cwt.	$2/cwt.	$3/cwt.

TABLE 12.9
LEAST-COST LOGISTICS PATTERN

	DISTRIBUTION CENTRE					
	NO. 1	NO. 2	NO. 3	NO. 4	NO. 5	TOTAL
Montreal		90 cwt.			60 cwt.	150 cwt.
Toronto	80 cwt.		20 cwt.			100 cwt.
Quebec City			80 cwt.	70 cwt.		150 cwt.

planning tool. Repeating the process for a number of optional warehouse or plant locations will establish the best of a number of optional systems. In each case the technique determines the lowest-cost assignment for a given set of warehouse–plant configurations. Comparison of the lowest-total-cost *assignments* will identify the lowest-total-cost *system*.

Variants of this technique can be used to allocate productive capacity to products and customers to shipping points, as well as warehouses to plants.

WAREHOUSE LOCATION

Frequently, management faces the task of selecting the best locations for depots or distribution centres in a local market area for a high-delivery-cost product. Typically this problem might apply to the delivery of beverages, baked goods, newspapers, etc. These products usually require a number of distribution points in a province or market area.

A number of techniques are available for the general class of problem. They can be represented by the following generalization:

D_1 — demand at Point 1, tons per year
D_2 — demand at Point 2, tons per year
D_i — demand at Point i, tons per year, etc.

S_1 — supply at Point 1, tons per year
S_2 — supply at Point 2, tons per year, etc.

r_1 — distance of supply Point 1
r_2 — distance of supply Point 2
d_1 — distance of demand Point 1
d_2 — distance of demand Point 2, etc.
C_d — cost per ton/mile for shipping outbound goods
C_s — cost per ton/mile for inbound flow of goods

The objective of the various techniques is to minimize the total cost, C_T, namely:

$$C_T = C_s (S_1 r_1 + S_2 r_2 + \ldots) + C_d (D_1 d_1 + D_2 d_2 + \ldots D_i d_i)$$

FIGURE 12.9

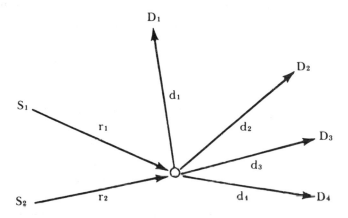

TRUCK ROUTING MODEL

Consider a fleet of trucks delivering goods from a central depot to a large number of delivery points. This operation is typical of many industries, such as newspapers, bread, milk, grocery products, gasoline and beverages. The objective is to assign trucks to routes so that all customer demands are met and the total distance covered is minimized. The measure of performance is total mileage covered by all trucks. We make simplifying assumptions, such as that we know the shortest route between each pair of delivery points, and that there are no customer priorities or delivery times. The constraints are the amounts required by each customer, vehicle capacities and the maximum number of deliveries per trip.

If there are 15 stores on one route, there are 653 billion different ways of routing the truck. Obviously most are not feasible, but thousands are. The chance of a clerk finding the optimum route is zero. The chances of a computer finding it are slim. But computer models have produced savings of 5% to 25% over conventional manual methods in Canada, the U.S.A. and the U.K.

A typical problem is shown in Figure 12.10 on page 380. The product is gasoline, to be delivered to 12 service stations from a central depot. There are three 6,000-gallon and two 5,000-gallon trucks. In one day each truck can travel up to 90 miles to make five deliveries, 120 miles for four deliveries and 150 miles for three deliveries. The mileage chart shows the mileages between the depot and each gas station, and between each pair of stations. Also shown on the left-hand side of the chart is the amount required by each gas station.

There are about 19 million possible solutions to this problem. The best solution that has been found is shown in Figure 12.11 on page 381. Four trucks are used. The amount delivered by each truck and its route are shown in the new mileage chart. For example, one truck starts at the depot with 5,100 gallons. It travels 25 miles to Station 6, 11 miles to Station 8, 6 miles to Station 9 and 38 miles back to the depot.

The model used is quite simple. It evaluates each pair of points and determines how many miles are saved by serving both points on one route rather than serving each separately from the depot. The model accepts route combinations where the largest savings are found and stops when it can find no more savings. No method has yet been found of determining an optimal solution that can be economically solved on present-day computers.

Logistics managers have to deal with more complex problems than this example. Some of the complications include:

• many different products
• different types of vehicles
• delays caused by breakdowns
• specified delivery times
• time taken to load and unload
• availability of drivers
• cost of overtime

Extensions of the basic approach described here have been built into complex, customized models which incorporate all such special conditions.

This illustrates the one common feature of using models. Rarely can a model developed for one purpose be used for any other purpose. Your reality is different from the next person's, though he or she may be in the same type of business and appear to have the same problem. If the model is any good, it will reflect your reality closely enough that you can have confidence in its results.

SIMULATING THE ENTIRE SYSTEM[2]

The above examples are concerned with making planning decisions for isolated parts of the logistics system.

When we get into very complex logistics systems — a large number of products, a large number of customers, many channels of distribution, many alternatives for locating facilities, many alternatives for modes of transportation — we run into an immediate problem in trying to evaluate the alternatives.

The problem is, of course, that all these trade-offs and alternatives have repercussions on all the other parts of the system. So far, except in the oil industry, there has been no way of developing analytic models for such systems. We have, however, been able to build simulation models. We want to be able to consider many, many combinations of all the alternatives and their combined effect on total costs and service levels. Because of the astronomical numbers of alternatives and their complexity, we tend to use a computer to do some or all of the calculations for us. For example, to consider one alternative location for each of seven warehouses, we have to evaluate 197 possible systems, before even considering different warehouses' sizes or different numbers of warehouses. Now, because of the twin development of management science and of computers, it is possible to build a model of a very complex system and simulate the effects of various alternatives.

How do we use this simulation? Having constructed a model of the entire system, we then ask questions of that model. What if we had so many warehouses of such and such a capacity in certain locations? What if we used this particular method of forecasting demand? What if we had this particular method of replenishing stocks from our district warehouses to our factory warehouses, or factory warehouses from the plant? What if we shipped from factory to district warehouse by rail, then from district warehouse to customer by road? Then, given all these choices of alternatives, the model takes all the customer orders and computes the effect of each alternative on the measures of performance, the objectives and the costs.

Why do we simulate? It is obviously much cheaper than trying to experiment in the real world, and it takes much less time. But, more important, we cannot really experiment in the real world, because we cannot control the real world. We can, however, look at a model of the real world we have built and attempt to see the effect of alternatives on the model. The question then is: how accurately does the model represent

---

[2] "Simulation — The Countemporary Approach to Distribution System Design," *Materials Handling in Canada* (November 1969).

FIGURE 12.10
TRUCK ROUTING PROBLEM

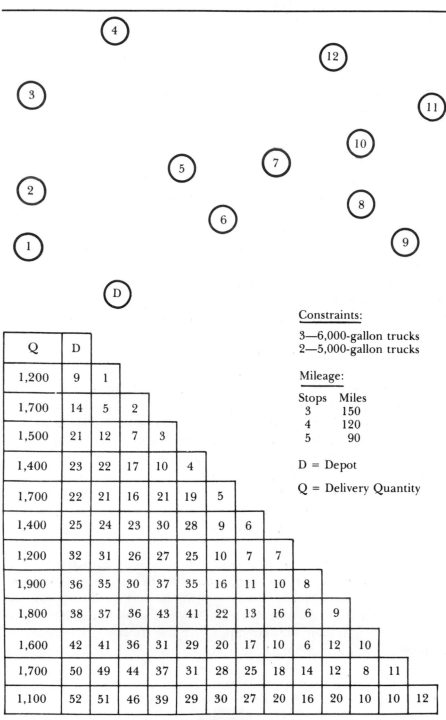

Constraints:

3—6,000-gallon trucks
2—5,000-gallon trucks

Mileage:

Stops	Miles
3	150
4	120
5	90

D = Depot

Q = Delivery Quantity

Q	D											
1,200	9	1										
1,700	14	5	2									
1,500	21	12	7	3								
1,400	23	22	17	10	4							
1,700	22	21	16	21	19	5						
1,400	25	24	23	30	28	9	6					
1,200	32	31	26	27	25	10	7	7				
1,900	36	35	30	37	35	16	11	10	8			
1,800	38	37	36	43	41	22	13	16	6	9		
1,600	42	41	36	31	29	20	17	10	6	12	10	
1,700	50	49	44	37	31	28	25	18	14	12	8	11
1,100	52	51	46	39	29	30	27	20	16	20	10	10	12

MILEAGE CHART

FIGURE 12.11
TRUCK ROUTING PROBLEM: "OPTIMUM SOLUTION"

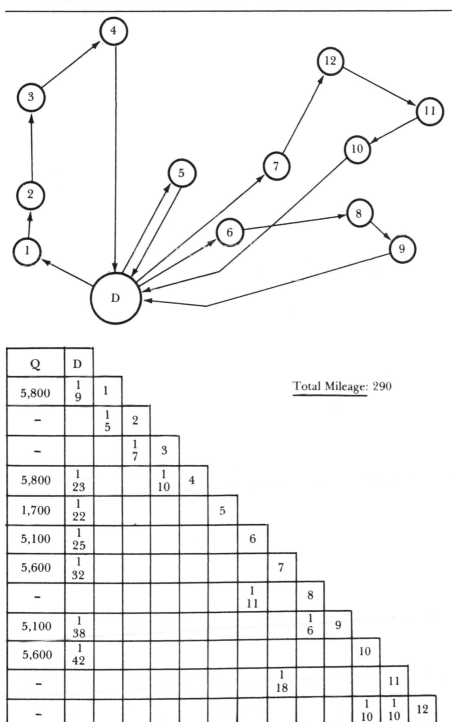

Q	D											
5,800	1 9	1										
–		1 5	2									
–			1 7	3								
5,800	1 23			1 10	4							
1,700	1 22					5						
5,100	1 25						6					
5,600	1 32							7				
–							1 11		8			
5,100	1 38								1 6	9		
5,600	1 42										10	
–							1 18				11	
–										1 10	1 10	12

Total Mileage: 290

the real world? We also use the simulation model when there is no way to find an optimal solution analytically, and when there are several measures of performance rather than just one. We can look at the results in terms of these several measures of performance. We use it when we want to see how sensitive the real world might be to a change in a particular alternative. For example, how sensitive is the level of service to changes in inventory policy?

Another advantage of simulation is that we can make it more like the real world than we can an analytic model. We do not have to make quite so many assumptions. We are not subject to more abstract mathematical theory. And, finally, we can compress time. We can look at a whole year and, in an hour's time, say, simulate the demand pattern week by week. Simulation is, so far, the only way we have found to study the entire complexity of a logistics system and evaluate the implications of all the trade-offs and interactions.

DESIGN OF A LOGISTICS SYSTEM FOR A PROVINCIAL LIQUOR BOARD

THE EXISTING SYSTEM

Before the study, the distribution system consisted of:

- 120 suppliers — from whom over 500 different items are purchased. Suppliers are located in Ontario, Quebec, the Atlantic provinces and Europe.
- Transportation — of cases of goods from suppliers to warehouses and stores, by road, rail and sea at varying frequencies and volumes. Some locally supplied goods are shipped direct to stores. Other goods are shipped via the warehouses. A few items are shipped from the central warehouse to other warehouses.
- Four warehouses — strategically located in the marketing area.
- Warehouse inventories — which buffer variable store requirements and the frequency and reliability of suppliers' shipments.
- Transportation — of goods between warehouses, and from warehouses to stores, by the company-owned truck fleet and, to a lesser extent, by common carriers.
- Fifty stores — each selling the full range of 500 items to the public in different cities and towns throughout a marketing area of 30,000 square miles.
- Store inventories — which balance the vagaries of consumer demand against the frequency of delivery from warehouses and suppliers. Total investment in warehouse and store inventories is $3,500,000.
- Cyclical demand — the peak demand (35% of annual sales) occurs in November and December. Total sales approximate $20,000,000.

HOW CAN THE SYSTEM BE ORGANIZED TO MAXIMIZE PROFITS?

Profitable management of the system implies two conflicting goals:

FIGURE 12.12
CONFIGURATION OF EXISTING SYSTEM

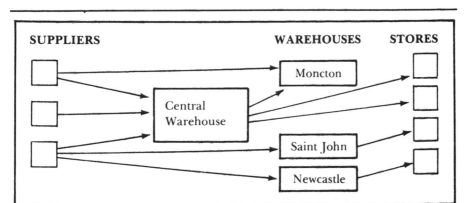

minimizing total costs and maintaining a satisfactory level of customer service. Minimizing total costs alone is not sufficient. This sub-optimal goal would be obtained through large, infrequent shipments to stores and warehouses, with minimal inventories. But service to the customer would decline and, in turn, sales and profits would be lost.

The best organization of the system reflects the need to maintain a specified level of service at the minimum overall cost. This was the objective of the study. It will be realized only when all the elements of the system are together operating most effectively. For the purposes of the study, these elements are:

- number, location and size of warehouses and appropriate manning
- number and types of warehouse equipment and methods of storage
- transportation modes and routes between suppliers and warehouses or stores
- inventory levels at warehouses and stores
- delivery frequencies and quantities to warehouses and stores
- whether to ship from suppliers direct to stores or via warehouses

The fixed, or uncontrollable, elements are:

- location and choice of suppliers
- products sold
- location and size of stores

The most effective system therefore consists of the optimum balance among all the possible combinations of routes and modes of transport, inventory levels, delivery frequencies and quantities, and warehouse configurations. Which combination will minimize overall costs while maintaining the desired level of service?

ELIMINATE WAREHOUSING?
Costly warehousing operations could be eliminated by shipping all goods

direct from suppliers to stores. But for small stores and small suppliers this would mean excessive inventories or transportation costs. Furthermore, warehouse operating costs per unit of throughput would increase as the volume of goods warehoused decreased. Thus, at what supplier-store volume does it become economical to by-pass the warehouse?

ONE LARGE WAREHOUSE?

Incoming freight charges can be minimized by shipping all goods in carload or truck-load lots to one central warehouse. By shipping the maximum possible quantities, the most favourable freight rates can be obtained. Suppliers' shipments could be combined at source to avoid excessive warehouse inventories. Total system inventories would be minimized. However, all goods will be shipped twice — from supplier to warehouse and from warehouse to store — and local delivery costs would increase compared to the present system.

NO CAPITAL INVESTMENT?

Capital costs would be minimized by using existing warehouses. Local delivery costs would be kept down. But to maintain a given level of customer service, higher inventories would be required and freight charges from suppliers to warehouses would be more expensive.

MORE FREQUENT INVENTORIES?

Inventories at stores and warehouses could be reduced if goods were shipped more frequently. But higher transportation and receiving costs may offset any gains.

The design of the best physical distribution system thus requires a number of conflicting decisions, each of which affects the others. Decisions on the number and location of warehouses influence shipping costs and, in turn, the relative economies of one or more warehouses.

In short, the system must be considered as an operating entity rather than a collection of isolated elements. The combined effects of all operating and investment decisions must be considered if management is to be assured of the greatest contribution to profit.

THE ANSWER

Simulation is a technique for testing the implications of possible policies without having to implement these policies. It is most useful, as in this instance, when the problem is highly complex and mathematically intractable and large volumes of data have to be manipulated. The power of computers makes feasible the massive computational effort required.

Simulation is carried out via a model which represents symbolically the real system as closely as possible. In this study it was used to evaluate two physical configurations under specified operating rules for:

FIGURE 12.13
ALTERNATIVE SYSTEM CONFIGURATIONS

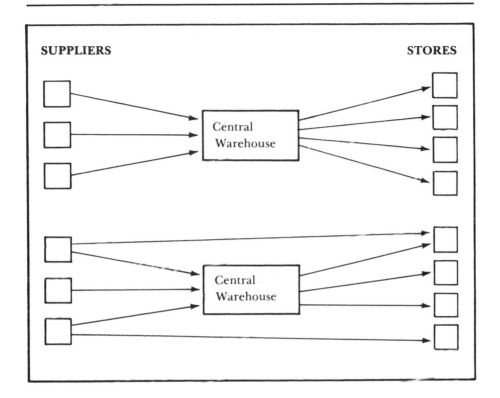

- sales forecasting
- consolidation of suppliers' shipments
- inventory review periods
- warehouse–store delivery routes
- supplier–store delivery routes
- transportation modes and rates
- lead times

The two configurations are illustrated in Figure 12.13. The first represents one warehouse with no direct shipment. The second is also based on one warehouse, but with direct shipment from suppliers to stores whenever the volume appears sufficient.

Each configuration, when combined with selected operating rules, constitutes a model. The model can be altered by changing the rules. Various combinations of rules can be tested to determine which leads to the minimum overall cost.

FIGURE 12.14

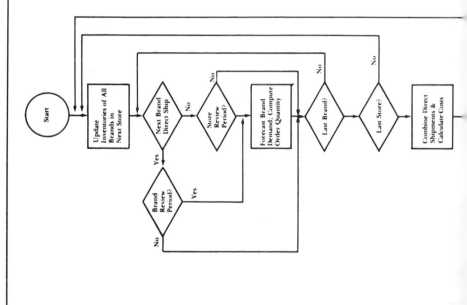

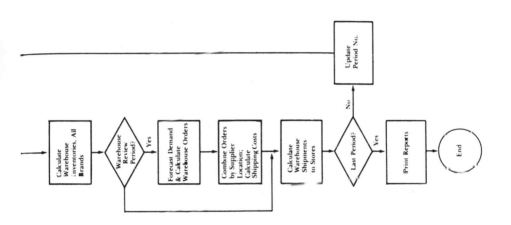

The simulation procedure, illustrated in Figure 12.14, can thus be used for any desirable set of rules. In this sense, it portrays a general model for the description and analysis of any distribution system. Any conceivable system can be evaluated in terms of its operating rules, investment decisions or overall configuration.

For each particular combination of rules the simulation model follows the flow of goods during a consecutive 52-week period. At the end of 52 weeks all costs, inventory levels and stock-outs are summarized so that management can evaluate the overall performance of the system under these rules. Change a rule, or any combination of rules, and different results are obtained.

Typical examples of the computer printouts are shown in Figures 12.15 and 12.16. Figure 12.15 shows the movement through Warehouse 1 in Weeks 47 and 48. In Week 47 goods were shipped to Stores 1, 3, 7, 9 . . . and 51. Altogether, 6,900 cases were shipped out, weighing 320,270 lb. Specifically we see that 1,190 cases were shipped to Store 1, 934 cases to Store 2, 1,327 cases to Store 30 and so forth. In the following week (48), 355 cases weighing 14,525 lb. were shipped to Store 19.

Inventory levels in this particular simulation resulted from a stated policy of giving a 99% level of service. This resulted in a stock of 92,778 cases valued at $1,917,495 in Week 47. For this stock, 79,964 cubic feet of storage space were required. In this week all demands were met — there were no stock-outs.

The right-hand side of the report shows goods received from suppliers. In Week 47 there were three receipts, of 3,328, 1,428 and 191 cases — 4,947 in total, weighing 438,941 lb. These shipments came in by rail and truck, the costs being $282 and $318 respectively.

Figure 12.16 represents the movement of goods at Store 5 during the period of Weeks 18 to 22. In Week 19, 1,861 bottles were sold. The inventory in the store amounted to 18,127 bottles — equivalent to 1,459 cases. It was valued at $7,017. The store was out of stock of two brands, but the total demand for these two brands was only three bottles — no great loss.

In the same week, 65 cases weighing 3,062 lb. were received from the central warehouse.

It will be seen that this store received goods both from the central warehouse and directly from suppliers. In Week 21, a shipment of 35 cases, weighing 2,857 lb., was received from a supplier at Location 4. This shipment cost $1,958.

Similar analysis and summaries were developed for all reasonable combinations of shipping frequency, routing, customer service levels, transportation modes, frequencies and rates and lead times.

FIGURE 12.15

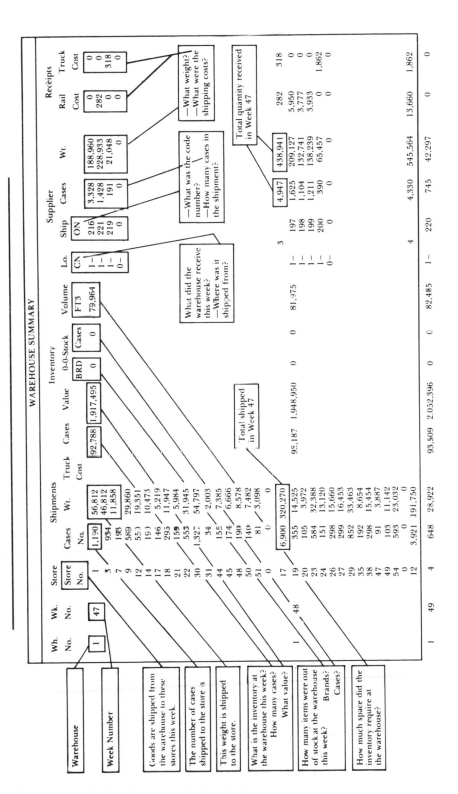

WAREHOUSE SUMMARY

FIGURE 12.16

No. 30

PHYSICAL DISTRIBUTION SIMULATION
STORE SUMMARY

Wh. No.	St. No.	Wk. No.	Sales Botls.	Inventory Botls.	Inventory Cases	Inventory Value	00-Stock BRD	00-Stock Botl.	Volume FT3	Wh. Receipts Cases	Wh. Receipts Wt.	Supplier Lo. CN	Supplier Ship No.	Supplier Receipts Cases	Supplier Receipts Wt.	Rail Cost	Truck Cost
1	5	18	1,919	18,370	1,488	5,836	13	172	791	0	0	6–	129	1,138	30,373	1	0
												2–	126	315	10,914	****	0
													2	1,453	41,287	****	0
		19	1,861	18,127	1,459	7,017	2	3	793	65	3,062	0–	0	0	0	0	0
													0	0	0	0	0
		20	1,859	16,869	1,367	6,051	2	7	733	0	0	0–	0	0	0	0	0
													0	0	0	0	0
		21	1,811	16,460	1,311	6,301	3	19	704	0	0	4–	149	35	2,857	0	1,958
													1	35	2,857	0	1,958
		22	1,994	15,143	1,212	5,438	9	40	640	0	0	0–	0	0	0	0	0

Store 5 is supplied from Warehouse No. 1.

Store No. 5

Week No. (19)

In Week 19, 1,861 bottles were sold in store No. 5.

In Week 19 there were 18,127 bottles, or

1,459 cases in stock

worth $7,017.

Two brands were out of stock—There was a demand for a total of 3 bottles of these brands.

Store inventory occupied 793 cu. ft.

Sixty-five cases weighing 3,062 lbs. were received from the warehouse.

In Week 21, shipment no. 149 was received from a supplier in Location 4.

It contained 35 cases weighing 2,857 lbs.

This shipment cost $1,958.

The result: an insight into how any system would work under various operating rules. In other words, management is able to test various operating, policy and investment decisions without disturbing the existing system. Instead of the former costly and time-consuming method of trial and error, management can now use a simulation model to select the best distribution system.

The results of this study more than justified the investment. The final set of distribution rules chosen resulted in projected savings of:

- 40% in inventories
- 7% in transportation costs
- 70% in warehouse operating costs

Annual logistics costs could be reduced by more than $300,000 on the basis of a capital investment of $400,000.

This study was exceptional in that all cost elements were reduced, some marginally, some substantially. More frequently, total costs are reduced but one or more elements may increase. In essence, this is why simulation is the answer. Other approaches might identify savings in one or more areas. But only simulation permits you to determine the effect on total logistics cost.

INDEX